Questions
From
Christians

Thom Thompson

Questions

From

Christians

ABOUT BAHA'U'LLAH AND
THE BAHA'I FAITH

Thom Thompson

Contents

DEDICATION

TO MY PARENTS, LACY AND EVA THOMPSON, WHO
BROUGHT ME TO CHRIST. I AM INDEBTED TO THEM IN A
WAY THAT ONLY GOD CAN REPAY.

TO WINSTON GILL EVANS, MY BAHA'I TEACHER, WHO
BROUGHT ME TO CHRIST RETURNED IN BAHA'U'LLAH.

TO DR. STANWOOD COBB, FOR HIS LIFE, HIS FRIENDSHIP,
HIS INFLUENCE AND FOR HIS BOOK, SECURITY FOR A
FAILING WORLD.

AND TO MY WIFE AND PARTNER, DOROTHY LEMON -
THOMPSON, SO LOVING AND SUPPORTIVE, FOR WHOM I
PRAY THE BLESSING OF FAITH IN BAHA'U'LLAH.

Frontispiece

"*Most assuredly, I say to you, unless one is born again, he cannot see the kingdom of God.*" John 3:3

Jesus Christ

"*For God so loved the world that He gave His only begotten Son, that whoever believes in Him should not perish but have everlasting life.*"

John 3:16

"*Lo! The Father is come, and that which ye were promised in the Kingdom is fulfilled!*"

Baha'u'llah

"*For the Son of Man will come in the glory of His Father with His angels, and then He will reward each according to his works.*"

Jesus Christ

"If ye be intent on crucifying once again Jesus, the Spirit of God, put Me to death, for He hath once more, in My person, been made manifest unto you."

Baha'u'llah

"Watch therefore, for you do not know what hour your Lord is coming. But know this, that if the master of the house had known what hour the thief would come, he would have watched and not allowed his house to be broken into. Therefore you also be ready, for the Son of Man is coming at an hour you do not expect."

Jesus Christ

"Open the doors of your hearts. He Who is the Spirit [that is, Jesus] verily standeth before them. Wherefore banish ye Him Who hath purposed to draw you nigh unto a Resplendent Spot? Say: We, in truth, have opened unto you the gates of the Kingdom. Will ye bar the doors of your houses in My face? This indeed is naught but a grievous error. He, verily, hath again come down from heaven, even as He came down from it the first time."

Baha'u'llah

"O God, my God! Thy forgiveness hath emboldened me, and Thy mercy hath strengthened me, and Thy call hath awakened me, and Thy grace hath raised me up and led me unto Thee."

Baha'u'llah

CHAPTER ONE

INTRODUCTION: WHY QUESTIONS FROM CHRISTIANS WAS WRITTEN

QUESTION: Why are you writing this book?

RESPONSE: As I will explain in chapter two, I come from a Christian background that was rich in the experience of Christ's Presence in my life and the life of my family. Christ's teachings and the salvation found in giving one's life over to Jesus Christ were an everyday, intimate understanding, a 'given' in our lives. A hymn that often plays in my memory was what my family treasured and taught: "Take my life, and let it be, consecrated Lord, to Thee."

When I encountered the Baha'i Faith and the Revelation seen and experienced in the person of Baha'u'llah, I had many questions. Some of these questions were answered very well, but some of the responses

I received from my questions were unclear or, worse, reflected too little knowledge of the Christ I knew so well and the Christian Faith I had cherished all my life.

So, I resolved that someday when I had the opportunity, I would attempt to answer my original questions and the many questions I have heard over the years from Christians who had just heard about Baha'u'llah and the Baha'i Faith. Baha'u'llah's name means 'The Glory of God.' It is pronounced phonetically, accenting the *second* and *fourth* syllables, as in Bah-**HAH**-o-**LAH**. Baha'i is pronounced accenting the *second* part of the word, as in Bah-**HIGH**.

QUESTION: Why should I read this book?

RESPONSE: One reason, I would think, is to learn about a new religion–the Baha'i Faith–that is organizing itself worldwide according to the plan and teachings of Baha'u'llah. Baha'i communities all over the planet are dedicated to the task of bringing the human race to its long-awaited consummation of oneness and unity. Another reason might be that the Baha'i Faith has very special teachings about Jesus, including a central teaching that Christ's Spirit and Person have appeared again in our contemporary world. Jesus taught us to pray: *"Thy Kingdom come, Thy will be done, on earth as it is in heaven."* Baha'is around the world believe they are building that 'Kingdom of God' here and now, on our common home–earth.

QUESTION: That's a very interesting development, but Christians also believe that God is bringing about the fulfillment of Christ's prayer and, anyway, you should know that I'm not looking for anything or anyone 'new.' Really, I'm satisfied with Jesus and what the Bible says.

RESPONSE: And we Baha'is believe that nothing should be allowed to undermine or weaken what a person already knows and understands. But, think with me for a moment: Couldn't a devout Jew of Jesus' time have said exactly what you just said, when someone invited him or her to learn about Jesus? Suppose that Jew encountered Jesus, but said: "I'm not looking for new teachings or a new messenger of God. I'm satisfied with what I have and what I know." Now…switch back to the present, but keep in mind what that Jewish person just said.

In saying that you aren't looking for anything or anyone new, what if today you encountered Baha'u'llah and He said to you, speaking of Jesus Christ: *"He hath once more, in My person, been made manifest unto you"?* (Baha'u'llah: *Gleanings*, Page: 101) What should a Jew have said two thousand years ago to Christ? What should you or anyone say now, to Baha'u'llah?

QUESTION: Well, wait a minute. Surely you know that many persons in history have claimed to be the returned Christ?

RESPONSE: True enough. However, as I believe you will find, Baha'u'llah's life and teachings are even more challenging that that claim seems, and we can discuss this in greater detail in the second chapter. The Revelation of God given through Baha'u'llah is not easily dismissed and the community created by God's fresh outpouring of 'Good Tidings' numbers six million worldwide (at the turn of the millennium) and is established in every country in the world. Baha'u'llah's Revelation and the Baha'i community flowing from it are living testimony to His life and teachings

QUESTION: Are you going to use the question/ response format throughout this book?

RESPONSE: Yes, but only because I think it is the most direct and genuine way to communicate with you. And, it keeps us focused on your questions, rather than just what I would like to have you hear and know.

QUESTION: Well, I can't really agree that these are my questions. As the reader, I can enter into a 'conversation,' but aren't you picking the questions?

RESPONSE: Yes and no. As I write, I am phrasing the questions, but they are questions that either came from Christian friends or were formed in my own mind as a Christian when I first encountered the Baha'i Faith. The reason I use the word 'response,' instead of 'answer' is that I don't presume to have answers. I do have information and the question/response format is a good way to process information.

Oh, one more thing: As often as possible, the response will not be from me, but from either Christ or Baha'u'llah. They are (with few exceptions) the only two people to be quoted in this book, except for several prayers and a few people quoted in chapter sixteen. The quotes from Christ are taken from the New King James Version of the Bible.

The question/response conversation also allows me to connect your question with Baha'u'llah's answer to that question. Like Jesus, who "taught with authority," you will see that the 'voice' with which Baha'u'llah speaks is one that invites the hearer to realize that they are in contact with a 'New Testament' of God's will for humankind.

QUESTION: You said earlier that you had some of the same questions as the ones that are in this book?

RESPONSE: Yes, many of these questions were the very ones I originally asked, from my Christian perspective. Other questions came from Christians when I spoke to groups in churches on the subject of the Baha'i Faith. Some questions were solicited from Christian friends when I began to do research for this book. Other Christian friends wrote, emailed and called me to suggest that certain questions be included. I'm thankful to them for their help.

Fourteen persons read the final draft of this book. Most of them have Christian backgrounds. One is a Christian minister. And all of them suggested changes, even new questions. As you read this book, you may have a question that has not been included. If so, please contact me. My address and email are in the chapter fifteen. I definitely want to hear from you.

QUESTION: So, let me hear more. I can have an open mind if you realize that I don't need something new. Why should I want more? My Christian Faith is everything that I want and need.

RESPONSE: I do realize and respect that. I felt very strongly the same way as a Christian (but, as you will learn as you read on, I still feel that I am a follower of Christ; more on this later). One of Baha'u'llah's teachings is that of 'independent investigation of the truth,' calling on all the people of Earth to investigate freely His claims and mission. This means that each individual, in his or her own way, is challenged and charged to make up her or his own mind, just as a Jew needed to do, twenty centuries ago when he or she encountered the 'Son of God.'

QUESTION: What is this book about and how is it arranged?

RESPONSE: This book is about the announcement of Baha'u'llah that He is the long awaited 'Promised One' of all faiths and religions. It is about His teachings and about the community that bears His name—the Baha'i Faith. The worldwide community of Baha'is is pursuing the specific mission entrusted to it by Baha'u'llah. Here is a description of that mission in Baha'u'llah's own words: *"That which God hath ordained as the sovereign remedy and mightiest instrument for the healing of the world is the union of all its peoples in one universal Cause, one common Faith. This can in no wise be achieved except through the power of a skilled, an all-powerful, and inspired Physician."* (Baha'u'llah: *Epistle to the Son of the Wolf,* Pages: 62-63)

QUESTION: Please! Stop right there! The idea of 'uniting the world' seems silly and grandiose. You only need to look around to know that a united, peaceful world is not about to happen anytime soon. The Twenty-First Century is here and there are conflicts all around the world, in Africa, Eastern Europe and the Middle East. Those conflicts have been brought to the United States in the horrific, terrorist acts occurring in Fall, 2001, yet you talk about 'world unity!'

RESPONSE: It would seem that you are right. However, the Baha'is in following Baha'u'llah are responding to One Who says He is: *"Him Whom Thou* *hast appointed as the Manifestation of Thine own Being* [that is, God's Being] *and Thy discriminating Word unto all that are in heaven and on earth.*" (Baha'u'llah: *Prayers and Meditations*, Page: 26) Even though Baha'u'llah Himself said: *"Darkness hath fallen upon every land, and the forces of mischief have encompassed all the nations,"* (Baha'u'llah: *Prayers and Meditations*, Page: 14) nevertheless, He announced He was bringing a fresh revelation of God's will to humanity, a *"Revelation whereby darkness hath been turned into light."* (Baha'u'llah: *Prayers and Meditations*, Page: 9)

Finally, Baha'u'llah constantly reminds us that this period of history is a *'new day,'* a spiritual *'springtime.'* Speaking of what God has done, He said: *"This is the hour when Thou hast unlocked the doors of Thy bounty".* (Baha'u'llah: *Prayers and Meditations*, Page: 144)

QUESTION: There you go again. Only you would call the Twentieth Century a time of divine springtime! Terrorist actions such as planes being flown into buildings in New York City and Washington, DC don't indicate a 'springtime.' The recent events of history just don't support this idea, do they?

RESPONSE: Right again, but I remind you that it is Baha'u'llah talking, not me. And, would you have called the years of Christ's birth and ministry a divine springtime? It really was, I know you would agree. But no person living then would have called it a time of special 'bounty,' especially not Jesus' own people, the Jews, who were subjugated by Roman legions and law. Apparently, we can't always easily tell, at any given moment, what is really happening and what it means until some time goes by to give us historical perspective.

QUESTION: I'll have to give you that one. No one, not even the Jews, knew or understood what was happening when Jesus walked the Galilean hills. They didn't recognize God's Son and they didn't realize that they were experiencing an event that would change history. But, you were going to tell me how the book is organized and what I can learn from it.

RESPONSE: The book is organized as follows: *Chapter One* is the chapter you are now reading. *Chapter two* tells how a Christian became a Baha'i. *Chapter Three* is a Short History of the Baha'i Faith, to orient you to the Faith's central figures and how the Baha'i Faith began. *Chapter Four* tells about a concept that, while not entirely new, will be new to many, called 'Progressive Revelation.' This concept is essentially a new way of understanding human history. *Chapter Five* explains a word that will seem new, but which is actually used in the New Testament several times. The word is 'Manifestation,' which is the Baha'i way of explaining how God chooses to reveal Himself in human history.

Chapter Six informs about how Baha'is view the person of Christ and His place in history. I think you will be quite interested in this and perhaps a bit surprised. *Chapter Seven* tells how a Christian might look at Baha'u'llah and His place in history. *Chapter Eight* brings you an introduction to Baha'u'llah's teachings and what they might mean for the world. *Chapter Nine* talks about similarities and differences between the Christian and Baha'i Faiths.

The Baha'i House of Worship in Wilmette, Illinois, a
Chicago suburb. There are houses of worship on every
continent.

QUESTION: You know, I'm just realizing that you
consider the Baha'i Faith a separate religion, instead of
what I thought, that you might be a denomination or
sect of the Christian Faith.

RESPONSE: That's true. It will become more understandable as we go along and I can promise you that
there is an interesting way in which the two Faiths are

still considered 'one.' I know that probably makes no sense now, but stay with me, it will.

Back to the contents of the book. *Chapter Ten* focuses on the famous quote of Christ for His followers to become *"fishers of men"* and the equally famous phrase of Baha'u'llah to His followers to become the *"quickeners of mankind"* and shows how the two commands are related and complementary. *Chapter Eleven* informs Christians that Baha'u'llah made a special appeal to them to become His followers in a new 'discipleship' from *"the Father,"* as Baha'u'llah called Himself.

QUESTION: That title, 'the Father,' sounds incredible and strange. It even sounds blasphemous to me, as if Baha'u'llah is claiming to be God!

RESPONSE: Maybe you are on the edge of a discovery! Just imagine how strange, incredible, blasphemous, even crazy it must have sounded to a Jew in Jesus' time for Jesus to be described as *"the Son of God"!* No wonder that some Jews tore their clothing, inflicted wounds upon themselves and plotted to kill this Person, who to them was a blasphemer. Then, imagine how shocked and angered they felt when He said, *"The Father and I are one."* More on this later in chapter seven mentioned above. For now, let's go back to the contents of the book.

Chapter Twelve introduces a thesis, shocking as it may sound at first hearing, namely, that committed Christians have compelling reasons to become followers of Baha'u'llah. As a Christian minister, I used to tell Jews that they had compelling reasons to become followers of Christ. If you are thinking that these two situations are not the same and the analogy fails, at least read this chapter to see if the analogy has any merit.

Chapter Thirteen actually issues an invitation to the

reader to become a follower of Baha'u'llah. I come by this 'invitation' honestly, since hundreds of times I have invited people to give their lives to Christ and become His follower. How can I do less when talking to Christians about One whom I believe to be the Return of Christ?

Chapter Fourteen talks about the rebirth of the individual that occurs when one becomes a follower of Baha'u'llah and the renewal that the world will experience when the teachings of Christ and of Baha'u'llah have spread into the world.

Chapter Fifteen invites you to contact me, to comment on the book, to ask a question and to dialog with me to suggest changes for revision. I list email and mail addresses. Please let me know your ideas, criticisms, suggestions and, especially, new questions, so that they can be included in the book upon revision.

Chapter Sixteen is a list of one hundred topics, alphabetically arranged, based on questions asked by Christians about the Baha'i Faith, with short responses and suggestions for further reading to learn more about Baha'u'llah and His teachings. *Chapter Seventeen* acknowledges the many people who have, directly and indirectly, helped me produce this book.

So, what do you think so far of the approach of the book and the material it will cover?

QUESTION: I don't exactly know how to say this, but I'm astounded and a little part of me wonders if you are in your right mind. Just listen to what you have said so far: You believe God has revealed Himself again, that there is a new revelation, which represents the return of the spirit of Christ, a new day of God, with new teachings and a community of followers who are trying to unite the world? How does that sound when you hear it fed back to you?

RESPONSE: I'll grant you that it seems to be a 'lot to swallow.' To give perspective, however, imagine again that same Jew in the time of Jesus, who hears Jesus say that His *"Father"* sent him with a 'new message,' that He and the Father (that is, God) were *"one"*, that His teachings represented *"salvation"* to the extent that He said *"He that believeth in me, though he were dead, yet shall he live: And whosoever liveth and believeth in me shall never die."* (John 11:25-26) Listening further, that Jew hears Jesus say that if the Jew does not believe in Him personally, that he would be as one *"dead"* and *"I am the way, the truth, and the life: no man cometh unto the Father, but by me."* (John 14:6)

Finally, the Jew hears his religion referred to as an *"old bottle"* that cannot contain the *"new wine"* of Jesus' teachings. Jesus looks at the young man and tells him to leave everything, even family, to follow Him to spread new tidings of salvation to everyone. He told another to give away everything he owned. And to another, He refuses time to go bury his father, saying: *"Follow Me, and let the dead bury their own dead."* (Matt 8:22)

What do you suppose *your* response would have been if you had been that Jew listening to Jesus? It's a curious thought, isn't it? Would you have thought a follower of Jesus just a little mad or off center? As a matter of fact, Jesus and His followers were accused more than once in the New Testament of being 'mad' or 'just plain crazy,' or worse. Would you, as that Jew, have thought the followers of Christ were grandiose, crazy or even blasphemous and destructive to your Jewish religion?

Or . . . would you have heard Him out?

QUESTION: But if all the things you just mentioned that Jesus said are true, why do we need another Faith?

RESPONSE: Wasn't this the primary question of the Jews in the time of Jesus? In their time, the *"Son of God"* appeared. Now we know they *did* need Him. And now, if the *'Father'* of all mankind appears, One who is the Return of the Christ Spirit, the 'Word,' we do need *Him*, especially if He is the One promised by Christ. Remember that important quote of Baha'u'llah about Christ that *"He hath once more, in My person, been made manifest unto you"*. (Baha'u'llah: *Gleanings*, Page: 101) Jesus promised many times to His disciples that He would return.

Sometimes Jesus described His Return in terms of the appearance of the *"Spirit of Truth."* Jesus said: *"But when the Helper comes, whom I shall send to you from the Father, the Spirit of truth who proceeds from the Father, He will testify of Me."* (John 15:26) Baha'u'llah very clearly claimed to be that *"Spirit of Truth."*

About the 'Spirit of Truth', Baha'u'llah said, *"Proclaim then unto all mankind the glad-tidings of this mighty, this glorious Revelation. Verily, He Who is the Spirit of Truth is come to guide you unto all truth. He speaketh not as prompted by His own self, but as bidden by Him Who is the All-Knowing, the All-Wise. Say, this is the One Who hath glorified the Son and hath exalted His Cause."* (Baha'u'llah: *Tablets of Baha'u'llah*, Page: 12)

When Jesus spoke of His Coming, He often said it would be hard to notice, that it would be stealthy, like a *"thief in the night"* and that the 'hour' of His Coming was unknown even to Him: *"But of that day and hour no one knows, not even the angels in heaven, nor the Son, but only the Father."* (Mark 13:32-33)

Baha'u'llah said: *"The Hour which We had concealed from the knowledge of the peoples of the earth and of the favoured angels hath come to pass.* (Baha'u'llah: *Tablets of Baha'u'llah*, Page: 11)

But back to your question of needing another Faith, it would seem to me that we do need someone—if He is the One promised by Christ, and if He is the One expected and awaited by all the religions and cultures of the world, the "Promise of All Ages." I would not hide from you what I believe to be the truth, beautiful and fulfilling to me, and probably quite challenging to you at this point, that Baha'u'llah said He was that Person Whom God had sent to fulfill the promises, prophecies and expectations of all the Faiths of the world.

Baha'u'llah wrote: *"Thou art He, O my God, Who hath raised me up at Thy behest, and bidden me to occupy Thy seat, and to summon all men to the court of Thy mercy. It is Thou Who hast commanded me to tell out the things Thou didst destine for them in the Tablet of Thy decree and didst inscribe with the pen of Thy Revelation, and Who hast enjoined on me the duty of kindling the fire of Thy love in the hearts of Thy servants, and of drawing all the peoples of the earth nearer to the habitation of Thy throne."* (Baha'u'llah: *Prayers and Meditations*, Page: 107)

If—and I realize it is a very big 'if' for you, but hear me out—if Baha'u'llah is who He says He is and if His call to spread a healing, uniting message into all the world is a reality and, finally, if He asks us to call this new message 'The Baha'i Faith,' then we have only as much right to say we are not comfortable with this new name and new Faith as a Jew would have had in Jesus' time to say: "No thanks, I don't want to hear about a new name or a new message and I certainly don't want to follow a new 'messenger.' I'm quite satisfied with what I have."

QUESTION: Okay, this almost seems overwhelming and my first thought is just to reject it and forget about it, but I know by now in our conversation that you will just say that's exactly what most Jews did. Right? So, I guess you should go on to tell me, as you promised, how you came to be a follower of Baha'u'llah. I must tell you, though that it seems very sad to me that you seem to have exchanged the Savior, Jesus, for another. How can you have done that?

RESPONSE: Very simply, I can tell you that I haven't done that. My closeness to Jesus, learned at my parents' knee and probably even in their arms is not only as strong today but I believe, even stronger. I am still a follower of Jesus Christ and a follower of Baha'u'llah at the same time. Sound confusing? I promise to clear it up in the next chapter and, again, later on, when we discuss a concept called 'progressive revelation,' a concept shared by Christians and Baha'is. This concept, which will be new to many people, has the power to give us a larger, more comprehensive understanding of history, an understanding that Baha'is believe can, indeed, unite the world.

So, yes, on to chapter two. I am happy to share a personal story of how a Christian became a Baha'i. But first, let me tell you that I am going to follow the practice of sharing a prayer with you at the end of each chapter. Most of the time, the prayer will be from Baha'u'llah.

"My God, my Adored One, my King, my Desire! What tongue can voice my thanks to Thee? I was heedless, Thou didst awaken me. I had turned back from Thee, Thou didst graciously aid me to turn towards Thee. I was as one dead, Thou didst quicken me with the water of life. I was withered, Thou didst revive me with the heavenly stream of Thine utterance which hath flowed forth from the Pen of the All-Merciful.

O Divine Providence! All existence is begotten by Thy bounty; deprive it not of the waters of Thy generosity, neither do Thou withhold it from the ocean of Thy mercy. I beseech

Thee to aid and assist me at all times and under all conditions, and seek from the heaven of Thy grace Thine ancient favor. Thou art, in truth, the Lord of bounty, and the Sovereign of the kingdom of eternity." (Baha'u'llah: *Prayers and Meditations*, Pages: 264-265)

And a prayer from His son, 'Abdu'l-Baha (which means 'Servant of Baha'u'llah.' It is pronounced, phonetically, Ab-**DUL**-bah-**HAH**):

"O compassionate God! Thanks be to Thee for Thou hast awakened and made me conscious. Thou hast given me a seeing eye and favored me with a hearing ear, hast led me to Thy kingdom and guided me to Thy path. Thou hast shown me the right way and caused me to enter the ark of deliverance. O God! Keep me steadfast and make me firm and staunch. Protect me from violent tests, and preserve and shelter me in the strongly fortified fortress of Thy Covenant and Testament. Thou art the Powerful. Thou art the Seeing. Thou art the Hearing.

O Thou the Compassionate God. Bestow upon me a heart which, like unto a glass, may be illumined with the light of Thy love, and confer upon me thoughts which may change this world into a rose garden through the outpourings of heavenly grace.

Thou art the Compassionate, the Merciful. Thou art the Great Beneficent God." 'Abdu'l-Baha: *Baha'i Prayers*, Pages: 71-72)

CHAPTER TWO

HOW A CHRISTIAN
BECAME A BAHÁ'Í

QUESTION: The first thought that comes to my mind is a sad one, or it could even be an angry one, which is: Have you replaced the precious Savior with someone else, this Baha'u'llah?! I can't even pronounce His name!

RESPONSE: Well, I believe I understand your question and your mood, because I once formed this exact question in my own mind, when I first heard about Baha'u'llah. I too would have been angry if anyone would try to replace Christ my Savior with another. No, I have not forsaken Jesus nor replaced Him with someone new. He is, after all, we would agree, irreplaceable. In the words of a hymn of my youth, "He's everything to me"; He is "The Lily of the Valley, the Bright and Morning Star, He's the fairest of ten thousand for my soul."

I can answer in more detail later in this conversation, but for now please accept my statement that Jesus Christ has not in any way been replaced or rejected by me. I sincerely believe my discipleship in following Baha'u'llah has come about precisely because of my strong, and continued, belief in Christ. As I said, I'll tell you more later, but for many years I have believed that Christ led me to Baha'u'llah, and that I hear the voice of my beloved Savior in the voice of Baha'u'llah.

The name Baha'u'llah is pronounced, phonetically, by accenting the second and fourth syllables, as follows: Bah-**HAH**-o-**LAH.** As you've already heard, His name means the 'Glory of God.'

QUESTION: There's a lot I don't understand or accept about your religion, and I have many questions, but maybe you should tell me something about yourself so I can see, as they say, "Where you are coming from."

RESPONSE: All right. My upbringing was in a household totally dedicated to Jesus Christ. My father was a Methodist minister in rural Iowa. He and my mother were truly good examples of persons expressing full discipleship in Christ. When I was an infant and near death, they prayed to God that if I were allowed to live, they would do everything in their power to dedicate my life completely to the Master.

In fact, they said in their prayer: "If you must take this child, we bow to Your Will, but if he can be allowed to live, we know he no longer belongs to us, but is Yours entirely." Several hours later, I made what the Doctor thought was a 'miraculous' recovery. My parents often told me this story and suggested to me that I had the task of struggling to understand what it meant. They told me what they thought but said that my spiritual quest was before me.

At age fifteen, while at an evangelistic service for teenagers, I moved to the altar, kneeled and gave my life to Jesus Christ, my Savior. My decision ratified what my parents had done earlier. To complete an answer I gave you earlier, it would have been unthinkable to me to accept the salvation of Jesus Christ, to give my life over to Him completely, then later take it back and give it to someone else!

QUESTION: But it seems that is exactly what you did!

RESPONSE: I suppose it does seem that way to you, but what you need to know is this: Baha'u'llah mentions Christ very often in His writings, usually using the phrase 'the Spirit' or 'the Son' to refer to Jesus. The quotation from Baha'u'llah that challenged me as a Christian to make a decision to follow Him was this one: (in a letter written to all the Christians of the world):

"Open the doors of your hearts. He Who is the Spirit [that is, Jesus] *verily standeth before them. Wherefore banish ye Him Who hath purposed to draw you nigh unto a Resplendent Spot? Say: We, in truth, have opened unto you the gates of the Kingdom. Will ye bar the doors of your houses in My face? This indeed is naught but a grievous error. He, verily, hath again come down from heaven, even as He came down from it the first time."* (Baha'u'llah: *Tablets of Baha'u'llah*, Page: 11)

In addition to this, I was struck by the following quote (the quote comes from a letter written to a community of Jews, many of whom became Baha'is after reading this letter): *"...If ye be intent on crucifying once again Jesus, the Spirit of God, put Me to death, for He hath once more, in*

My person, been made manifest unto you." (Baha'u'llah: *Gleanings,* Page: 101)

There are numerous other quotes such as these, many of which will be included in this book in later chapters, but for now let us both notice that these quotes just given are very direct, too forthright to be interpreted in some way other than exactly what they plainly say. I couldn't evade them, or quickly deny them without investigation. So, when I encountered these quotes and others like them, I knew I had to make a decision for or against Baha'u'llah. I proceeded to investigate with all my energy. I read, I prayed, I pondered and meditated, prayed some more, and finally I realized I believed that Baha'u'llah was the new Manifestation of God's Will for today, and, more importantly, I believed that He was, for me, the return of Jesus Christ.

QUESTION: You claim that Baha'u'llah is the return of Christ? How do you support this claim? What proofs do you have? Surely you realize that hundreds or thousands of charlatans or madmen have made this very claim?

RESPONSE: Agreed. However, Baha'u'llah's life and writings are an 'open book.' His Revelation contains over ten thousand documents, including prayers, meditations, books and letters. We can study His words and His life to decide the truth for ourselves. In fact, Baha'u'llah referred to Himself as the *"Living Book"* which was open to the people of the world to read and understand. As for support for this claim, I hope this conversation-book will supply much of what you are looking for.

And, don't forget that the words of Jesus *"The Fa-*

ther and I are one" must have come as a blasphemous bombshell to Jews, who saw that claim as absurdly wrong and may have even caused them to see Jesus as a madman or a charlatan. One Christian theologian said that when you look at Jesus, you can only see Him in one of three ways. Either He is a madman, a charlatan and trickster, or the only other alternative is that: He is Who He says He is. The same test can be applied to Baha'u'llah. He is either mad, a charlatan or He just may be the Promised One of all religions.

QUESTION: What do you mean by the 'Promised One' of all religions? I thought what we were talking about was Baha'u'llah claiming to be the Return of Christ. And, couldn't Baha'u'llah be a false prophet or the Anti-Christ or even the Devil? That Christian theologian had only three categories. It seems to me there are several more.

RESPONSE: One of the most striking aspects of the appearance in history of Baha'u'llah is that He claimed to be what one writer called 'The Promise of All Ages.' I'll tell you more about His life and His Mission in chapter three—'How it all Began.' Some Christians are aware of the fact (but others may not be) that their religion is not the only one that expects a 'return' of their Manifestation or Messenger or a 're-expression' of the Spirit that was in the original Messenger of their religion.

Some Moslems expect two 'Manifestations' of God to appear. This Baha'i expression—'Manifestation of God—refers to One (such as Christ or Baha'u'llah), Who brings to earth the very 'presence' of God. Baha'u'llah taught that God causes these 'Manifestations of Himself' to be sent, from time to time, to earth and earth's people. Jews, for example, still expect the Messiah. Buddhists expect the Fifth Buddha, while Hindus, Zoroastrians and others are all looking for a 'Promised One.' The Three Wise Men who sought out the baby Jesus were Zoroastrian Priests who were expecting a fresh 'Manifestation of God.' The word 'manifestation' is used in the New Testament (though not exactly the way Baha'is use it. See Luke 1:80).

Others, like Native Americans and indigenous peoples all over the world have prophecies in their religions relating to a golden age when a great Prophet or Manifestation of God will appear or reappear in fulfillment of many prophecies. This great 'Promise of all Ages' will bring about, they say, a kingdom of unity and justice about which Jesus also prayed: *"Thy kingdom come. Thy will be done in earth, as it is in heaven."* (Matt 6:10, *King James Version*; most quotes are taken from the New King James Version). What is interesting to me is that these prophecies—and Christ's Prayer—all state that this Kingdom will be built right here, *on earth.*

As for Baha'u'llah possibly being the Antichrist or the Devil in some disguise or a 'false prophet'— against which Christ warned—I can only say that when Jesus appeared, He was thought by the Jews to be 'false', to be the Devil (Matt. 12:24 for example), or a destroyer of true religion. Apparently, whenever a new Manifestation of God appears, some people, even many or most people, read bad motives into His appearance. A century or two later, however, their great, great, great grandchildren all believe in the 'new' prophetic figure, whether Jesus, Buddha, or in this day, Baha'u'llah.

QUESTION: But, Christians believe that Jesus was

the fulfillment of most of the prophecies of other religions, except perhaps for Muslims.

RESPONSE: Yes, the Muslim prophecies could not at all refer to Jesus, since they were made more than six centuries after Jesus' death and Resurrection. Also, the Muslims were expecting the appearance of *two* prophets, or as Baha'is say, 'Manifestations of God.'

Another problem is that all these prophecies speak of the 'end of history,' of a time when prophecy ends and fulfillment of prophecy begins, a time of peace, justice, and unity for all the people of earth. While Jesus was the Son of God and His life and teachings a central unfolding of God's design and purpose, He cannot have been the 'Promise of all Ages' because, first and most importantly, He never claimed to be. Second, no such Kingdom of unity, peace and justice has been erected in twenty centuries.

By contrast, Baha'u'llah clearly and forcefully told the people of the world that: *"The Revelation which, from time immemorial, hath been acclaimed as the Purpose and Promise of all the Prophets of God, and the most cherished Desire of His Messengers, hath now, by virtue of the pervasive Will of the Almighty and at His irresistible bidding, been revealed unto men. The advent of such a Revelation hath been heralded in all the sacred Scriptures. Behold how, notwithstanding such an announcement, mankind hath strayed from its path and shut out itself from its glory."* He referred to Himself in the same passage as: *"Him Who is the Promise of all nations."* (Baha'u'llah: *Gleanings,* Page: 5)

Another view of Mt. Carmel, the 'Mountain of the Lord,' showing the Shrine of the Bab, with Terraces below and above the shrine, from the sea to Mt. Carmel's brow.

More information about Baha'u'llah's mission and teachings will come later in this book, but for now I will list His teachings in brief. Please consult Chapter Eight: 'Baha'u'llah's Teachings: What they Could Mean to Christians, and to the World.' You will get much more detail on Baha'u'llah's teachings in that chapter, but here is a brief list:

BAHA'U'LLAH TAUGHT:

1. That there is only one God. The God of the Jews, the Christians, the Buddhists, the Moslems, the Hindus, is one God, not many Gods.
2. That this one God has been the motivating force and the 'Planner' behind the general movement of human history. Thus, history has a 'direction' and a purpose. And, God is 'progressively' unfolding this purpose by fulfilling a promise never to leave man alone and unaided.
3. That this one God has manifested His full 'Presence' in history not just one time, but many times, in a 'progressive' way. Thus, this one God is seen as the reality within all of the Messengers of History, or Manifestations of God, as Baha'u'llah called them. Therefore, Baha'u'llah taught that all the Manifestations are 'from' this one God, including Moses, Buddha, Jesus, Muhammad, Krishna, Zoroaster and, in this day, Baha'u'llah, Himself.
4. That Mankind is One, truly spiritually and physically united (as science also tells us), even though we have not yet realized this truth. Thus, many cultures, many religions, many ethnic groups, but only one human race.
5. That it is God's Will for today that this human race both realize its oneness and enact it by forging ahead into human unity. When we do create that unity, and Baha'u'llah says it is a certainty that it will happen, as it is God's Will for today, we will then realize the truth of His saying: *"The earth is but one country, and*

11935-THOM

mankind its citizens." (Baha'u'llah: *Gleanings*, Page: 250)

6. That there must be absolute equality of women and men. Neither can fulfill their ultimate destiny without acknowledgment and cooperation from the other.

7. That there must be agreement between science and religion, so that empty and meaningless materialism on the one hand and superstition and fanaticism on the other hand may both be rooted out to be replaced with a marriage of faith and reason.

8. That there must be universal education for every child on the planet, with special emphasis on educating girls because they will someday become the first teacher of their own children.

9. That humankind should choose a universal language with everyone learning both their original language and the universal language so that communication between all peoples can be assured. There cannot be unity of the human race, Baha'u'llah said, without this accomplishment. Baha'u'llah stressed that diversity of culture should be maintained, even while unity remains the bright goal of humankind. Thus, the universal language should not blot out or obscure the original language of each culture.

10. That the people of the world should meet in a world assembly to freely vote upon and choose a planetary government, to reduce arms only to those needed for the internal stability of each state and country of the world, and to choose the universal language mentioned above.

11. That what Baha'u'llah called 'extremes' of both wealth and poverty be abolished. This is to be accomplished, He said, not primarily by political means, nor by rules or any bureaucratic solution, but by application of spiritual principles. Baha'u'llah said that there

would still be income levels, based on effort and talent, but that there should be no class of people that is in abject poverty and no class that has thousands of times more wealth than they can ever use in a lifetime. Incidentally, both Jesus and Baha'u'llah made comments that indicate that it will be difficult for the rich man or woman to enter into the 'Kingdom of Heaven.'

12. That humankind was now ready to leave its 'adolescence' and enter into maturity. As a manifestation of this 'maturity', human beings must now learn to 'think for themselves' instead of blindly following authority figures. This is why one of Baha'u'llah's teachings is 'The Independent Investigation of Truth.' One cannot be mature without this ability to weigh things for oneself and make independent, informed decisions. Humanity's first act of maturity will be to unite the planet and the power to do so will be supplied by the coming of Baha'u'llah, *"the Father"* of all mankind and the 'Promise of All Ages.'

There are many other teachings of Baha'u'llah, but this is a short list of His central and important ideas and teachings, which He tells us are the Will of God for today. Chapter eight will give you more detail about His teachings.

Baha'u'llah also told the people of the world (and His message was, at many times, particularly directed toward Christians) that the long awaited appearance of the Manifestation of God, called *'the Father'* was realized in His own Coming. His words tell it more clearly than I ever could:

Speaking about God, the Divine Being, Baha'u'llah says: *"From everlasting Thou hast been a treasure hidden from the sight and minds of men and shalt continue to remain the same for ever and ever."* But then He says*: "In Thy holy Books, in Thy Scriptures and Thy Scrolls Thou hast promised all the peoples of the world that Thou Thyself shalt appear and shalt remove the veils of glory from Thy face"* (Baha'u'llah: *Tablets of Baha'u'llah*, Page: 114) and then *"I bear witness that Thou hast in truth fulfilled Thy pledge and hast made manifest the One Whose advent was foretold by Thy Prophets."* (Baha'u'llah: *Tablets of Baha'u'llah*, Page: 115)

QUESTION: Did I understand you to say that Baha'u'llah not only directly claimed to be the Return of Christ but also to be the appearance of God, as we speak of Him as 'God, the Father'? This sounds preposterous, even crazy!

RESPONSE: Baha'u'llah never said that He was "God, the Father,' nor did Jesus. Again, we have to remember that Jesus said: *"He who has seen Me hath seen the Father"* and *"the Father and I are One."* But He also said that the Father had knowledge that He didn't have. *"But of that day and hour no one knows, not even the angels in heaven, nor the Son, but only the Father."* (Mark 13: 32-33) On another occasion, He stated: *"Why do you call me good? No one is good but One, that is, God."* (Luke 18:19)

But when Jesus said, *"The Father and I are one"* and *"he who has seen me has seen the Father,"* we must remember the impact that these phrases, these claims, had on Jewish believers: Blasphemy, absurdity, an unreal quality. If you are feeling the same way as you listen to the claims of Baha'u'llah, I understand. I felt this way myself upon first hearing these words of Baha'u'llah However, I appeal to you to listen to Baha'u'llah, so that you do not reject Him without a hearing as the Pharisees did with Jesus.

In Baha'u'llah's words: *"Say, Lo! The Father is come, and that which ye were promised in the Kingdom is fulfilled! This is the Word which the Son concealed, when to those around Him He said: 'Ye cannot bear it now.' And when the appointed time was fulfilled and the Hour had struck, the Word shone forth above the horizon of the Will of God.*

"Beware, O followers of the Son, that ye cast it not behind your backs. Take ye fast hold of it. Better is this for you than all that ye possess. Verily He is nigh unto them that do good. The Hour which We had concealed from the knowledge of the peoples of the earth and of the favoured angels hath come to pass. Say, verily, He (that is, Jesus) *hath testified of Me, and I do testify of Him."* (Baha'u'llah: *Tablets of Baha'u'llah*, Page: 11)

QUESTION: The claim of Baha'u'llah to be *"the Father"* seems over-whelming. And a little ridiculous. Surely the context of His words would show His claim to be less than that?

RESPONSE: Let me give you a strong assurance that I will not quote words of Baha'u'llah 'out of context,' so that the meaning would be different if you read the entire paragraph or page. However, please do investigate for yourself. I suggest a reading list in chapter sixteen. Read, and judge for yourself. As you will read in coming chapters of this conversation/book, both Jesus and Baha'u'llah seemed at some times to be claiming 'oneness' with God, while at other times they were very clear that they were not God.

When Baha'u'llah speaks of Himself as *"the Father,"* He is not claiming to be God, anymore than Jesus was claiming to be identical with God. Jesus went out of His way several times to distinguish Himself from God, by saying once, as we saw above that He didn't want to be called 'good' because, in His words: *"No one is good but One, that is, God."* Also, Jesus pointedly said (Mark 13:32-3), as quoted above, that He as *"the Son"* did not know the time of His Return to earth.

In the same vein as these two comments from Christ, Baha'u'llah once said that when He *"turneth His eyes toward His own self, He findeth it the most insignificant of all creation. When He contemplates, however, the bright effulgences He hath been empowered to manifest, lo, that self is transfigured before Him into a sovereign Potency permeating the essence of all things visible and invisible."* Later, in the same passage, He said: *"Glory be to Him, Who, through the power of truth, hath sent down the Manifestation of His own Self and entrusted Him with His message for all mankind."* (Baha'u'llah: *Gleanings*, p. 102)

In a letter written directly to Christians (I'll show you this entire letter later in this conversation), He said: *"Tell Me then: Do the sons* [that is, the Christians] *recognize the Father, and acknowledge Him, or do they deny Him, even as the people aforetime denied Him (Jesus)?"* (Baha'u'llah: *Proclamation of Baha'u'llah*, Page: 97)

QUESTION: This is almost too much to take in. It seems either that it must be true, or it has to be the greatest falsehood ever told, but then, that was the case with Jesus, wasn't it? It has to be one or the other. There is nothing much 'in between' with Jesus, the *"Son of God,"* or with Baha'u'llah, Who claims to be *"the Father."* Maybe you had better tell me something of the story of Baha'u'llah's life, His teachings and His mission.

RESPONSE: Let's do just that. To close this part of our conversation, here is another prayer from the pen of Baha'u'llah:

"Magnified be Thy name, O Lord my God! Thou art He

Whom all things worship and Who worshipeth no one, Who is the Lord of all things and is the vassal of none, Who knoweth all things and is known of none. Thou didst wish to make Thyself known unto men; therefore, Thou didst, through a word of Thy mouth, bring creation into being and fashion the universe. There is none other God except Thee, the Fashioner, the Creator, the Almighty, the Most Powerful.

"I implore Thee, by this very word that hath shone forth above the horizon of Thy will, to enable me to drink deep of the living waters through which Thou hast vivified the hearts of Thy chosen ones and quickened the souls of them that love Thee, that I may, at all times and under all conditions, turn my face wholly towards Thee.

"Thou art the God of power, of glory and bounty. No God is there beside Thee, the Supreme Ruler, the All-Glorious, the Omniscient." (Baha'u'llah: *Prayers and Meditations*, Pages: 6-7)

And a prayer from His son, 'Abdu'l-Baha, who is a central figure in the Baha'i Faith, as you will hear in chapter three:

"O Thou kind Lord! Thou hast created all humanity from the same stock. Thou hast decreed that all shall belong to the same household. In Thy Holy Presence they are all Thy servants, and all mankind are sheltered beneath Thy Tabernacle; all have gathered together at Thy Table of Bounty; all are illumined through the light of Thy Providence.

"O God! Thou art kind to all, Thou hast provided for all, dost shelter all, conferrest life upon all. Thou hast endowed each and all with talents and faculties, and all are submerged in the Ocean of Thy Mercy.

"O Thou kind Lord! Unite all. Let the religions agree and make the nations one, so that they may see each other as one family and the whole earth as one home. May they all live together in perfect harmony. O God! Raise aloft the banner of

the oneness of mankind. O God! Establish the Most Great Peace. Cement Thou, O God, the hearts together.

"O Thou kind Father, God! Gladden our hearts through the fragrance of Thy love. Brighten our eyes through the Light of Thy Guidance. Delight our ears with the melody of Thy Word, and shelter us all in the Stronghold of Thy Providence.

"Thou art the Mighty and Powerful, Thou art the Forgiving and Thou art the One Who overlooketh the shortcomings of all mankind."

('Abdu'l-Baha: *Promulgation of Universal Peace*, Pages: 100-101.)

CHAPTER THREE

HOW IT ALL BEGAN: THE COMING OF BAHA'U'LLAH AND THE BEGINNING OF THE BAHA'I FAITH

QUESTION: It may sound strange to you but I've never heard of the Baha'i Faith and no one I know has ever heard about it, so I need you to give me information about where, when and how the Baha'i Faith began.

RESPONSE: Actually, in Christian terms, it's pretty fascinating, as you will see. During the mid 1800's, the time of your great, or great, great grandfather, Christians were strong in their expectation of the imminent return of Jesus, which they thought would be immediate. They were fervently awaiting Him and they thought it would happen any day. One Christian minister, William Miller, even picked the year, using biblical prophecy, as 1843. Christians in the United States and around the world heard and believed this prediction and eagerly awaited Christ's Return.

When the promised return did not occur, Rev. Miller looked again at his calculations and discovered that he had, he said, made a mistake about the "time of the end" and now pronounced that the Return of Jesus would happen on October 22, 1844, one year later than earlier predicted. His followers, the Millerites, from whom several modern-day churches derive, were disappointed when the promised return still did not occur. The spiritual descendants of the Millerites, including the Jehovah's Witnesses and the Seventh Day Adventists, among others, have often referred to this experience as "The Great Disappointment." Not only these smaller groups, but Methodists, Presbyterians, Baptists and even Episcopalians were excited about the imminent return of Christ.

However, from the Baha'i perspective, Christ's Return *did* occur, but in a different way than was expected by Rev. Miller, his followers, and millions of Christians around the world, who were caught up in a 'millennial fervor.' It was not just the 'Millerites' who believed this. It was widely believed by millions of people of Christian background around the world, of all classes. Speeches were made in the United States Congress about it.

QUESTION: You are saying Christ's Return *did* occur?

RESPONSE: Baha'is believe that it did occur, that when Baha'u'llah appeared He was the Return of Christ to the world. If that is a shocking statement, I can relate very well to how you might feel, since I experienced a whole range of feelings when I first heard this claim, from disgust, to anger, to curiosity and, finally, to the point of wanting to know more.

History is often ironic, isn't it? Especially in this case, since May 23, 1844 is the date on which the Baha'i Faith begins, with a fresh outpouring of God's Grace and an event that signaled, Baha'is believe, the Return of Christ. Baha'is believe Rev. Miller was right, somehow spiritually 'attuned' and should not have felt 'disappointed.' And, though it is not known to most Christians, part of the Moslem world also expected an announcement of a prophetic messenger around the same date. In fact, all the other major faiths, even the religions of the Native Americans and other indigenous peoples pointed to this general time in history as the time of fulfillment of prophesy.

QUESTION: So Baha'u'llah appeared in 1844?

RESPONSE: No, because just as was the case with Jesus, Who was preceded by John the Baptist announcing His coming, Baha'u'llah also had a forerunner, a young merchant of Shiraz, Persia (modern day Iran) who proclaimed to the world that the 'Promise of All Ages' was about to appear. The young merchant, a Manifestation of God in His own right, Baha'is believe, is known by His title: The Bab (which means 'Gate'). The symbolism was clear, namely, that 'the Bab' was the 'Gate' through which the long awaited Promised One of all Religions would walk. The Bab called this Promised One *"Him Whom God shall make manifest"* (The Bab: *Selections from the Bab*, Page: 7) The Bab's name is pronounced with an 'ah' sound, rather than with a short 'a', almost as if saying 'bob.'

I think that the next chapter may help. It's about a

new way of looking at history and trying to understand it in a radically new way. When you understand
what Baha'is mean by 'Progressive Revelation,' I hope
you will begin to see why they are so excited about
the prospect of human unity expressed by an oft-used
Baha'i phrase: 'One God, One Planet, One People.'

We spoke of the Bab, Baha'u'llah's predecessor a
moment ago. When the Bab set forth His mission and
began His ministry, the whole of Persia (modern Iran)
was set into an uproar, for many people responded to
His message and followed His new Faith. His central
message was the imminent coming of the Promised
One of all Ages. His followers began to eagerly await
the appearance of *"Him Whom God shall make manifest"* which was soon to happen.

The Bab said that this Promised One would appear for the sake of the whole world, to unite the
world's peoples, to bring together the races, religions
and cultures of that world and to bring about the
Golden Age of fulfillment of the prophecies of all religions.

In an historical moment reminding us of John the
Baptist and Jesus, there was a follower of the Bab
named Mirza Husayn Ali (known later as Baha'u'llah).
As mentioned earlier, the birth name of Jesus was Jesus
of Nazareth while His title later on was 'Christ', meaning 'The Anointed One.' In this same way, Baha'u'llah
had both a birth name and a title, Baha'u'llah, which
means 'The Glory of God.' Just as Jesus began His
ministry as a follower of John the Baptist (even going
to John to be baptized), Baha'u'llah began His ministry as a follower of the Bab.

But going back to the Bab, His religion grew so
quickly that the state and religious leaders were
alarmed. Remember Annas and Caiaphas (religious

leaders in the time of Jesus) and Pilate (leader of the state) who were alarmed at how the people were responding to Jesus? For that matter, these same religious leaders and state leaders were greatly alarmed at the following of John the Baptist. The same thing happened to the Bab as happened to both John the Baptist and Jesus. The clergy and the state had the Bab executed on July 9, 1850. An account of the apparently miraculous martyrdom of the Bab can be found in the *Encyclopedia Britannica*, but let me whet your interest by telling you that even though seven hundred fifty rifles were used to attempt to execute the Bab, He was unscathed and nowhere to be found after the first fusillade of rifle fire and the clearing of the tremendous cloud of smoke.

Prison guards eventually found Him back in His cell, where He told them that they could now carry out their intention, as His mission was finished. And, they now carried out His execution in the same fashion. Look up this entire story or have a Baha'i friend tell it to you in detail because it is a fascinating historical moment, including a Christian Captain of the rifle forces who refused to carry out the Bab's final execution. His name was Sam Khan and he is well remembered by the Baha'is.

I will include here the last words that the Bab spoke before seven hundred fifty bullets tore through His body. The words were spoken to 10,000 people who had gathered in a barracks square and on the rooftops to witness His execution. A young man had begged the Bab to be allowed to die with Him. The Bab spoke to those assembled before Him and said:

"O wayward generation!" were the last words of the Bab to the gazing multitude, as the regiment prepared to fire its volley, *"Had you believed in Me every one of*

*you would have followed the example of this youth, who
stood in rank above most of you, and would have willingly
sacrificed himself in My path. The day will come when you
will have recognized Me; that day I shall have ceased to be
with you.*" (Quoted in Shoghi Effendi: *God Passes By*, Page:
53)

QUESTION: What happened then? And where does
Baha'u'llah come into the picture?

RESPONSE: As I began to tell you earlier,
Baha'u'llah was a follower of the Bab, just as Jesus at
one point was a follower of John the Baptist. The Bab
was martyred in 1850. Persia was still in chaos, with
the government and clergy intent upon exterminat-
ing the community of the followers of the Bab. They
martyred 20,000 or more people who chose to die
rather than give up their Faith. Most of them were
offered life if they would utter one word of denial but
few chose that path. The Bab's followers were true to
His central message that God would very soon make
Himself known in a way awaited by the entire world.
They were eagerly awaiting the appearance of *"Him
Whom God shall make manifest."*

In 1853, three years after the martyrdom of the
Bab, Baha'u'llah had been cast into a prison dungeon
called 'The Black Pit,' along with other followers of
the Bab. It was in this dark, oppressive dungeon that
Baha'u'llah received God's Revelation, fully realizing
for the first time that He was *"Him Whom God shall
make manifest"* and the One sent by God, the 'Promised One of All Ages.'

When Jesus was baptized, a dove, symbolizing the
Holy Spirit, hovered above His head and there was,

the New Testament tells us, a voice that said: *"You are My beloved Son; in You I am well pleased."* Luke 3:22

Baha'u'llah's experience in the dungeon bears a striking similarity to the story of the Holy Spirit descending upon Jesus in the form of a dove. This is what happened: There appeared before Baha'u'llah, suspended in the air above His head, that same Holy Spirit, symbolized by a beautiful maiden, who pointed at His head and said: *"Verily, We shall render Thee victorious by Thyself and by Thy pen. Grieve Thou not for that which hath befallen Thee, neither be Thou afraid, for Thou art in safety. Ere long will God raise up the treasures of the earth—men who will aid Thee through Thyself and through Thy Name, wherewith God hath revived the hearts of such as have recognized Him."* (Quoted in Shoghi Effendi: *God Passes By*, Page: 101)

We are allowed a 'rare' glimpse at what happens when a 'Manifestation' of God begins to realize that God will be speaking and acting through Him as Baha'u'llah shares with us what happened next. He is still in the dungeon:

"During the days I lay in the prison of Tihran [the dungeon was in the capital city of Iran, now spelled as Teheran] ... *though the galling weight of the chains and the stench-filled air allowed Me but little sleep, still in those infrequent moments of slumber I felt as if something flowed from the crown of My head over My breast, even as a mighty torrent that precipitateth itself upon the earth from the summit of a lofty mountain. Every limb of My body would, as a result, be set afire. At such moments My tongue recited what no man could bear to hear."* (Quoted in Shoghi Effendi: *God Passes By*, Page: 101)

Later in His ministry, Baha'u'llah referred to a time when He was well aware of the Divine Presence in His life and His Ministry. He said: *"And whenever I chose to hold my peace and be still, lo, the voice of the Holy Ghost, standing on my right hand, aroused me, and the Supreme Spirit appeared before my face, and Gabriel overshadowed me, and the Spirit of Glory stirred within my bosom, bidding me arise and break my silence."* (Baha'u'llah: *Gleanings*, Page: 103)

When Baha'u'llah was released, He was banished from Persia to Baghdad, Iraq, then to Constantinople (now Istanbul), then to Adrianople (now Edirne), and finally, to a prison city—Akka, Palestine (now Israel). The clergy of Iran and the Sultan of the Islamic empire were attempting to remove Baha'u'llah so far from Persia that His influence on His followers would wane. They did not realize that the 'Divine Light' cannot be extinguished, not in a dungeon nor in a faraway prison city. Many writers and scholars of the Baha'i Faith have noted that Baha'u'llah's successive banishment and imprisonment seemed to be in fulfillment of Biblical prophecy. We can talk more about this later.

His final banishment was to the city of Akka, in the vicinity of Mt. Carmel, the 'Mountain of the Lord' of the Old Testament. This is where the Baha'i World Center now exists and it is also where the remains of the Bab lie in a beautiful shrine. The city of Haifa, Israel, lies at the foot of the 'Mountain of the Lord' and its citizens look up to the Baha'i Shrines in the bosom of that mountain. In the early part of the Twenty-First Century, more than one non-Baha'i writer has referred to the Gardens and Terraces of the Shrine of the Bab as the 'Eighth Wonder of the World.'

The Shrine of the Bab sits astride Mt. Carmel–the Mountain of the Lord, in Haifa, Israel.

On the eve of His banishment from Baghdad (April, 1863), Baha'u'llah spent several days in a garden called Ridvan (the name in Arabic means 'Paradise'). He had waited a full ten years to announce His Mission to the world, which He now did, while camped in that Garden. Over the next thirty years, though He was subject to continuous banishment, imprisonment or house arrest, He

continued to pour forth the stream of God's new Revelation. Neither torture, nor isolation, nor condemnation
by the authorities could keep Him from unfolding God's
Will for humanity.

QUESTION: Let me interrupt you a moment! It
sounds as if Baha'u'llah was a criminal. The state pun-
ished Him, put Him in prison, banished Him and kept
Him under house arrest. Was He a criminal? If so, why
are you talking about Him in this reverential way?

RESPONSE: Well, I can understand your confusion.
Do we consider Christ to be a criminal? Of course not!
We don't think that way about Christ at all, do we? But
we have to remember that Jesus was 'legally' executed as
a criminal on several criminal charges put forth by religious and state leaders. He was condemned by the top
religious leaders and the leader of the state, Pilate.

So I guess it's a point of view: Pilate thought Christ
was a criminal, and the Sultan of the Ottoman Empire
thought Baha'u'llah was a criminal, but now that time
has gone by, we realize that those religious and tempo-
ral leaders were not only short-sighted, but wrong. Pilate
missed recognizing the *'Son of God'*—Jesus. Likewise,
Sultan Abdu'l-'Aziz, missed recognizing the *'Father'*—
Baha'u'llah. (Quoted in Shoghi Effendi: *God Passes By*,
Page: 17)

Now, to get back to the story of Baha'u'llah. Even
though He was undergoing banishment and imprisonment over the next thirty years (1863–1892), He steadily
revealed what God had commissioned Him to give to
humanity. A mighty torrent of scripture poured forth,
all of which we have in His handwriting or under His
seal in their original form. There are more than ten

thousand documents, papers and letters and several dozen book-length writings.

Baha'u'llah suffered all His life, saying, on one occasion: *"I have been, most of the days of My life . . . sitting under a sword hanging on a thread."* (Baha'u'llah: *Epistle to the Son of the Wolf,* Page: 94) However, Baha'u'llah said His sufferings had a purpose. *"I have accepted to be tried by manifold adversities for no purpose except to regenerate all that are in Thy heaven and on Thy earth."* (Baha'u'llah: *Prayers and Meditations,* Page: 198) And He said that He *"hath consented to be bound with chains that mankind may be released from its bondage, and hath accepted to be made a prisoner within this most mighty Stronghold that the whole world may attain unto true liberty. He hath drained to its dregs the cup of sorrow, that all the peoples of the earth may attain unto abiding joy, and be filled with gladness."* (Baha'u'llah: *Gleanings,* Page: 99)

QUESTION: Baha'u'llah may have gone to prison, but Jesus was sacrificed upon the cross for the sins of the world. God sacrificed His own Son! Don't you appreciate the significance of that?

RESPONSE: This sacrifice was amazing and significant. Baha'u'llah speaks of it often. But regarding being sent to prison, which He accepted as God's Will, Baha'u'llah spoke of Himself as the One *"Whom Thou hast sacrificed that all the dwellers of Thine earth and heaven may be born anew, and Whom Thou hast cast into prison that mankind may, as a token of Thy bounty and of Thy sovereign might, be released from the bondage of evil passions and corrupt desires."* (Baha'u'llah: *Prayers and Meditations,* Page: 44) You will hear, as we continue our conversation, that Baha'u'llah teaches that God has sacrificed over and over again in the sending of Manifestations of Himself to humanity. Each of them has suffered and sacrificed in a significant way. Each time, this sacrifice, this suffering, has been for the sins of the world and the salvation of all.

Also, regarding the purpose of His imprisonment, Baha'u'llah said: *"My body hath endured imprisonment that ye may be released from the bondage of self."* (Baha'u'llah: *Tablets of Baha'u'llah*, Page: 12) Christians believe that Christ's suffering was for the salvation of the world. Baha'is believe the same thing about Christ. The difference is that Baha'u'llah taught that His own suffering and the suffering of all the Manifestations of God was also for the world's salvation and regeneration. More on this later in Chapter Nine: 'Similarities and Differences of the Christian and Baha'i Faiths.'

In 1892, Baha'u'llah's Spirit ascended. He left a Will and Testament, naming His Son, 'Abdu'l-Baha (His name means 'Servant of Baha'u'llah) to lead the community of Baha'is and, more importantly, to be what He called the *"Center of my Covenant"* with the Baha'is and with all humankind. Baha'u'llah said that God has always set forth a *"Covenant"* with mankind and that whenever a new Manifestation of God's Being appears in our human history, this 'Covenant' is being renewed.

Likewise, each Manifestation makes a 'Covenant' with His followers. Baha'u'llah's 'Covenant' with mankind involved telling His followers to turn toward 'Abdu'l-Baha as the only one who was authorized to interpret the meaning of His revelation. In this way, unity, so important not only to the Baha'is but to the world, could be maintained. As a result, 'Abdu'l-Baha is central in the Baha'i Faith, and His writings and prayers are very dear to the Baha'is and considered part of our Scripture. I will conclude this chapter with several prayers from 'Abdu'l-Baha.

Baha'u'llah asked that the Baha'is embrace and vigorously pursue the task of healing and uniting the world. He indicated this would prove impossible *"unless the peoples of the world unite in pursuit of one common aim and embrace one universal faith."* (Baha'u'llah: *Tablets of Baha'u'llah*, Page: 69) He also charged the Baha'is with the task of electing a *"House of Justice"* (a governing body) in every community in the world where there are nine or more Baha'is. These 'Houses of Justice' are called 'Local Spiritual Assemblies' at this time in Baha'i history. (There are many tens of thousands of them around the world.)

Finally, He asked that when the Faith had spread throughout the world (which was finally accomplished in the 1950's) that the worldwide Baha'i Community should elect a 'Universal House of Justice.' This institution, the direct creation of Baha'u'llah and drawn from all over the world, was elected for the first time in 1963. Baha'u'llah called this Universal House of Justice (and all of the Local and Spiritual Assemblies around the world) *"the Trustees of the All-Merciful"* and *"the Trustees of God among His servants and the dayspring of authority in His countries."* (Baha'u'llah: *Tablets of Baha'u'llah*, Pages 26-7) Therefore, Baha'is see these institutions as divinely ordained, having the task of administering all the affairs of the worldwide Baha'i Community.

Baha'u'llah left a great legacy of scripture to guide the Baha'is but said that for anything not covered in His Revelation, the Baha'is were to turn to this Universal House of Justice. They would decide based upon what Baha'u'llah called *"the needs and requirements of the time"* (Baha'u'llah: *Tablets of Baha'u'llah*, Page 27) He gave them the task of being *"a shelter for the poor and needy"* (Baha'u'llah: *Tablets of Baha'u'llah*, Page 128) and charged them to act in the *"protection and safeguarding"* of humankind. (Baha'u'llah: *Tablets of Baha'u'llah*, Page: 27,69,91)

Most important of all, Baha'u'llah assured that this institution would have Divine Guidance, saying: *"God will verily inspire them with whatsoever He willeth."* He asked them to *"take counsel together regarding those things which have not outwardly been revealed in the Book"* (Baha'u'llah: *Tablets of Baha'u'llah,* Page: 68), telling them once again that they would be the *"recipients of divine inspiration from the unseen Kingdom".* (Baha'u'llah: *Tablets of Baha'u'llah,* Page: 27

Because of His appointment of His son 'Abdu'l-Baha as the sole interpreter of His Revelation and because of the guidance of God that He bestowed on the Universal House of Justice, the Baha'i Faith has not fallen victim to disunity, which very often occurs quickly after the founder of a religion has died, as sadly happened in both Christianity and Islam.

QUESTION: You said a moment ago that the Baha'i Faith had spread over the entire planet. I doubt that. Wouldn't I have heard about it if it were so widespread?

RESPONSE: The Baha'i Faith is not trying to be silent or stealthy. Every Baha'i would like to 'shout from the rooftops' but yes, somehow this interesting development has occurred right now in the Twentieth Century. I guess most of humanity has been looking the other way, just as they were when Christ came. The world at large took almost no note of the Christian faith for several hundred years. When they did take note, it was to see Christianity as a 'dangerous cult' with atheistic tendencies (Christians refused to believe in or to sacrifice to the Roman 'gods,' so to Roman citizens, they were atheists, as strange as that sounds.)

If you would like a reference on the spread of the Baha'i Faith, consult the Encyclopedia Britannica again, which in 1996 declared the Baha'i Faith to be the world's most widespread religion, second only to Christianity. Let me tease you; maybe you were looking the other way at wars, cold wars, atomic explosions, revolutions, terrorism, and the like, while *"the Father"*—Baha'u'llah— put in His appearance. Two thousand years ago, many Romans were definitely 'looking the other way' and missed the appearance of *"The Son of God."*

The Baha'is have received a definite charge from Baha'u'llah, a mission to unite the world. You have already told me that this mission sounds grandiose, but I don't have a choice about whether or not to tell you about it because that is precisely what Baha'u'llah asked Baha'is to do. We believe humanity's accomplishment of this mission of unity and peace is God's Will for today's world and today's people. Baha'is have already been hard at work in the Twentieth Century, while the people of the world were 'looking the other way,' to spread the Faith of Baha'u'llah and to broadcast His teachings. We believe those teachings will have a transforming effect on a world so much in need.

So, while the world seemed to be 'coming apart' in the Twentieth Century, as destruction and devastation and planetary breakdown seemed to be the order of the day, there was another process going on—a process of a new and different world slowly, surely being built, a new world that mankind has been long awaiting, a world of peace, unity and fulfillment. This is the way Baha'u'llah put it:

"O friends! It behoveth you to refresh and revive your souls through the gracious favors which in this Divine, this soul-stirring Springtime are being showered upon you. The Day Star of His great glory hath shed its radiance upon you, and the clouds of His limitless grace have overshadowed you. How high the reward of him that hath not deprived himself of

so great a bounty, nor failed to recognize the beauty of his Best-Beloved in this, His new attire."(Baha'u'llah: *Gleanings,* Page: 94)

"Say: O men! This is a matchless Day. Matchless must, likewise, be the tongue that celebrateth the praise of the Desire of all nations, and matchless the deed that aspireth to be acceptable in His sight. The whole human race hath longed for this Day, that perchance it may fulfil that which well beseemeth its station, and is worthy of its destiny. Blessed is the man whom the affairs of the world have failed to deter from recognizing Him Who is the Lord of all things." (Baha'u'llah: *Gleanings, Page: 39*)

And: *"This is the Day whereon the Ocean of God's mercy hath been manifested unto men, the Day in which the Day Star of His loving-kindness hath shed its radiance upon them, the Day in which the clouds of His bountiful favor have overshadowed the whole of mankind. Now is the time to cheer and refresh the down-cast through the invigorating breeze of love and fellowship, and the living waters of friendliness and charity."* (Baha'u'llah: *Gleanings,* Page: 7)

"Take heed lest anything deter thee from extolling the greatness of this Day—the Day whereon the Finger of majesty and power hath opened the seal of the Wine of Reunion, and called all who are in the heavens and all who are on the earth. Preferrest thou to tarry when the breeze announcing the Day of God hath already breathed over thee, or art thou of them that are shut out as by a veil from Him?" (Baha'u'llah: *Gleanings,* Page: 28)

Also: *"Say: He Who is the Unconditioned is come, in the clouds of light, that He may quicken all created things with the breezes of His Name, the Most Merciful, and unify the world, and gather all men around this Table which hath been sent down from heaven."* (Baha'u'llah: *Epistle to the Son of the Wolf,* Page: 46) *"Darkness hath been chased away by the dawning light of the mercy of thy Lord, the Source of all light.*

The breeze of the All-Merciful hath wafted, and the souls have been quickened in the tombs of their bodies." (Baha'u'llah: *Tablets of Baha'u'llah*, Page: 118)

Finally: *"The hands of bounty have borne round the cup of everlasting life. Approach, and quaff your fill . . . "* (Baha'u'llah: *Gleanings*, Page: 32)

So, charged by Baha'u'llah, Baha'is labored mightily to take the healing message of the Faith into every corner of the Earth. As I told you, this was accomplished by 1963, so that the Universal House of Justice could be elected. The Baha'is are still concentrating on bringing this message to every human being on the planet. While this 'outreach' is occurring, the Baha'is are also constructing a World Center in Haifa, Israel, as I mentioned earlier.

This nerve center in the Holy Land (now 'holy' to four Faiths—Judaism, Christianity, Islam and Baha'i) is serving to coordinate and energize the spread of the message of the coming of Baha'u'llah and His teachings. The goal of this world center and of the Baha'is over the entire world is none other than the unification of the human race, under one God. Daunting? Impossible? Consider this: Wouldn't it have been well nigh impossible to have told the early Christians that they wouldn't be able to fulfil the commandment of Christ to *"Go into all the world, and preach the gospel to every creature."*? (Mark 16:15) Baha'is, like those early Christians, are confident that they can, with divine assistance, take this message to every person in the world.

QUESTION: To me, you seem a little vague when you talk about a 'healing, uniting message.' Just how do the Baha'is even hope to make an impact on a world like the one we have now, so disunited, violent, and angry?

RESPONSE: Two ways. First, wherever there are Baha'is, there is a community of men and women, youth and children, who live their lives by a renewed power of the Holy Spirit instilled in them by Baha'u'llah and by a set of teachings given by Baha'u'llah, teachings that are remarkable by any standard. These are teachings that affect individual behavior, then go on to affect the way a community of people act and react toward each other and to the world at large. I'll tell you more about Baha'u'llah's teachings in chapter eight, but for the moment, imagine the following:

Imagine that you are driving through the mid west of the United States or through Spain or through sub-Saharan Africa or in South America or through Indonesia. Imagine yourself to be *anywhere* on the planet and the person riding with you says: "Did you know that an unusual group of people live in the town (or village) just ahead?" You reply: "Why are they so different?"

Your friend says: "Listen to this. The people in this village or town all believe in the equality of men and women, *every last one of them.* They *all* are trying very hard to eradicate all forms of prejudice from their individual and community lives. They *all* believe not only in Jesus, but also in Buddha, Muhammad, Moses, Zoroaster and all the manifestations of God that have appeared in human history. They *all* believe in the oneness of religion, the oneness of God, the oneness of the human race. Many of them intermarry between the so-called 'races' and even promote intermarriage."

You probably would say: "That couldn't be true, could it?" Your friend continues that everyone in this small village considers themselves 'world citizens' and that they support the establishment of a universal language. Then, finally, because you don't believe him at all, your friend tells you that the village ahead is a Baha'i village and that, in fact, wherever Baha'is live on the planet, in whatever country, they are conducting their lives by these values and beliefs given them by Baha'u'llah, who said: *"I can utter no word, O my God, unless I be permitted by Thee, and can move in no direction until I obtain Thy sanction. It is Thou, O my God, Who hast called me into being through the power of Thy might, and hast endued me with Thy grace to manifest Thy Cause."* (Baha'u'llah: *Prayers and Meditations*, Page: 208)

Today, there is a worldwide network of Baha'is, all united in the set of objectives mentioned above, all of them focused on a goal of the recognition and the creation of human unity.

QUESTION: You said there was a second way, besides your teachings and your community life that Baha'is would use to make a practical impact upon the world. You certainly do know that nice and beautiful teachings alone won't really do much. What about human nature, and what about 'sin'?

RESPONSE: You couldn't be more right about that last point. If all that the Baha'i Faith had to offer were a new set of teachings, it wouldn't be enough, no matter how beautiful or compelling. In fact, the teachings are secondary to the appearance of Baha'u'llah, who brings the Divine energy needed for these tasks that the teachings propose and, more importantly, Baha'u'llah brings salvation not just for individuals, but also for a dying, failing world.

One of the proofs of Jesus Christ, when He appeared the first time, was that those who followed Him began to lead changed, transformed lives, full of new and more positive values and beliefs, people who were energized with a new set of goals and who led individual and community lives that expressed a new ethic, a new culture and, in essence, a new world.

This is exactly what is happening when a person follows Baha'u'llah. Baha'u'llah tells us He is the Return of Christ to the world as well as the appearance of *"The Father"* of all mankind. This follower, this person is transformed, saved, brought into a new life, infused with new values and ideas and charged with a mission to enact, with others, the reality of a united humanity. The old saying that the proof is in the pudding probably applies here.

Take a look at the Baha'i communities and witness what is going on. If they are not leading those transformed lives, if their communities are not vibrant examples of a unifying force for humanity, then your question of who Baha'u'llah is gets really easy. In that event, He is probably just a mystic, a wise man, maybe a saint, someone to study, but not Who He says He is.

On the other hand, of course, if you take that look at the Baha'is and their communities and you see what I have described, then maybe your decision on who Baha'u'llah is gets 'heated up' and becomes quite important not only in your life but in the lives of every individual on this planet.

No, it's not just new teachings, though they are powerful and energizing. It is the fact that the Promise of all Ages has showed up, the Return of Christ has occurred and there is a fresh outpouring of Divine guidance in the person of Baha'u'llah, the *"Father"* of all mankind. Baha'u'llah said that God had given many wonderful *"gifts"* to humankind, but: *"That which is preeminent above all other gifts, is incorruptible in nature, and pertaineth to God Himself, is the gift of Divine Revelation. Every bounty conferred by the Creator upon man, be it material or spiritual, is subservient unto this.*

" It is, in its essence, and will ever so remain, the Bread which cometh down from Heaven. It is God's supreme testimony, the clearest evidence of His truth, the sign of His consummate bounty, the token of His all-encompassing mercy, the proof of His most loving providence, the symbol of His most perfect grace. He hath, indeed, partaken of this highest gift of God who hath recognized His Manifestation in this Day. " (Baha'u'llah: *Gleanings*, Page: 195)

QUESTION: The truth is I'm still uncertain about what you are saying. It all sounds so new, so unlikely, and I've been wondering, how could all this have been happening without my notice. As I said before, why didn't I hear about it until now? Why, if it's so great, hasn't it been in the news, why isn't the world taking notice? Oh, I heard you when you said that the world didn't take notice of the Christian Faith for over a hundred years and more, but these are modern times, with instant communication, a thousand newspapers and books and every form of media. I just don't get it!

RESPONSE: To help you to know the actual growth and spread of the Baha'i Faith, statistics released in the year 2000 showed the following: The Baha'i Faith was established in 190 countries of the world. It had nearly 6,000,000 adherents. There were 2,112 races, tribes and ethnic groups represented and literature existed in 803 languages. National Spiritual Assemblies existed in 182 countries. Local Spiritual Assemblies were counted at 12,591 and Baha'is lived in 129,949 localities around the globe. The Encyclopedia Britannica, in 1996, referred to the Baha'i Faith as the most widespread religion in the world, save for Christianity.

And maybe this will help. We are probably at the point, here in the Twenty-First century of the Common

Era, where the world will begin to take proper notice of the Baha'i Faith and the Baha'i community, which will soon be too large to ignore and, more importantly, so effective in changing lives and building vibrant, successful communities, that the world will be quite ready to notice and, perhaps, to emulate. That is our hope, that we can provide a guiding light, a successful example of the presence of unity in the world. We believe that this 'presence of unity' will draw the people of earth to the long-promised time of resurrection and reunion that, in some way, all Faiths have predicted and prophesied.

As we've said before, the Christian community was extremely small and little noticed in the great Roman Empire for more than one hundred years. Witness the fact that (with only one or two minor exceptions) not one well-known person was a Christian for three centuries, not one poet or scholar, nor general nor governor nor anyone of note. But then, suddenly, Christianity broke out into the world's attention and within a short few decades, everyone seems to know about it.

I'll bet some people who were around in 100 AD said what you said, that they just couldn't understand, if the Christian Faith was so great, why hadn't they heard about it and why it wasn't being talked about in the Roman Senate? You can test this with your own memory. Can you think of a well-known Christian in the first three centuries after the beginning of the Christian Faith, other than the Paul and the Apostles and companions of Christ?

My own answer to this question is this: When you brought this up before, I said that all I can figure out is that this is 'God's way of doing things,' slow and steady, person by person, transformed life by transformed life, toward new spiritually empowered, task-oriented communities and finally, on to a broadly changed, new and better world. Christians, if they understand the history of the early Church, know what I am talking about. The very thing that happened in early Christianity is happening again in the world as we speak, within Baha'i individuals and Baha'i communities. Take a look at the Baha'is and the Baha'i Community to see whether or not I am telling a true story. I assure you that I am, but nothing beats finding out for yourself.

It's easy enough to do. Reading this book and entering into this conversation is just a first step. Next, find the Baha'is and take a look at them. *Chapter fifteen* tells you not only how to contact the author to 'join the conversation' but also how to find the Baha'is, if they are not already a presence in your community. If you have a computer or access to one, log onto www.Bahai.org for complete information.

Finally, as to your expressed confusion, I think that the next chapter may help. It's about a new way of looking at history and trying to understand history in a new and radically different way. When you understand what Baha'u'llah means by 'progressive revelation,' you will begin to see why the Baha'is are so excited about the prospect of human unity expressed by a Baha'i phrase—'one God, one planet, one people'.

To close this chapter, here are three prayers, one from Baha'u'llah, followed by two from 'Abdu'l-Baha, His Son. I promised you these prayers from 'Abdu'l-Baha and I think you may enjoy them quite a bit.

First from Baha'u'llah:

"O my God! O my God! Unite the hearts of Thy servants, and reveal to them Thy great purpose. May they follow Thy commandments and abide in Thy law. Help them, O God, in their endeavor, and grant them strength to serve Thee. O God! Leave them not to themselves, but guide their steps by the light of Thy knowledge, and cheer their hearts by Thy love.

Verily, Thou art their Helper and their Lord." (Baha'u'llah: *Baha'i Prayers* (US), Page: 206)

And from 'Abdu'l-Baha:

"*O my God! O my God! Verily, I invoke Thee and supplicate before Thy threshold, asking Thee that all Thy mercies may descend upon these souls. Specialize them for Thy favor and Thy truth.*

"*O Lord! Unite and bind together the hearts, join in accord all the souls, and exhilarate the spirits through the signs of Thy sanctity and oneness. O Lord! Make these faces radiant through the light of Thy oneness. Strengthen the loins of Thy servants in the service of Thy kingdom.*

"*O Lord, Thou possessor of infinite mercy! O Lord of forgiveness and pardon! Forgive our sins, pardon our shortcomings, and cause us to turn to the kingdom of Thy clemency, invoking the kingdom of might and power, humble at Thy shrine and submissive before the glory of Thine evidences.*

"*O Lord God! Make us as waves of the sea, as flowers of the garden, united, agreed through the bounties of Thy love. O Lord! Dilate the breasts through the signs of Thy oneness, and make all mankind as stars shining from the same height of glory, as perfect fruits growing upon Thy tree of life.*

"*Verily, Thou art the Almighty, the Self-Subsistent, the Giver, the Forgiving, the Pardoner, the Omniscient, the One Creator.*" ('Abdu'l-Baha: *Baha'i Prayers* (US edition), Pages: 204-205)

Keeping in mind that so many of the world's peoples are caught up in the destructive passions and false gods of racism, nationalism, sexism and are deprived of any idea or any hope of unity with other cultures, religions and races, this following prayer of Abdul-Baha seems directly keyed to the needs of the masses of people around the world.

"*O Thou, my God, Who guidest the seeker to the pathway that leadeth aright, Who deliverest the lost and blinded soul out of the wastes of perdition, Thou Who bestowest upon the sincere great bounties and favours, Who guardest the frightened within Thine impregnable refuge, Who answerest, from Thine all-highest horizon, the cry of those who cry out unto Thee. Praised be Thou, O my Lord! Thou hast guided the distracted out of the death of unbelief, and hast brought those who draw nigh unto Thee to the journey's goal, and hast rejoiced the assured among Thy servants by granting them their most cherished desires, and hast, from Thy Kingdom of beauty, opened before the faces of those who yearn after Thee the gates of reunion, and hast rescued them from the fires of deprivation and loss—so that they hastened unto Thee and gained Thy presence, and arrived at Thy welcoming door, and received of gifts an abundant share.*

"O my Lord, they thirsted, Thou didst lift to their parched lips the waters of reunion. O Tender One, Bestowing One, Thou didst calm their pain with the balm of Thy bounty and grace, and didst heal their ailments with the sovereign medicine of Thy compassion. O Lord, make firm their feet on Thy straight path, make wide for them the needle's eye, and cause them, dressed in royal robes, to walk in glory for ever and ever.

"Verily art Thou the Generous, the Ever-Giving, the Precious, the Most Bountiful. There is none other God but Thee, the Mighty, the Powerful, the Exalted, the Victorious." ('Abdu'l-Baha: *Selections,* Page: 317)

CHAPTER FOUR

PROGRESSIVE REVELATION: A NEW WAY OF UNDERSTANDING HISTORY

QUESTION: What do you mean by 'A new way of understanding history?' And what does this phrase 'progressive revelation' mean? It sounds rather strange to me, a Christian. God has revealed Himself only once, in His Son.

RESPONSE: Well, while I understand what you are saying, aren't you forgetting that God revealed His Will at least one other time in a very direct way, through Moses? Upon reflection, we can surely agree that Christians believe in at least two 'revelations' of God and, in that earlier revelation, God actually appeared to Moses as a 'burning bush' and spoke to Him. Later, He even allowed Moses to see Him, if you recall (Exodus 33: 23).

No one ever compares the words, prophecies and

teachings of Jeremiah and Isaiah, great as they were, to the revelation of the Ten Commandments, which were revealed very directly by God to Moses. God spoke to Moses directly, the Bible says, something that He did not even do with Jesus, according to the New Testament. Jesus, however, often speaks to God in the New Testament.

Additionally, Christians await the Return of Christ, which would be a new, fresh outpouring of revelation. This would be a third revelation, counting Moses, Christ's first Advent and His Second Coming, still expected by Christians. In these three revelations, one can see 'progressive' stages of revelation in Christian thinking. A Christian minister, who was one of the 'readers' of this book, remarked that progressive revelation is seen by some Christians in the sacraments and in the life of the Church itself.

QUESTION: I hadn't ever thought of it that way. But surely you realize that Christians don't see Moses on the same level as Christ?

RESPONSE: I do realize that. Nor do Christians see Muhammad, Buddha or Krishna on the same level. But Baha'u'llah taught that Jesus, Buddha, Muhammad, Zoroaster, Moses, Krishna and all of the Manifestations of history are from the same God, are Manifestations of that one God and all have been carrying out God's Divine Plan, a Plan that is apparently larger than we have ever known. A quote from Baha'u'llah that highlights this idea: *"If thou wilt observe with discriminating eyes, thou wilt behold Them all abiding in the same tabernacle, soaring in the same heaven, seated upon the same throne, uttering the same speech, and proclaiming the same Faith."* (Baha'u'llah: *Gleanings*, Page: 52)

And when Baha'u'llah brought God's Will to today's humanity, He did not just call it a 'new Revelation,' but rather said this: *"This is the changeless Faith of God, eternal in the past, eternal in the future."* (Baha'u'llah: *Gleanings*, Page: 136)

Baha'u'llah says that God has revealed Himself many times in history, saying: *"And when Thou didst purpose to make Thyself known unto men, Thou didst successively reveal the Manifestations of Thy Cause, and ordained each to be a sign of Thy Revelation among Thy people, and the Day-Spring of Thine invisible Self amidst Thy creatures."* (Baha'u'llah: *Prayers and Meditations*, Page: 128)

QUESTION: What does that word 'Dayspring' mean? I'm not familiar with it.

RESPONSE: Take a look at Luke 1:78. This is a word that is used in the New Testament (Actually, the New Testament is quoting the Jewish Scriptures—the Old Testament—at the time.) Dayspring is a word for the sun, as our source of light and as a symbol of spiritual light. Here is the complete quote: *" Through the tender mercy of our God, With which the Dayspring from on high has visited us; To give light to those who sit in darkness and the shadow of death, to guide our feet into the way of peace."*

In another place, Baha'u'llah points out that God had always come to man in this way, that is, by causing Manifestations of Himself *"to appear out of the realm of the spirit, in the noble form of the human temple."* (Baha'u'llah: *Gleanings*, Page: 47) Baha'u'llah said that God had revealed Himself in this way from "the *beginning that hath no beginning"* and would continue to do so *"until the end that hath no end."* Here is the full quote:

"There can be no doubt whatever that if for one moment the tide of His mercy and grace were to be withheld from the

world, it would completely perish. For this reason, from the beginning that hath no beginning the portals of Divine mercy have been flung open to the face of all created things, and the clouds of Truth will continue to the end that hath no end to rain on the soil of human capacity, reality and personality their favors and bounties. Such hath been God's method continued from everlasting to everlasting." (Baha'u'llah: *Gleanings*, Pages: 68-69)

QUESTION: But what Christians believe is that history has a 'center' and that 'center' was formed when He sent His 'only-begotten Son' for the salvation of mankind. Don't you see that 'only-begotten' prevents Christians from seeing God's Revelation in anyone else?

RESPONSE: Baha'is do not dispute that Jesus is the only Manifestation Who has the station and the name of *'Son.'* And He is certainly and truly 'only-begotten' in the sense that there cannot be another *"Son."* You have already heard that Baha'u'llah not only refers to Christ as *'the Son'* and to Himself as the Return of Christ and His Spirit to the world, but Baha'u'llah also says—in a letter written to the Christians of the world—*"The Father hath come."* (That is, the *"Father"* of all mankind.)

QUESTION: Baha'u'llah saying He is *'the Father'* really sounds insulting and crazy. Can you mean what you are saying? Could *He* have meant it!?

RESPONSE: I do mean it because I know Baha'u'llah meant it. He said it directly, forcefully and repeatedly. The only suggestion I can possibly make, as you hear what to you is astounding and almost blasphemous, is this: You could remember how difficult it must have been for Jewish ears in Christ's time to hear Jesus saying *"All* *power is given unto me in heaven and in earth"* and to have His disciples call Him *'The Son of God."* It must have been confusing and challenging for them, just as it is now for you to hear Baha'u'llah call Himself *'The Father."*

And, as for Jesus being the center of history, a careful reading of the New Testament causes many Christians to think that while Jesus' first advent was all important to the world and to history, it will be His Second Coming that will be the true central event of all history, the time of consummation, of fulfillment and of the building of the Kingdom of God and the expression of His Will: *"on earth as it is in Heaven."*

QUESTION: Are you saying that Baha'u'llah teaches that God has revealed Himself many times in history? Aside from Moses, Christians don't believe that, but it sounds intriguing. I would like to know more.

RESPONSE: Yes. Baha'u'llah says that every time God reveals Himself it is a central and critical moment in history. Each time such a new revelation takes place, Baha'u'llah calls it a 'Manifestation' of God, a fresh outpouring of the 'Word of God.' From a Christian point of view, this 'Word of God' is the reality of Christ. But, as Baha'is, we are taught by Baha'u'llah that the 'Word of God' was in *all* the Manifestations. This 'Word of God,' or this 'Christ Spirit' is the animating force in each and every Manifestation of God. That is why I say that the Baha'i teachings bring us a 'Larger Christ' than we have ever known.

Christians finally decided, five centuries after Jesus (at the Council of Chalcedon, in 451 AD), that Christ was 'fully man' as well as 'fully God,' seeing that Christ had both a human and a divine station. Baha'is realize that the Manifestations are different, in their 'human' capacity, or station. In fact, Baha'u'llah taught that all the Manifestations are quite different in this human station, or what Baha'u'llah calls the *'station of distinction'*, which *"pertaineth to the world of creation, and to the limitations thereof. In this respect, each Manifestation of God hath a distinct individuality, a definitely prescribed mission, a predestined revelation, and specially designated limitations. Each one of them is known by a different name, is characterized by a special attribute, fulfils a definite mission, and is entrusted with a particular Revelation"* (Baha'u'llah: *Gleanings*, Page: 52)

However, these Manifestations or High Prophets are seen by Baha'u'llah as *"one and the same"* when viewed in their second station, the *"station of unity."* In this station, Baha'u'llah tells us: *"they are all but one person, one soul, one spirit, one being, one revelation."* (Baha'u'llah, *Gleanings*, Page 54). He also says: *"No distinction do We make between any of His Messengers. For they, one and all, summon the people of the earth to acknowledge the unity of God."* (Baha'u'llah: *Gleanings*, Page: 51)

Finally, Baha'u'llah says that the Manifestations of God are those *"Who have appeared clothed in divers attire. If thou wilt observe with discriminating eyes, thou wilt behold them all abiding in the same tabernacle, soaring in the same heaven, seated upon the same throne, uttering the same speech, and proclaiming the same Faith."* (Baha'u'llah: *The Kitab-i-Iqan*, Pages: 153-154)

Therefore, even though the Manifestations are different historical personages, they have a 'oneness' as described by Baha'u'llah. This oneness can be characterized in many ways, I suppose, but my way is to think of the New Testament's 'pre-existent Word of God' being in all of them. This is what I think

Baha'u'llah may mean by His description of many lamps (the historical persons of the Manifestations) but only one light (the presence of God in history when any and all of these Manifestations appeared in historical time).

QUESTION: So what do Baha'is believe in? Everything and everyone? If so, that seems to me to weaken their message, rather than strengthen it.

RESPONSE: Well, we have many times been called 'the world religion,' probably because we believe that God has always been guiding the world by sending many Manifestations of Himself into our historical world. When one becomes a follower of Baha'u'llah, one recognizes and believes in Moses, Jesus, Muhammad, Buddha, Krishna, Zoroaster, as well as Baha'u'llah—all of them—as Manifestations and revelations of God. This may be why many people, in becoming followers of Baha'u'llah, say that it feels like a 'homecoming,' a harmony of all of history, of all the religions and cultures that have made our world what it is. They don't feel weakness in this; rather, strength and 'wholeness.'

A Jew, for example, cannot become a Baha'i without recognizing Christ and Muhammad. A Christian must recognize not only Baha'u'llah, but Buddha, Muhammad and Moses, as well as the other Manifestations of God. When one follows Baha'u'llah and His teachings, which Baha'is believe are God's Will for humanity today, he embraces all of history, seeing (perhaps for the first time) that there was, all along, a thread of purpose, a direction, a larger plan of God than ever imagined.

Baha'i House of Worship in New Delhi, India. It resembles a Lotus Flower and has received world-wide recognition as an architectural marvel.

QUESTION: When did this process of 'progressive revelation' begin? And I suppose you are going to tell me that it ended with Baha'u'llah?

RESPONSE: According to Baha'u'llah, God has caused 'Manifestations' of Himself to be *"sent down from time immemorial"* (*Gleanings*, p. 174) from His *"celestial throne"* at various times in history. They *"are all sent down from the heaven of the Will of God, and as they all arise to proclaim His irresistible Faith, they, therefore, are regarded as one soul and the same person. For they all drink from the one Cup of the love of God, and all partake of the fruit of the same Tree of Oneness."* (Baha'u'llah: *Gleanings*, Page: 50)

This is apparently God's way of guiding humankind and Baha'u'llah says it will go on in this fashion *"to the end that hath no end to rain on the soil of human capacity, reality and personality their favors and bounties. Such hath been God's method continued from everlasting to everlasting."* (Baha'u'llah: *Gleanings*, Pages: 68-69)

Using the phrase *"City of God"* as a metaphor for the appearance of a Manifestation of God in history, He said: *"Once in about a thousand years shall this City be renewed and readorned . . . ."* (Baha'u'llah: *Gleanings*, Page: 269)

The direct answer to your question is that Baha'u'llah said He is *not* the last Manifestation of God that God will 'send' to humanity. Baha'u'llah did say that no Manifestation would appear before another full thousand years. However, Baha'is certainly *do* expect a fresh outpouring of God's Will to occur again and again in human history, as taught by Baha'u'llah. He promises that God will never leave man alone and unaided. Thus, Baha'u'llah is not the last Manifestation of God Who will appear in human history.

In fact, Baha'u'llah said, *"a single breath from the breezes of the Day of Thy Revelation is enough to adorn all mankind with a fresh attire."* (Baha'u'llah: *Prayers and Meditations*, Page: 252) Baha'is believe that without this *"fresh attire"* the world would slide further into the kind of spiritual degradation and oblivion that we see throughout the Twentieth Century. Never has God's power and the Voice of the Divine been so needed, something upon which almost everyone on earth seems to agree.

Baha'u'llah observed that the world seems to be dying, in need of medicine, an elixir, to bring it back to life. He said: *"what else but the Elixir of His potent Revelation can cleanse and revive it?"* (Baha'u'llah: *Gleanings*, Page: 200) And, a dying patient would need a physician to administer the medicine. Baha'u'llah says: *"This can*

*in no wise be achieved except through the power of a skilled,
an all-powerful, and inspired Physician.*" (Baha'u'llah: *Epistle
to the Son of the Wolf,* Pages: 62-63)

Baha'u'llah tells us that He is that *"Physician"* sent by
God. *"The All-Knowing Physician hath His finger on the pulse
of mankind. He perceiveth the disease, and prescribeth, in
His unerring wisdom, the remedy. Every age hath its own
problem, and every soul its particular aspiration. The remedy
the world needeth in its present-day afflictions can never be
the same as that which a subsequent age may require. Be
anxiously concerned with the needs of the age ye live in, and
center your deliberations on its exigencies and requirements.*

*"We can well perceive how the whole human race is en-
compassed with great, with incalculable afflictions. We see it
languishing on its bed of sickness, sore-tried and disillusioned.
They that are intoxicated by self-conceit have interposed themselves between it and the Divine and infallible Physician.*"
(Baha'u'llah: *Gleanings,* Page: 213)

QUESTION: What you say is all well and good, but
Jesus is still the Son of God, and you are forgetting, it
seems to me, that He said, flatly: *"No one comes to the
Father except through me."* (John 14:6)

RESPONSE: Jesus *is* still the Son of God. Nothing
can change that. Baha'u'llah claims not only to be Christ's
Return (*"in my person,"* as He puts it) but also says He is
"The Father" of all mankind, manifested by God to mankind, as was Jesus. As for the quote from Jesus that *"No
one comes to the Father except through Me",* that was true
when Jesus came. Now, in the day of the appearance of
Christ Returned in the Glory of the Father, Baha'u'llah
says: *"No man can obtain everlasting life, unless he embraceth
the truth of this inestimable, this wondrous, and sublime Revelation."* (Baha'u'llah: *Gleanings,* Page: 183)

What Baha'u'llah taught was this: That whenever a Manifestation of God appears in human history and reveals God's fresh, new message, representing the Will of God for that Day, everyone must turn to Him for salvation and everlasting life. To turn away is not only to reject Him, as a Manifestation of God, say Jesus or Baha'u'llah, but to reject the God Who sent Him.

QUESTION: You seem to be saying that Baha'u'llah is God? Surely you can't be saying something so outlandish and blasphemous?

RESPONSE: Let's consider statements of both Jesus and Baha'u'llah. Jesus said: *"The Father and I are One,"* but on another occasion, He said: *"Why callest thou me good? there is none good but one, that is, God."* (Matt 19:17) Baha'u'llah likewise says: *"When I contemplate, O my God, the relationship that bindeth me to Thee, I am moved to proclaim to all created things 'verily I am God'; and when I consider my own self, lo, I find it coarser than clay!"* (Baha'u'llah: *Kitab-i-Aqdas*, Notes, Page: 234) But on the other hand, like Jesus, He says something that (if we didn't know better) seems contradictory: *"If it be your wish, O people, to know God and to discover the greatness of His might, look, then, upon Me."* (Baha'u'llah: *Gleanings*, Page: 272)

The problem of whether we should consider the Manifestations of God Divine and how we might be better able to understand this is taken up in the next chapter. We will talk about an entirely new way of understanding God's Messengers or Manifestations, as Baha'u'llah calls them. Each of them has a title. Jesus was the 'Son of God,' for example; Muhammad was the 'Friend of God,' Baha'u'llah is called 'the Father.'

When Jesus spoke of His mission and His Person and gave His teachings, one man tore at his clothing and seemed so agitated as to do himself harm. What he heard seemed to be blasphemous, namely, that Jesus seemed to be saying that He was God. When Baha'u'llah says something comparable, it probably provokes or at least challenges the Christian listener in a similar way.

I can imagine that Jew being confused and provoked when Jesus said *"The Father and I are One"* just as I can imagine a Christian being uncertain, even angry when he hears Baha'u'llah talk about His own appearance: *"He Who, from everlasting, had concealed His Face from the sight of creation is now come."* (Baha'u'llah: *Gleanings,* Page: 31) and *"Speed out of your sepulchers. How long will ye sleep? The second blast hath been blown on the trumpet. On whom are ye gazing? This is your Lord, the God of Mercy."* (Baha'u'llah: *Gleanings,* Page: 44)

Let's go on to consider how God reveals Himself to human beings. As I told you, I want to introduce you to a totally new way of looking at the method God uses to bring His very presence into human history.

QUESTION: Before you do, let me be certain I understand what you mean by 'progressive revelation.' Is this what you are saying, that God has revealed Himself many times instead of just once or twice and that these revelations are the same or equal?

RESPONSE: Well, you have it mostly right. Baha'u'llah does teach that God has revealed Himself many, perhaps uncountable, times and that these revelations have brought salvation to individual men and women as well as mankind and have progressively unfolded His purpose. They have guided us up to a moment of historical consummation and fulfillment.

Now, Baha'u'llah teaches that His Revelation is that moment of completion and realization of the many prophetic dreams of mankind's long history. He says: *"The Revelation which, from time immemorial, hath been acclaimed as the Purpose and Promise of all the Prophets of God, and the most cherished Desire of His Messengers, hath now, by virtue of the pervasive Will of the Almighty and at His irresistible bidding, been revealed unto men. The advent of such a Revelation hath been heralded in all the sacred Scriptures."* (Baha'u'llah: *Gleanings,* Page: 5)

However, Baha'u'llah didn't say that the Revelations were the same or even equal. Remember earlier we talked about a 'station of distinction' where each of the Manifestations is quite distinct in their person and their message? When the Manifestations appear, they teach what people are able to hear and understand, not what is beyond them, or things they would be quite unable to accept.

Jesus said that there were teachings He would like to have given, but *"Ye cannot bear them now."* I have often thought that ending human slavery would have been one of those. Jesus certainly would have been against slavery, but His followers wouldn't have been able to hear it because slavery was so entrenched in the ancient world. This is why Jesus never mentions what we would think to be an important topic and why St. Paul even tells a runaway slave to return to his master.

This doesn't make the Christian Faith any less good, does it? It simply is exactly as Jesus said, that there are certain things that people are not ready to hear or accept. This is yet another reason why revelation needs to be 'progressive,' as God sends yet another, fresh Manifestation of Himself to tell us in a later day what we then need to hear and are ready to accept and enact in our individual lives and in our communities.

World unity and the oneness of mankind, two of Baha'u'llah's central teachings, could not have been taught two thousand years ago, nor even fourteen hundred years ago when Muhammad appeared, because knowledge of the world and its peoples was not at a stage where that could even be understood. Baha'u'llah could not teach to us now what we will need two or five thousand years from now, but He teaches that God will again manifest Himself with guidance and renewing power.

So, the Manifestations teach what can be understood and what people need most at that particular moment of history in which they appear. This is what makes the Manifestations appear different, but Baha'u'llah tells us: *"They* [the Manifestations] *only differ in the intensity of their revelation."* (Baha'u'llah: *Gleanings*, Page: 48)

But even with this apparent difference, they are still in reality *"one person, one soul, one spirit, one being, one revelation"* (Baha'u'llah: *Gleanings*, Page: 54) Baha'u'llah closes His remarks on this 'oneness/difference' explanation by saying about all the Manifestations: *"No distinction do We make between any of them."* (Baha'u'llah: The *Kitab-i-Iqan*, Page: 176)

QUESTION: This idea of progressive revelation still sounds very new to me, even though I do understand the progressive nature of God's Revelation of the Ten Commandments, then later the Revelation of Jesus Christ, His Son. I'm still puzzled how you even came up with this idea.

RESPONSE: I want you to know that I didn't 'come up with' this idea. Baha'u'llah taught very directly on this subject. Progressive Revelation is seen in another religion–Islam. But here is another way to look at progressive revelation. Think of a school with classes. You don't teach in the third grade what must wait until high school to be understood, based upon the capacity of the student, not the teacher. However, teachers, whether teaching in kindergarten or high school, all have the same knowledge and receive the same training in college. While this analogy works, we should remember this: Baha'u'llah made it clear that each and every one of the Manifestations of God had complete divine knowledge and could have given to the people of His time every part of that knowledge, if only the people of that time could have been able to hear it (as Christ said).

As we hear about 'progressive revelation,' we need to entertain a radically new and challenging idea: That God has been the mover of history all along, much more than we ever realized, that He will never leave us alone or to ourselves. Having already learned that: *"God so loved the world that He gave His only begotten Son,"* (John 3:16) we now learn that, finally, He came Himself in the glory of *"the Father."* Baha'u'llah also put it this way: *"He that was hidden from the eyes of men is revealed, girded with sovereignty and power!"* (Baha'u'llah: *Gleanings*, Page: 31) And: *"He Who, from everlasting, had concealed His Face from the sight of creation is now come . . . He Who is the sovereign Lord of all is made manifest."* (Baha'u'llah: *Gleanings*, Page: 31)

Progressive revelation means that there has been only one God in human history, though He may have appeared with different names. That one God has revealed Himself at those times when mankind most needed His Grace and guidance. Slowly but surely, God was guiding us all along through centuries of time to a moment of historic fulfillment when humankind would achieve unity and peace. This, in turn, would enable humankind to progress toward the goal of an ever-advancing civilization that would more and more reflect the divine purpose and will. This entire process would result in a promise being realized, the promise Christ made in the Lord's

Prayer where He prayed *"Thy Kingdom come, thy Will be done, on earth, as it is in Heaven."* (Matt. 6:10)

As you read the following prayer of Baha'u'llah, remember that just as Jesus was scourged and crucified, Baha'u'llah was tortured and imprisoned for nearly His entire life. He wrote this prayer from prison for His followers to pray, much as Jesus gave His disciples the Lord's Prayer to pray.

"Many a chilled heart, O my God, hath been set ablaze with the fire of Thy Cause, and many a slumberer hath been wakened by the sweetness of Thy voice. How many are the strangers who have sought shelter beneath the shadow of the tree of Thy oneness, and how numerous the thirsty ones who have panted after the fountain of Thy living waters in Thy days!

"Blessed is he that hath set himself towards Thee, and hasted to attain the Day-Spring of the lights of Thy face. Blessed is he who with all his affections hath turned to the Dawning-Place of Thy Revelation and the Fountain-Head of Thine inspiration. Blessed is he that hath expended in Thy path what Thou didst bestow upon him through Thy bounty and favor. Blessed is he who, in his sore longing after Thee, hath cast away all else except Thyself. Blessed is he who hath enjoyed intimate communion with Thee, and rid himself of all attachment to any one save Thee.

"I beseech Thee, O my Lord, by Him Who is Thy Name, Who, through the power of Thy sovereignty and might, hath risen above the horizon of His prison, to ordain for every one what becometh Thee and beseemeth Thine exaltation.

"Thy might, in truth, is equal to all things." Baha'u'llah: *Prayers and Meditations*, Pages: 33-34)

Here is a prayer from 'Abdu'l-Baha:

"O Thou kind Lord! O Thou Who art generous and merciful! We are the servants of Thy threshold and are gathered

beneath the sheltering shadow of Thy divine unity. The sun of Thy mercy is shining upon all, and the clouds of Thy bounty shower upon all. Thy gifts encompass all, Thy loving providence sustains all, Thy protection overshadows all, and the glances of Thy favor are cast upon all. O Lord! Grant Thine infinite bestowals, and let the light of Thy guidance shine. Illumine the eyes, gladden the hearts with abiding joy.

Confer a new spirit upon all people and bestow upon them eternal life. Unlock the gates of true understanding and let the light of faith shine resplendent. Gather all people beneath the shadow of Thy bounty and cause them to unite in harmony, so that they may become as the rays of one sun, as the waves of one ocean, and as the fruit of one tree. May they drink from the same fountain. May they be refreshed by the same breeze. May they receive illumination from the same source of light. Thou art the Giver, the Merciful, the Omnipotent."

('Abdu'l-Baha: *Promulgation of Universal Peace*, Page: 116)

CHAPTER FIVE

MANIFESTATION: A NEW WAY OF UNDERSTANDING HOW GOD REVEALS HIMSELF TO MAN

QUESTION: Baha'is always seem to use the word 'Manifestation' to refer to Jesus, Baha'u'llah and other founders of world religions. Why invent some new word? Is it a brand new word?

RESPONSE: It's not really a new word. It is used in the New Testament (Remember, I am using the New King James Version for quotes from the Bible). (Luke 1:80 and I Cor. 12:7) But the reason Baha'is use the word is because Baha'u'llah used it. He used it in a somewhat different way than in the New Testament. In Luke 1:80, for example, it refers to a 'showing forth' (from the Greek word 'anadeixis') of John the Baptist to the people of Israel. When Baha'u'llah uses the word, it refers not to a 'showing forth' ('shewing' in the KJV), but to God's way of sending and 'Manifesting' His own 'Presence' into human history in the form of a person.

You mentioned that Baha'is may have 'invented' things, but I want to assure you that since the Coming of Baha'u'llah, Baha'is haven't 'made things up' because they haven't needed to do so. The stream of God's Revelation through Baha'u'llah lasted almost forty years and contains over ten thousand documents, letters, papers, and books. It is very complete and the ideas and teachings that I am sharing with you come directly from Baha'u'llah, with little interpretation on my part.

The second reason Baha'is use the word 'Manifestation' is that it makes a clean, clear distinction between the word 'Prophet' (which means to 'speak for God') of which Jeremiah and Isaiah would be examples, and the word 'Manifestation,' which indicates those who bring the very 'Presence' of God into human affairs and human history. 'Prophets' deliver a message for God; 'Manifestations' bring God's Presence into history.

Baha'u'llah taught and Baha'is believe that when Jesus, Muhammad, Zoroaster or Baha'u'llah speak, they are not speaking 'for' God; instead, they *are* God being 'manifested' in history. When you see them, hear them, respond to them, you are seeing, hearing and responding to God in a direct way, in fact, in the only way that man can ever 'know' God. Jesus said: *"He that hath seen me hath seen the Father"* (John 14:9) and Baha'u'llah said: *"If it be your wish, O people, to know God and to discover the greatness of His might, look, then, upon Me."* (Baha'u'llah: *Gleanings*, Page: 272)

The Manifestations of God, Jesus, Baha'u'llah, and others, clearly drew distinctions between themselves and God. For example, Jesus said: *"My Father is greater than I."* (John 14:28-29) and *"Why do you call Me good? No one is good but One, that is, God."* (Matt 19:17) thus distinguishing Himself from God, even though His other quotes such as" "The *Father and I are One"* seem to be contradictory. Baha'u'llah likewise seems sometimes to be claiming oneness with God, but at other times, just like Jesus, seems to utter something seemingly contradictory, as in this statement below:

"When I contemplate, O my God, the relationship that bindeth me to Thee, I am moved to proclaim to all created things 'verily I am God'; and when I consider my own self, lo, I find it coarser than clay! " (Baha'u'llah: *Kitab-i-Aqdas*: Notes, Page: 234)

So, in summary, both Jesus and Baha'u'llah declare oneness with God or at least tell their followers that to look upon them is to look upon God, and at other times they disclaim being one with God.

QUESTION: But Christians have never been confused about this. They have always known who Jesus was, namely, the Son of God, the Second Person of the Trinity.

RESPONSE: Well, I don't know exactly how to tell you this if you've never heard it before, but Christians took several centuries to decide Who Jesus was. They fought doctrinal battles so severe that they often ended with banishment or execution for the 'losing side.' The quotes from Jesus that I've just given you, two or three paragraphs above, perplexed Christians and, as a result, many fanciful and heretical ideas were concocted and set forth, even as late as four centuries after Christ. One idea was that Jesus was only a man and not God; another that He was God, but not a man. This was finally resolved five centuries later at the Council of Chalcedon in 451 AD, when Jesus was declared to be one person with two natures.

QUESTION: Didn't Christians simply follow the Gospel? It all seems so clear now.

RESPONSE: Yes, it does, but it didn't seem clear then at all, partly because the four familiar Gospels were not settled on as reliable scripture for over a century. Actually, there were originally between 60 and 125 'gospels' in existence. Many church councils were held to decide which Gospels were the ones to be included in the New Testament. The argument about what was to be included in scripture was not entirely settled for over two hundred years and even as late as the fifteenth century, Martin Luther was still considering whether the book of James should continue to be included in the New Testament. Some Christians to this day include the 'Apocrypha' (an additional number of books of the Bible accepted by Catholic Christians), while others do not, so the issue of what is 'Holy Scripture' has never been settled entirely within Christianity.

QUESTION: None of this weakens my faith in Christ or the Bible.

RESPONSE: It shouldn't and I certainly didn't put it forth for that reason. Baha'is seek to strengthen Faith, extend it, enlarge it, never to water it down or weaken it. And Baha'is strive to show believers of any religion how their beliefs are closely related to the beliefs of other Faiths. I've said to you before, and it's not to be taken in any critical or insulting way, the Baha'i Faith teaches a 'greater God' and a 'larger Christ.' Not a different Christ, but the very same Christ we have always known but now understood as having played a much 'larger' role in history than we ever knew.

QUESTION: What about the concepts of incarnation, the belief that God dwelt 'bodily' in the Person of Christ, and the Holy Trinity, the concept of the 'Three in One.' What do Baha'is believe about those key Christian doctrines?

RESPONSE: It may be shocking to realize that these two doctrines of Trinity and Incarnation do not appear anywhere in what Christ says or elsewhere in the New Testament by those exact names. These words were only in use decades or hundreds of years later, in an attempt to explain the nature and meaning of Christ's Person and Revelation. Usually these questions of doctrine were voted on in Church Councils, quite often in response to some threatening heresy that had developed.

I have often heard Christians explain, and I agree, that this ability to come to terms with these confusing issues was one of the strengths of their Revelation, that they were able to 'work things out' with the help of the Holy Spirit. It was often painful, sometimes confusing, but ultimately, they did come to conclusions that helped them understand who Christ was and what the meaning of His Revelation was.

By contrast, what Baha'is believe is always taken very directly from Baha'u'llah's teachings. As I've indicated to you, we don't hold a council or vote on what Baha'u'llah's teachings mean, since He was so explicit, detailed and complete, and since His teachings are either written in His own hand, or authenticated with His seal. All of these writings are at the Baha'i World Center in Haifa, Israel. If you visit Israel, don't fail to go to the

Baha'i Shrines in Haifa. Among those shrines is a building called the 'Center for the Study of the Texts.'

All of Baha'u'llah's writings, His Revelation, in the original documents, are contained in vaults within that building. And since Baha'u'llah appointed His Son 'Abdu'l-Baha as the official and only interpreter of the meaning of His words, this has helped to avoid debate and conflict about what Baha'u'llah meant by what He said.

Center for the Study of the Texts, located on Mt. Carmel, housing all the Baha'i Scriptures and the Holy Texts of All Religions.

The idea of Trinity was a theological innovation, which seems to be very close to the truth of Christ's Revelation. It speaks of God the Father, God the Son and God the Holy Ghost (or Spirit). Without this formulation, the Christian Faith would have broken apart very early into many sects. In fact, splintering had begun early after the death of the original disciples and only a series of Church Councils and the development of ideas such as the Trinity enabled the Christian Faith to maintain some degree of unity for eleven centuries.

The Christian Faith divided very early into 'Eastern' and 'Western' branches, with some very different ideas and practices, and even some differences on the nature of Christ's Person and Revelation. The Protestant Reformation, coming fourteen centuries later, was a split occurring within European or 'Western' Christianity.

Today, Christianity is sadly divided, as the Church itself admits. It is trying to unify itself, but the reality is that there is a diversity of hundreds of separate and sometimes conflicting ideas and beliefs. This disunity and division is not only in the Christian Faith. It is in the other major religions as well, including Islam, Buddhism, Judaism and others.

Baha'u'llah commanded the Baha'is—His followers—to be apostles and examples of unity to the world, first and foremost among themselves, and then offering this new idea of world unity to others. As we turn into the Twenty-First Century, Baha'is have finished over one and one half centuries of the development of their Faith with no significant or lasting divisions. There have been unsuccessful and short-lived attempts to divide the Baha'i Faith, but because of Baha'u'llah's clear, direct and detailed writings and because He strongly and clearly named His Son 'Abdu'l-Baha as His successor and only interpreter, the unity of the Baha'is has remained intact.

QUESTION: Christians can discover their unity if only they would unite around Christ, Whom we believe to be God incarnate. The entire situation of disunity could be changed, if only they would listen to Christ and be true to the Bible instead of following their own imaginations.

RESPONSE: So true. Probably the Buddhists and Moslems and Hindus or even the Jews could unite, if only they were able to be true to their founder, Who manifested God to them. As far as 'incarnation' is concerned, the word never appears in the Gospels, as I've mentioned to you before. However, the basic concept is stated in other words. Strangely, and this is not known by many Christians, the concept of incarnation was similar to an idea used by pagan religions of the time of Jesus. This was also true of the concept of Virgin Birth. Incarnation was a concept known to ancient peoples. In Christ's time, it literally meant 'in the body,' meaning that a God would 'come down' to earth, taking an earthly form.

In that day and time of the beginning of Christianity, the biographies of many emperors, famous poets, victorious generals all included the fact that their births were divinely caused and miraculous (a virgin birth), or (in the case of some) that a god had taken human form, had intercourse with a human female, and their birth resulted. In still other cases, some important ancient figures were said to be gods who had descended to earth taking human form (literally, 'incarnation').

Of course, none of this means that the story of Jesus should not be understood basically as we do understand it. Just because there is an unusual and unfortunate history around this word incarnation does not mean that we should not understand that the very presence of God was in Christ.

QUESTION: That's right! You had me worried for a while there, as if you were trying to invalidate my Faith. You said you wouldn't do that, but from your last statement, I see that was not your purpose. And I agree that just because other pagan faiths that existed at the time of Christianity claimed incarnations and virgin births doesn't mean that they are true or that they are somehow equal with what Christ taught and what Christians know to be true from the Bible.

RESPONSE: Exactly! Among all the fanciful claims of other pagan faiths, Jesus made a true claim that God was so fully manifest in Him that He could truthfully say *"the Father and I are One"* and *"if you have seen Me, you have seen the Father."*

Baha'u'llah does use the word 'incarnate' several times in His writings, once to indicate that we should not take literally the idea that the God of the universe descends bodily into human form, but in another place to indicate that the Manifestations show the 'attributes' of God in their human form. About Himself he said, for example: *"He doth verily incarnate the highest, the infallible standard of justice unto all creation."* (Baha'u'llah: *Gleanings*, Page: 175)

What Baha'u'llah teaches is that the concept of 'Manifestation' gives us all of the good parts of the idea of 'incarnation' without the parts that are tied too strongly to pagan sources and without teaching something that goes strongly against common sense. That would also go against a central Baha'i teaching that science, reason and religion should agree, not disagree. To summarize, the Baha'i concept of Manifestation is quite close to that of incarnation, but it is easier to understand and, less confusing.

QUESTION: Some of what you say seems to indicate to me that you are still denying the reality of the incarnation.

RESPONSE: I hope not. Let me clear it up. Baha'is believe that God was in Christ, a key Christian concept. Whether that full presence of God is best understood through the idea of Incarnation or the idea of Manifestation is the only difference we might have. In both cases, both Christians and Baha'is believe that the full presence of the pre-existent Word of God is present in Christ. Baha'is believe that this 'full presence of God,' the Word that existed before the beginning of historical time, was in all the other Manifestations of God as well, including Baha'u'llah.

In the case of incarnation, we have the problem of the similarity to pagan examples and the likelihood that early Christian writers drew upon pagan sources to develop the concept. We also have the problem that it asks us to go contrary to reason. While I realize that we cannot always go by our reason alone, surely it is good to do so when we can. In the final analysis, however, both Christians and Baha'is turn not to reason, but to divinely revealed scripture to guide us.

The concept of Manifestation helps us to understand that God is truly present in all the Manifestations, to the extent that Jesus or Baha'u'llah or any of the others can say that if you have seen them, you see God, if you listen to them, you are listening to God, if you recognize and obey them, you are recognizing and obeying god.

Faced with the pressing need to define the Person of Christ, the early Church fathers came to explain Christ's human and Divine station with the concept of incarnation. By contrast, we have the clear teaching of Baha'u'llah about Manifestation that includes the very best of the idea of incarnation without its pagan baggage. However, I believe that when one steps back to take a more careful view, the two concepts are very much more alike than they are different.

QUESTION: Give me as much as you can about what Baha'u'llah Himself said. I'm interested in your opinion, but I really want to give careful consideration to Baha'u'llah's Revelation. I can see now that it is not something that can be easily ignored. It seems to me that I will have to accept it or clearly reject it. There doesn't seem to be a middle ground.

RESPONSE: It does seem that way, I agree. If you ran into Jesus in A D 31, you probably couldn't go home that day and just forget about Him and about His call to *"follow me."* You would have to respond or know *why* you weren't responding. And you would have to know that if you did follow Jesus, your parents, family, friends and religious leaders would say you were betraying your faith. What a striking and serious thought! Jesus passes your way, you stop and listen and your whole life is changed, whether you follow Him or not!

It's probably like that with Baha'u'llah. To reject Him or accept Him as a new Manifestation of God and as the Return of Christ will have serious meaning and consequences for your life, no matter which way you decide.

QUESTION: Can we get back to Incarnation and Manifestation? I want to hear more so that I'm sure what the Baha'i position is.

RESPONSE: Yes, I want to be sure that we have a mutual understanding, too. In fact, I don't want to be seen as saying that there is anything basically wrong about the idea of incarnation, short of taking it too literally. If taken literally, I think it may be confusing to some people and may distort the real beauty of what we are trying to describe. By contrast, I think the concept of 'manifestation' succeeds in doing what 'incarnation' tries but fails to do.

Let's put it this way: If incarnation means that God is fully present in this human person of the Manifestation, it is true and helpful. As I said, Baha'u'llah Himself used the term several times. However, if incarnation means that the God of the universe literally descends (as in pagan mythology) into a human form, this is what Baha'u'llah says:

"Know thou of a certainty that the Unseen can in no wise incarnate His Essence and reveal it unto men." (Baha'u'llah: *Gleanings*, Page: 49) However, while God does not incarnate His *"essence"*, He nevertheless says *"Thy presence hath appeared through Thy Manifestation unto all who are in Thy heaven and all who are on Thy earth."* (Baha'u'llah: *Prayers and Meditations*, Page 272)

It appears that if one decides to deal not so much with 'words' as with 'meaning,' that the concepts of incarnation and manifestation, while clearly not the same, have very much in common.

Earlier, I mentioned that the idea of incarnation was a popular, non-Jewish, non-Christian, pagan concept that existed many centuries before Christ was born. In the secular as well as religious traditions several centuries before Christ, an extraordinary man would be portrayed as a God, or a son of a God, Who has come down to earth. To ancient peoples, this explained the man's unusual career, his might, power, or wisdom. With manifestation as the concept, the confusion about *"the Father and I are One"* disappears, while the essential truth of God's full presence among us fully manifested in a human form is retained.

You asked a moment ago for more from Baha'u'llah

on this subject. Here are several quotes that I think may help. Referring to the Manifestations, calling them 'Ancient Beings,' He says:

"These ancient Beings, though delivered from the womb of their mother, have in reality descended from the heaven of the will of God. Though they be dwelling on this earth, yet their true habitations are the retreats of glory in the realms above. Whilst walking amongst mortals, they soar in the heaven of the divine presence. Without feet they tread the path of the spirit, and without wings they rise unto the exalted heights of divine unity." (Baha'u'llah: *The Kitab-i-Iqan*, Page: 67)

Indicating the importance of the Manifestations to humanity and to history, Baha'u'llah tells us: " . . . *all else besides these Manifestations, live by the operation of Their Will, and move and have their being through the outpourings of Their grace."* (Baha'u'llah: *Gleanings*, Page: 179)

Baha'u'llah calls Himself: *"Him in Whom Thou Thyself art manifest."* (Baha'u'llah: *Prayers and Meditations*, Page: 235) In another passage, He refers to Himself as *"Him Whom Thou hast appointed as the Manifestation of Thine own Being."* (Baha'u'llah: *Prayers and Meditations*, Page: 26) The key understanding, however, is that Baha'u'llah saw all the Manifestations, not just Jesus and not just Himself, as being *"Manifestations of Thine own being"*. He taught that every Manifestation of God is One " . . . *in Whom Thou Thyself art manifest."*

One more quote: In a prayer, Baha'u'llah refers to Himself (and by implication, to all the Manifestations) as *"Him in Whom Thy Godhead is manifest."* (Baha'u'llah: *Prayers and Meditations*, Page: 196)

QUESTION: As you remarked a while ago, the two concepts, incarnation and Manifestation don't seem all that different. Surely you know that Christians don't use the term incarnation in the same way pagans used it,

even though it is very similar and even though the early
Church may have used a concept that they thought people
were familiar with.

RESPONSE: Of course, I agree, but bear in mind
that the Manifestation concept allows us to see Jesus,
Buddha, Muhammad, Zoroaster, Baha'u'llah, all the
Messengers of God in an entirely new way, without using
a borrowed, pagan concept that seems to raise barriers
to belief, rather than supporting true faith.

With this 'new way' of looking at the Manifestations,
we can see that the 'Word of God' was in all of them, the
same 'Word of God,' that existed before the foundation
of the world. Therefore, we can begin to see that God
has been at work in a larger way than we had ever conceived. We can see, as I mentioned before, a 'greater
God' and a 'larger Christ.' It's very challenging, I agree,
but it seems to be the road ahead for people from every
culture and religion to begin to see the possibilities of
unity and oneness.

QUESTION: What you have just said is strange and
quite unacceptable to me. You are obviously paraphras-
ing the New Testament, when you talk about the 'Word
of God,' but I believe that 'the Word' refers to Jesus alone,
not to anyone else. In my understanding, that pre-existent 'Word' cannot be in anyone else. Jesus is Alpha and
Omega, the 'First and Last.'

RESPONSE: We are at the heart of the matter, aren't
we? The 'Word,' which was in Christ is truly 'Alpha and
Omega,' 'first and last,' but the teaching of Baha'u'llah
shows us for the first time in human history, that this pre-
existent 'Word' that the Bible tells us was 'made flesh,'
this same 'Word of God' (not a different one) has ap-

peared before and will appear again in what Baha'u'llah called *"the human temple."* Thus, the 'Word' is 'First and Last,' but it has appeared from time to time in history in the different Manifestations of *"the Self of God."*

This 'Word' made flesh (which is just another way of saying 'in the human temple') is understood now as the Manifestations of God, whom God sends us from time to time, bringing salvation to us by His presence and progressively revealing His purpose for us. These revelations of His 'Word made flesh' propel us toward our destiny, toward the great consummation in history that God has planned for us, the beginning of which is peace and human unity and the end of which we can only know when God shows it to us through His continuing love and guidance.

We now could ask: Which is the more helpful idea for our understanding of how God dwells amongst men, how He enters history and how His full presence charges it with meaning, direction and purpose? Does 'incarnation' help us the most, or does 'manifestation' work the best for a more deep and complete understanding?

Think for a moment about our discussion of 'progressive revelation.' With that in mind, the idea of 'manifestation' tells us that from time to time in human history God 'manifests' Himself so fully into a human being, into a 'human temple', that this Manifestation is the very presence of God Himself among us. I understand that the typical Christian believes this happened only once, but Baha'u'llah reveals that God has acted in this way not once, but many times.

And each time, to see the Manifestation, whether Buddha, Jesus, Muhammad or Baha'u'llah, was to see God. To know Him was to know God. To follow Him, respond to him, was to respond to God and to His Will. Each time one of these Manifestations appeared, Baha'u'llah says, salvation was possible *only* through following Him and to turn away from Him was to be as if you were a dead person. As we have noted several times, Jesus said the same thing.

Before you think I'm exaggerating, remember that Jesus regarded those who did not believe in Him as 'dead,' didn't He? Jesus said: *"Let the dead bury the dead"* and Baha'u'llah said: *"Vouchsafe Thy strength, O Almighty One, unto Thy weak creatures, and quicken them who are as dead, that haply they may find Thee, and may be led unto the ocean of Thy guidance"* (Baha'u'llah: *Epistle to the Son of the Wolf,* Page: 10)

QUESTION: I'm glad you see that we Christians believe that the 'Word of God made flesh' happened only once. I cringe when you seem to be putting the Savior of the World, Jesus, down to the same level as others, with very great, perhaps prophetic figures, but nevertheless, those who are lesser men. In fact, that's it, just men, as compared to the Son of God.

RESPONSE: First, let me say, and I have tried to emphasize this all along, that Baha'is believe that Jesus was the *"Son of God,"* that the 'Word of God' was in Christ, that God was in Christ. Baha'is, in fact, believe almost everything about Jesus that Christians believe. The difference is that they are taught by Baha'u'llah that this 'Word' has appeared in history many times and has appeared today in Baha'u'llah. I've mentioned many times that Baha'u'llah said that Christ had again come to humanity *"in my Person"* and that His coming represented the appearance of *"The Father"* of all mankind. He spoke often of the Word of God being the animating force in His Revelation.

Let's turn again to Baha'u'llah to see what He can

tell us about the unity of the Manifestations. He tells us that the *"essence"* of all the Manifestations of God *"is one and the same. Their unity is absolute. God, the Creator, saith: There is no distinction whatsoever among the Bearers of My Message. They all have but one purpose; their secret is the same secret. To prefer one in honor to another, to exalt certain ones above the rest, is in no wise to be permitted."* (Baha'u'llah: *Gleanings,* Page: 78)

Baha'u'llah tells us to look deeply within: *"Contemplate with thine inward eye."* We will then see, He says, that *"each one of these Manifestations hath been sent down through the operation of the Divine Will and Purpose, that each hath been the bearer of a specific Message, that each hath been entrusted with a divinely-revealed Book . . . "* (Baha'u'llah: *Gleanings,* Page: 74)

The Manifestations are *" . . . all sent down from the heaven of the Will of God, and as they all arise to proclaim His irresistible Faith, they, therefore, are regarded as one soul and the same person."* (Baha'u'llah: *Gleanings,* Page: 50) He further says: *"These Manifestations of God have each a twofold station. One is the station of pure abstraction and essential unity. In this respect, if thou callest them all by one name, and dost ascribe to them the same attributes, thou hast not erred from the truth."* (Baha'u'llah: *Gleanings,* Pages: 50-51)

Baha'u'llah then states one of my favorite passages of His Revelation: *"It is clear and evident to thee that all the Prophets are the Temples of the Cause of God, Who have appeared clothed in divers attire. If Thou wilt observe with discriminating eyes, thou wilt behold Them all abiding in the same tabernacle, soaring in the same heaven, seated upon the same throne, uttering the same speech, and proclaiming the same Faith."* (Baha'u'llah: *Gleanings,* Pages: 51-52)

A moment ago, we quoted Baha'u'llah as saying that the Manifestations have 'two stations' and we heard His words on the 'station of unity.' Here is what He says about the other station: *"The other station is the station of distinction, and pertaineth to the world of creation, and to the limitations thereof. In this respect, each Manifestation of God hath a distinct individuality, a definitely prescribed mission, a predestined revelation, and specially designated limitations. Each one of them is known by a different name, is characterized by a special attribute, fulfils a definite mission, and is entrusted with a particular Revelation."* (Baha'u'llah: *Gleanings*, Page: 52)

Thus, we see from Baha'u'llah that we can think of the Manifestations as being different persons in history, but at the same time, we can have a sense that they are *"as one Person"* when we think of the pre-existent 'Word of God' that animates each and every one.

QUESTION: Surely, Baha'u'llah doesn't mean the same person came back again and again?

RESPONSE: No, not at all. Baha'u'llah said, that the manifestations have two 'stations', the station of unity and the station of distinction or difference. In the station of distinction, they can be seen as very different persons, with a cultural identity, speaking a certain language, growing up with a certain religious faith, etc. In the station of unity, when we remember the 'Word of God' that is in them all, we can see them, spiritually, *"as one person."*

QUESTION: I can't really agree yet with what you are telling me, even though I begin to understand it, or I think I do. Let me try this out: You are saying that Baha'u'llah teaches that one God has operated in history, progressively revealing Himself, caring for and guiding mankind by 'manifesting' Himself in a full, present way in the lives of several Messengers. Right? And you are saying further that you *do* recognize that Jesus is the Son of God? You did say this earlier, didn't you? Now: This is my question: When God sent His only begotten Son, what more was needed for the salvation of the world?

RESPONSE: Baha'u'llah tells us that the lack of response of man is never to be laid at the door of the Manifestation. Each of the Manifestations possesses all power and all knowledge, He tells us. When they appear in the world, it is usually when they are most needed, when the world is at a very low point. From their teachings arise new individuals and new communities; the world is changed.

Much later, things begin to deteriorate. When that happens, it is not the fault of the religion that the Manifestation left for man; rather, it is the fact that man has 'drifted away.' We are in a state today of having drifted away and the Twentieth Century appears to present a low point in human history. This low point cannot be blamed on Jesus or Muhammad or Buddha. It is our own lack of response that has brought us where we are.

But it is precisely at such a low point that God again manifests Himself as He has done now, in our own time, in the person of Baha'u'llah. He said His Coming was *"to revive the world, to ennoble its life, and regenerate its peoples"* (Baha'u'llah: *Gleanings,* Page: 271) and that He would *"quicken all created things with the breezes of His Name, the Most Merciful"* would *"unify the world"* and would *"gather together the whole of mankind"* around *"this Table which hath been sent down from heaven."* (Baha'u'llah: *Epistle to the Son of the Wolf,* Page: 46 and 92)

Maybe a parable of Jesus would help in our understanding at this point. Remember the parable of the man who owned a vineyard? (Luke 20: 9) He was away from the vineyard, so he sent several representatives, who were

chased away by the workers in the vineyard. Then he
sent His only son, Jesus tells us. Surely, the man thought,
they would respect my son. But the workers also killed
the son. Jesus then says that the owner of the vineyard
plans to come himself and Jesus asks His disciples to
ponder what the owner of the vineyard will do when he
comes.

In the sense of this parable, it is clearly God Who is
the owner of the vineyard. Jesus plainly states in this parable that *"The Son"* (Jesus) comes to the vineyard and is
killed. Then He states that the vineyard owner will come
Himself (Baha'u'llah—Who comes as *"The Father"* as
Baha'is would see it). Baha'u'llah says over and again
"The Father hath come." This is the One Who had *"concealed His Face"* throughout all of human history, but
Who has now appeared. Here is the full quote:

*"There hath appeared what hath never previously ap-
peared. He Who, from everlasting, had concealed His Face
from the sight of creation is now come . . . All eyes are glad-
dened, for He Whom none hath beheld, Whose secret no one
hath discovered, hath lifted the veil of glory, and uncovered
the countenance of Beauty."* (Baha'u'llah: *Gleanings*, Page:
31) When Jesus, *"the Son"* appeared in history, salvation
for individuals and for the world could only be obtained
by turning to Him. Baha'u'llah tells that whenever *any*
Manifestation of God appears in history, salvation can
only be experienced by turning to Him and following
Him. Today, Baha'u'llah says, He has come as *"the Father"* of all mankind, to bring salvation to all the individuals on the planet and, additionally, to gather the
people of earth into a new day of unity and peace.

But back to your question of "what more was needed
after God sent Jesus, His only Begotten Son?" Baha'u'llah
says that if mankind had responded fully to *any* of the
Manifestations of Himself, this world would have become

a paradise. Mankind is never able, as Jesus says, to 'hear' all that the Manifestation could tell them. This is why, Baha'u'llah tells us, that God will send Manifestations of Himself throughout human history. Whenever mankind is in the greatest need, God will send another Manifestation of His Presence into the world. Whenever that happens, it will be, in Baha'u'llah's words, a new *'springtime.'*

Inevitably, mankind will fall away from the purity and the beauty of what is taught to them and will need a fresh Revelation of God's Presence in human history. However, Baha'u'llah tells us that, in this day, the day of the dawning of human unity, we will never fall again into chaos and disunity. Though a new Manifestation will someday be needed, nevertheless, the Day which now dawns on humanity is a Day in which mankind will achieve a state of full recognition of God's Will, especially God's design for human unity. Baha'u'llah assures us that this New Day is the Day of 'fulfillment of prophecy' and that His Coming and His Revelation could be described in this way: *"Indeed He is a Light which is not followed by darkness and a Truth not overtaken by error."* (Baha'u'llah: *Tablets of Baha'u'llah*, Page: 108)

As we look about our world today, it is anything other than a paradise. It is, in fact, a hell of division, hatred, killing, and misunderstanding based on race, religion, and cultural differences. Make no mistake about it, however, Baha'u'llah has said that the long-awaited, long-promised human unity is about to be enacted and realized. In a sense, this event will signal the real and true beginning of humanity's journey toward fulfillment and purposeful, divinely oriented progress. Where are we going? To what destination? We certainly do not know. However, Baha'u'llah has laid out the plan for mankind to begin to create the unity that will be requisite for the tasks ahead that can only be imagined.

QUESTION: Let me try again to understand what you are saying. Are you saying that Baha'u'llah is the Return of the Spirit of Christ, the 'Word of God' expressed again, with the title of *"The Father"* of mankind? That all sounds so bizarre to me, so far out of anything that I've ever heard that I don't know whether to laugh or to be angry.

RESPONSE: I can only agree with you that it must sound bizarre or blasphemous, if you are hearing it for the first time. But even as we say these things, we realize this is the same way the words of Jesus sounded to Jewish crowds who heard Him say *"The Father and I are One"* and *"No man cometh unto the Father but by Me,"* or when they observed what to them was a wandering, unemployed carpenter saying that He would soon be seen to be *"sitting at the right hand of God"* and that *"all power"* had been placed into His hands. Unless you knew who Jesus was, these statements sounded weird and, yes, bizarre. And they certainly sounded blasphemous to His Jewish hearers and the Sanhedrin, the Jewish Priests and Doctors of Law of Jesus' day.

As I see it, you are beginning to realize that Baha'u'llah cannot be ignored, that He must be put into one of those three famous categories: (1) A Madman; (2) A charlatan or trickster; or the only other choice: He is Who He says He is.

QUESTION: I can't really see Baha'u'llah as a madman or a charlatan, but couldn't Baha'u'llah or anyone else making these claims be the Antichrist?

RESPONSE: If you remember, I mentioned this earlier, that Baha'u'llah theoretically could be accused of being the Antichrist or even the Devil himself! Jesus was thought by many who heard Him to be the Devil, as is reported in the Gospels several times. He was certainly thought to be a corrupter of religion, which is the role of Antichrist.

What I say to you is this: If you investigate prayerfully and with an open mind, as I think you are ready and willing to do, the Holy Spirit will lead you to the truth. But, we must remember that some Jews *did* see Christ as the Devil or as a corrupter of religion, and I suppose some Christians will see Baha'u'llah as the Antichrist. You will have to decide for yourself through reading, study, search and prayer. Here are two quotes from Baha'u'llah on the subject of Who He Said He is:

"He Who leadeth to true victory is come. By the righteousness of God! He is fully capable of revolutionizing the world through the power of a single Word." (Baha'u'llah: *Tablets of Baha'u'llah*, Pages: 259-260) And: *"Fix your gaze upon Him Who is the Temple of God amongst men. He, in truth, hath offered up His life as a ransom for the redemption of the world. He, verily, is the All-Bountiful, the Gracious, the Most High."* (Baha'u'llah: *Gleanings*, Page: 315)

And: *"Bestir yourselves, O people, in anticipation of the days of Divine justice, for the promised hour is now come. Beware lest ye fail to apprehend its import and be accounted among the erring . . . Call out to Zion, O Carmel, and announce the joyful tidings: He that was hidden from mortal eyes is come!"* (Baha'u'llah: *Gleanings*, Page: 16-17)

One more thing: As to whether Baha'u'llah might be the Antichrist or a 'false prophet,' you can actually use what I call the 'test of Christ' to decide this. You may be aware, but many people are not aware that when Jesus speaks in the Gospels, He speaks about His Return about twenty percent of the time. He obviously felt His Return was very important.

In one talk that Jesus has with His disciples, He warns them so severely about 'false prophets' that they ask Him the obvious question, namely, "How are we going to be able to recognize the true appearance of your return from that of a 'false prophet?' After all, you've warned us that your return will be an event that may be hard to understand, even hard to notice, since you have compared it to the coming of a thief in the night." Jesus had told them a story or parable of a man who would have guarded his house better if he had only known the time when the 'thief' would come.

Here is the reference: *"But know this, that if the master of the house had known what hour the thief would come, he would have watched and not allowed his house to be broken into. Therefore you also be ready, for the Son of Man is coming at an hour you do not expect."* (Matt 24:43-44) The disciples realized from this that it would indeed be difficult to know or even to recognize Jesus at His Second Coming. They wanted guidance on this.

Do you remember what Jesus told them? Actually, He advised them in a number of ways, but the striking, memorable thing He told them was that they would be able to distinguish the true Return from 'false prophets' in this way: *"Therefore, by their fruits you will know them."* (Matt 7:20) Even with the difficulty that Jesus speaks of in recognizing His Return, Baha'u'llah nevertheless said that 'some' individuals in this day would be so attuned to His coming as the Return of Christ in the Glory of *"The Father"* that they would immediately and instinctively turn to Him once they became aware of His Message and His person.

Indeed, this kind of instantaneous recognition of Baha'u'llah has happened numerous times in the last century and one half. However, it is not the way for most people like you and me. We seem to have to go through a process of study, search and prayer. Or, at least, that is what I had to do. I know you should speak for yourself. But, if as you hear what has been said about Baha'u'llah, you find that you instantly know Who Baha'u'llah is and you decide to declare your Faith in Him instinctively and immediately, I would like to know about it, to rejoice with you in your spiritual insight and your process of instant discovery. See chapter fifteen for a way to contact me to share your experience.

I mention this 'instant discovery' process because it happened many times with Jesus and with Baha'u'llah. Some individuals recognized Jesus instantly, in a burst of spiritual insight and intuition. Just as was the case with Jesus, some people were around Baha'u'llah only for minutes, simply looking upon Him, not even having heard anything from His lips, before they fell on their knees at the feet of their Lord. This would all happen without Baha'u'llah or the person saying anything. But as I have said, most individuals are not granted this kind of spiritual insight and need to think, pray, analyze and investigate.

One of the teachings of Baha'u'llah is the 'Independent investigation of truth' and He gave a formula for investigating, just as Christ gave a formula for deciding the truth of His Reappearance and Return to the world. In one scriptural passage, Baha'u'llah says: *"The first and foremost testimony establishing His truth is His own Self. Next to this testimony is His Revelation. For whoso faileth to recognize either the one or the other He hath established the words He hath revealed as proof of His reality and truth."* (Baha'u'llah: *Gleanings*, Page: 105)

Here is another quote, where Baha'u'llah acknowledges that knowledge of God in a complete and full sense is not possible and tells us that this is the very reason that God sends 'Manifestations of Himself' to the world:

"The door of the knowledge of the Ancient Being hath ever been, and will continue for ever to be, closed in the face of men. No man's understanding shall ever gain access unto His holy court. As a token of His mercy, however, and as a proof of His loving-kindness, He hath manifested unto men the Day Stars of His divine guidance, the Symbols of His divine unity, and hath ordained the knowledge of these sanctified Beings to be identical with the knowledge of His own Self.

"Whoso recognizeth them hath recognized God. Whoso hearkeneth to their call, hath hearkened to the Voice of God, and whoso testifieth to the truth of their Revelation, hath testified to the truth of God Himself. Whoso turneth away from them, hath turned away from God, and whoso disbelieveth in them, hath disbelieved in God. Every one of them is the Way of God that connecteth this world with the realms above, and the Standard of His Truth unto every one in the kingdoms of earth and heaven. They are the Manifestations of God amidst men, the evidences of His Truth, and the signs of His glory." (Baha'u'llah: *Gleanings*, Pages: 49-50)

QUESTION: What else did Baha'u'llah say about His Person that would cast light for me on the subject of 'Manifestation' and, at the same time, help me to decide if He is or isn't a 'Manifestation of God'?

RESPONSE: Here are some words of Baha'u'llah that I think are directly relevant to your question. At least, I hope so. Whenever I offer Baha'u'llah's words to you, please remember that you can start the process of investigation on your own. In fact, in my view, that would be better. If that is what you would like to do, or if you would like a reference to use while you engage in the rest of this conversation, get a copy of *Gleanings* from the library or from a Baha'i friend. This book is a book of 'gleanings' of Scripture from the writings of Baha'u'llah, compiled by His Great Grandson, Shoghi Effendi. It contains many of the central ideas and statements of Baha'u'llah and should be quite helpful to you, in my opinion.

Here are those words of Baha'u'llah: Speaking of all the Manifestations of God: *"We recognize in the manifestation of each one of them, whether outwardly or inwardly, the manifestation of none but God Himself, if ye be of those that comprehend. Every one of them is a mirror of God, reflecting naught else but His Self, His Beauty, His Might and Glory, if ye will understand."* Gleanings, p.73)

Specifically, you asked what Baha'u'llah said about Himself. Here are several statements that may be helpful: Remembering the 'two-fold station' of the Manifestations, being both human and divine, this what Baha'u'llah says: *"When I contemplate, O my God, the relationship that bindeth me to Thee, I am moved to proclaim to all created things "Verily I am God";* [the 'divine station'] *and when I consider my own self, lo, I find it coarser than clay!"* [The 'human station'] (Baha'u'llah: *Kitab-i-Aqdas,* Notes, Page: 234) This statement puts us in mind of the words of Jesus where He first says, *"The Father and I are one,"* [the 'divine station'] but then says in Matt 19:17 *"Why do you call Me good? No one is good but One, that is, God."* [referring to the 'human station']

Speaking of Himself and of the *"Word"* of God that is in every Manifestation (and therefore in Him) Baha'u'llah says that the *"spiritual resurrection"* of all humanity is dependent upon *"Him through Whose coming the world was made the recipient of this promised glory, this wondrous favor. Behold how the generality of mankind hath been endued with the capacity to hearken unto God's most exalted Word.*" (Baha'u'llah: *Gleanings*, Pages: 96-97)

In the same passage where He speaks about the role He will play in mankind's *"spiritual resurrection,"* He also says that He is *"the Word of God"* and *"God's most exalted Word—the Word upon which must depend the gathering together and spiritual resurrection of all men . . . ."* (Baha'u'llah: *Gleanings*, Page: 97)

In a passage where Baha'u'llah laments the sad state of affairs in the world today, He nevertheless gives us the 'good news,' that by *"the movement of our pen"* [that is, His Revelation] He has *"breathed new life"* into every human soul and has called forth, as bidden by God, *"world-wide regeneration."*

Here is the full quote: *"Justice is, in this day, bewailing its plight, and Equity groaneth beneath the yoke of oppression. The thick clouds of tyranny have darkened the face of the earth, and enveloped its peoples. Through the movement of Our Pen of glory We have, at the bidding of the omnipotent Ordainer, breathed a new life into every human frame, and instilled into every word a fresh potency. All created things proclaim the evidences of this world-wide regeneration."* (Baha'u'llah: *Gleanings*, Pages: 92-93)

Finally, keeping in mind Baha'u'llah's life-long sufferings and tribulations, this quote: *"I have accepted to be tried by manifold adversities for no purpose except to regenerate all that are in Thy heaven and on Thy earth."* (Baha'u'llah: *Prayers and Meditations*, Page: 198)

QUESTION: Did Baha'u'llah say anything specific about the purpose of God in revealing Himself again, as Baha'u'llah put it, *"in the Glory of the Father"?*

RESPONSE: He said quite a bit, and I will give you only several quotes, but this would probably be a good place to begin, as I said above, to do your own 'digging' and investigating. However, here are the statements He revealed that I think come the closest to relating to your question:

First, He tells us that this new Revelation is in fulfillment of prophecy, not only those of the Christian Faith, but the prophecies of all faiths, throughout all history. *"The Revelation which, from time immemorial, hath been acclaimed as the Purpose and Promise of all the Prophets of God, and the most cherished Desire of His Messengers, hath now, by virtue of the pervasive Will of the Almighty and at His irresistible bidding, been revealed unto men. The advent of such a Revelation hath been heralded in all the sacred Scriptures."* (Baha'u'llah: *Gleanings*, Page: 5)

Second, the world is in trouble and travail. It is, many would agree, in great need of divine intervention. With this in mind, Baha'u'llah said: *"The vitality of men's belief in God is dying out in every land; nothing short of His wholesome medicine can ever restore it. The corrosion of ungodliness is eating into the vitals of human society; what else but the Elixir of His potent Revelation can cleanse and revive it?"* (Baha'u'llah: *Gleanings*, Page: 200)

One might ask how does Baha'u'llah plan to carry out this 'revival' of the world, especially in the face of so much division and anger? Later in that same passage, Baha'u'llah tells us *"the task of converting satanic strength into heavenly power is one that We have been empowered to accomplish."* (Baha'u'llah: *Gleanings*, Page: 200) Baha'u'llah further says: *"This can in no wise be achieved except through the power of a skilled, an all-powerful, and inspired Physician."* (Baha'u'llah: *Epistle to the Son of the Wolf*, Pages: 62-63)

And, *"That which is conducive to the regeneration of the world and the salvation of the peoples and kindreds of the earth hath been sent down from the heaven of the utterance of*

Him Who is the Desire of the world. [that is, God] *Give ye a hearing ear to the counsels of the Pen of Glory.* [One of the titles of Baha'u'llah] *Better is this for you than all that is on the earth.* " (Baha'u'llah: *Tablets of Baha'u'llah*, Page: 223)

Speaking of the purpose of God in sending Him to the world with this new Revelation, He says: *"I confess that Thou hast no desire except the regeneration of the whole world, and the establishment of the unity of its peoples, and the salvation of all them that dwell therein.* " (Baha'u'llah: *Gleanings*, Page: 243

Telling us that God is the source of this Revelation, Baha'u'llah says: *"He, the Glory of God (Baha),* [short form of Baha'u'llah's name] *hath spoken not from mere impulse. He that hath given Him a voice is He that hath given a voice unto all things, that they may praise and glorify Him.* " (Baha'u'llah: *Epistle to the Son of the Wolf*, Page: 9)

Closing this section, Baha'u'llah says His Revelation is like an *"ocean"*: *"My holy, My divinely ordained Revelation may be likened unto an ocean in whose depths are concealed innumerable pearls of great price, of surpassing luster. It is the duty of every seeker to bestir himself and strive to attain the shores of this ocean, so that he may, in proportion to the eagerness of his search and the efforts he hath exerted, partake of such benefits.* " (Baha'u'llah: *Gleanings*, Page: 326)

Later in the same passage, Baha'u'llah appeals to every man and woman and youth on the planet to accept God's Grace: *"This most great, this fathomless and surging Ocean is near, astonishingly near, unto you. Behold it is closer to you than your life-vein! Swift as the twinkling of an eye ye can, if ye but wish it, reach and partake of this imperishable favor, this God-given grace, this incorruptible gift, this most potent and unspeakably glorious bounty.* " (Baha'u'llah: *Gleanings*, Page: 326)

QUESTION: You have heard this from me before, I realize, but I have to say it again. I still feel that you are 'lowering' the station of Jesus by 'lumping' Him together with Buddha, Muhammad, Moses, Baha'u'llah, and others. I keep trying to tell you that Jesus is the one and only begotten Son of God. You knew that once. Have you forgotten it, or denied it?

RESPONSE: This is one thing that I am certain I will never forget nor deny. In responding to you, I've agreed with you each time you say that Jesus is the **'Son of God.'** Jesus is indeed the Son of God and I've always tried, gently but energetically, to remind you that Baha'u'llah is *"The Father."* Baha'u'llah tells us that *"The Father hath come"* and links His appearance with an assurance to Christians that the Return of Christ has been fulfilled in His coming. By now you are very familiar with His statement (speaking of Jesus Christ): *"O Jews! If ye be intent on crucifying once again Jesus, the Spirit of God, put Me to death, for He hath once more, in My person, been made manifest unto you."* (Baha'u'llah: *Gleanings*, Page: 101)

Baha'u'llah summarizes His mission and gives again the purpose of God's new Revelation: *"The measure of the favors of God hath been filled up, His Word hath been perfected, the light of His countenance hath been revealed, His sovereignty hath encompassed the whole of creation, the glory of His Revelation hath been made manifest, and His bounties have rained upon all mankind."* (Baha'u'llah: *Gleanings*, Page: 259)

QUESTION: How can I make this any plainer! You are still not dealing with my central question or my belief that Jesus stands alone, as the 'Son of God,' not just 'one of a group'!

RESPONSE: It's true that Jesus stands alone, as does every other Manifestation of God, in Baha'i teaching. Each one is unique; there can be no other one like that particular Manifestation of God. But I'm still appealing to you to open up your heart and mind to a totally new concept of Manifestation and progressive revelation that does not 'lower' Jesus but actually *raises* His station, while at the same time raising the station of all the other Manifestations.

The concept of 'Manifestation' says that the pre-existent 'Word of God,' through which the world was created, has been the forceful, complete presence of God in the 'human form' of all the Manifestations; it has been God appearing in the *"human temple."* Further, that this full presence of God has appeared many times in history and will appear again.

In a special and unique way, there was, in our Christian understanding, a Manifestation—Jesus—Who had the title of *"The Son."* Again, in a special way today, there is a Manifestation of God—Baha'u'llah—Who has the title of *"The Father."* He says that Christians and all others should see Christ Returned in Him. He has appeared, He tells us, to draw history and the people of the world into a fulfillment period in which all the dreams and hopes of a beleaguered, dispirited and disunited humanity will be realized and enacted. He said this would be a period in which prophecies and promises of a *"Kingdom of God"* would be realized and fulfilled *"on earth as it is in Heaven."*

Baha'u'llah tells us in many places in His Revelation that this time of History, which He once called *"the Day of Days"* and *"the Day of God, Himself"* is very great. So great, He says, that it is beyond our ability to conceive and only future generations will fully understand and comprehend what is happening now, as the ground of historical change moves more rapidly beneath our feet.

This is a very great Day in the history of the world, says Baha'u'llah. Here are several quotes about this *"Day of God,"* as He calls it: *"Verily I say, this is the Day in which mankind can behold the Face, and hear the Voice, of the Promised One. The Call of God hath been raised, and the light of His countenance hath been lifted up upon men. It behoveth every man to blot out the trace of every idle word from the tablet of his heart, and to gaze, with an open and unbiased mind, on the signs of His Revelation, the proofs of His Mission, and the tokens of His glory.*

"Great indeed is this Day! The allusions made to it in all the sacred Scriptures as the Day of God attest its greatness. The soul of every Prophet of God, of every Divine Messenger, hath thirsted for this wondrous Day." (Baha'u'llah: *Gleanings*, Pages: 10-11)

Calling this *"the King of Days"*, Baha'u'llah again appeals to the people of the world, and to you! *"Say: O people! The Day, promised unto you in all the Scriptures, is now come. Fear ye God, and withhold not yourselves from recognizing the One Who is the Object of your creation. Hasten ye unto Him. Better is this for you than the world and all that is therein. Would that ye could perceive it!"* (Baha'u'llah: *Gleanings*, Page: 314)

Referring to this Day as a *"soul-stirring springtime,"* Baha'u'llah says: *"O friends! It behoveth you to refresh and revive your souls through the gracious favors which in this Divine, this soul-stirring Springtime are being showered upon you. The Day Star of His great glory hath shed its radiance upon you, and the clouds of His limitless grace have overshadowed you. How high the reward of him that hath not deprived himself of so great a bounty, nor failed to recognize the beauty of his Best-Beloved in this, His new attire."* (Baha'u'llah: *Gleanings*, Page: 94)

Finally, though, I do agree with you that you still have a burning question about Who Baha'is think Christ is. Let's turn to that question in the next chapter. Jesus asked His disciples: *"Who do men say that I am?"* Let's find out who Baha'is say He is. Your other pressing question, if I understand it, is: Who is Baha'u'llah in relation to Jesus Christ? I think you are in for something of a surprise when you hear Baha'u'llah's testimony about the identity and mission of Jesus Christ. I have not seen anywhere in Christian literature such a moving tribute, as the one Baha'u'llah gives Christ.

Here, as usual for the end of a chapter, are two prayers: one from Baha'u'llah and another from his Son, 'Abdu'l-Baha.

"All praise, O my God, be to Thee Who art the Source of all glory and majesty, of greatness and honor, of sovereignty and dominion, of loftiness and grace, of awe and power. Whomsoever Thou willest Thou causest to draw nigh unto the Most Great Ocean, and on whomsoever Thou desirest Thou conferrest the honor of recognizing Thy Most Ancient Name. Of all who are in heaven and on earth, none can withstand the operation of Thy sovereign Will. From all eternity Thou didst rule the entire creation, and Thou wilt continue for evermore to exercise Thy dominion over all created things. There is none other God but Thee, the Almighty, the Most Exalted, the All-Powerful, the All-Wise.

"Illumine, O Lord, the faces of Thy servants, that they may behold Thee; and cleanse their hearts that they may turn unto the court of Thy heavenly favors, and recognize Him Who is the Manifestation of Thy Self and the Day-Spring of Thine Essence. Verily, Thou art the Lord of all worlds. There is no God but Thee, the Unconstrained, the All-Subduing."
(Baha'u'llah: *Prayers and Meditations*, Pages: 94-95)

And a prayer from 'Abdu'l-Baha:

"O God, my God! Shield Thy trusted servants from the

evils of self and passion, protect them with the watchful eye of Thy loving kindness from all rancor, hate and envy, shelter them in the impregnable stronghold of Thy care and, safe from the darts of doubtfulness, make them the manifestations of Thy glorious Signs, illumine their faces with the effulgent rays shed from the Dayspring of Thy Divine Unity, gladden their hearts with the verses revealed from Thy Holy Kingdom, strengthen their loins by Thy all-swaying power that cometh from Thy Realm of Glory. Thou art the All-Bountiful, the Protector, the Almighty, the Gracious! ('Abdu'l-Baha: *Will and Testament,* Pages: 9-10)

CHAPTER SIX

"WHO DO MEN SAY THAT I AM?": A BAHA'I CONSIDERS THE PLACE OF JESUS CHRIST IN HISTORY.

QUESTION: Well, yes, please do tell me what you think about Jesus. I am worried that you think He is just a man, a philosopher, or a wise person, instead of the 'Son of God.'

RESPONSE: First and foremost, for me, He is my Lord and Savior. As I told you before, there was a time, and I remember it quite vividly, when I became not only rationally convinced but also emotionally convicted that my life should 'belong' to Jesus Christ. My parents had dedicated me to Him as an infant, and at fifteen, I fell to my knees in a promise of commitment to Jesus Christ that has not and will not end.

The one and only reason I am a Baha'i today is that

I believed Jesus when He said He would return and I believe Baha'u'llah when He says He is the return of the Spirit of Christ and when He says, rather directly: *"He* [that is, Jesus] *hath once more, in My person, been made manifest unto you."* (Baha'u'llah: *Gleanings,* Page: 101)

I know and you know that a person cannot truly dedicate his or her life to Christ, literally give it over to Him and then, somehow, take it back or give it to someone else. At least, I couldn't do that. If I didn't believe that Baha'u'llah was *"The Father"* and the reality of the return of the Word of God, the Christ, I certainly would not be a Baha'i.

QUESTION: You really do confuse me sometimes, and frankly, I have wondered if you weren't a little confused or befuddled yourself. Not crazy, just somehow 'mixed up'?

RESPONSE: Believe it or not, I don't mind your observation at all. Early Christians were accused of being 'drunk' or 'mad' because of their extreme joy and strong, utter belief in what they were teaching and preaching. So, it would not surprise me if you saw me that way at times. St. Paul was called a 'fool' so many times that he finally decided to call himself a 'Fool for Christ'. (I Cor 3:18)

Therefore, if I need to be a 'Fool for Baha'u'llah' while we talk, the role is one that I can relish very consciously, as did St. Paul. St. Paul may have recognized the truth of what Baha'u'llah's Son, 'Abdu'l-Baha once said: " *Seeking the approval of man is many times the imperiling of the approval of God."* (From the journal, *Star of the West,* Vol. 6, p.45).

Besides, what we are talking about will either start making more and more sense or it will continue to seem senseless and wrong, depending on your own search, your inclination, your spiritual sense of adventure and your willingness to consider the reality of Baha'u'llah's claims and teachings. Imagine a committed Jew who stays at the fringe of the crowd while listening to Jesus. Day after day, he hears challenging words, feels some degree of attraction, but fears that this Jesus may be 'of Beelzebub,' meaning, of the devil. (As the New Testament reports, many felt Jesus might be a manifestation of Satan: Matt. 10:25; Mark 3:22 and Luke 11: 18)

What is this devout, well meaning Jew to do? He must, we can agree, do one of two things, either leave, go home, try to forget this possibly crazy teacher, this perhaps satanic or confused rabbi *or*, he must move in a little closer, perhaps start to talk to Jesus, listen carefully and maybe even draw closer to Him, maybe even become a follower.

What if you were not this devout Jew but a great and good friend of his? He comes to you and tells you about Jesus. Might you not think that he had 'flipped his lid,' or perhaps been 'attracted to a cult'? Jews and Romans alike thought of Christianity for over a hundred years as 'a cult.' But back to how you might advise your friend, this devout Jew. Might you not warn him that hanging around Jesus could be dangerous, that this Jesus might draw him into an emotional-spiritual decision to become His disciple?

QUESTION: Before saying anything to that friend, I would have gone to see for myself and, if I had, I think I would have become a disciple of Jesus, but I begin to see the point that if I had gone in a doubting mood, I might not have seen Jesus in the right light. Still, I hope that I would have had an open mind.

RESPONSE: Yes, and now you don't need to do any

more than that, to bring an open mind to this question of Baha'u'llah. I see that you are that kind of person, willing to listen, to consider, to investigate for yourself, as you said you would have done in the case of Jesus.

But let's return to what you might have said to your Jewish friend. I hear you that you would have gone to investigate for yourself, but I think you might have been tempted to tell your friend that someone had heard Jesus shockingly say to a disciple and follower of His that the disciple should not go home to bury his father, but should follow Him instead, telling the man: *"Let the dead bury the dead."*

You or someone else might tell him that Jesus advocated people leaving their family to follow Him, even saying that one could not be His disciple unless they loved Him more than family. I'm sure you recognize both of those statements as being from the New Testament. You might have warned him that this advice sounded like a 'cult.' Surely you or someone would warn this man in order to save him from what could be considered the rigors and spiritual dangers of discipleship with this 'strange new Jesus'?

QUESTION: O.K. I told you that I would go see for myself, but I can agree that someone, perhaps his mother or brother might have said them. Being fearful for his soul, I suppose I might have said them myself.

RESPONSE: In any case, whatever you imagine yourself doing or saying in response to that young man who has just learned about Jesus, I am going . . .

QUESTION: Don't even bother. I know what you are going to say now. You are going to tell me to do the same now for myself with relation to deciding who Baha'u'llah is? Right?

RESPONSE: Right! Are you reading my mind? As I was saying, whatever you imagine yourself saying to that young man, or whatever you imagine yourself doing in that example of your advice to the young devout Jew, then yes, do that same thing. If you gave the warning against Jesus (which you said you wouldn't without investigating), I am, believe it or not, going to give you the same warning about Baha'u'llah. Don't get too close, don't listen, don't investigate, don't let yourself learn His claims and don't discover Who He said He was because . . . you could become a follower, just as that young Jew might have done if he got too close to Jesus.

If, on the other hand, (having the knowledge that you now have of Who Jesus was) you gave your friend the advice to investigate Jesus in a careful and thorough way, then I now say to you: Follow your own advice, take your time, study, read, pray, investigate Baha'u'llah in a complete way. You can even take the attitude of one of Jesus' disciples that I am named after, 'Doubting Thomas,' who definitely was one of those kinds of people who had to find out 'for himself.' I'm a lot like my namesake, so I understand those kinds of people. I'm beginning to think you are like that, too.

QUESTION: Say, I thought you were going to tell me what Baha'u'llah said about Who Christ was and how Baha'is see Christ's place in history.

RESPONSE: O.K. Let's start out with a quote from Baha'u'llah that I think will set a good tone for our discussion. It will also surprise and inspire you, if I'm not mistaken.

"Know thou that when the Son of Man yielded up His breath to God, the whole creation wept with a great weeping. By sacrificing Himself, however, a fresh capacity was infused into all created things. Its evidences, as witnessed in all the peoples of the earth, are now manifest before thee. The deepest wisdom which the sages have uttered, the profoundest learning which any mind hath unfolded, the arts which the ablest hands have produced, the influence exerted by the most potent of rulers, are but manifestations of the quickening power released by His transcendent, His all-pervasive, and resplendent Spirit.

"We testify that when He came into the world, He shed the splendor of His glory upon all created things. Through Him the leper recovered from the leprosy of perversity and ignorance. Through Him, the unchaste and wayward were healed. Through His power, born of Almighty God, the eyes of the blind were opened, and the soul of the sinner sanctified.

"Leprosy may be interpreted as any veil that interveneth between man and the recognition of the Lord, his God. Whoso alloweth himself to be shut out from Him is indeed a leper, who shall not be remembered in the Kingdom of God, the Mighty, the All-Praised. We bear witness that through the power of the Word of God every leper was cleansed, every sickness was healed, every human infirmity was banished. He it is Who purified the world. Blessed is the man who, with a face beaming with light, hath turned towards Him."
(Baha'u'llah: *Gleanings,* Pages: 85-86)

QUESTION: I must admit that this statement of Baha'u'llah is the most striking quote about Jesus Christ I've ever heard. Are you sure it isn't from a Christian source?

RESPONSE: No, it is definitely from the Revelation of Baha'u'llah. Here is another quote, especially for those who feel, as one of my friends once said, that Baha'u'llah's name is 'strange sounding': *"Say, O followers of the Son!* [that is, Christians] *Have ye shut out yourselves from Me by reason of My Name? Wherefore ponder ye not in your hearts? Day and night ye have been calling upon your Lord, the Omnipotent, but when He came from the heaven of eternity in His great glory, ye turned aside from Him and remained sunk in heedlessness."* (Baha'u'llah: *Tablets of Baha'u'llah*, Page: 9) I'm sure you recall that in Revelations 2:17 and 3:12, the Bible reveals that not only will there be a 'New Jerusalem,' but that God will also give the true believer His 'new Name.' *"And I will write on him My new name."* Rev 3:12-13

QUESTION: So, if I understand you correctly, you Baha'is believe Jesus is the Son of God, the 'Word of God,' the pre-existent Word, the Word made flesh, but you believe that this same 'Word of God' was manifest also in Buddha, in Moses, in Muhammad (and others) and you believe that this same 'Word of God' is now manifest in the person of Baha'u'llah? I don't agree with you, at least not yet, but at last I see where you are coming from.

You said something several chapters ago that caused me to 'go into a boil.' It really made me angry, to tell you the truth, when you said that the Baha'is were talking about a 'larger' Christ. But, in the light of what we've just been talking about, I can at least understand why you said it. It still doesn't make me too comfortable to hear it, but it makes 'some' sense, at least from your point of view.

RESPONSE: I would never have followed Baha'u'llah if I felt I had to begin to believe in a 'smaller' Christ. The two reasons I became a Baha'i are first, that

I began to believe that Baha'u'llah was Christ Returned and second, I realized that Baha'u'llah saw Christ in a much larger role in history than I had ever imagined.

QUESTION: Well, I have to tell you I don't feel assured on that point, just that I am starting to see what you believe and why. But there is something else bothering me. There seems to be no mention of the role of the Holy Spirit in all of this. Why?

RESPONSE: That is my error. The existence and the role of the Holy Spirit is a strong theme in Baha'u'llah's Revelation. Here are several quotes about the Holy Spirit from the Baha'i Writings

"And to Jesus, Son of Mary, We gave manifest signs, and We strengthened Him with the Holy Spirit." (Baha'u'llah: *Gleanings*, Page: 52)

Baha'u'llah speaks of the Word of God, saying: *"... a single word of which quickeneth to fresh, new life the bodies of the dead, and bestoweth the Holy Spirit upon the moldering bones of this existence."* (Baha'u'llah: *Seven Valleys and Four Valleys*, Page: 20)

Baha'u'llah felt He was under the constant guidance of the Holy Spirit. Once, while speaking He said: *"Methinks that I hear the Voice of the Holy Spirit calling from behind Me saying: Vary Thou Thy theme, and alter Thy tone, lest the heart of him who hath fixed his gaze upon Thy face be saddened."* (Baha'u'llah: *Gleanings*, Page: 37)

One more quote, of the many hundreds of times the Holy Spirit is mentioned in the Baha'i Scriptures: Speaking to the 'peoples of the earth' He said: *"O ye peoples of the earth! Turn yourselves towards Him* [that is, toward Baha'u'llah] *Who hath turned towards you. He, verily, is the Face of God amongst you, and His Testimony and His Guide unto you ... The voice of the Burning Bush is raised in the midmost heart of the world, and the Holy Spirit calleth aloud among the nations: 'Lo, the Desired One is come with manifest dominion!' "* (Baha'u'llah: *Epistle to the Son of the Wolf,* Page: 48)

QUESTION: Sometimes I wonder if you realize how challenging some of these statements are, but for right now, let me go on to see if I understand how you Baha'is are thinking about my Jesus . . .

RESPONSE: It's my turn to 'butt in' this time. He certainly is 'your Jesus,' but don't forget that He is 'my Jesus' too and always will be. I think of Jesus every day of my life and several Baha'i prayers remind me to think of Jesus, including one that I like to pray every day, since the prayer asks me to call upon God in the name of all the Manifestations. In this prayer the Manifestations are called *"the Daysprings of thine invisible essence"* and Baha'is know that Baha'u'llah often used the word 'Dayspring' to refer to the Manifestations (Dayspring referring to the rising of the sun; the word 'Dayspring' is used in the New Testament, in the same way that Baha'u'llah uses it.) (Luke 1: 78)

So let me remind you that Jesus belongs to you, to me, to all the Moslems of the world, to all the Jews and Buddhists and, especially, to every Baha'i, as you will see in our discussion.

QUESTION: Let me apologize. I didn't mean to be 'possessive' about Jesus. The fact is I agree that Jesus does belong to the entire world, and I am just beginning to be aware that Baha'is revere Jesus as I do, but I'm not quite convinced. You will need to show me much more. But before you do, I was about to continue with what I have learned from you to check whether my understanding of what you are saying is correct.

As I understand so far, you Baha'is believe that one God—not many Gods—has been operating in human history, progressively revealing Himself, leading up to the event you call the consummation of history, the coming of what you call the *"Father."* Also, that this consummation of history is the Return of Christ, with Jesus 'coming again' in the Person of Baha'u'llah. With Baha'u'llah's coming, with this Return of Christ, the world will experience a realization of human unity, the establishment of peace and the beginning of what Christians call God's Kingdom and the expression of His Will, *"on earth as it is in heaven."*

I hope I've got this mostly right, because when I leave our conversation and go off on my own to pray, read, investigate and just 'think all this over,' I don't want to be laboring under any misconceptions. And, I do have a question that just occurred to me: Don't you Baha'is realize that when most Christians think of the 'time of the end,' they think of the destruction of this world?

RESPONSE: Your summary was masterful. You have it so right that I'm jealous. The last time this happened, with someone picking up very quickly on the Baha'i message, was on a day when I spoke in a Pentecostal Church. I was amazed at how quickly and how correctly one person heard what I said. I even felt that somehow 'the Holy Spirit' might have assisted him! And, I felt that maybe it wasn't coincidental that it was among the Pentecostals that this happened.

So yes, you have it right, very right. Right on the heels of that compliment, I have to remind you that there is nothing that Christians have disagreed about more than the 'time of the end' (the end of history). The study of 'the time of the end,' called eschatology, has filled thousands of books, and there are literally hundreds of ideas of how this will take place. Some of the theories are literal, some figurative, some fanciful. Thus, there is no one theory of the 'time of the end' to which most Christians subscribe.

Baha'u'llah has a beautiful and striking passage in which He talks about the time of the end as being a metaphor for the 'Resurrection' that is now taking place in the world as a result of the Return of Christ in His [that is, Baha'u'llah's] Person. *"The Father"* of all mankind has come to gather together His many children into the unity of the oneness of mankind–a true Resurrection of humanity. As one reads Baha'u'llah, one realizes that the 'old world order' is, in fact, going to be destroyed, to be replaced by the 'Kingdom of God on earth' about which Christ spoke.

Here is the quote from Baha'u'llah on the 'time of the end.' In it, He lists the questions that men will ask at that time and gives (in metaphor, as in the Old Testament) answers that refer to His coming: *"Among them are those who have said: 'Have the verses been sent down?' Say: 'Yea, by Him Who is the Lord of the heavens!' 'Hath the Hour come?' 'Nay, more; it hath passed, by Him Who is the Revealer of clear tokens! Verily, the Inevitable is come, and He, the True One, hath appeared with proof and testimony. The Plain is disclosed, and mankind is sore vexed and fearful. Earthquakes have broken loose, and the tribes have lamented, for fear of God, the Lord of Strength, the All-Compelling.'*

"Say: 'The stunning trumpet-blast hath been loudly raised, and the Day is God's, the One, the Unconstrained.' 'Hath the Catastrophe come to pass?' Say: 'Yea, by the

Lord of Lords!' 'Is the Resurrection come?' 'Nay, more; He Who is the Self-Subsisting hath appeared with the Kingdom of His signs.' 'Seest thou men laid low?' 'Yea, by my Lord, the Exalted, the Most High!' 'Have the tree-stumps been uprooted?' 'Yea, more; the mountains have been scattered in dust; by Him the Lord of attributes!' They say: 'Where is Paradise, and where is Hell?' Say: 'The one is reunion with Me; the other thine own self'. . ." (Baha'u'llah: *Epistle to the Son of the Wolf*, Pages: 131-132)

Another quote from Baha'u'llah on the 'time of the end' is this: *"The blast hath been blown on the trumpet . . . Speed out of your sepulchres. How long will ye sleep? The second blast hath been blown on the trumpet. On whom are ye gazing? This is your Lord, the God of Mercy."* (Baha'u'llah: *Proclamation of Baha'u'llah*, Page: 98) And still another passage, where God is speaking to Baha'u'llah: *"We have chosen thee to be our most mighty Trumpet, whose blast is to signalize the resurrection of all mankind."* (Baha'u'llah: *Gleanings*, Page: 31)

Finally: *"Say: O men! This is a matchless Day. Matchless must, likewise, be the tongue that celebrateth the praise of the Desire of all nations, and matchless the deed that aspireth to be acceptable in His sight. The whole human race hath longed for this Day, that perchance it may fulfil that which well beseemeth its station, and is worthy of its destiny. Blessed is the man whom the affairs of the world have failed to deter from recognizing Him Who is the Lord of all things."* (Baha'u'llah: *Gleanings*, Page: 39)

Baha'i House of Worship, Apia, Samoa.

QUESTION: We've drifted away from how Baha'is see Christ, haven't we?

RESPONSE: Yes, I suppose so, but I'm trying to follow where you lead and that takes us down different paths, but probably what we've been talking about isn't so far afield if you consider the close connection between *"The Son"* and *"The Father"* and if you constantly keep in mind that Baha'u'llah claims to be the Return of Christ *"in my Person."*

Here are several other quotes from Baha'u'llah about Christ: In this quote, He makes clear that Jesus 'testified' of Him and had His coming in mind when He told the disciples to await His Return: *"Say, Lo! The Father is come, and that which ye were promised in the Kingdom is fulfilled! This is the Word which the Son* [that is, Jesus] *concealed, when to those around Him He said: 'Ye cannot bear it now.' And when the appointed time was fulfilled and the Hour had struck, the Word shone forth above the horizon of the Will of God.*

"Beware, O followers of the Son, that ye cast it not behind your backs. Take ye fast hold of it. Better is this for you than all that ye possess. Verily He is nigh unto them that do good. The Hour which We had concealed from the knowledge of the peoples of the earth and of the favoured angels hath come to pass. Say, verily, He [that is, Jesus] *hath testified of Me, and I do testify of Him. Indeed, He hath purposed no one other than Me."* (Baha'u'llah: *Tablets of Baha'u'llah*, Page: 11)

In a passage where Baha'u'llah refers to Jesus as 'The Spirit' (a title He often uses for Jesus), Baha'u'llah says: *"Give ear unto that which the Spirit imparteth unto thee from the verses of God, the Help in Peril, the Self-Subsisting, that His Call may attract thee to the Summit of transcendent glory and draw thee nigh unto the Station where thou shalt behold thine entire being set ablaze with the fire of the love of God in such wise that neither the ascendancy of the rulers nor the whisperings of their vassals can quench it, and thou wilt arise amidst the peoples of the world to celebrate the praise of thy Lord, the Possessor of Names. This is that which well beseemeth thee in this Day."* (Baha'u'llah: *Tablets of Baha'u'llah*, Page: 265)

Can you begin to see how I, as a Baha'i from a Christian background, believe that I am as true as ever to my commitment to Christ? In fact, I often feel that my commitment is stronger and deeper than ever before. And many other Christians who have become Baha'is have given the same witness. Some say their 'discovery' of Who Christ was has become not only stronger but has also become endued with deeper meaning.

When I was twenty, my Christ was everything to me and I proceeded into the ministry. I could not imagine that there could be a larger concept of Christ. Then I learned about Baha'u'llah and about progressive revelation, about God Manifesting Himself many times in

history by sending the pre-existent Word into the world
in *"the form of the human temple"* as Baha'u'llah put it.
Though it seemed confusing and even insulting when I
first heard it, finally I understood that there could indeed be a 'greater God' and a 'larger Christ.'

QUESTION: I'm glad that you realize that what you
just said can sound insulting to Christian ears. You say
you even felt that way yourself when you first heard it. So
I guess you realize that when you say that, it makes me
feel as if you are saying to me: "Your Christ is too small."

RESPONSE: The way you heard what I said is, as
you say, exactly how I first heard it, though I quickly
learned that the Baha'i spirit is to unite, not to disunite.
Baha'is don't intend to criticize or belittle. They try very
hard not to say something that is hurtful to the feelings
of others. Dispute and argument are avoided. The bot-
tom line is that Baha'is have been commissioned by *"The
Father"* of all mankind to work to support and promote
human unity. They couldn't do that if they went around
criticizing and insulting people.

So, instead of hearing me say, "Your Christ is too
small," please hear me say that Christ is everything in
the world to me and to you and to anyone who has experienced His salvation and carries Him in their hearts.
And then, hear me say that your idea, my idea, anyone's
idea and concept of Christ can be 'larger' than it was
before, greater than ever imagined.

If the Pre-existent Word of God that was in Christ
was also in all the other Manifestations of God, then from
a Christian point of view, 'Christ' as the 'Word of God'
has been active across the entire history of the world and
is present again today in the Person of Baha'u'llah. So,
rather than hearing me say that your Christ is too small,

I offer you instead a new vision of the Person of Christ. Our vision of Him can get as large as we want it to be and as powerful as our new understanding of history will allow.

And, let me share that Baha'is have a sense of 'joy' as we have learned to expand our belief to include all the appearances or Manifestations of the Word of God. Baha'is feel they begin to understand history in a new and radically expanded way that represents a complete, full understanding in which the Christ Spirit is seen in many places and times in history and in many different *"human temples"* of the Manifestations of other religions.

QUESTION: I don't want you to think that I am 'stuck' on this question, but I have to be sure, very sure, that you are not trying to 'downsize' Jesus Christ, to make Him smaller, lesser, than what He is. I do hear you that you are actually trying to enlarge my idea and the world's idea, of Jesus, but how can I be sure that you are sincere in this?

RESPONSE: It is my wish and my hope to present Baha'u'llah to you with sincerity and humbleness, but also with a sense of joy and maybe a bit of the elation that the early Christian believers felt. You can question or test my sincerity (I won't mind) but that isn't even the point.

It is your decision as to Who Baha'u'llah is that really counts. Is He or is He not the Return of Christ, as He very clearly and forcefully claims to be? Answer that one and you won't trouble yourself with whether I am or am not sincere. I do hope that sometime soon in this conversation, you will see that I am sincere in what I am saying to you. Also, I hope that you will see that I have been true to the Christian Scriptures and to the Baha'i

Scriptures, as well. When I quote from either of those sources, I quote 'in context,' so that the original meaning is carefully maintained. That's important to me, because I wouldn't want anything I say in a clumsy, wrong way or incomplete way to 'turn you off' from investigating the Person of Baha'u'llah.

So, no, it is not any concept of a smaller or lesser Christ that I present. Quite the contrary, I believe I am introducing to you a way to see your Christ (and mine) in a larger way, as One Whose Presence permeates all of human history and Who is present today in Baha'u'llah's coming.

QUESTION: It is still beyond my belief at this point, or my desire to believe, that Baha'u'llah is Jesus, my Savior, Returned.

RESPONSE: Baha'u'llah says in His writings (with the 'Voice of God' speaking): *"And to Jesus, Son of Mary, We gave manifest signs, and We strengthened Him with the Holy Spirit."* (Baha'u'llah: *The Kitab-i-Iqan*, Pages: 176-177) Then He continues, stating that Jesus has announced the Revelation of Baha'u'llah: *"If ye have resolved to shed the blood of Him Whose . . . Revelation Jesus Christ Himself hath announced, behold Me standing, ready and defenseless, before you. Deal with Me after your own desires."* (Baha'u'llah: *Gleanings*, Page: 102)

Finally, Baha'u'llah wrote letters to all the world leaders of His day (the time of your great, great grandfather, if you are twenty years old around the turn of the millennium) and said to them: *"O kings of Christendom! Heard ye not the saying of Jesus, the Spirit of God, 'I go away, and come again unto you'? Wherefore, then, did ye fail, when He did come again unto you in the clouds of heaven, to draw nigh unto Him, that ye might behold His face, and be of them that attained His Presence?*

"In another passage He saith: 'When He, the Spirit of Truth, is come, He will guide you into all truth.' And yet, behold how, when He did bring the truth, ye refused to turn your faces towards Him, and persisted in disporting yourselves with your pastimes and fancies. Ye welcomed Him not, neither did ye seek His Presence, that ye might hear the verses of God from His own mouth, and partake of the manifold wisdom of the Almighty, the All-Glorious, the All-Wise.

"Ye have, by reason of your failure, hindered the breath of God from being wafted over you, and have withheld from your souls the sweetness of its fragrance. Ye continue roving with delight in the valley of your corrupt desires. Ye, and all ye possess, shall pass away. Ye shall, most certainly, return to God, and shall be called to account for your doings in the presence of Him Who shall gather together the entire creation . . . " (Baha'u'llah: *Gleanings*, Pages: 246-247)

QUESTION: I do have to admit that Baha'u'llah cannot be lightly or easily dismissed. He does seem to speak with authority, but I still have the lingering doubts that He may be a madman or one of the many thousands in history who have falsely claimed to be the return of Christ. We are having this conversation at the turn of the millennium. Is He perhaps one of those that we could call 'millenarian enthusiasts'?

RESPONSE: First, Baha'u'llah declared His mission in 1863, so no, He couldn't be an enthusiast of the turn of the millennium. But, please recall what you heard in the third chapter ('How it all Began'). Christians had great fervor for the Return of Christ in the early and middle parts of the 1800's. A minister, William Miller, picked the date of 1844 as the time of arrival of the Returned Christ. Christians of nearly all denominations all over the world thought He would return on this date. It seems to me that it wasn't a coincidence that Baha'u'llah's predecessor—The Bab—His 'John the Baptist,' if you will, declared His mission during that very year.

What was the Bab's Mission? To prepare the way for the appearance of Baha'u'llah, Who, like Jesus, was a follower of His predecessor. This is a very interesting story as you look into it. And, a number of modern day Churches, including the Seventh Day Adventists and the Jehovah's Witnesses, stem from the original preaching of William Miller. Thus, these churches are historically very close to the spirit of the Baha'i Faith, something that I think will come up within those denominations as time goes by.

At any rate, Baha'u'llah's claim is not just to be the Return of Christ, but more. Just as Jesus said: *"He who has seen Me has seen the Father"* (John 14:9) Baha'u'llah said: *"If it be your wish, O people, to know God and to discover the greatness of His might, look, then, upon Me . . . "* (Baha'u'llah: *Gleanings*, Page: 272)

QUESTION: It certainly is true that no other prophetic figure such as Jeremiah, Isaiah or Hosea ever claimed that they were the Presence of God, as Jesus Christ and Baha'u'llah did. Both of them made unequivocal claims to represent the reality of God in human history, so much so, that to look upon them, hear them, obey them was to see, hear and obey God. But please remember that Jesus said: *"I am the way, the truth, and the life. No one comes to the Father except through Me."* (John 14:6)

RESPONSE: And Baha'is support that when Jesus came, that was exactly true. Whenever a Manifestation comes, Baha'u'llah says, no one can respond to the Will of God that is brightly evident in that new Messenger of the Word of God without recognizing and following Him. But remember that Jesus once said that He would return *"in the glory of His Father."* (Matt 16:27) I would have to add the thought that, because of my background, I came to Baha'u'llah through Jesus. Additionally, no person becoming a Baha'i can do so unless they realize Jesus as the *"Son of God"* anymore than they can become a Baha'i without realizing that Baha'u'llah is *"the Father"* of all mankind.

QUESTION: The rest of that quotation about the *'Glory of the Father'* continues with some words that I think you shouldn't leave out, so let me quote the full verse: *"For the Son of Man will come in the glory of His Father with His angels, and then He will reward each according to his works."* (Matt 16:27)

RESPONSE: I'm glad you corrected me. Baha'u'llah often spoke of 'angels' as in this challenging passage: *"Say, God is my witness! The Promised One Himself hath come down from heaven, seated upon the crimson cloud with the hosts of revelation on His right, and the angels of inspiration on His left, and the Decree hath been fulfilled at the behest of God, the Omnipotent, the Almighty. Thereupon the footsteps of everyone have slipped except such as God hath protected through His tender mercy and numbered with those who have recognized Him through His Own Self and detached themselves from all that pertaineth to the world."* (Baha'u'llah: *Tablets of Baha'u'llah*, Pages: 182-183)

Now, to Baha'is who believe that *"The Father"* has come (and remember that the name 'Baha'u'llah' means 'the Glory of God'), Baha'u'llah says this: *"Arise, and lift up your voices, that haply they that are fast asleep may be awakened. Say: O ye who are as dead! The Hand of Divine bounty proffereth unto you the Water of Life. Hasten and drink your fill.* " Then, in a statement similar to a saying of Jesus: *"Whoso hath been re-born in this Day, shall never die; whoso remaineth dead, shall never live.* " (Baha'u'llah: *Gleanings*, Page: 213)

QUESTION: I've been doing some reading as we carry on this conversation. You told me to do some checking of sources on my own, rather than just accepting what you tell me. I see from my reading that there is another similarity between what Christ said and what Baha'u'llah said. Something about the Divine Physician?

RESPONSE: Christ Himself did not speak directly of being the Divine Physician (but see Matt. 9:12, where He implied it). Many others throughout the ages have referred to Jesus in this way, as one Who can heal hearts and minds, as well as the body. Baha'u'llah has a strikingly similar passage, in which He refers to Himself in this way:

"The All-Knowing Physician hath His finger on the pulse of mankind. He perceiveth the disease, and prescribeth, in His unerring wisdom, the remedy. Every age hath its own problem, and every soul its particular aspiration. The remedy the world needeth in its present-day afflictions can never be the same as that which a subsequent age may require. Be anxiously concerned with the needs of the age ye live in, and centre your deliberations on its exigencies and requirements.

"We can well perceive how the whole human race is encompassed with great, with incalculable afflictions. We see it languishing on its bed of sickness, sore-tried and disillusioned. They that are intoxicated by self-conceit have interposed themselves between it and the Divine and infallible Physician. "
(Baha'u'llah: *Proclamation of Baha'u'llah*, Pages: 116-117)

QUESTION: And something else seems similar, something about 'Fishers of Men'?

RESPONSE: Yes. This refers to Christ's statement to His disciples, as you know, where He commands them to be *'Fishers of Men.'* The statement of Baha'u'llah is one where He tells His disciples today to follow Him in becoming the *'quickeners of mankind.'* 'Quicken' is a word not in everyday use so we can remind ourselves that in the New Testament, it means 'to bring a person from death to life.' In both Christian and Baha'i scriptures, it means that people are considered spiritually 'dead' until they recognize the reality of the Manifestation of God in their day.

Once they do recognize and accept Jesus, Christians would say they are brought from a spiritual condition of 'death' to a 'life' of salvation in Christ. Similarly, Baha'u'llah says (quoted earlier) that until a person recognizes Him in this Day, that person is, in the spiritual sense, 'dead' and is brought to life by recognizing Him, turning to Him, and following His teachings.

There is no contradiction between *'fishers of men'* and *'quickeners of mankind.'* Both Christians and Baha'is obviously try to do both, but the accent in Christianity is the salvation of the individual soul, while the emphasis in the Baha'i Faith is the *'quickening'* and the *'resurrection'* of all mankind, bringing them not only to life, but to a life of unity and peace. While there is a focus by Baha'u'llah on the state of the world, nevertheless, He frequently calls upon all men and women to realize their need for personal or individual salvation. And while the emphasis of the Christian Faith is clearly on personal and individual salvation, nevertheless, Christians are also concerned about the state of the world. We could both

probably agree here that while there are some differences of emphasis, the two Faiths are concerned about
both personal salvation and the needs of the world.

Do you remember in an earlier chapter, that I said
that Baha'u'llah teaches that each Manifestation has a
'prescribed mission'? Here is the full quote: *"Each Manifestation of God hath a distinct individuality, a definitely prescribed mission, a predestined revelation, and specially designated limitations. Each one of them is known by a different
name, is characterized by a special attribute, fulfils a definite
mission, and is entrusted with a particular Revelation."*
(Baha'u'llah: *Gleanings,* Page: 52)

Clearly, from the New Testament, Christ's mission
was for the salvation of individual lives, such as happened
with me and, I'm sure, with you. Christians have often
called Jesus the Prince of Peace, even though Jesus said:
*"Do not think that I came to bring peace on earth. I did not
come to bring peace but a sword."* (Matt 10:34-35) To anyone who truly understands the spirit of Jesus Christ, we
know that, in spite of this particular statement, He ultimately wanted peace for the nations. But there is only
one statement in Christ's direct teaching about peace,
*"Blessed are the peacemakers, for they shall be called sons of
God."* (Matt 5:9-10) and it must be one of those areas
where Jesus said He had much more to tell us, but we
couldn't 'bear it' at that particular time in history. Apparently, we weren't ready. I guess the proof of this
unreadiness is that peace has not occurred in twenty centuries.

The fact is that early Christians were not too interested in the state of the world, because many or most of
them were expecting Christ to return very soon, even
tomorrow or the day after tomorrow. When your focus
is on staying ready for an imminent return, you don't
talk so much about today's news or the needs of the world.

Later, a century and more, Christians certainly did begin to think about the state of the world and to put their teachings to work to make the world better. Still, Christianity stayed focused upon the return, as you will agree. As we discussed earlier, Christian attention to the Return of Christ rose up to a fever pitch in the early and middle part of the Nineteenth Century—exactly the time of Baha'u'llah's appearance.

As time went by, Christian teaching penetrated into the entire world and wherever it has gone, it has been effective in creating a somewhat more civilized, kind and gentle world. (I'm not forgetting about the negative and destructive effects of European colonialism, as I say this; Mahatma Ghandi was once asked, during a visit to England, "Mr. Ghandi, what do you think of Western Civilization?" Ghandi replied: "I think it would be a very good thing.")

But even with a certain civilizing, organizing influence from the western world, no peace was evident, even between Christian nations. Both 'World Wars' in the Twentieth Century were fought mostly between Christian nations (save for the Japanese). Someone calculated that at the turn of the millennium, there were over 180 wars and ethnic conflicts currently being waged, both between and among nations. Roughly five million people were killed by these conflicts in the 1980's and the 1990's seem to be worse, with more than that killed within the first five years of the decade.

QUESTION: Well, I am still going to think of Jesus as the 'Prince of Peace.' And I hope you are not saying the Christian religion is to blame for world wars and the lack of peace. Christianity has always been on the side of peace, hasn't it?

RESPONSE: Let me put it this way. Christianity, *at its best,* has always been a force for peace. When Christian nations were not at their best, they supported wars, slavery, colonization of the developing world, predatory and unbridled domination of the economies of the world and other not so admirable actions. Many of these actions were done in the name of Christianity.

When that happened, I believe you and I would agree that it wasn't Christianity speaking, but people, institutions, or governments who had 'hijacked' Christianity, who pretended to represent it, but were really using it for their own twisted, selfish or evil purposes. Witness the actions of *all* the Christian churches (except for the Quakers) in the southern United States during the Civil War, who supported slavery strongly, based on the Bible! This wasn't Christianity at its best, was it? Nor even Christianity at all, as I see it.

Nor was Christianity at its best when western nations, Christian in belief, colonized the non-European world in a predatory way. Nevertheless, even with these negative examples, Christianity and Christian nations have been a 'force for peace', based upon the spirit of their Christian belief and the Savior who taught it.

Jesus has been portrayed as the 'Prince of Peace' in poetry and song for twenty centuries. When peace comes, as Baha'u'llah tells us it now *will* come (and soon, He says) it will be not only because of the coming of Baha'u'llah but also because of the mission and person of Christ, when He came the first time. If Christ is present in the person and mission of Baha'u'llah, as Baha'u'llah tells us, then Christ has been (all along) and is (now) central to the establishment of human unity and peace.

What is the role of the Baha'i Faith, and of Baha'u'llah, Christ Returned? Baha'u'llah tells us His role is to bring the power of God's guidance and the stimulation of an energized community of followers drawn from all religions and cultures to create a new day of unity and peace.

Here is a quote from Baha'u'llah in which He refers to God as *"the Great Being."* He says: *"That one indeed is a man who, today, dedicateth himself to the service of the entire human race. The Great Being saith: Blessed and happy is he that ariseth to promote the best interests of the peoples and kindreds of the earth."* Then, in one of the best known and most often quoted passages of Baha'u'llah, He says: *"It is not for him to pride himself who loveth his own country, but rather for him who loveth the whole world. The earth is but one country, and mankind its citizens."* (Baha'u'llah: *Gleanings*, Page: 250)

Thus, Baha'is believe, we will have peace because the true Divine Physician—Christ Returned in the Glory of the Father—will now minister to the needs of the world. We will attain the long-promised unity, fellowship and 'spirit of love' spoken of by Baha'u'llah and by Christ and by all the other Manifestations of God. Baha'u'llah says, speaking to all the people of the world: *"O wellbeloved ones! The tabernacle of unity hath been raised; regard ye not one another as strangers. Ye are the fruits of one tree, and the leaves of one branch."* (Baha'u'llah: *Gleanings*, Page: 218)

Where are we headed after peace and human unity arrives? We do not know. What we do know is that it will not be just a materialistic advancement. There is much work to do in the material area, such as schooling, housing, health care and more security for everyone on the planet. But what then? Again, we don't know. The only thing that seems certain is that it will have some kind of spiritual character, both for individuals and for humanity collectively.

Baha'u'llah says below that we human beings have

been created to move toward *"an ever-advancing civiliza-tion."* To advance, we must be advancing in the direction of some goal. There are many social, spiritual and global goals set forth in the Baha'i teachings, but in my view, we won't know the 'grand goal' of it all until later, perhaps much later. For now, it is enough for me to know that the goals of the coming centuries have been clearly and well set by yet another Manifestation of the *"Self of God"*—Baha'u'llah.

We have one big 'hint' about that future 'grand goal' when we realize that Baha'u'llah tells us that the central task on planet earth is to recognize and enact our unity as one people, one race. I have a hunch or a guess that when we achieve human unity, which Baha'u'llah calls *"The Most Great Peace,"* that we will then see more clearly along and up the road ahead.

Baha'u'llah said: *"All men have been created to carry forward an ever-advancing civilization."* (Baha'u'llah: *Gleanings*, Page: 215) He continues to say: *"Say: O friends! Drink your fill from this crystal stream that floweth through the heavenly grace of Him Who is the Lord of Names. Let others partake of its waters in My name, that the leaders of men in every land may fully recognize the purpose for which the Eternal Truth hath been revealed, and the reason for which they themselves have been created.*

"The Great Being saith: O ye children of men! The fundamental purpose animating the Faith of God and His Religion is to safeguard the interests and promote the unity of the human race, and to foster the spirit of love and fellowship amongst men." (Baha'u'llah: *Gleanings*, Page: 215)

We can be certain that this *"ever advancing civilization"* will have a spiritual character that will be revealed and discovered later on when we are able to hear a new interpretation of the meaning of our individual and collective lives. This is where 'progressive revelation' comes in. God will again manifest Himself in the future when we are able or capable of hearing things that we could not now hear or understand, as Jesus told us.

QUESTION: Well, there you go again! I understand faith and hope, but how can you utter these platitudes and these pious hopes and dreams when the world around us is literally falling apart! It makes no sense and, although I'm not trying to hurt your feelings, it makes you sound terribly naive.

RESPONSE: You know, I just had a funny thought, actually a memory. When I first heard the Baha'is talking, I had almost the same reaction, so I certainly can't take offense. I called the Baha'is worse names in my head than you have voiced. Naive, yes. How about foolish? Or unknowing? How about people who just aren't 'connected,' who just don't know what is happening in the world? Then, I remembered something. It was very embarrassing to me to have forgotten it. That is exactly how people who were around the early Christians viewed them, as fools, naive, even unconnected to reality. I had to back up entirely and look past what seemed to be naiveté to see if these Baha'is were 'onto something.' I finally decided they were.

As for someone being pessimistic, as your statement seemed to be, listen to Baha'u'llah, speaking in the 1870's: *"How long will humanity persist in its waywardness? How long will injustice continue? How long is chaos and confusion to reign amongst men? How long will discord agitate the face of society? . . . The winds of despair are, alas, blowing from every direction, and the strife that divideth and afflicteth the human race is daily increasing.*

"The signs of impending convulsions and chaos can now be discerned, inasmuch as the prevailing order appeareth to

be lamentably defective. I beseech God, exalted be His glory, that He may graciously awaken the peoples of the earth, may grant that the end of their conduct may be profitable unto them, and aid them to accomplish that which beseemeth their station." (Baha'u'llah: *Gleanings*, Pages: 216-217)

That doesn't sound too naive, does it? Nor does it sound hopeless, since Baha'u'llah implies that through the assistance of the Almighty God, mankind will be awakened and aided in the tasks of healing and unification that lie ahead. He said: *"Every word that proceedeth out of the mouth of God is endowed with such potency as can instill new life into every human frame . . . "* (Baha'u'llah: *Gleanings*, Page: 141)

Baha'u'llah continues with an appeal to all humanity: *"O contending peoples and kindreds of the earth! Set your faces towards unity, and let the radiance of its light shine upon you. Gather ye together, and for the sake of God resolve to root out whatever is the source of contention amongst you."* (Baha'u'llah: *Gleanings*, Pages: 216-217) But even though this appeal was made, there was also a warning, a prediction: *"The prevailing order appeareth to be lamentably defective"* and that *"Soon will the present-day order be rolled up, and a new one spread out in its stead."* (Baha'u'llah: *Gleanings*, Page: 7)

At another time, He referred to the 'old order' of things in this way: *"The day is approaching when We will have rolled up the world and all that is therein, and spread out a new order in its stead."* (Baha'u'llah: *Gleanings*, Page: 313)

There will be more on this later, but now is probably a good time to take note of what Baha'u'llah said about His Coming and His Revelation. He tells us in the following passage that God has released a power in His Coming, a 'revolutionary' power that will be able to transform the earth and its peoples: *"Through the movement of*

Our Pen of glory We have, at the bidding of the omnipotent Ordainer, breathed a new life into every human frame, and instilled into every word a fresh potency. All created things proclaim the evidences of this world-wide regeneration." (Baha'u'llah: *Gleanings*, Pages: 92-93)

Baha'u'llah describes the Day in which we live: "*Say: O men! This is a matchless Day. Matchless must, likewise, be the tongue that celebrateth the praise of the Desire of all nations, and matchless the deed that aspireth to be acceptable in His sight. The whole human race hath longed for this Day, that perchance it may fulfil that which well beseemeth its station, and is worthy of its destiny. Blessed is the man whom the affairs of the world have failed to deter from recognizing Him Who is the Lord of all things.*" (Baha'u'llah: *Gleanings*, Page: 39)

But as to being naive, Baha'u'llah says: "*Witness how the world is being afflicted with a fresh calamity every day. Its tribulation is continually deepening . . . neither hath the world been tranquillized, nor have the hearts of its peoples been at rest. At one time it hath been agitated by contentions and disputes, at another it hath been convulsed by wars, and fallen a victim to inveterate diseases.*

"*Its sickness is approaching the stage of utter hopelessness, inasmuch as the true Physician is debarred from administering the remedy, whilst unskilled practitioners are regarded with favor, and are accorded full freedom to act. . . . The dust of sedition hath clouded the hearts of men, and blinded their eyes. Erelong, they will perceive the consequences of what their hands have wrought in the Day of God. Thus warneth you He Who is the All-Informed, as bidden by One Who is the Most Powerful, the Almighty.*" (Baha'u'llah: *Gleanings*, Pages: 39-40)

These and other passages will, I hope, show you why Baha'is are richly confident about humankind's near future, as well as its far distant future, stretching out through many eons of time.

QUESTION: You haven't sufficiently answered for me what Christians regard as a central truth of their religion, that Christ is the 'only begotten Son' of God. 'Only begotten' seems clearly, to me, to rule out others that you call other Manifestations of God. And Jesus never referred to any such thing as other Manifestations.

RESPONSE: Well, first we could remember that Jesus does speak of 'other sheep' that He has, which certainly could mean the followers of other Manifestations. *"And other sheep I have which are not of this fold; them also I must bring, and they will hear My voice; and there will be one flock and one shepherd."* (John 10:16) Also, I should mention the fact that Jesus did refer to Moses and to other prophetic figures in the Old Testament. Christians, I have noticed, sometimes tend to forget that the Old Testament was the scripture of another religion for a thousand years before Christ appeared.

Let's concentrate, instead, on what Baha'is believe, namely, that Jesus had a central, all-important and unique place in history. Remember that quote of Baha'u'llah about Jesus Christ that opened this chapter. Go back and read it again to be reminded of the uniqueness of Jesus in Baha'u'llah's thinking. Also, keep always in mind that Baha'u'llah, when not referring to Jesus as *'The Spirit,'* referred to Him as *'The Son.'* And it is Baha'u'llah's reference to Himself as the Return of Christ *'in My Person'* that links Jesus to Baha'u'llah in such a way that if the station of one is high, the station of the other must also be high.

No teaching of the Baha'i Faith will make Christ lesser or deny that He is the only-begotten Son of God. In one absolutely fascinating passage Baha'u'llah writes of a 'conversation' between Christ and Himself in which Christ speaks to Baha'u'llah saying: " . . . *in these days whereon the Christ exclaimeth: 'All dominion is Thine, O Thou the Begetter of the Spirit (Jesus)'* (Baha'u'llah: *Prayers and Meditations*, Page: 68) Combining this unusual description, in which Christ refers to Baha'u'llah as His begetter (i.e., *'The Father,'*) with Baha'u'llah's frequent designation of Jesus as *'The Son'* will serve, I hope, to clarify this particular point.

I hope you are ready for something very challenging. I believe you are. Here is a passage from Baha'u'llah that will perhaps be the most striking of all: *"In Thy holy Books, in Thy Scriptures and Thy Scrolls Thou hast promised all the peoples of the world that Thou Thyself shalt appear and shalt remove the veils of glory from Thy face"* (Baha'u'llah: *Tablets of Baha'u'llah*, Page: 114)

"I bear witness that Thou hast in truth fulfilled Thy pledge and hast made manifest the One Whose advent was foretold by Thy Prophets, Thy chosen ones and by them that serve Thee. He hath come from the heaven of glory and power, bearing the banners of Thy signs and the standards of Thy testimonies.

"Through the potency of Thine indomitable power and strength, He stood up before the faces of all men and summoned all mankind to the summit of transcendent glory and unto the all-highest Horizon, in such wise that neither the oppression of the ecclesiastics nor the onslaught of the rulers was able to deter Him. He arose with inflexible resolve and, unloosing His tongue, proclaimed in ringing tones: 'He Who is the All-Bountiful is come, riding aloft on the clouds. Advance, O people of the earth, with shining faces and radiant hearts!'" (Baha'u'llah: *Tablets of Baha'u'llah,* Page 115)

QUESTION: 'Riding aloft in the clouds'?! Is

Baha'u'llah emotionally unbalanced? Mentally ill? Only individuals with grandiose, mentally ill tendencies say things like that!

RESPONSE: What about this statement from Jesus as He was standing before the High Priest, who asked Him: "Are You the Christ, the Son of the Blessed?" And Jesus said, *"I am. And you will see the Son of Man sitting at the right hand of the Power, and coming with the clouds of heaven."* (Mark 14:61-62) Jesus told them: *"Hereafter the Son of Man will sit on the right hand of the power of God."* (Luke 22:69-70) Jesus also said: *"Most assuredly, I say to you, before Abraham was, I AM."* (John 8:58)

Finally, Jesus said: *"All authority has been given to Me in heaven and on earth."* (Matt 28:18) Was Jesus mentally ill? Of course not! Nevertheless, He was uttering statements of the kind that if we did not already know Who He was, we would undoubtedly say He was mad, would we not?

QUESTION: I guess I have to 'back up' on that comment I made. It seems sensible when Jesus says something like that, because I know what He meant. He wasn't speaking literally, but figuratively, and I know you are going to say Baha'u'llah was speaking figuratively as well.

RESPONSE: This reminds me of a joke my minister father told. He had a great sense of humor. He said his definition of a 'sect' was a religion 'other than our own and smaller than our own.' I gathered from what he said that we understand our own religion the best and can accept things that were said by the Manifestation of our own religion, no matter how 'outlandish' or 'peculiar' they might sound to someone outside the 'magic circle' of our own understanding.

We know what Jesus meant and means by *"sitting at the right hand of power"* because we have the benefit of hindsight. But if a person today said: *"The Father and I are One"* or indicated that He was sitting at the *'right hand of God'* in Heaven, we might well hustle that person off to a mental hospital for his own good.

Baha'u'llah, like Jesus, is helping us to understand that whenever Manifestations of God appear, they truly have all power, though to the outward eye, they can be beaten, crowned with a crown of thorns, reviled, crucified or in the case of Baha'u'llah, beaten, tortured, chained, imprisoned, exiled and ignored by the world at large (as was Christ, let us not forget). It is a serious thought as to whether we would be able to see Christ, bound as a criminal in Herod's Palace and know, nevertheless, that He was telling the truth when He said that He would soon be seen to be *"sitting at the right hand of God."* I don't believe Herod or Annas saw that, do you? Are we entirely sure we would have seen it? It certainly wasn't obvious to the casual onlooker, was it?

To return to your recent question, Baha'is do believe that Jesus is truly the 'only begotten' Son of God. There is no other person Who fills this role or assumes the title of the Son of God, just as no other Manifestation other than Baha'u'llah has claimed to be the long awaited *"Father"* of all mankind. Baha'u'llah announced His appearance as: *"The Father hath come,"* the One Who, as promised and prophesied, has finally come Himself removing all the *"veils of glory,"* showing us, for the first time *"the face of God."* Yes, Baha'u'llah did say all these things. Check for yourself, investigate. Maybe a Jew of Jesus' time would have sent Him to a mental hospital. Maybe you will decide to send Baha'u'llah to a mental hospital, maybe not.

Say, listen, let's do a little speculation, if you are 'up

to it.' Do you wonder what you would have done if you were the court psychiatrist at Herod's Palace? If you had interviewed Christ, what would you have thought? Savior or paranoid schizophrenic? Son of God or grandiose thinker? Sitting at the right hand of God or delusional and hallucinating? And, as Herod's psychiatrist, what *would* you have recommended to him, as to what to do with this Jesus?

QUESTION: I guess I honestly have to say I am not sure, but I hope that I would have recognized Christ. If you are saying that recognition of Him would be difficult, I agree. Also, I agree that it would have been a severe test, because at that time, in Herod's Palace, I would have been interviewing a prisoner and supposed criminal. And I think I see the point that deciding Who Baha'u'llah is will be an equally severe test, one that I would like to pass on the side of truth, whatever that may be.

But I have another question. Christians believe that without Christ, they would be doomed to lives of sin and destruction, that salvation through Christ lifts them up to a new plane of living and transforms their lives, giving them meaning, purpose and direction.

RESPONSE: I am intimately aware of that belief and the effect that dedicating a life to Christ and accepting His salvation can have. It happened to me. Baha'is have no desire to have Christians think less of Christ; rather, we want them to see that Christ has played a larger part in history than any of us had imagined. I am proposing not a lesser Christ, but a larger, expanded Christ, a Christ Who, as the Word of God that existed before the world began, was and is the same yesterday, today and forever.

Part of that yesterday, Baha'u'llah teaches, was in

Buddha, Moses, Muhammad and other Manifestations, and part of the today is Baha'u'llah's coming as *"The Father"* of all mankind. The forever part is Baha'u'llah's teaching that God will continue to manifest Himself and His 'Word' *"until the end that hath no end."*

As I have previously discussed, Baha'i teachings say that when any Manifestation appears in history, salvation can only happen through Him and Him alone. He must be followed and obeyed. To obtain salvation, life must be lived in terms of His new teachings. This salvation and the following of the teachings of the new Manifestation does indeed transform individuals and creates a new 'community' in which those individuals can begin to transform those around them and make the kind of impact on history that we see after the coming of Moses, Jesus, Buddha, Muhammad or, today, Baha'u'llah.

No one can look at history and say that the centuries following the appearance of any of these (and other) Manifestations were not periods of immense and important growth for humankind. And, though past renewals have seen inevitable decline, Baha'u'llah tells us that the new day that will dawn for mankind is *"the king of days,"* *"the 'Day of God Himself,"* and especially this: *"the Day which shall never be followed by night,"* *"the Springtime which autumn will never overtake."* (Quoted in Shoghi Effendi: *God Passes By*, Page: 99) This does not mean that other Manifestations of God will not come in the future. Baha'u'llah makes it clear that they will arise, as sent by God, appearing when we need them most.

You have reminded me of a scriptural passage that I remember quite well. Jesus said: *"No man cometh unto the Father but by Me."* Closely related to this comment is one from Baha'u'llah: *"No man can obtain everlasting life, unless he embraceth the truth of this inestimable, this wondrous, and sublime Revelation."* (Baha'u'llah: *Gleanings*, Page: 183)

Jesus said: *"For what profit is it to a man if he gains the whole world, and loses his own soul?"* (Matt 16:26) (that is, by not recognizing and following Him) and Baha'u'llah said, in a strikingly similar passage: *"What would it profit man, if he were to fail to recognize the Revelation of God?"* (that is, following Baha'u'llah and His Revelation). Baha'u'llah answers His own question *"Nothing whatsoever".* Baha'u'llah: *Gleanings*, Page: 146)

QUESTION: You have brought up several quotations from Baha'u'llah that are similar to those of Christ. Was Baha'u'llah copying Christ's statements? Why were they so similar?

RESPONSE: No, Baha'u'llah was not copying Christ at all. It's just that the situation is so similar when a Manifestation appears that they are bound to say some things that sound similar. Baha'u'llah quotes Jesus frequently or refers to Him hundreds of times in His Revelation and, as I have said, the two religions have a special affinity, because of the symmetry of *"The Son"* and *"The Father"* and because Baha'u'llah was so specific and forceful in His comments that Jesus had appeared again, as Baha'u'llah put it, *"in my person."* It is interesting to note that Baha'u'llah never formally studied Christianity and, in fact, never entered or studied in any school, as a youth or as an adult. The Manifestations, He tells us, have innate knowledge that is not acquired by 'learning.'

When you add in the teaching of Baha'u'llah that the Manifestations are *"all but one person, one soul, one spirit, one being, one revelation."* (Baha'u'llah: *Gleanings*, Page: 54) it is not surprising for them to say some things that sound similar. For the most part, the Revelation of

Baha'u'llah is truly a New Testament of God's Will, as I think you may find when you begin to investigate.

Finally, don't forget that Jesus quoted from the scriptures of another religion numerous times, including a direct quotation when He issued His 'Great Commandment' which was actually two quotations from the Jewish Scripture: *"The first of all the commandments is: 'Hear, O Israel, the LORD our God, the LORD is one.' 'And you shall love the LORD your God with all your heart, with all your soul, with all your mind, and with all your strength.' This is the first commandment. And the second, like it, is this: 'You shall love your neighbor as yourself.' There is no other commandment greater than these."* (Mark 12:29-32) (The 'Old Testament' Jewish Scripture that Jesus is quoting—literally—is from Deut. 6:4 and Lev. 19:18)

QUESTION: Well, did any of the other Manifestations say things similar to the quotations you gave above from Jesus and Baha'u'llah?

RESPONSE: Yes, as a matter of fact, Muhammad, Buddha, Krishna, Zoroaster, and the Bab, Baha'u'llah's predecessor, all the Manifestations, uttered similar statements. Let me quote again Baha'u'llah's famous statement on the unity of the Manifestations: *"If thou wilt observe with discriminating eyes, thou wilt behold Them all abiding in the same tabernacle, soaring in the same heaven, seated upon the same throne, uttering the same speech, and proclaiming the same Faith."* He also says that the Manifestations of God may have different names and, so to speak, wear different clothes, that is, they come from different cultures, speak different languages, but nevertheless *"are the Temples of the Cause of God, Who have appeared clothed in divers attire."* (Baha'u'llah: *Gleanings*, Page: 52)

QUESTION: But that's just it! They *don't* proclaim the same Faith. The Buddhist Faith and Islam and Christianity are not the same! These Faiths are really quite different. Don't you see that?

RESPONSE: On the surface, and in terms of their laws and in their 'outer' aspects, they certainly are different, but often not as much as you would think. When you study them, as I have and others have, you find a great deal of similarity not too far below the surface, if not even on the surface itself. However, when you go a little deeper, begin to plumb the depths, when you take a careful, studied look farther down beneath that surface, you find that the core of all religions is quite similar and in many respects, the same, in the deepest spiritual sense. Many scholars have testified that they feel or sense what I discovered in studying the world's religions, namely, that the Holy Spirit of God has been at work in all of them.

So, my understanding is that the religions may be different, quite a bit similar, or nearly the same, and it all depends on whether you are concentrating on the surface or whether you are willing to look at deeper aspects. What Baha'u'llah says is that the religions are different on the surface and even several layers below, precisely because the Manifestation of God gives teachings and laws that are specific to the needs of that day and those people. So, we should expect the religions to be different in this way, but this is no contradiction to the reality of their oneness at a deeper level.

The greatest way in which the Religions are one is that they proceed from the Will of One God, not many Gods. This is a major teaching of Baha'u'llah.

QUESTION: Are you saying that the Christian God

has been *that* active, has been the 'Prime Mover' in all of the world's Religions and Revelations?

RESPONSE: Yes, that is exactly what I am saying.

QUESTION: Well then, I'm beginning to see the picture you are putting forth. Not that I can yet agree, but this concept of a 'larger Christ' and a 'greater God' that insulted me so much the first time I heard it, is now intriguing. I want to think long and hard about it. It may be the key that I need to be able to make a decision about Baha'u'llah.

RESPONSE: You mentioned an active God? I like that phrase. You are the second person to make that observation to me. When I talked to a class in a Christian seminary, one of the graduate students made that observation. The God of the Baha'is is (this student said) is 'a pretty busy and active God.' I'm not even sure that the student meant it as a compliment, but I took it that way. God, says Baha'u'llah, has been with us all along, closer than we realized, more active than we knew, more influential in our guidance, more inspiring for our lives and for human history than we ever thought or dreamed.

Now, this 'more active' God has decided to show Himself in Baha'u'llah in a way that commands us to decide the truth of His Revelation. We can dream a new dream of all humanity, which will be united in history as never before understood and moving under God's instruction toward a destiny that can only be revealed when that unity becomes our common victory.

Christians expect Christ to come again 'on the clouds,' something that I purposely decided not to bring up when you were so challenged by Baha'u'llah's statement about exactly that, where He said that He

(Baha'u'llah) was *"riding aloft on the clouds."* The full quote is: *"He Who is the All-Bountiful is come, riding aloft on the clouds. Advance, O people of the earth, with shining faces and radiant hearts! Great indeed is the blessedness of him who attaineth Thy presence . . . "* (Baha'u'llah: *Tablets of Baha'u'llah*, Pages: 115-116)

QUESTION: All right, I will admit that Baha'u'llah does challenge me—very greatly! He is, as you keep on saying, either a madman, a charlatan or trickster, or, the only other choice is:

He is Who He says He is.

But I want to be very sure of this one thing: Are you Baha'is saying that you have not abandoned Christ, you still believe in Him, and if you are from a Christian background, He is still your personal Savior and you have become a Baha'i only because you believe Baha'u'llah is the Return of Christ and the Appearance of *"The Father,"* Who will lead all humankind into their destined unity and peace?

I want to be sure that I understand 'the Baha'i position' correctly, especially what you believe about Jesus. As I now understand it, you feel you have not 'demoted' Christ or painted Him as a 'lesser' figure; rather, you say you believe that your concept of Christ is an enlarged, expanded Christ. And God is seen as greater than we have ever imagined, a God Who has been and is 'very active' across all of human history? I'm certainly not a believer in Baha'u'llah yet. I don't know if I ever can be, but I want to be certain that I have it right, in terms of what you believe.

RESPONSE: You are close, very close, to the Baha'i position. I know you have other questions and as I respond to them, you will see, I hope, other aspects of

Baha'i belief, all of which serve to strengthen belief in a 'larger Christ.' It's worth noting that wherever Baha'is go, wherever they teach the Faith of Baha'u'llah, they teach Jesus as the 'Son of God' and it would be just impossible to find a Baha'i who did not recognize Jesus as a Manifestation of God, including Baha'is of Jewish, Islamic and Hindu backgrounds, for example.

There is a great story of the famed missionary, E. Stanley Jones (one of my favorites in the modern Christian missionary history) who was teaching in India, when his guide said of a remote village: "Everyone in the village up ahead already believes in Christ." Jones thought that, as far as was known, there were no Christians at all in this part of India. He said he did not believe it. When he arrived, it was a village of Baha'is that had been taught decades before by a teacher sent out by Baha'u'llah to India. Jones marveled at this finding, and decided to move on to another village in pursuit of those who had not yet heard of Christ. Said Jones of the Baha'i village: "They do know of Jesus here." Perhaps Jones should have stayed awhile, for those simple villagers could have taught him about Jesus having returned in Baha'u'llah!

QUESTION: I have an important question to ask. I've been 'saving' it. I need to have you understand really well what this question is. It is this: Christians hold Christ in their hearts as 'Lord and Savior,' as you say you did and still do, but to Christians 'Savior' means that Christ has redeemed us from sin, has brought us from a 'lost' sinful condition into bright salvation, a salvation that we believe can only come from Christ. As I told you before, Christ is for us 'Alpha and Omega,' 'first and last,' 'all in all.' We have no need for other 'Saviors' or, as you call them, 'Manifestations'. What about that?

RESPONSE: As I have consistently said in this conversation, and I'm happy to see that you recognize it, Jesus is, in fact, my Lord and Savior, as He is and has to be for every Baha'i of Christian background who was inspired by a 'salvation' experience. If their Christian past was authentic and they experienced salvation and understood that Jesus is Lord and Savior of their lives, they cannot and do not (nor would they be able to) 'unload' their belief in and commitment to Jesus Christ.

A Baha'i of Christian background, such as myself, could agree with nearly everything you just said, except the 'exclusivity' of your statement. As we have discussed, the Baha'i understanding of progressive revelation leads Baha'is to a plane of 'new thinking' that sees a greater, more active God and a larger Christ. Though we have discussed how I am using this phrase, I want to say again that it is not meant in an insulting way. It is meant in the same way that—several decades ago—a Christian theologian, J. B. Phillips, meant it when he said to Christians 'your Christ is too small.' He explained that, unless we are careful to see Christ in all His 'fullness,' our view of Christ could be too narrow to hold all that Christ can mean to the world.

This more active God has been ever-present in history. Baha'is believe that the Christ spirit, as the pre-existent Word of God, has been present in the appearance of all the Manifestations. Christ and the Christ Spirit, in this new thinking, is infused into all of history, and we see that the reality of Christ and of Muhammad and of Buddha and others is the reality of the Word of God and the Will of God.

This 'new thinking' is, understandably, a big stretch to take in our view of history, of God and of Christ, but it leads to a great coming together of millions of former

Hindus, Christians, Zoroastrians, Jews, Muslims, and others into a new unity of belief and action, as Baha'is, believers in Baha'u'llah.

This new 'Gospel' of thinking shows us that all the Manifestations of history were infused with the pre-existent Word of God, or what Christians can best understand as the Christ Spirit. And, this 'New Testament' of belief shows us further that the sacrifices, sufferings and deaths of the Manifestations of God all represented salvation and redemption from sin for the people of the world at the time of their appearance.

Understandably, because it is what they have been taught throughout their lives, Christians see Christ as the one and only Word of God or Manifestation of God. But what if Christ as the Christ Spirit has been at work both before Jesus and after His first coming? What if the pre-existent Word of God has, in effect, been the prime mover of all history?

Another way of saying this is for both of us to ask the question, in a sincere and open way: "Has God acted only once in human history (or twice, if you count Moses and the Ten Commandments) or are we beginning to learn that God has acted countless times, sending Manifestations of Himself to guide, protect, redeem, and educate mankind?" And the final question could be: "Has God finally Manifested Himself as *'the Father,'* showing His Face to the children of men, fulfilling and enacting the prophecies and promises of history, drawing all humanity into a long-awaited peace and unity?"

QUESTION: A moment ago I asked you about sin and redemption and I don't think you addressed this question. Please tell me what Baha'u'llah said about this, if anything.

RESPONSE: He said that His suffering and imprisonment had a purpose for the world and its people, just
as Christ's suffering and crucifixion had a purpose.
Baha'u'llah, speaking of the terrible prison into which
He had been thrown by religious leaders and political
rulers, put it this way: *"The Ancient Beauty* [a title of
Baha'u'llah] *hath consented to be bound with chains that
mankind may be released from its bondage, and hath accepted
to be made a prisoner within this most mighty Stronghold that
the whole world may attain unto true liberty."*

He continues: *"He hath drained to its dregs the cup of
sorrow, that all the peoples of the earth may attain unto abiding joy, and be filled with gladness. This is of the mercy of
your Lord, the Compassionate, the Most Merciful. We have
accepted to be abased, O believers in the Unity of God, that
ye may be exalted, and have suffered manifold afflictions,
that ye might prosper and flourish."* Baha'u'llah closes this
passage by describing Himself as *"He Who hath come to
build anew the whole world"*. (Baha'u'llah: *Gleanings*,
Pages: 99-100)

In another passage, Baha'u'llah, prays to God about
His banishment to the prison city of Akka (in Israel):
*"Thou seest and knowest full well, O my God, how He hath
been made to dwell within the most desolate of cities, so that
He may build up the hearts of Thy servants, and hath been
willing to suffer the most grievous abasement, that Thy creatures may be exalted."* (Baha'u'llah: *Prayers and Meditations*, Page: 37)

As for salvation, Baha'u'llah explains why God sent
Him into the world: *"We, verily, have come for your sakes,
and have borne the misfortunes of the world for your salvation. Flee ye the One Who hath sacrificed His life that ye may
be quickened? Fear God, O followers of the Spirit (Jesus),
and walk not in the footsteps of every divine that hath gone
far astray . . .*

"Open the doors of your hearts. He Who is the Spirit (Jesus) verily, standeth before them. Wherefore keep ye afar from Him Who hath purposed to draw you nigh unto a Resplendent Spot? Say: We, in truth, have opened unto you the gates of the Kingdom. Will ye bar the doors of your houses in My face? This indeed is naught but a grievous error." (Baha'u'llah: *Proclamation of Baha'u'llah*, Page: 92)

Using the language of the story of Noah and the Ark, Baha'u'llah calls upon the people of the world to enter the *"Ark which God hath ordained"* (Baha'u'llah: *Epistle to the Son of the Wolf*, Page: 139), and says of those Who decide to follow Him, that is, to 'enter this Ark': *"He that entereth therein is saved, and he that turneth aside perisheth."* (Baha'u'llah: *Epistle to the Son of the Wolf*, Page: 139)

Baha'u'llah continues in this passage to describe what will happen when a person enters this 'Ark of Salvation' of belief in Him: *"Thereupon, will the doors of the Kingdom be flung wide before thy face, and thou wilt behold what eyes have never beheld, and hear what ears have never heard."* (Baha'u'llah: *Epistle to the Son of the Wolf*, Page: 140)

He concludes: *"This is the day whereon all created things cry out, and announce unto men this Revelation, through which hath appeared what was concealed and preserved in the knowledge of God, the Mighty, the All-Praised."* (Baha'u'llah: *Epistle to the Son of the Wolf*, Page: 140)

In Chapter Sixteen, there are sections that deal with 'sin' and 'salvation.' You may be able to find other material there that speaks to the question of sin. For the moment, you may remember that Jesus angered the Pharisees by telling a man *"Son, your sins are forgiven you."* (Mark 2:5) Jesus said He did this *"That you might know that the Son of Man has power on earth to forgive sins."* (Mark: 2:10)

Likewise, Baha'u'llah forgave sin, offering forgiveness to a man, saying: *"We have attired his temple with the robe of forgiveness and adorned his head with the crown of pardon . . . Say: Be not despondent. After the revelation of this blessed verse it is as though thou hast been born anew from thy mother's womb. Say: Thou art free from sin and error. Truly God hath purged thee with the living waters of His utterance in His Most Great Prison.* " (Baha'u'llah: *Tablets of Baha'u'llah*: Page 77) At the time He freed this man from sin, Baha'u'llah was writing from a terrible prison in Akka, Palestine (now Israel) into which He had been thrown by the forces opposing Him, the same forces who opposed Jesus Christ—clergy and kings.

QUESTION: You say the next chapter deals with how a Christian might look at the place of Baha'u'llah in history. Let's go on to that. I'm beginning to see that the one and only question that matters is to decide Who Baha'u'llah is. And, for the Christian, to decide if Baha'u'llah does represent what Christians have longed for these twenty centuries, namely, the Return of Christ.

RESPONSE: I agree with you on that one. It's absolutely the central question and if you do answer it, many other areas are immediately illumined. When a Jew in the time of Jesus could take that step to see Jesus as the 'Son of the Living God,' as did the Jew named Simon Peter, the rest of his questions faded quickly away just as Peter's questions faded away and were answered. Today, it is probably the same: If someone can take the step of seeing Baha'u'llah as the Father of all mankind and the Return of Christ, there will still be many discoveries to make, but the main and important question will have been answered.

Here is a short prayer from Baha'u'llah:

"Create in me a pure heart, O my God, and renew a tranquil conscience within me, O my Hope! Through the spirit

of power confirm Thou me in Thy Cause, O my Best-Beloved, and by the light of Thy glory reveal unto me Thy path, O Thou the Goal of my desire! Through the power of Thy transcendent might lift me up unto the heaven of Thy holiness, O Source of my being, and by the breezes of Thine eternity gladden me, O Thou Who art my God! Let Thine everlasting melodies breathe tranquillity on me, O my Companion, and let the riches of Thine ancient countenance deliver me from all except Thee, O my Master, and let the tidings of the revelation of Thine incorruptible Essence bring me joy, O Thou Who art the most manifest of the manifest and the most hidden of the hidden!" (Baha'u'llah: *Prayers and Meditations*, Pages: 248-249)

And another prayer from His Son, 'Abdu'l-Baha:

"O Thou compassionate Lord, Thou Who art generous and able! We are servants of Thine sheltered beneath Thy providence. Cast Thy glance of favor upon us. Give light to our eyes, hearing to our ears, and understanding and love to our hearts. Render our souls joyous and happy through Thy glad tidings. O Lord! Point out to us the pathway of Thy kingdom and resuscitate all of us through the breaths of the Holy Spirit. Bestow upon us life everlasting and confer upon us never-ending honor. Unify mankind and illumine the world of humanity. May we all follow Thy pathway, long for Thy good pleasure and seek the mysteries of Thy kingdom. O God! Unite us and connect our hearts with Thine indissoluble bond. Verily, Thou art the Giver, Thou art the Kind One and Thou art the Almighty." ('Abdu'l-Baha: *Promulgation of Universal Peace*, Page: 397)

CHAPTER SEVEN

IN THE GARDEN,
A NEW FLOWER "HATH BEGUN TO
BLOOM": HOW A CHRISTIAN MIGHT
LOOK AT BAHA'U'LLAH AND HIS PLACE
IN HISTORY.

QUESTION: Really, I have to tell you that I don't know what to think about Baha'u'llah. He doesn't seem to be insignificant in terms of history, but over time there have been many wonderful thinkers, saints, poets, mystics, even prophets. Perhaps He is one of those?

RESPONSE: The critical point is this: Not one of those saints, mystics, poets, philosophers or 'great thinkers' or even prophets the likes of Jeremiah has ever claimed to be 'the Father of all mankind.' Wait, I do remember that you reminded me earlier that there have been unbalanced or unprincipled persons in the last two thousand years who claimed, as did Baha'u'llah, to be Christ's Return. But as time goes by, those claims and charlatans have faded away and been quickly forgotten. They left nothing behind except a footnote in history. And the key issue here is that even those as great as Jeremiah or Martin Luther King, Jr. or Mother Teresa simply did not make the claims that both Christ and Baha'u'llah did.

At the close of the Twentieth Century, Baha'u'llah's Revelation has been around for more than one hundred fifty years. His teachings, His message are empowering the new community He is assembling from all over the world, a community that is functioning, not fading. It is actually growing as a unifying force, a vibrant gathering together of the people of earth.

QUESTION: You are right about that, I guess, but I'm still uneasy over Baha'u'llah's claims. Sometimes He doesn't seem 'sane' to me. Could He have been mentally unbalanced? I even heard from another Baha'i that Baha'u'llah claimed that when the people of the world turned to Him that they would see the *"face of God"* and *"hear His Voice."* (that is, the 'Voice of God'). You will have to forgive me, but that just sounds plain crazy!

RESPONSE: Well, I can only agree with you that, taken literally, it sounds crazy. Let me give you one of the quotes that speaks of this: *"Verily I say, this is the Day in which mankind can behold the Face, and hear the Voice, of the Promised One. The Call of God hath been raised, and the light of His countenance hath been lifted up upon men."* (Baha'u'llah: Gleanings, Pages: 10-11)

Baha'u'llah taught that when a people see a new Manifestation of God appearing in human history, they are

looking at the *"face of God."* For example, He said
that the Jews, because of their lack of spiritual response
to the Christ: *"remained deprived of recognizing the beauty
of Jesus and of beholding the face of God."* (Baha'u'llah:
The Kitab-i-Iqan, Page: 19) Also, speaking of all the
Manifestations: *"From their knowledge, the knowledge of
God is revealed, and from the light of their countenance,
the splendour of the Face of God is made manifest."*
(Baha'u'llah: *The Kitab-i-Iqan*, Page: 142)

To sharpen even further the challenging nature
of these words and to see how they apply to God's
latest Manifestation, Baha'u'llah said that to behold
Him was to behold *"the face of God Himself."*
(Baha'u'llah: *The Kitab-i-Iqan*, Page: 4)

Still sounds crazy, does it? Well, consider this following experiment that may help us decide this question of whether or not Baha'u'llah was 'crazy.' I call
this the 'Mall Experiment'. Let's say you leave your
house and drive to a nearby shopping Mall. You notice there is a large crowd in the parking area. A man
is preaching. You are curious, so you stand at the edge
of the crowd and hear the man say: "I have come
down from heaven, not to do my own will, but the will
of Him that sent me."

Next, he says: "Before Abraham was, I am" and
finally, this Mall Preacher says: "He that has seen me
has seen the Father.' By now, you are ready to walk
away and you have certainly concluded that this
preacher is crazy, haven't you? As you walk away in
disgust, you hear him shout: "I am the way, the truth
and the life" and "no man comes to the Father but by
me!"

QUESTION: Say, listen, you are just being silly.

You are having this 'Mall Preacher' say the same things that Jesus said!

RESPONSE: Yes, but there's more to the experiment. Just bear with me. Now, take yourself back two thousand years. You are now a Jew who knows very little or nothing about Jesus. You are riding a donkey to go to the market. As you pass through the Judean hills, you come across an itinerant preacher or teacher. It's Jesus! But remember, you haven't heard of Him; you know little or nothing at all about Him, or, you may have heard some negative things. (Hangs with a 'bad crowd,' a bunch of drunks, and a prostitute; gets into fights at the Temple, breaks religious laws and says blasphemous things. All of these were reported in the New Testament, weren't they?)

You may have heard some good things, that He is known as a healer, that He has beautiful and compelling new teachings, that He seems to be kind and caring. You aren't sure what to think. But there is a crowd. You are curious. You stop at the edge of the crowd and you hear Him say those same things:

1. Before Abraham was, I am.

2. He that hath seen Me, hath seen the Father.

3. I have come down from heaven, to do the will of Him that sent me.

4. I am the Way, the Truth and the Life; no man cometh unto the Father but by Me.

QUESTION: I think I see the point. You are saying it really is hard to tell 'crazy people' from the *'Son* *of God'* - Jesus. Or, it would be hard to tell a deranged person from, as you call Him, the *'Father'* of all Mankind'—Baha'u'llah.

RESPONSE: Please remember that it isn't me who calls Baha'u'llah *"the Father."* It is Baha'u'llah Himself. Here are several quotes from Baha'u'llah supporting this: *"The Word which the Son* [that is, Jesus] *concealed is made manifest. It hath been sent down in the form of the human temple in this day. Blessed be the Lord Who is the Father! He, verily, is come unto the nations in His most great majesty. Turn your faces towards Him, O concourse of the righteous . . . This is the day whereon the Rock (Peter) crieth out and shouteth, and celebrateth the praise of its Lord, the All-Possessing, the Most High, saying: 'Lo! The Father is come, and that which ye were promised in the Kingdom is fulfilled!'"* (Baha'u'llah: *Proclamation of Baha'u'llah*, Pages: 84-85)

And, in writing to Christian clergymen, Baha'u'llah said: *"O concourse of bishops! Trembling hath seized all the kindreds of the earth, and He Who is the Everlasting Father calleth aloud between earth and heaven. Blessed the ear that hath heard, and the eye that hath seen, and the heart that hath turned unto Him Who is the Point of Adoration of all who are in the heavens and all who are on earth . . . ."* (Baha'u'llah: *Proclamation of Baha'u'llah*, Page: 93)

In a striking passage of Baha'i Scripture, Baha'u'llah speaks and Jesus answers: *"He Who is the Father is come, and the Son (Jesus Christ), in the holy vale, crieth out: 'Here am I, here am I, O Lord, my God!'. . . The All-Bounteous is come mounted upon the clouds! Blessed is he that draweth nigh unto Him, and woe betide them that are far away."* (Baha'u'llah: *Epistle to the Son of the Wolf*, Page: 57)

And finally, as I have quoted to you before: *"Tell Me then: Do the sons* (that is, the Christians) *recognize the Father, and acknowledge Him, or do they deny Him, even as the people aforetime denied Him (Jesus)?"* (Baha'u'llah: *Proclamation of Baha'u'llah*, Page: 97)

QUESTION: You said earlier that a Christian theologian once said that Jesus had to be viewed in one of only three ways: As a madman, as a charlatan or trickster or, the only other choice would be to see Him as Who He said He was. I guess the same must be true of Baha'u'llah?

RESPONSE: Well, yes, but when we talked about this before, I mentioned that there are several other choices, as well. He could be the Devil himself. Remember that some people who heard Jesus accused Him of being the Devil, or working His miracles through satanic power. Or, Baha'u'llah could be the Antichrist.

What I believe you will quickly conclude, if you study Baha'u'llah's life, Writings, teachings and His Revelation in general, is that He is not the Antichrist and not the Devil. When you apply Christ's criteria, the standard by which false prophets are contrasted with the true Return, you will know that Baha'u'llah is not a false prophet. Here is what Jesus said: *"Beware of false prophets, who come to you in sheep's clothing, but inwardly they are ravenous wolves. You will know them by their fruits."* (Matt 7:15-16)

According to this, you can do what I did when I first encountered the Baha'i Faith. I looked at the *"fruits"* represented not just in the teachings of the Baha'i Faith, but also in the lives of the Baha'is themselves, their communities, their goals and accomplishments. When you do the same, I believe you will certainly conclude that Baha'u'llah is not the Antichrist or a false prophet. But, on something as important as this, you must check for yourself. I did.

And, that does leave only the choices that you mentioned:

1. A madman, someone crazy, deranged, mentally unbalanced; (2) A charlatan, a trickster, someone trying to mislead; OR: (3) He could be Who He said He was—Christ Returned in the Glory of the Father.

As an historical note, let's remind ourselves again that many in Jesus' time thought He was mad or crazy, or the devil. Baha'u'llah tells us that when Manifestations of God appear in history, they are accused, as Jesus and Baha'u'llah were of being 'mad', perverters of the scriptures or plagiarists, and worse. Moses was called a *'Sorcerer'* and *'impostor!'* (Baha'u'llah: *Epistle to the Son of the Wolf,* Page: 64) Other Manifestations of God, Baha'u'llah says, have been *"held to be possessed, others were called impostors, and were treated in a manner that the pen is ashamed to describe."* (Baha'u'llah: *Epistle to the Son of the Wolf,* Page: 92)

QUESTION: This whole situation is so confusing! How can I, or anyone decide such a thing?

RESPONSE: It has always been confusing, I guess. Apparently, God tests us in every age when He sends His Pre-Existent Word into history, as Baha'u'llah said, in *"the form of a human temple."* When this 'Word of God' comes to us, sent by God in the appearance of what Baha'u'llah called 'Manifestations of God,' our faith, our judgment, our willingness to respond to the divine message, is severely tested.

Think of the test when God sent His 'only begotten

Son'! Jesus was not at all what the Jews wanted or expected. They had views of the Messiah that were distinctly different from the kind of person Jesus was or the teachings He gave. They wanted a nationalist, a spiritual, but also military leader who could restore their greatness and cast out the hated oppressors–the Romans.

Then, think of the test when Baha'u'llah, the Glory of God Himself appears in human history, showing His Face, allowing us to hear His Voice. Think of the trial for some people when they hear that Christ is returned *"in the glory of His Father."* (Matt 16:27) Think of the test when Christians realize that the Return of Jesus is in the appearance of One Who has a different name? Certainly the test was very great when those around Jesus *"The Son"* heard Him proclaim, *"The Father and I are one."* Equally, the test is strong when Baha'u'llah, *"The Father"* appears in human history saying: *"The Father hath come."*

Neither Christians nor Baha'is are confused about these statements, however, because Christians see Christ as God, *'the Son,'* a different 'Person' of the Trinity and not God the Father. Baha'is realize that while God is fully manifested in Baha'u'llah and even though He carries the title *'the Father,'* He is not God.

But come to think of it, if the test were not there, if it were easy to decide, there would be no true disciples, no devoted and committed followers, no real 'believers' who would even give up their all, even their very lives, to follow Jesus, or Baha'u'llah.

**Baha'i House of Worship in Kampala, Uganda, on the
African Continent.**

QUESTION: You have used the phrase 'Promise of
All Ages' several times in this conversation. What exactly
do you mean by that?

RESPONSE: Well, the phrase 'Promise of all Ages'
is not directly from Baha'u'llah, but from the writings of
His great grandson, Shoghi Effendi, the leader of the
Baha'i Faith for the first half of the Twentieth Century. A
great Baha'i teacher, George Townshend, who was a
Canon of the Episcopal Church in Ireland, left the min-
istry to become a follower of Baha'u'llah. A great teacher,
He served the Baha'i Faith faithfully and long and wrote

a well-known book about Baha'u'llah's Coming, which I recommend to you—*The Promise of All Ages.*

However, Baha'u'llah spoke of Himself frequently as *"The Promised One"* and wrote on this theme often, saying (what every scholar of religions knows) that every religion, every culture, in fact, all the peoples and ethnic groups of the entire planet are expecting the appearance or re-appearance of a great divine teacher. Christians expect the 'Return of Christ'; Buddhists the 'Fifth Buddha'; some Moslems expect two great teachers, which Baha'is believe were fulfilled by the Bab and Baha'u'llah.

Native Americans, Hindus, Zoroastrians, in fact all people everywhere across the earth expect some divinely-sent Person to appear Who will usher in a Golden Age of harmony, unity and peace, and start the process of what Jesus prayed for, namely, the building of the 'Kingdom of God on Earth'.

Baha'u'llah clearly and forcefully said, time and again, that these promises, these prophecies, these hopes and expectations, all refer to Him, to His Message, His Teachings and to the community of united believers that He has called into being. He is, if He is correct, the 'Promise of All Ages' in that His coming, His Advent, His appearance in history, fulfills not one, not several, but *all* of these prophecies and expectations that mankind has recorded.

QUESTION: This is almost more than I can take! How dare you say such things? The statements you are making are ludicrous and blasphemous, even stupid-sounding!

RESPONSE: It's difficult at times to say things in such a way that you won't get too 'riled up,' as my Grandfather used to say. I'm worried that I will tell you one too many times that I am not the one saying these things at all! It is Baha'u'llah Who is saying them. I'm just repeating them to you, passing along to you what He said.

As you think about how 'stupid-sounding' and 'blasphemous' these things sound, remember how that Jew in the time of Jesus felt when Jesus said that He would soon be seen to be *"sitting at the right hand of the power of God."* (Luke 22:69-70) or: *"All authority has been given to Me in heaven and on earth."* (Matt 28:18)

I'm sure some Jew in the crowd around Jesus must have said to himself or even out loud: "Now, that really sounds stupid!" Some other Jews were so upset at what they thought were blasphemous sayings of Jesus that they planned to kill him. Of course, they finally did execute Him, largely for saying things that seemed blasphemous and 'crazy.'

QUESTION: Well, that brings up another point I want to make. Jesus, as you say, was finally crucified, dying on the cross for the sins of the world and for the salvation of all the people of earth. But from what I can make out, Baha'u'llah died in bed.

RESPONSE: Baha'u'llah taught that all of the Manifestations suffered greatly for the people of the world. I know that Christians are accustomed to think that only Jesus suffered and died for salvation, but Baha'u'llah teaches that each one of them suffered greatly, some were killed (like Jesus and the Bab, Baha'u'llah's predecessor, Himself a Manifestation), others suffered and sacrificed their lives over long years for the salvation of humanity.

Muhammad experienced years of suffering, and Baha'u'llah suffered for most of His adult life, including nearly forty years of banishment from His native land, lengthy house arrest or imprisonment and numerous tortures. He was beaten, poisoned, put in chains, and from about the age of twenty-seven, he never knew freedom from banishment, prison or house arrest.

No one who understands the spirit of the Manifestations would say that life-long suffering is greater than the suffering of Jesus on the Cross; nor would anyone sensibly argue the opposite, that the pain of death by crucifixion is greater than a lifetime of chains, torture and prison. The point is that the suffering of the Manifestations is always for the same purpose, namely, for the salvation of individual souls. In Baha'u'llah's case, His sacrifice was not only for individual salvation but also for the salvation of the entire world. He said His Coming represented the Will of God to bring together earth's peoples into a long promised unity and peace and the building of 'The Kingdom of God on Earth.'

From the beginning of His realization of His Mission, Baha'u'llah accepted God's Plan for His life and the suffering it entailed. *"From the very day Thou didst reveal Thyself unto me, I have accepted for myself every manner of tribulation."* (Baha'u'llah: *Prayers and Meditations*, Pages: 108-109) Why this 'acceptance'? He said: *"I have accepted to be tried by manifold adversities for no purpose except to regenerate all that are in Thy heaven and on Thy earth."* (Baha'u'llah: *Prayers and Meditations*, Page: 198)

Baha'u'llah's life was constantly threatened, as was the life of Jesus. And like Jesus, He gives us assurance of His purpose: *"We desire to regenerate the world, yet they have resolved to put an end to My life."* (Baha'u'llah: *Tablets of Baha'u'llah*, Page: 244) And, commenting on His imprisonment: *"Consider these days in which He Who is the Ancient Beauty* [one of the titles of Baha'u'llah] *hath come in the Most Great Name, that He may quicken the world and unite its peoples. They, however, rose up against Him with sharpened swords . . . until in the end they imprisoned Him in the most desolate of cities."* (Baha'u'llah: *Epistle to the Son of the Wolf,* Page: 63)

Baha'u'llah tells us He was willing to sacrifice, to bear tribulations and manifold suffering for mankind. Why? He said it was done *". . . for the sake of the regeneration of their souls, that they may haste to attain the River that is Life indeed . . . "* (Baha'u'llah: *Prayers and Meditations,* Page: 198) All this suffering, He continued, was accepted *"so that He may build up the hearts of Thy servants"* and He was *"willing to suffer the most grievous abasement, that Thy creatures may be exalted."* (Baha'u'llah: *Prayers and Meditations,* Page: 37)

He concludes with a comment that helps us understand that all the Manifestations of God sacrifice themselves for a purpose: *"I yield Thee thanks, O my God, for that Thou hast offered me up as a sacrifice in Thy path, and made me a target for the arrows of afflictions as a token of Thy love for Thy servants, and singled me out for all manner of tribulation for the regeneration of Thy people."* (Baha'u'llah: *Prayers and Meditations,* Page: 154)

My mother's favorite passage from scripture was John 3:16: *"For God so loved the world that He gave His only begotten Son, that whoever believes in Him should not perish but have everlasting life."* (John 3:16) It has occurred to me that these two quotations show that the emphasis on salvation is on the individual in Christianity, while the emphasis from Baha'u'llah is on the 'regeneration' of the entire world. But there is no real difference here, since, as John says 'God so loved the world' and Baha'u'llah says over and again that each human individual must seek salvation on his or her own.

QUESTION: Wait! Are you trying to say that Baha'u'llah suffered and died for our sins? That happened once and for all with Jesus Christ. It is eternal. It doesn't need to happen again!

RESPONSE: Jesus did sacrifice Himself for us. What Baha'u'llah is trying to get us to understand is that so did Buddha and Moses and Muhammad. So did Baha'u'llah. Christians have been so accustomed (and I understand this, from my Christian background) to thinking of their religion as 'the one and only' that it must be challenging indeed to hear that there are other religions that have similar claims.

In the case of Baha'u'llah, He made it very clear that He suffered chains, torture and life-long imprisonment and *"endured manifold sufferings, hardships and tribulations"* in order *"to quench the fire of animosity and hatred which burneth fiercely in the hearts of the peoples of the earth . . . that fire may turn into light, and hatred may give way to fellowship and love."* (Baha'u'llah: *Tablets of Baha'u'llah*, Page: 44)

QUESTION: But I've told you before, and you seem to be skirting around the question, that Jesus said: *"No one comes to the Father except through Me."* (John 14:6)

RESPONSE: Yes, I do remember we discussed this before and I think I quoted to you that Baha'u'llah said that *"He Who is everlastingly hidden from the eyes of men can never be known except through His Manifestation, and His Manifestation can adduce no greater proof of the truth of His Mission than the proof of His own Person."* (Baha'u'llah: *Gleanings*, Page: 49) Baha'u'llah continued to explain that whenever a Manifestation appears, no man can 'come to God' in the Day of that Manifestation except through accepting and following that Manifestation. Thus, when

Jesus appeared, the people of Moses could only attain salvation, so say Christians, by accepting Christ.

Baha'u'llah tells us that if a follower of Christ were around Muhammad (not many were, of course, although some were) he could only experience salvation through recognition of Muhammad and following Him with a committed life.

As for the statement of Jesus that *"no man cometh unto the Father but by Me"* (John 14:6) listen to this statement of Baha'u'llah: *"No man can obtain everlasting life, unless he embraceth the truth of this inestimable, this wondrous, and sublime Revelation."* (Baha'u'llah: Gleanings, Page: 183) And then, this statement of Baha'u'llah, similar again, to that same saying of Jesus: *"Attainment unto the Divine Presence can be realized solely by attaining His* [that is, Baha'u'llah's] *presence."* (Baha'u'llah: *Tablets of Baha'u'llah*, Page: 50)

QUESTION: I'm learning many new things about Baha'u'llah, but I doubt very greatly that He will ever replace Christ for me. In fact, you can count on that.

RESPONSE: Christ cannot and should not be replaced. That certainly didn't happen in my case, as you can see from reading chapter two of this conversation. A Jew in the time of Jesus didn't 'give up' Moses to follow Christ, did he? Rather, that Jew followed Christ because he believed Jesus was the promised Messiah. The Jewish person who listened to Jesus recognized that Jesus frequently quoted the Old Testament. One of the best examples is the following: Jesus was, you could say, irritated that the people of His day kept asking for a 'sign,' some irrefutable, totally believable sign that would unmistakably certify Jesus as truly being from God.

He told them, I'm sure you recall, that the only sign

they would get was the sign of Jonah. Every Jewish listener—Jesus never, or almost never preached or taught to anyone other than Jews—understood that Jesus was referring to the reappearance of Jonah after he was swallowed by a whale. We now know that His mention of Jonah was referring to His own Resurrection after three days.

QUESTION: That brings up another question. Some friends of mine said that Baha'is don't believe in Christ's Resurrection. What about that?

RESPONSE: Baha'is *do* believe in the Resurrection of Christ. What your friend probably heard was that Baha'u'llah's Son, 'Abdu'l-Baha, said that the Resurrection, the central event of Christianity, was to be understood in a spiritual way, instead of a material way. You can turn to the sixteenth chapter of this book and look up 'Resurrection' for a longer statement on this. There have been several apparently miraculous events in other religions, which of course Christians tend to explain by rational and logical reasoning. As I mentioned before, read about the Bab, Baha'u'llah's predecessor, Who remained alive after facing an execution squad of 750 rifles. You can read about this in the Encyclopedia Britannica. (Look under 'Babism')

But to come back to Jesus being replaced. Baha'is would never suggest this; in fact, quite the opposite, Baha'is are constantly asking the people of the world who are not Christians to believe in Jesus.

QUESTION: Please, get real! What on earth are you talking about? You are making Baha'is sound like Christian teachers or missionaries!

RESPONSE: In a way, Baha'is are exactly that—Christian missionaries—of a sort. Because, whenever they teach Buddhists or Jews or Hindus, they teach Christ as being the Son of God and as a Manifestation of God, and they patiently, carefully, tactfully point out that belief in Baha'u'llah is not possible without belief in Christ. They don't have to point this out to Muslims, since Muslims (unbeknownst to many Christians) already believe in Jesus Christ.

QUESTION: Without wanting to hurt your feelings, I have to tell you that I'm much more interested in what Baha'u'llah said about Himself than I am in what you say about Him.

RESPONSE: That doesn't hurt my feelings at all. Your decision about Baha'u'llah shouldn't rest on my words or testimony, but rather on what you decide after you have listened carefully and well to what Baha'u'llah Himself said. So, I'm in perfect agreement with you. Therefore, here are some selected quotations from Baha'u'llah on the subject of Who He was, His identity.

From these quotations, I hope you will have an opportunity to become clearer as to your decision about Him. The central question, as we have said before, is the question Christ asked of His disciples: *"Who do men say that I am?"* Likewise, the central question being asked by Baha'u'llah of you is to make your decision about Who He is.

Here are the quotations from Baha'u'llah about Who He is: *"He that was hidden from the eyes of men is revealed, girded with sovereignty and power!" This is the Paradise, the rustling of whose leaves proclaims: "O ye that inhabit the heavens and the earth! There hath appeared what hath never previously appeared. He Who, from everlasting, had concealed His Face from the sight of creation is now come.* " (Baha'u'llah: *Gleanings*, Page: 31)

"Speed out of your sepulchers. How long will ye sleep? The second blast hath been blown on the trumpet. [This refers to the first 'Trumpet Blast' of His predecessor, the Bab and to Himself as the 'Second Blast' of the 'Trumpet'] *"On whom are ye gazing? This is your Lord, the God of Mercy. Witness how ye gainsay His signs!"* (Baha'u'llah: *Gleanings*, Page 44)

And then using the symbolic language Christians are acquainted with in the Bible: *"This is the Day whereon the All-Merciful hath come down in the clouds of knowledge, clothed with manifest sovereignty. He well knoweth the actions of men. He it is Whose glory none can mistake, could ye but comprehend it. The heaven of every religion hath been rent, and the earth of human understanding been cleft asunder, and the angels of God are seen descending . . . the mountains have passed away, and the heavens have been folded together, and the whole earth is held within His grasp, could ye but understand it."* (Baha'u'llah: *Gleanings*, Pages: 44-45)

Baha'u'llah speaks of Himself as being *" . . . Him through Whose coming the world was made the recipient of this promised glory, this wondrous favor. Behold how the generality of mankind hath been endued with the capacity to hearken unto God's most exalted Word—the Word upon which must depend the gathering together and spiritual resurrection of all men . . . ."* (Baha'u'llah: *Gleanings*, Pages: 96-97)

Baha'u'llah also said: *"The peoples of the world are fast asleep. Were they to wake from their slumber, they would hasten with eagerness unto God, the All-Knowing, the All-Wise. They would cast away everything they possess, be it all the treasures of the earth, that their Lord may remember them to the extent of addressing to them but one word . . . So*

bewildered are they in the drunkenness of their evil desires,
that they are powerless to recognize the Lord of all being,
Whose voice calleth aloud from every direction: 'There is none
other God but Me, the Mighty, the All-Wise.'" (Baha'u'llah:
Gleanings, Page: 137)

Using the analogy we spoke of before, where
Baha'u'llah calls Himself the 'Pen' that is being held in
God's hands, indicating that what He says is not from
Himself, but from God, He says that He has: *"through the*
Pen of the Most High, unlocked the doors of men's hearts.
Every verse which this Pen hath revealed is a bright and
shining portal that discloseth the glories of a saintly and pious
life, of pure and stainless deeds. The summons and the mes-
sage which We gave were never intended to reach or to benefit
one land or one people only.

"Mankind in its entirety must firmly adhere to whatso-
ever hath been revealed and vouchsafed unto it. Then and
only then will it attain unto true liberty . . . The whole earth
is illuminated with the resplendent glory of God's Revela-
tion." Baha'is believe this Revelation came from God
through Baha'u'llah

"We beseech God to strengthen thee with His power, and
enable thee to recognize Him Who is the Source of all knowl-
edge, that thou mayest detach thyself from all human learn-
ing, for, 'what would it profit any man to strive after learning
when he hath already found and recognized Him Who is the
Object of all knowledge?'" (Baha'u'llah: *Gleanings,* Pages:
176-177)

Speaking of Himself as *"the Promised One"* He referred
to the many martyrs who gave their lives for His Cause
and Who now reside in Heaven as *"the Concourse on High."*
And speaking of the reaction of the world to His coming,
Baha'u'llah says: *"And when the Promised One came unto*
them, they recognized Him not, and disbelieved in Thy signs,
and repudiated Thy clear tokens, and strayed so grievously

from Thy path that they slew Thy servants, through the brightness of whose faces the countenances of the Concourse on high have been illumined. " (Baha'u'llah: *Prayers and Meditations,* Page: 97)

He continues: *"Thou art He, O my God, Who hath raised me up at Thy behest, and bidden me to occupy Thy seat, and to summon all men to the court of Thy mercy. It is Thou Who hast commanded me to tell out the things Thou didst destine for them in the Tablet of Thy decree and didst inscribe with the pen of Thy Revelation, and Who hast enjoined on me the duty of kindling the fire of Thy love in the hearts of Thy servants, and of drawing all the peoples of the earth nearer to the habitation of Thy throne.* " (Baha'u'llah: *Prayers and Meditations,* Page: 107)

And: *"I have no will but Thy will, O my Lord, and cherish no desire except Thy desire. From my pen floweth only the summons which Thine own exalted pen hath voiced, and my tongue uttereth naught save what the Most Great Spirit hath itself proclaimed in the kingdom of Thine eternity. I am stirred by nothing else except the winds of Thy will, and breathe no word except the words which, by Thy leave and Thine inspiration, I am led to pronounce.* " (Baha'u'llah: *Prayers and Meditations,* Page: 108)

Also, this striking passage that shows God working within Baha'u'llah: *"Glory be to Thee, O my God! My face hath been set towards Thy face, and my face is, verily, Thy face, and my call is Thy call, and my Revelation Thy Revelation, and my self Thy Self, and my Cause Thy Cause, and my behest Thy behest, and my Being Thy Being, and my sovereignty Thy sovereignty, and my glory Thy glory, and my power Thy power.* " (Baha'u'llah: *Prayers and Meditations,* Page: 231)

Baha'u'llah was in a terrible prison-city—Akka, Palestine (now Israel)—for a good portion of His life. Listen to Him to see if He sounds like a prisoner or, if not, we are challenged to decide Who is speaking: *"O my God! Thou beholdest the Lord of all mankind confined in His Most Great Prison, calling aloud Thy Name, gazing upon Thy face, proclaiming that which hath enraptured the denizens of Thy kingdoms of revelation and of creation. O my God! I behold Mine own Self captive in the hands of Thy servants, yet the light of Thy sovereignty and the revelations of Thine invincible power shine resplendent from His face, enabling all to know of a certainty that Thou art God, and that there is none other God but Thee.*

"Neither can the power of the powerful frustrate Thee, nor the ascendancy of the rulers prevail against Thee. Thou doest whatsoever Thou willest by virtue of Thy sovereignty which encompasseth all created things, and ordainest that which Thou pleasest through the potency of Thy behest which pervadeth the entire creation. (Baha'u'llah: *Tablets of Baha'u'llah*, Page: 233)

Ask yourself Who was in charge when Jesus stood a captive in Herod's palace? Or in Pilate's mansion? You and I know the answer. Then ask Who was in charge in Baha'u'llah's prison cell? Was it the ruler that sent Him there? Again, it seems, to me at least, that the answer is clear. What do you think?

He also said (and you asked to hear from Him, didn't you?): *"He Who was hidden from mortal eyes exclaimeth: 'Lo! I am the All-Manifest.' This is the Word which hath caused the limbs of disbelievers to quake. Glorified be God! All the heavenly Scriptures of the past attest to the greatness of this Day, the greatness of this Manifestation, the greatness of His signs, the greatness of His Word . . . "* (Baha'u'llah: *Tablets of Baha'u'llah*, Page: 258)

Finally, Baha'u'llah said of Himself: *"He it is Who in the Old Testament hath been named Jehovah, Who in the Gospel hath been designated as the Spirit of Truth,"* (Quoted in Shoghi Effendi: *World Order of Baha'u'llah*, Page: 104)

QUESTION: Stop! Stop! Stop! Is Baha'u'llah claiming to be Jehovah, to be God Himself? Surely that shows that Baha'u'llah is just a mentally unbalanced person?

RESPONSE: Well, we don't call Jesus mentally unbalanced, when He says, *"the Father and I are One,"* do we? Nor do we call Jesus 'unbalanced' when He says: *"Most assuredly, I say to you, hereafter you shall see heaven open, and the angels of God ascending and descending upon the Son of Man."* (John 1:51)

We know that Jesus was sane. And we know that He was the Son of God. Jesus, while talking with the Chief Priests and scribes at His trial, spoke of Himself in this way: *"Hereafter the Son of Man will sit on the right hand of the power of God."* (Luke 22:69-70) If this were anyone else but Jesus, especially if we encountered a man preaching in a tent alongside a modern highway, who said such a thing, we would undoubtedly think the man 'mentally unbalanced.'

That statement by Jesus could certainly have qualified Him as 'mentally unbalanced' by those who heard Him but did not understand His station as God's Son. Also, as we've said before in this conversation, Jesus said: *"The Father and I are One"* and *"if you have seen me, you have seen the Father."* That certainly sounded as if Jesus was saying: "I'm God," didn't it? Small wonder that many in the crowd turned away from Jesus, for this was just too much for them to bear, too strange, too much like what one might hear from a mentally deranged person. Some of them (let me tease you a little) might have said to Jesus: 'Stop! Stop! Stop!'

The statements of Jesus do seem to be saying, "I'm God", don't they? But remember, Jesus at other times denied being God very vehemently, just as Baha'u'llah did. Though the above quotes do sound as if He is saying He is God, other quotes clearly indicate that He did not claim to be God. There is a mystery that we find in the words of Christ that took the Christian Church over four hundred fifty years to understand (the Council of Chalcedon, you recall, was the final turning point, after which there was more agreement on these points than before.) The quote about *"Jehovah"* needs to be understood in the same way that we understand the quote about *"the Father and I are one."*

Baha'is weren't confused about the identity of Baha'u'llah. His identity was well understood by them, even in Baha'u'llah's lifetime. Why? Because He wrote so clearly and forcefully on this point. I don't want to repeat what we discussed in chapters four and five, but in brief review, Baha'u'llah tells us that the Manifestations have two natures (very close to the solution of the Council of Chalcedon, when you get down to it) and that therefore, they can sometimes speak as a man, while at other times, they speak as God amongst men.

The Manifestations of God, he says, are men, but more than men. Baha'u'llah said, on one occasion: *"We call aloud unto thee saying: In truth there is no God but Me, the All-Knowing, the All-Wise."* (Baha'u'llah: *Tablets of Baha'u'llah,* Page: 246) and at another time, He said *"Were any of the all-embracing Manifestations of God to declare: 'I am God', He, verily, speaketh the truth . . . "* (Baha'u'llah: *Gleanings,* Page: 53-54)

The Manifestations have a 'twofold station'—both Divine and human—just as Christians finally realized and decided about Jesus four hundred fifty years after Jesus lived and just as Baha'u'llah taught in His writings: He said: *"When I contemplate, O my God, the relationship that bindeth me to Thee, I am moved to proclaim to all created things 'verily I am God'; and when I consider my own self, lo,*

I find it coarser than clay!" (Baha'u'llah: *The Kitab-i-Aqdas*: Notes, Page: 234)

QUESTION: This all sounds so confusing! Christians don't see a contradiction with Christ because they see Him as man and as God. But this Baha'u'llah–isn't He just a man claiming to be God one minute and disclaiming it the next?

RESPONSE: Remember, that when Jesus was on this earth, people felt the same way you are feeling now about Baha'u'llah. Jesus made both kinds of statements, namely, that He was God *"I and My Father are one,"* (John 10:30) and that He was not God: *"Why callest thou me good? there is none good but one, that is, God."* (Matt 19:17)

Again, I refer to chapters four and five where we discussed what Baha'u'llah taught about the Manifestations of God, but maybe we should delve back into that a little. Baha'u'llah said the Manifestations of God (there are many, but let's use Christ and Baha'u'llah as examples, just for now) have *"two natures,"* one physical (related to the *"world of matter"*) and one spiritual, *"born of the substance of God Himself."* Baha'u'llah: *Gleanings*, Page: 66)

In addition to these two natures, each Manifestation has, Baha'u'llah says, two *"stations."* In the one station, the Manifestation is seen as *"One Whose voice is the voice of God Himself."* With the other station, each of the Manifestations could say, as Baha'u'llah did, *"I am but a man like you,"* or as Christ did *"Why callest thou me good; there is none good but God."*

QUESTION: Well, maybe that does help a little to clear up the confusion, at least somewhat. But it doesn't mean I accept Baha'u'llah as being *"the Voice of God Himself."*

RESPONSE: Not many people would come quickly to such a conclusion. A Jew following Jesus through the Judean hills and into Galilee would probably be alternately convinced and confused, then more certain, then doubtful and finally, he would either come to accept Jesus as the Son of God or he would have to relieve the tension by turning away.

It's worth remembering, as we have discussed before, that in both cases—Christ and Baha'u'llah—a few persons followed them instantly, with no prayer, no lengthy thought process, no 'deliberation,' no weighing of the pros and cons, just an immediate surrender, without reservation. They realized immediately that their lives belonged to Him. For most of us, however, this process is longer, more complicated, sometimes tortuous and often arrived at only after prolonged prayer and decision making, leading finally to commitment.

QUESTION: I'm learning how to be ahead of you. I suspect you are now going to tell me that I have the same challenge with Baha'u'llah that the Jew had with Christ?

RESPONSE: You are getting way ahead of me, actually. What I say is this: I do believe you have before you the 'decision of a lifetime.' All I can suggest is that you acquaint yourself with Baha'u'llah and His Writings. And, that you pray earnestly to Christ for guidance on this decision. I cannot remember a time when I did not believe in Jesus, His power and His care over us. Therefore, I believe that the Holy Spirit will inspire you and Jesus will answer your prayer and will give you the guidance you seek, leading you to the answer for your life. At least, that is what He did for me.

Your Jesus and my Jesus said: *"So I say to you, ask, and it will be given to you; seek, and you will find; knock, and it will be opened to you."* (Luke 11:9) And there is a hymn, like so many others, playing in my mind: 'May I hear Thee say to me, Jesus Savior, pilot me.' If you need a 'Pilot' for this journey, you and I know the best one possible. Our Jesus.

But remember one important thing. Jesus had, out of thousands who heard Him, only a tiny handful of true believers. On the day of His death, even His closest disciples were filled with uncertainty. His chief disciple, Peter, even betrayed Him three times! When you think about it, what we are saying is that more than ninety-nine percent of all who heard Jesus did *not* follow Him, even after seeing Jesus, being around Him, listening to His teachings and witnessing numerous miracles. So . . . I guess trying to be a follower of both Jesus and Baha'u'llah in this day will be no easier than being a Jewish follower of Christ (without denying Moses and Judaism) two thousand years ago.

QUESTION: So I have a choice to make, is that it? To decide Who Baha'u'llah is?

RESPONSE: That was the choice I felt I had to make. Rather than say anything more, let me offer Baha'u'llah's words. They present the best evidence for the making of this decision, this choice for or against Baha'u'llah. His words, not mine, are the guidance I think you need, along with fervent prayer to Christ for Him to guide and 'pilot' you to the truth. Ask Jesus what His will is for you in the question of Baha'u'llah. There can be no better advisor than the Master.

Baha'u'llah wrote a letter especially to Christians, another to Moslems, still another to Jews and special letters to other religious groups. He wrote to common people and to Kings. In a letter to the Kings of the Western world, He said: *"O kings of the earth! He Who is the sovereign Lord of all is come. The Kingdom is God's, the omnipotent Protector, the Self-Subsisting. Worship none but God, and, with radiant hearts, lift up your faces unto your Lord, the Lord of all names. This is a Revelation to which whatever ye possess can never be compared, could ye but know it."* (Baha'u'llah: *Gleanings*, Page: 210)

In this same passage, He says that Jesus is calling those same kings to turn to Baha'u'llah: *" . . . from the heights of the Kingdom the Voice of the Spirit of God* [that is, Jesus] *is heard proclaiming: "Bestir yourselves, ye proud ones of the earth, and hasten ye unto Him."'* (Baha'u'llah: *Gleanings*, Page: 211) Baha'u'llah also refers in His letter to these Kings in this way:

"Ye are but vassals, O kings of the earth! He Who is the King of Kings hath appeared, arrayed in His most wondrous glory, and is summoning you unto Himself, the Help in Peril, the Self-Subsisting. Take heed lest pride deter you from recognizing the Source of Revelation, lest the things of this world shut you out as by a veil from Him Who is the Creator of heaven. Arise, and serve Him Who is the Desire of all nations, Who hath created you through a word from Him, and ordained you to be, for all time, the emblems of His sovereignty." (Baha'u'llah: *Gleanings*, Page: 211)

The Kings did not respond, anymore than Pilate and Herod responded in the day of Jesus. Baha'u'llah then announced to the world: *"From two ranks amongst men power hath been seized: kings and ecclesiastics."* (Quoted in Shoghi Effendi: *God Passes By*, Page: 230) In another passage, Baha'u'llah speaks of His coming and Jesus speaks in response: *"He, verily, is come with His Kingdom, and all the atoms cry aloud: 'Lo! The Lord is come in His great majesty!' He Who is the Father is come, and the Son (Jesus), in the holy vale, crieth out: 'Here am I, here am I, O Lord, My God!'"* (Baha'u'llah: *Proclamation of Baha'u'llah*, Page: 27)

Just as Jesus told His disciples: *"He who has seen Me has seen the Father,"* (John 14:9) Baha'u'llah taught the Baha'is to pray: *"I bear witness that he who hath known Thee* [that is, Baha'u'llah] *hath known God, and he who hath attained unto Thy presence hath attained unto the presence of God."* (Baha'u'llah: *Prayers and Meditations*, Page: 311)

Baha'u'llah speaks of the spiritual nature of His Mission: *"Say: By the righteousness of the Almighty! The measure of the favors of God hath been filled up, His Word hath been perfected, the light of His countenance hath been revealed, His sovereignty hath encompassed the whole of creation, the glory of His Revelation hath been made manifest, and His bounties have rained upon all mankind."* (Baha'u'llah: *Gleanings*, Page: 259)

But then, referring to Himself as *"the Eternal Truth"* He speaks in practical terms of what God has commissioned Him to accomplish: *" . . . the purpose of Him Who is the Eternal Truth hath been to confer everlasting life upon all men, and ensure their security and peace... "* (Baha'u'llah: *Gleanings*, Page: 116)

In another place, He tells us that God's purpose in sending all the Manifestations, including Himself: *" . . . is twofold. The first is to liberate the children of men from the darkness of ignorance, and guide them to the light of true understanding. The second is to ensure the peace and tranquillity of mankind, and provide all the means by which they can be established. The Prophets of God should be regarded as physicians whose task is to foster the well-being of the world and its peoples, that, through the spirit of oneness, they may heal the sickness of a divided humanity."* (Baha'u'llah: *Gleanings*, Pages: 79-80)

Finally: Baha'u'llah said that God's Will, as expressed

through Him, was for " . . . *the regeneration of the whole world, and the establishment of the unity of its peoples, and the salvation of all them that dwell therein.*" (Baha'u'llah: Gleanings, Page: 243). For Christians, the central question could be whether they will recognize Baha'u'llah as the Father of all Mankind: *"Tell Me then: Do the sons recognize the Father, and acknowledge Him, or do they deny Him, even as the people aforetime denied Him (Jesus)?"* (Baha'u'llah: *Proclamation of Baha'u'llah*, Page: 97)

QUESTION: Something is still confusing me. It seems you have said two contradicting things. First, you say that Baha'u'llah claims to be the Return of Christ. Then, second, that He claims to be the appearance in history of the long-awaited *'Promised One,'* who is called, in this Day, *"the Father."*

RESPONSE: This could be very confusing, I agree, but only if you forget Baha'u'llah's teaching about the Manifestations of God. When these Manifestations come, they always represent the 'return' of the reality of God's direct Presence in human history, the 'Word of God.' Baha'u'llah compared the appearance of the Manifestations to the *"light of the Sun,"* pointing out that the sun that dawns today is a 'new' sun but also the return of the same life-giving sun, providing light and warmth. He tells us we do not say: "This is an absolutely new and different sun" as it dawns. He reminds us that we know it is the same sun, with the same precious, life-giving light, even though the day is new and the sun is rising at a different point on the horizon.

In the same way, Baha'u'llah teaches, Christ represents a 'new' Sun, but the Divine Light, the 'Word' is the same as that of Moses and the Burning Bush. Clearly, the Ten Commandments were, as the Old Testament tells us forcefully, the 'Word of God'. When Christ appears, it is that same 'Word of God', not a different word of God that shines through Him upon us.

And, when Baha'u'llah appears, it is the same light as the one that shined so brilliantly in Jesus.

QUESTION: Wait a minute! Jesus and Baha'u'llah were two completely different historical figures.

RESPONSE: Yes, of course, you are right. But, they were still one, said Baha'u'llah, one in their origin—being from God—and one in their commission from God to bring salvation to humanity and to guide them to a destiny of unity and fulfillment. They are 'one' in another way, in that Baha'u'llah claimed to be the Return of the Spirit of Christ to this world.

Think of the many Manifestations of God, including Moses, Jesus, Muhammad, Buddha, Krishna, the Bab and Baha'u'llah Himself. About these Manifestations, *all of them*, Baha'u'llah said: *"It is clear and evident to thee that all the Prophets are the Temples of the Cause of God, Who have appeared clothed in divers attire. If thou wilt observe with discriminating eyes, thou wilt behold Them all abiding in the same tabernacle, soaring in the same heaven, seated upon the same throne, uttering the same speech, and proclaiming the same Faith.*

"Such is the unity of those Essences of Being, those Luminaries of infinite and immeasurable splendor! Wherefore, should one of these Manifestations of Holiness proclaim saying: 'I am the return of all the Prophets', He, verily, speaketh the truth." (Baha'u'llah: *Gleanings*, Page: 52)

QUESTION: There's a big problem here, which I don't think you see. The Son of God and the 'Manifestations' as you call them do *not* proclaim the same faith. Their teachings are quite different. Don't you realize that?

RESPONSE: All my life, I've been interested in the different religions and one of the most attractive things to me about the Baha'i Faith is that it allows me to see history, *all* history, in a connected, meaningful and purposeful way. It also allows me to believe not only in Jesus and Moses, but also in Buddha, Krishna, Muhammad, as well as the Bab and Baha'u'llah. But to answer your question more directly, we need to remember what we discussed in chapter four, when we talked about something called 'progressive revelation.' This is one of the central teachings of Baha'u'llah.

To start with, yes, you are right, the Manifestations always give 'new' teachings, new laws, new understandings of God's Will. But they always preserve some of the past as well. As I mentioned before, Jesus quoted the Old Testament numerous times and His 'Great Commandment' is a nearly exact quotation from the scriptures of Judaism.

But, even though there is freshness and newness in every divine revelation, there is a core of religion and faith that is always the same: Love of God, love of your neighbor, love of yourself; upright conduct, honest behavior and the Golden Rule, which is in every religion, not just Christianity. Dig deeply into any religion, Christianity, Hinduism, Buddhism, Islam, or the Baha'i Faith, and the deeper you go, the closer you get to a body of belief that is strongly similar, though not exactly the same. So, on the surface of any religion, you see obvious differences, deeper down, great similarities. When we go to the very core of any religion, we see 'oneness.'

QUESTION: You are missing the point, or I think

so at least. In Christianity, God sends His only begotten Son to save the world and every individual from the grip of sin. No other religion offers this teaching, does it?

RESPONSE: Baha'u'llah says that the situation was and is the same in every single religion, in every appearance of a Manifestation. When the Manifestation, the 'Word' appears, everyone must turn to Him for salvation. To turn away is to turn away not only from salvation, but also from the chance for the whole world to be renewed and revitalized, even revolutionized in the direction of something better and more 'whole.' In the case of the Baha'i Faith, that 'something better' would be unity and peace across the entire planet.

But to return to the dire prospect of 'turning away' from Jesus or from Baha'u'llah or from any of the Manifestations, any failure to respond to them, says Baha'u'llah, any 'turning away' represents sinfulness at its worst.

In the coming of Baha'u'llah, He clearly says He is the Return of Christ, as in the statement: *"If ye be intent on crucifying once again Jesus, the Spirit of God, put Me to death, for He hath once more, in My person, been made manifest unto you. Deal with Me as ye wish, for I have vowed to lay down My life in the path of God."* (Baha'u'llah: *Gleanings*, Page: 101) Christ once said to the Pharisees, *"had ye believed Moses, ye would have believed me: for he wrote of me"* (John 5:46) clearly indicating that those who did not believe in Him had not truly believed in Moses and the Prophets.

Reading the quote of Baha'u'llah above, where He says that Jesus is once more appearing in the world in the form of Baha'u'llah's Person, one can shudder to realize that if Baha'u'llah is Who He said He was and is, then to turn away from Him is also to turn away from Christ.

QUESTION: I really don't like what you just said. Do you have to be that challenging? It almost seems 'pushy'! And, I could resent it.

RESPONSE: 'Pushy' is something Baha'is don't want to be. Baha'u'llah commissioned us to be apostles of unity and concord. I hope you realize that what is upsetting you is not what I'm saying but what Baha'u'llah is saying–to you. And, I'm sure you realize that what He said is not qualitatively different from what Christ said, as I just quoted. Was Jesus being 'pushy?' Neither you nor I think that He was. Both Jesus and Baha'u'llah were authoritative, strong, challenging, even demanding, such as when Jesus told one man to give away all his wealth, told another to leave his family to follow Him and still another was denied 'leave time' to go bury his father! But, we don't criticize Jesus for these things, do we? And we shouldn't.

Baha'u'llah said that the Manifestations, when they come, when they appear *"out of the invisible heaven"* are to be listened to as if one is hearing God talking. He said that each Manifestation *"doeth whatsoever He willeth"* (Baha'u'llah: *Epistle to the Son of the Wolf,* Page: 1) and is not to be questioned about His teachings and His guidance and any commands He may give. Baha'u'llah is trying to get us to realize that when these Manifestations appear, they are the 'Word of God' in our midst.

QUESTION: Well, to get back to the question I raised before, and I don't think it's been answered well enough, how about putting it this way? If Baha'u'llah was and is the Return of Christ, how can He also be *'the Father'* of all mankind, the 'Promised One of All Ages'? I told you once before that sometimes it seems as if Baha'u'llah claimed to be everything to everyone, and that just seems ridiculous!

RESPONSE: Yes, and I suppose that two-thousand years ago, it seemed ridiculous when Christ told His listeners that He would soon be seen to be *"sitting at the right hand of the Power"* (that is, at God's right hand) (Mark 14:62), and *"All authority has been given to Me in heaven and on earth."* (Matt 28:18)

When Jesus said these things, He appeared to His listeners to be an unemployed carpenter, a simple, un-educated man, a wandering teacher, with no observable means of support. Can't you imagine someone in the back of the crowd muttering: 'Yeah, sure, Ridiculous!" and then walking away from the Person we now know is the Son of God.

Think of the impact on that man's life, from 'turning away.' So, I cannot apologize when I say to you that the consequences of turning away from Baha'u'llah are immense, especially for the Christian believer. As I remember, you said earlier that you do begin to realize that this is a fateful and fearful decision, either way, with great consequences for being right or wrong, no matter what is decided.

So, it seems to me we must be careful what and whom we call ridiculous. Is it just a wandering, unemployed carpenter, or is it the Son of God? And is Baha'u'llah just a wise man, maybe a madman, a prisoner, even a criminal (remember that both Christ and Baha'u'llah were accused of committing crimes) or, is Baha'u'llah the Return of Christ, the Father of all mankind, and the Promise of All Ages? Which is He?

In the case of Jesus, we know the answer instantly.

But—would we have known it back then, two thousand years ago? You have already admitted that it would have been pretty difficult if you had been there with Jesus back in those times. And it's difficult now, too, to decide Who Baha'u'llah is, I agree. Difficult in both cases, it seems to me, if you are there at the time that they are first making their claims. Several hundred years later, it's a 'breeze' to make the decision, because by then you begin to see the 'fruits' of their revelation appearing on the 'tree' of the community they established and the changed individual lives that result from the power they release.

But, there was another part of your question I haven't addressed. About Baha'u'llah being 'everything to everyone.' I've never heard it put that way before, but in a strange way, that is exactly what He was and is—everything to everyone. The Father to all on the planet, the Return, not only of Christ but the Return of the true spirit, the 'Word' that was in Buddha, Krishna, Moses and Muhammad and others.

He truly was 'everything to everyone' as the 'Promise of All Ages,' the One often prophesied in the many religions of the past, the One long awaited, the One expected fervently by all religions and cultures. He is the One Who, at His coming, ushers in a millennial age of fulfillment of prophecy, One Who will guide us, lead us, inspire us, and infuse us with power and energy to build, finally, Christ's Kingdom of God *"on earth as it is in heaven."*

Everything to everyone? It sounds right and true, not ridiculous, to one who knows Christ returned in Baha'u'llah. Baha'is feel they are currently witnessing the coming together, the divine ingathering of all peoples into a new era of oneness, unity, and peace. We feel we are blessed to be witnesses of and participants in what has often been described in scripture and poetry as a 'golden age' of fulfillment and deeper realization of our purpose here on earth.

QUESTION: You are still not answering one of my central questions to my satisfaction. How can Baha'u'llah be the Return of Christ and "The Father"? Which is it? He can't be both!

RESPONSE: There may be a way that Baha'u'llah *can* be both the return of Christ (*"He has once more been made manifest to you in my Person"*) and, at the same time, *"the Father."* Remember this: Christ said clearly that *"The Father and I are One,"* so for Baha'u'llah to announce that He is the Return of Christ in one breath and that He is the final, long awaited appearance of *"the Father"* of all mankind in another breath may not be so illogical.

All we need to do is to remember Christ's statement about the 'oneness' of the *'Son'* and the *'Father.'* Jesus also said: *"He that hath seen me hath seen the Father."* Baha'u'llah, in a letter written directly to Christian believers uttered this challenging statement: *"Do the sons* [that is, the Christians] *recognize the Father?"* clearly expecting true Christians to recognize Him both as the Return of Christ and as *'the Father.'*

QUESTION: You have mentioned, several times, the letter that Baha'u'llah wrote to the Christians of the world. When do I get to see it? If it was written to Christians, then I would like to look it over for myself.

RESPONSE: I do intend to show you the full letter. Before we look at it, however, I'd like to tell you something about Baha'u'llah's teachings, something about similarities and differences between the Christian and Baha'i Faiths and, finally, I'd like to show you why Christians and Baha'is share a special trust to rebuild the world, in Christ's words, as *"fishers of men"* and, in Baha'u'llah's phrase, *"quickeners of mankind."*

If I may, I will tease your interest in that letter by telling you that the letter was written to the world's first Christian to become a follower of Baha'u'llah. His name was Faris Effendi. He was a Syrian physician. Baha'u'llah's letter to him is often called "The Letter to the Christians." I believe, as do most Baha'is, that this letter was written to all the Christians of the world, as well as to Faris Effendi.

I'll show you the letter soon, but for now, I maintain that since this letter was written to all Christians, it is Baha'u'llah's letter—to you!

Of all the prayers of Baha'u'llah, here is one of the best-known and most oft-quoted, the *'sweet-scented streams'* prayer. When I first read it, I thought it sounded like one of the Psalms of the Old Testament:

"From the sweet-scented streams of Thine eternity give me to drink, O my God, and of the fruits of the tree of Thy being enable me to taste, O my Hope! From the crystal springs of Thy love suffer me to quaff, O my Glory, and beneath the shadow of Thine everlasting providence let me abide, O my Light! Within the meadows of Thy nearness, before Thy presence, make me able to roam, O my Beloved, and at the right hand of the throne of Thy mercy, seat me, O my Desire!

"From the fragrant breezes of Thy joy let a breath pass over me, O my Goal, and into the heights of the paradise of Thy reality let me gain admission, O my Adored One! To the melodies of the dove of Thy oneness suffer me to hearken, O Resplendent One, and through the spirit of Thy power and Thy might quicken me, O my Provider!

"In the spirit of Thy love keep me steadfast, O my Succorer, and in the path of Thy good-pleasure set firm my steps, O my Maker! Within the garden of Thine immortality, before

Thy countenance, let me abide for ever, O Thou Who art merciful unto me, and upon the seat of Thy glory stablish me, O Thou Who art my Possessor! To the heaven of Thy lovingkindness lift me up, O my Quickener, and unto the Day-Star of Thy guidance lead me, O Thou my Attractor!

"Before the revelations of Thine invisible spirit summon me to be present, O Thou Who art my Origin and my Highest Wish, and unto the essence of the fragrance of Thy beauty, which Thou wilt manifest, cause me to return, O Thou Who art my God!

"Potent art Thou to do what pleasest Thee. Thou art, verily, the Most Exalted, the All-Glorious, the All-Highest." (Baha'u'llah: *Prayers and Meditations*, Pages: 258-259)

Here is a selection from Baha'u'llah's book *Hidden Words*, speaking about a 'New Garden':

"O YE DWELLERS IN THE HIGHEST PARADISE! Proclaim unto the children of assurance that within the realms of holiness, nigh unto the celestial paradise, a new garden hath appeared, round which circle the denizens of the realm on high and the immortal dwellers of the exalted paradise. Strive, then, that ye may attain that station, that ye may unravel the mysteries of love from its wind-flowers and learn the secret of divine and consummate wisdom from its eternal fruits. Solaced are the eyes of them that enter and abide therein!" (Baha'u'llah: *Hidden Words*, Page: 18)

And here is a prayer of 'Abdu'l-Baha:

"O Thou, my God, Who guidest the seeker to the pathway that leadeth aright, Who deliverest the lost and blinded soul out of the wastes of perdition, Thou Who bestowest upon the sincere great bounties and favours, Who guardest the frightened within Thine impregnable refuge, Who answerest, from Thine all-highest horizon, the cry of those who cry out unto Thee. Praised be Thou, O my Lord!

"Thou hast guided the distracted out of the death of unbelief, and hast brought those who draw nigh unto Thee to the

journey's goal, and hast rejoiced the assured among Thy servants by granting them their most cherished desires, and hast, from Thy Kingdom of beauty, opened before the faces of those who yearn after Thee the gates of reunion, and hast rescued them from the fires of deprivation and loss—so that they hastened unto Thee and gained Thy presence, and arrived at Thy welcoming door, and received of gifts an abundant share.

"O my Lord, they thirsted, Thou didst lift to their parched lips the waters of reunion. O Tender One, Bestowing One, Thou didst calm their pain with the balm of Thy bounty and grace, and didst heal their ailments with the sovereign medicine of Thy compassion. O Lord, make firm their feet on Thy straight path, make wide for them the needle's eye, and cause them, dressed in royal robes, to walk in glory for ever and ever.

"Verily art Thou the Generous, the Ever-Giving, the Precious, the Most Bountiful. There is none other God but Thee, the Mighty, the Powerful, the Exalted, the Victorious. " ('Abdu'l-Baha: *Selections from the Writings of 'Abdu'l-Baha,* Page: 317)

CHAPTER EIGHT

BAHA'U'LLAH'S TEACHINGS: WHAT THEY COULD MEAN FOR CHRISTIANS AND FOR THE WORLD

QUESTION: My first thought about Baha'u'llah's 'teachings' is that Christians don't need any new teachings. If they would only live up to the ones they already have, this world would be a much better place.

RESPONSE: I think you are right, or mostly right. Baha'u'llah Himself said many times that if the teachings of any of the world's great religions were actually followed carefully and well, this world would already have become a 'Paradise.'

The reason I said you were 'mostly right' is that I can think of many of Baha'u'llah's teachings that are not in the Christian revelation. Of the many, here are two: The abolition of human slavery and the equality of men and women.

QUESTION: Are you trying to minimize or put down the Christian religion!? I thought you said that Baha'is would never do such a thing?

RESPONSE: They wouldn't. And I wouldn't. Jesus Himself said: *"I still have many things to say to you, but you cannot bear them now."* (John 16:12-15) You and I know that Jesus Christ would, most certainly, have been against slavery. But the New Testament does not forbid slavery. In fact, St. Paul tells 'bondservants' (read 'slaves'), *"Bondservants, be obedient to those who are your masters"* (Eph 6:5)

Should we wonder why Jesus didn't speak on this? We don't know, but it seems obvious to me that His explanation in John 16:12 is sufficient: *"I still have many things to say to you, but you cannot bear them now."*

Human slavery was so widespread that humanity at that time was simply not ready for a teaching that it must be abolished. The people of Jesus' time would not have been able to conceive of a world without slavery. St. Paul, Christ's chief disciple after the original twelve and His major interpreter, sent a Christian, who was a slave—Onesimus—back to his master. While he told the master to receive him as a 'brother,' he pointedly did not ask the master to free him. (Philemon: 8-14) It is one of the most unfortunate moments in Christian history, that slave masters in the American South constantly used this biblical reference to justify human slavery.

QUESTION: But Christians believe that it is the Spirit of Truth that Christ promised to send that *"will guide you into all truth"* that will allow us to discover needed truths, for example, of the horror of slavery. And slavery was abolished, mainly through Christian pressure.

RESPONSE: Well, again, yes and no. It certainly was abolished in Christian nations first (it still goes on in the Sudan, for example) but not without every Christian denomination in the Southern United States breaking away during the Civil War and supporting slavery. They quoted the Bible passages I just mentioned above (twisting their meaning) to support the idea that slavery was, in fact, divinely ordained! Only the Quakers stood firm on this issue.

Christians often exerted pressure upon rulers for more humane treatment of slaves, although this was sadly lacking in the pre-civil war American South. Largely from Christian influence, Roman rulers passed a law in 337 AD outlawing the murder of slaves, but even then there was no outcry for the abolishment of slavery, for people could not yet, as Christ said, hear this truth. Slavery was still just assumed to be part of the normal landscape and Christian families with any wealth owned slaves, just as they did for 1500 more years.

You mentioned the *"Spirit of Truth"* that Christ promised would appear. It is important for you to know that Baha'u'llah said He was that *"Spirit of Truth."* Let's first consult what Christ said, then Baha'u'llah. First Christ: *"I still have many things to say to you, but you cannot bear them now. However, when He, the Spirit of truth, has come, He will guide you into all truth; for He will not speak on His own authority, but whatever He hears He will speak; and He will tell you things to come. He will glorify Me, for He will take of what is Mine and declare it to you."* (John 16:12-15)

This is what Baha'u'llah said: *"Lo! He Who is the Ruler is come. Step out from behind the veil in the name of thy Lord, He Who layeth low the necks of all men. Proclaim then unto all mankind the glad-tidings of this mighty, this glorious Revelation. Verily, He Who is the Spirit of Truth is come to guide you unto all truth. He speaketh not as prompted by His own self, but as bidden by Him Who is the All-Knowing, the All-Wise.*

"Say, this is the One Who hath glorified the Son [that is, Jesus] *and hath exalted His Cause. Cast away, O peoples of the earth, that which ye have and take fast hold of that which ye are bidden by the All-Powerful, He Who is the Bearer of the Trust of God."* (Baha'u'llah: *Tablets of Baha'u'llah*, Page: 12)

The Baha'i Writings also call unreservedly for recognition of the equality of women and men, and for full 'gender equality' in all areas. Neither Jesus, Muhammad, or Buddha, nor any of the previous Manifestations until Baha'u'llah said much if anything about this now all-important social topic. Does this mean that these earlier religions are deficient? It certainly does not! Does it mean that they are somehow less good? Definitely not! What it means is what Jesus said: That a Manifestation teaches as much as men and women are able to hear when He comes. He gives to the world as much as they can 'bear,' but does not try to teach them what they certainly could not hear, understand or accept.

To mention just one more instance of the 'newness' of Baha'u'llah's teachings, He forbids consumption of alcohol and drugs. Jesus said nothing of this and the only instance of understanding His attitude toward wine is that He turned water into wine at a wedding feast at Cana. It had to have been real wine, because the New Testament records that the guests said something like: "Why did you save the best until last?" Also, St. Paul advises one of his disciples to drink wine for medicinal purposes. But here is the important point: Is one religion better than another because it has a teaching that an earlier one did not have? No, not at all.

That is what Baha'u'llah is trying to get us to understand. When a Manifestation comes at any time in human history, His teachings are *exactly* what are needed for that time and those people. Baha'u'llah reminds us that there is only one God, not many. One and the same God sent each and every one of the Manifestations.

Therefore, none of what we have been talking about means that the Christian Faith is deficient or that Christ would not have been for equality of men and women and against alcohol consumption and slavery. Rather, it means only what Christ said, in effect, I have additional teachings and lessons that I would like to tell you now, but you wouldn't even be able to understand them. But, as you said a moment ago, He then said: *"However, when He, the Spirit of truth, has come, He will guide you into all truth"* (John 16:13)

Who is this *"Spirit of Truth"*? Baha'u'llah said not just once (as in the quote above) but numerous times He was that *"Spirit of Truth"* of which Jesus spoke and promised. Baha'u'llah said very directly that He was the return of the Spirit of Christ and told the people of the world that Christ was now to be seen again *"in my person."* Most important, He said that He was the appearance in history of *"the Father"* of all mankind.

Another quote about the *"Spirit of Truth"* is taken from a letter Baha'u'llah wrote to the Kings of Christian nations: *"O kings of Christendom! Heard ye not the saying of Jesus, the Spirit of God, 'I go away, and come again unto you'? Wherefore, then, did ye fail, when He did come again unto you in the clouds of heaven, to draw nigh unto Him, that ye might behold His face, and be of them that attained His Presence? In another passage He saith: 'When He, the Spirit of Truth, is come, He will guide you into all truth.' And yet, behold how, when He did bring the truth, ye refused to turn your faces towards Him, and persisted in disporting yourselves with your pastimes and fancies."* (Baha'u'llah: *Gleanings*, Page: 246)

Baha'u'llah said that this *"Father,"* this *"Spirit of Truth"* would shower upon all the men and women of the entire earth, the knowledge, the teachings and the spiritual power needed to build a free, united, peaceful world that could appropriately be called 'the Kingdom of God on earth'. Jesus prayed for this in the 'Lord's Prayer' and Baha'is believe that it is to be realized in the period of history in which we are now living.

QUESTION: I'll grant you that there may be new teachings, but a Christian can come to realization of those same teachings through prayer and careful study of the scriptures, if they will just be true to the Spirit of Jesus.

RESPONSE: That's true. But even today Christians don't agree on the equality of men and women, do they?

QUESTION: True Christians do, I believe.

RESPONSE: I'd have to agree with that, but let me ask you whether Christians who believe that men and women are *not* equal would agree that they are not true Christians? We know they would disagree with that, to the extreme. And, the fact remains that during the United States Civil War, almost all Christian Churches and Christians in the Southern United States broke away, using sources in the Bible (incorrectly) to support their belief in slavery, even claiming slavery to be 'God's Will.' Many Christians even today use biblical verses to support paternalism, male superiority and male dominance over women. It might be worth mentioning that many Moslems do the same thing, even today, quoting sacred scriptures from the Qur'an (narrowly and intolerantly) to support the same things.

The point I am making is that Baha'is could not experience this confusion or disunity, simply because Baha'u'llah and His Son 'Abdu'l-Baha spoke out so forcefully, clearly and directly on those issues and many others. No Baha'i group could 'break away,' saying that we don't want to believe in the oneness of humanity, or the need to do away with racial prejudice or gender inequality in our community. I'm not saying that Baha'is are perfect. Indeed, individual Baha'is and Baha'i communities always need to 'grow' in their recognition of the full meaning of their teachings. What I *am* saying is that no Baha'i Community or national Baha'i group could get away with being 'for' gender inequality or racial prejudice or being against interracial marriage.

QUESTION: Well, I can't help wondering why you didn't just learn these teachings and remain within the Christian Faith, remaining true to Christ?

RESPONSE: Maybe the understanding that we need here should come from Jesus. When He was asked why His teachings couldn't just be added to the wonderful Jewish traditions and religion, do you remember what He said? I know you do. He said: *"And no one puts new wine into old wineskins . . . "* (Luke 5:37) That must have been hard for Jewish ears to hear from Jesus, but it was nevertheless true. The same is true today. This 'new wine' cannot really be contained in the 'old wineskins' or bottles of tradition and old institutions.

No less important, I suspect that Peter, Paul, John and others felt that they remained true to their Jewish Faith, even while following Jesus; in that same way, I feel true and real in my commitment to Jesus Christ today, as much so as when I fell on my knees at fifteen to give my life to Him.

QUESTION: I'm ready to hear what Baha'u'llah's other teachings are but you should know that I still believe I have all that I need. But as we said before, it's better to have an open mind and to be willing to investigate. After all, if those around Christ had not had an open mind, they would have missed His Truth and Reality.

RESPONSE: Your statement about an open mind is really important, and I'm glad that you are open to investigation and discussion. Let's actually start with Jesus. As I understand it, His most important teaching was that He had appeared as the Word of God, that He was the one who would be, as He said: *"Sitting at the right hand of Power* [that is, God]. *"* When Jesus said this, He was at His trial for blasphemy and the so-called criminal acts with which He had been charged. However, Jesus knew and we now know that He was possessed of the power of God, that He was God's *"only begotten Son," "the Way, the Truth, and the Life,"* and that *"no man cometh unto the Father but by Me."* Finally, most importantly, Jesus taught that the sacrifice of His life brought salvation to humanity.

Now, and it's not a contrast at all, let's look at Baha'u'llah's most important teaching: It was that He, *"the Father"* had come, that He was the Return of the Spirit of Christ—the actual reappearance of Christ *"in my person"*-that He was the *"Spirit of Truth"* that Christ had said would *"guide you into all truth."*

Baha'u'llah said: *"Thou art He, O my God, Who hath raised me up at Thy behest, and bidden me to occupy Thy seat, and to summon all men to the court of Thy mercy. It is Thou Who hast commanded me to tell out the things Thou didst destine for them in the Tablet of Thy decree and didst inscribe with the pen of Thy Revelation, and Who hast enjoined on me the duty of kindling the fire of Thy love in the hearts of Thy servants, and of drawing all the peoples of the earth nearer to the habitation of Thy throne.*" (Baha'u'llah: *Prayers and Meditations*, Page: 107)

Also, *"Call out to Zion, O Carmel, and announce the joyful tidings: He that was hidden from mortal eyes is come!"* (Baha'u'llah: *Gleanings*, Page: 16) and *"Speed out of your sepulchers. How long will ye sleep? The second blast hath been blown on the trumpet. On whom are ye gazing? This is your Lord, the God of Mercy.*" (Baha'u'llah: *Gleanings*, Page: 44)

He told the people of the world, *"Fix your gaze upon Him Who is the Temple of God amongst men. He, in truth, hath offered up His life as a ransom for the redemption of the world.*" (Baha'u'llah: *Gleanings*, Page: 315)

QUESTION: Really, I have to stop you there. Christ died for our sins and provided, once and for all time, the 'ransom' for the redemption of the world. Christians cannot accept that anything further is needed in terms of redemption.

RESPONSE: I realize that this is the Christian position. What Baha'u'llah asks of us is to continue our 'core belief,' but to widen it, expand it, to see that there is a work of a 'Greater God' in history. He asks us to realize that what Christians believe about Christ's redemptive power is true not only for Christ but that all the other Manifestations have also provided redemption through their sufferings and, in some cases, their deaths.

Whenever God's full presence, His 'Word' appears

in human history, God is acting to 'redeem' us from our worst mistakes and to 'save' us from our folly and our unwillingness to see the truth. Each and every Manifestation, says Baha'u'llah, provides this ransom and redemption and, as well, salvation.

Baha'u'llah referred to Himself as: *"Him Who is the Word of Truth amidst you."* (Baha'u'llah: *Gleanings*, Page: 316) and advised His followers to *"Keep your gaze centred on Him Who is the Sovereign Word of Truth: place your whole reliance upon Him, and beg of Him to destine for you what is meet and fitting."* (Baha'u'llah: *Trustworthiness*, Page: 333)

Finally, echoing Jesus' statement about being seated at *"the right hand of Power* [that is, God]," Baha'u'llah said He came *"from the invisible heaven, bearing the banner 'He doeth whatsoever He willeth' and is accompanied by hosts of power and authority . . . "* (Baha'u'llah: *Tablets of Baha'u'llah*, Page: 108)

And, just as Christ said: *"No man cometh unto the Father but by me"* Baha'u'llah said: *"No man can obtain everlasting life, unless he embraceth the truth of this inestimable, this wondrous, and sublime Revelation."* (Baha'u'llah: Gleanings, Page: 183) and while Christ said: *"If you have seen me you have seen the Father,"* Baha'u'llah said: *"If it be your wish, O people, to know God and to discover the greatness of His might, look, then, upon Me . . . "* (Baha'u'llah: *Gleanings*, Page: 272)

As to salvation and the sacrifice made by all the Manifestations and in this day by Baha'u'llah, He said: *"We, verily, have come for your sakes, and have borne the misfortunes of the world for your salvation. Flee ye the One Who hath sacrificed His life that ye may be quickened? Fear God, O followers of the Spirit (Jesus), and walk not in the footsteps of every divine* [the clergy] *that hath gone far astray . . . Open the doors of your hearts. He Who is the Spirit (Jesus) verily, standeth before them.*" (Baha'u'llah: *Proclamation of Baha'u'llah*, Pages: 91-92)

He also said: *"Blessed the soul that hath been raised to life through My quickening breath and hath gained admittance into My heavenly Kingdom."* (Baha'u'llah: *Tablets of Baha'u'llah*, Page: 16) and in a prayer to God, Baha'u'llah speaks of Himself as *"Him Whom Thou hast sacrificed that all the dwellers of Thine earth and heaven may be born anew, and Whom Thou hast cast into prison that mankind may, as a token of Thy bounty and of Thy sovereign might, be released from the bondage of evil passions and corrupt desires."* (Baha'u'llah: *Prayers and Meditations*, Page: 44)

QUESTION: I can agree that the most important 'teaching' of the Christian Faith is that God revealed Himself and His Will in Jesus Christ and manifested salvation to the world through Jesus' sacrifice on the cross, so I guess I can understand why Baha'is might see Baha'u'llah's coming as the main 'teaching' of their Faith and even why His sufferings and imprisonment are important.

But, exactly what are the specific and main teachings of Baha'u'llah? Can you spell them out to me in some detail?

RESPONSE: The teachings of Baha'u'llah fall into four categories, as I understand them. First, some ideas about God and humanity and the way God reveals His will to humankind and the way He manifests Himself in history. Second, social teachings designed to hasten the building of a new social order that can fittingly be named 'the Kingdom of God on earth' (as envisioned and prayed for by Jesus). Third, laws given by Baha'u'llah, such as those governing marriage, the family, burial, abstinence from alcohol and drugs, and other laws. Fourth, teach-

ings and writings about prayer, meditation, fasting and
spiritual growth.

QUESTION: Tell me first, if you will, of the Baha'i
teachings about God and man and the way God reveals
His will to mankind, although it seems we have just been
talking a lot about this subject in the last two chapters,
haven't we?

RESPONSE: You are right, so just let me summarize those teachings:

1. **There is only one God.** Several generations ago, we
   spoke of 'false gods' when we referred to the religions of other peoples and cultures. We tended to
   think of the God of our religion as 'the True God'
   and the God of, say, the Muslims or Buddhists as a
   'false god.' Some people still think this way but many
   Christians and others realize the truth of Baha'u'llah's
   teaching that there is and has always been only one
   God, the Father of us all.
2. **There is only one humankind.** Beneath all the cultures, religions, 'races', ethnic groups, languages,
   customs, beneath it all, we are one, Baha'u'llah tells
   us. He says it is God's Will that we recognize and
   enact this oneness. Here is perhaps His most famous
   quote: *"The earth is but one country, and mankind its
   citizens."* (Baha'u'llah: *Gleanings*, Page: 250) He also
   said that God's wish, expressed through Him, was to
   behold *"the entire human race as one soul and one body."*
   (Baha'u'llah: *Gleanings*, Page: 214)
3. **This one God has always been lovingly guiding this
   one humanity in this one place, earth, toward an
   eventual time in history when prophecies of peace**

and unity would be fulfilled in a 'golden age' or a 'Kingdom of God' on earth.'

4. **The way God provides this guidance is first and foremost through sending progressive and successive Manifestations of Himself to earth and its people.**

Baha'u'llah said that God *"hath in every age and cycle, in conformity with His transcendent wisdom, sent forth a divine Messenger to revive the dispirited and despondent souls with the living waters of His utterance."* (Baha'u'llah: *Tablets of Baha'u'llah*, Page: 161)

He tells us that God *"hath ordained the knowledge of these sanctified Beings to be identical with the knowledge of His own Self. Whoso recognizeth them hath recognized God. Whoso hearkeneth to their call, hath hearkened to the Voice of God, and whoso testifieth to the truth of their Revelation, hath testified to the truth of God Himself.*

"Whoso turneth away from them, hath turned away from God, and whoso disbelieveth in them, hath disbelieved in God. Every one of them is the Way of God that connecteth this world with the realms above, and the Standard of His Truth unto every one in the kingdoms of earth and heaven. They are the Manifestations of God amidst men, the evidences of His Truth, and the signs of His glory." (Baha'u'llah: *Gleanings*, Page: 50)

After ages of promise and prophecy, Baha'u'llah reveals that God Himself stepped forth into history: *"He that was hidden from mortal eyes is come! His all-conquering sovereignty is manifest; His all-encompassing splendor is revealed."* (Baha'u'llah: *Gleanings*, Page: 16) and *"He Who, from everlasting, had concealed His Face from the sight of creation is now come."* (Baha'u'llah: *Gleanings*, Page: 31)

QUESTION: I'm still frankly confused. You told me earlier that Baha'u'llah did not claim to be God, but here it seems pretty clear that He did make that claim. It seems contradictory!

RESPONSE: Well, I don't want to repeat everything we discussed in chapters four through seven, so you may want to review them, but both Jesus and Baha'u'llah made what seem to be, *at first*, contradictory statements. They both spoke of being 'one' with God, but both also vehemently denied being God. We know now that these statements aren't contradictory at all, but simply are statements that speak of the full presence of the 'Word of God' that is within them, as well as the fact that they appear in a human form, as Baha'u'llah says, *"the human temple."*

The Manifestations are human beings, 'fully man,' as Christian doctrine says, but they also represent God to man in such a full way that to look at them is to see God, to hear them is to hearken to God, to obey them is to obey God. There is a passage just a page or two above that you may want to reread, that speaks to this, which brings us to the fifth, all important aspect of Baha'u'llah's teachings.

5. Baha'u'llah represented the fulfillment of mankind's age-long hopes, dreams and prophecies.

Baha'u'llah announced that He was:

First: The Return of Christ and the One Whom Christ called the *"Spirit of Truth."*

Second: The spiritual 'Return' of all of the figures awaited by all the world's religions and cultures. Thus, He is the 'Promise of all Ages.'

Third: The appearance of *"The Father"* of all mankind, come at long last after centuries of hope and expectation. He was, He said, the One Who would empower individual men and women and youth of all humanity to begin to build, finally, a united, peaceful world in which the long-awaited 'Kingdom of God' would be increasingly recognized.

Thus, to summarize: One world, one humanity, and one God, guiding humanity toward an era of fulfillment, by Manifesting Himself to different peoples, in different times and places, then finally stepping forth Himself from behind *"veils"* that had hidden Him. Now, He appears in such a way, as Baha'u'llah put it, that mankind cannot mistake His coming.

"Verily I say, this is the Day in which mankind can behold the Face, and hear the Voice, of the Promised One. The Call of God hath been raised, and the light of His countenance hath been lifted up upon men. It behoveth every man to blot out the trace of every idle word from the tablet of his heart, and to gaze, with an open and unbiased mind, on the signs of His Revelation, the proofs of His Mission, and the tokens of His glory. (Baha'u'llah: *Gleanings*, Pages: 10-11)

And one more important point, especially important to me and to other Baha'is from a Christian background, we have found and experienced that if one becomes a Baha'i, that is, a follower of Baha'u'llah, one renews and deepens faith in Christ.

This renewal and 'deepening' occurs when the new believer in Baha'u'llah acknowledges not only Faith in Baha'u'llah, but also faith in God's other Manifestations of Himself, namely, Moses, Buddha, Zoroaster, Krishna and Baha'u'llah and others. He now sees what he understands as the Spirit of Christ, the pre-existent Word of God at work in all the Manifestations. By this acknowledgment and declaration of faith, the new Baha'i becomes a 'citizen of the world' and all of human history now belongs to him. All people are 'his people.' The word 'foreign' can no longer be used by him in a spiritual way. He now fully understands the truth of Baha'u'llah's words: *"It is not for him to pride himself who loveth his own country, but rather for him who loveth the whole world. The earth is but one country, and mankind its citizens."* (Baha'u'llah: *Gleanings*, Page: 250)

QUESTION: I'm not sure I understand at all what you mean by 'all history now belongs to him'. Doesn't history belong to everyone anyway? What do you mean?

RESPONSE: Well, I may be guilty of some exuberance, but a person who becomes a Baha'i has a 'rush' of realization that all of the religions, the cultures, the ethnic groups of all history are now seen to be a parts of a larger pattern, formed and fashioned by God, with the pattern finally 'making sense' in the coming of Baha'u'llah and in His teachings. In this way, all of history *does* belong to this new Baha'i. If you would ask any Baha'i in the world (no matter what background they come from, Hindu, Jewish or Buddhist, for example), they would say that Christ is central to their Baha'i belief in a way that any Christian would respect and admire.

He sees that all people are his people, that the religions are, in their essence, one. God's purpose is seen in that He has 'progressively' revealed His Will in many places, many times, laying down many prophetic hopes and dreams. Now, this Baha'i feels that he is a 'witness' to a new day in which God has *"stepped forth"* into the world with a fresh revelation designed to gather all humankind into the fulfillment of those dreams and the realization of the many prophecies of peace, oneness and unity.

QUESTION: You sound as if you are saying that all people are alike and that all the religions are the same?

RESPONSE: No, not at all, although when people hear the Baha'i message for the first time, that often seems to be what they hear. However, it is subtle and more meaningful than that. The religions are different, in some ways very different, on the surface and especially in terms of social teachings, given by God for the day in which that Manifestation of God appeared.

When God appeared in the persons of Jesus or Muhammad or Buddha, the needs of the people were different and the social teachings were therefore special and distinct, targeted to the needs of that day. A famous example would be Moses telling the Israelites not to eat pork, which would be dangerous for a desert-living, nomadic people, but not problematic at all in an age of refrigeration.

But, as we have discussed before, if you go below the surface, to the deeper 'core' of any religion, you find great similarity and a zone of true 'oneness.' Not 'sameness' but 'oneness.' The reason you find this oneness is that the next finding you make, at the deepest level of all religions is, not surprisingly, God Himself, Who has been the mover and initiator of all the religions, as Baha'u'llah taught.

The religions are different, very different on the surface. Deeper down, similar. At the deepest level, they are 'one.'

Baha'is believe God was the motive force and initiator of all the religions by sending into history many Manifestations of His *"own Being."* Baha'u'llah spoke of Himself as *"Him Whom Thou hast appointed as the Manifestation of Thine own Being and Thy discriminating Word unto all that are in heaven and on earth, to gather together Thy servants beneath the shade of the Tree of Thy gracious providence."* (Baha'u'llah: *Prayers and Meditations*, Page: 26)

We can realize, first, that the Manifestations, all of them, are not only 'fully man' in the sense of appearing in *"the human Temple"*, but also are God in the sense of the *"Presence"* of God that is within them. Then it becomes easier to understand the following statement of Baha'u'llah about the Manifestations (such as Muhammad, Buddha, Jesus, and others):

"It is clear and evident to thee that all the Prophets are the Temples of the Cause of God, Who have appeared clothed in divers attire. If thou wilt observe with discriminating eyes, thou wilt behold Them all abiding in the same tabernacle, soaring in the same heaven, seated upon the same throne, uttering the same speech, and proclaiming the same Faith." (Baha'u'llah: Gleanings, Page: 52) and *"they are all but one person, one soul, one spirit, one being, one revelation."* (Baha'u'llah: *Gleanings*, Page: 54)

Baha'i House of Worship in Sydney, Australia.

QUESTION: What about the 'social teachings' you said each Manifestation gives? What social teachings did Baha'u'llah give?

RESPONSE: We always have to remember that Baha'u'llah, like Christ, said that He said nothing and did nothing but that which God asked Him to convey to humankind. *"I can utter no word, O my God, unless I be permitted by Thee, and can move in no direction until I obtain Thy sanction. It is Thou, O my God, Who hast called me into being through the power of Thy might, and hast endued me with Thy grace to manifest Thy Cause."* (Baha'u'llah: *Prayers and Meditations*, Page: 208)

With the spiritual confidence that could only come from the realization that God was speaking through Him, He said: *"Neither the hosts of the earth nor those of heaven can keep me back from revealing the things I am commanded to manifest. I have no will before Thy will, and can cherish no desire in the face of Thy desire."* (Baha'u'llah: *Prayers and Meditations*, Page: 184)

We have already mentioned several of those social teachings, but before we list the others, let us realize that the social teachings of Baha'u'llah flow out of the spiritual teachings listed just above, which focus on God's work in history, so let us review:

Baha'u'llah teaches that there is only one God, not many Gods, and that all the religions were initiated by this one God, who 'sent' a Messenger or Manifestation of Himself (in the case of the Christian Faith, that Manifestation was His own *'Son'*). Each of these Manifestations gave teachings, started a religion and empowered individuals and communities to live salvation-changed, renewed lives, thus transforming the earth.

That God has been progressively revealing Himself to man, preparing man for 'the Promised Day' of 'Resurrection' when all humanity would be brought into peace and unity; that Baha'u'llah finally appeared on earth, as a Manifestation of God's *"own Self"* (Baha'u'llah, *Gleanings*, Page 102), as *"the Father"* of all mankind to fulfill past prophecies of all religions and to establish and build the 'Kingdom of God' that would express His Will *"on earth as it is in heaven."*

Based upon these spiritual concepts, the following social teachings are those revealed by Baha'u'llah:

1. Mankind is one.

Properly speaking, there is only one race, the human race. Science agrees with Baha'u'llah's teaching that although there certainly are different ethnic groups, cultures, religions, customs, nevertheless, there is only one race on this earth. Speaking of all humanity, Baha'u'llah says: *"Ye are all the leaves of one tree and the drops of one ocean."* (Baha'u'llah: *Tablets of Baha'u'llah*, Page: 129)

Also: *"Ye are the fruits of one tree, and the leaves of one branch. Deal ye one with another with the utmost love and harmony, with friendliness and fellowship. He Who is the Day-Star of Truth beareth Me witness! So powerful is the light of unity that it can illuminate the whole earth."* (Baha'u'llah: *Epistle to the Son of the Wolf*, Page: 14)

2. All prejudice toward people of other 'races', ethnic groups or cultures must cease.

The virus of prejudice is beginning to cease within Baha'i communities across the planet, as Baha'is are striving in many practical ways to raise 'prejudice-free children.' We realize and welcome the efforts of Christians, Moslems, Jews and others who are working toward the same goal. Baha'u'llah said He gave God's Will for today to mankind and stated God's major wish: *"He Who is*

your Lord, the All-Merciful, cherisheth in His heart the desire
of beholding the entire human race as one soul and one body."
(Baha'u'llah: *Gleanings*, Page: 214)

However (and this is important) diversity of cultures and customs is appreciated. An interesting footnote to this worldwide plan to wipe out prejudice in Baha'i communities is that, in elections, if there is a tie between two individuals and one is of a minority, the elected post is automatically awarded to the minority person.

Baha'is are seeing success within their communities in this campaign to carry out God's Will for today and they are doing it in such a way as to preserve diversity. Baha'is often say: Unity, but with diversity. No one wants enforced, false unity that covers up the beautiful shades of color and the different customs and ways of the many people of earth.

3. There must be equality between men and women.

This must happen in our thinking and in our practice. It must be in our methods of childrearing and in our schools, in business and government. It must begin to permeate all that we do. Baha'u'llah revealed: *"Women and men have been and will always be equal in the sight of God. The Dawning-Place of the Light of God sheddeth its radiance upon all with the same effulgence. Verily God created women for men, and men for women."* (Baha'u'llah: *Women*, p. 379) It is fascinating to see in the words of Baha'u'llah that God did not create one gender for the benefit of the other; rather, both man and woman were created for each other.

Baha'u'llah's Son, 'Abdu'l-Baha said: *"For the world of humanity possesses two wings: man and woman. If one wing remains incapable and defective, it will restrict the power of the other, and full flight will be impossible. Therefore, the*

completeness and perfection of the human world are depen-
dent upon the equal development of these two wings. " ('Abdu'l-
Baha: *Promulgation of Universal Peace,* Page: 318)

A fascinating exception to this is stated explicitly:
Baha'u'llah said that if a family has limited income and
only one child at a time can be funded for education,
the preference must go to the female child to be educated first. He explained that this is because of the
woman's all-important role as the first educator of children. But aside from this exception, Baha'is are again
seeing success worldwide in making discoveries about
what the equality of women and men can and should
mean. They are acting this out in a 'practical' way in
their communities.

4. Extremes of poverty and riches should end.

Toward that goal, the teachings of Baha'u'llah fore-
shadowed by a century the concepts of Social Security,
progressive taxation, and profit sharing, among others.
The saying of Christ that *"the poor you have with you al-*
ways" (John 12:8) must not be misused to justify 'extreme'
poverty nor to permit unlimited acquisition of wealth,
Baha'u'llah tells us.

He explains that there will always be those who have
less and those who have more, based on effort and am-
bition, but that extremes on both ends must be elimi-
nated. Many of His teachings work in the direction of
blunting both extremes of the very poor and the very
rich. The *"Houses of Justice"* to be elected in every country by Baha'is have been given the task, among many
others, of insuring the well being of those less fortunate.
However, Baha'u'llah teaches that every person should
engage in some form of work or trade and that begging
or idleness are not to be allowed.

5. Recognizing our oneness and achieving the unity of mankind is the highest, brightest goal for the peoples of the world

Baha'u'llah taught that this unification of the human race is the Will of God for today and that it will definitely come to pass in this new era.

6. Unity or oneness must be established in such a way as to respect differences and diversity.

In fact, the unity we seek must even 'celebrate' this diversity and the 'specialness' of various peoples and cultures. Dr. Carl Lee, a Baha'i friend, feels that we must, in fact, go beyond 'celebration' of diversity. He points out that the Baha'i Universal House of Justice in its statement on 'The Prosperity of Humankind' enjoins us to recognize that diversity has an absolutely critical role in providing the 'social genetic diversity' that is needed for the survival and flourishing of mankind.

Baha'is speak of 'unity with diversity' to remind ourselves that no one would want to have or to accept a sterile 'unity' in which our wonderful differences, our beautiful and stunning diversity would be lost or swallowed up in some shallow, half-baked concept of 'oneness.'

'Abdu'l-Baha said: *"Let us look rather at the beauty in diversity, the beauty of harmony, and learn a lesson from the vegetable creation. If you beheld a garden in which all the plants were the same as to form, colour and perfume, it would not seem beautiful to you at all, but, rather, monotonous and dull. The garden which is pleasing to the eye and which makes the heart glad, is the garden in which are growing side by side flowers of every hue, form and perfume, and the joyous contrast of colour is what makes for charm and beauty."* ('Abdu'l-Baha: *Paris Talks,* Pages: 52-53)

7. The people of the world should adopt a universal language.

To insure our diversity, every child on the planet should learn two languages, the language of her or his own culture and people and the universal language. This universal language would be chosen by the people of the world, meeting in a gathering, perhaps at the United Nations, or some other world forum. Baha'u'llah advised the Kings and rulers of the world, as well as the people of the world, *"to adopt one of the existing languages or a new one to be taught to children in schools throughout the world, and likewise one script. Thus the whole earth will come to be regarded as one country."* (Baha'u'llah: *Tablets of Baha'u'llah*, Page: 22)

In another place, Baha'u'llah said: *"The day is approaching when all the peoples of the world will have adopted one universal language and one common script. When this is achieved, to whatsoever city a man may journey, it shall be as if he were entering his own home."* (Baha'u'llah: *Gleanings*, Pages: 249-250)

8. The peoples of the world and their governments should meet together to vote upon and freely choose a united form of planetary government.

This should not be something forced upon them, or foisted upon them, but something they would freely choose. Baha'is around the world are themselves ready for this, to a person, and are spreading the idea of world unity.

From the Revelation of Baha'u'llah: *"The Great Being,* [that is, God] *wishing to reveal the prerequisites of the peace and tranquillity of the world and the advancement of its peoples, hath written: The time must come when the imperative necessity for the holding of a vast, an all-embracing assemblage of men will be universally realized. The rulers and kings of the earth must needs attend it, and, participating in its deliberations, must consider such ways and means as will lay the foundations of the world's Great Peace amongst men. Such a peace demandeth that the Great Powers should resolve, for the sake of the tranquillity of the peoples of the earth, to be fully reconciled among themselves.*

"Should any king take up arms against another, all should unitedly arise and prevent him. If this be done, the nations of the world will no longer require any armaments, except for the purpose of preserving the security of their realms and of maintaining internal order within their territories. This will ensure the peace and composure of every people, government and nation." (Baha'u'llah: *Gleanings*, Page: 249) Note: This teaching about unity and no longer needing armaments is paramount in importance. Why? Because the trillions of dollars that are poured into armaments each decade are more than enough to materially transform the planet, bringing greater access to food, shelter, health and education to every man, woman and child on earth. A world without these armaments expenditures would be a world greatly changed in two to three generations.

9. Science and religion must agree.

In much of the Nineteenth century and nearly all of the Twentieth, religion and science have tended to disagree or even be enemies. A well-known book was written in the early years of the Twentieth Century speaking of the 'warfare' between science and religion. Baha'u'llah said we must strive to realize that faith and reason can, should and must live together in our minds. Faith is not 'turning off' reason, and reason is not the shunning of Faith. Our minds are such that we can accommodate and integrate both of these great human faculties. Doing so will lead to great progress as we enter the Twenty-First century.

This is what Baha'u'llah's Son, 'Abdu'l-Baha said: *"Religion and science are the two wings upon which man's intelligence can soar into the heights, with which the human soul can progress. It is not possible to fly with one wing alone! Should a man try to fly with the wing of religion alone, he would quickly fall into the quagmire of superstition, whilst on the other hand, with the wing of science alone, he would also make no progress, but fall into the despairing slough of materialism."*

'Abdu'l-Baha also says in that same passage that in many ways the teachings of the world's religions *"have fallen . . . out of harmony with the true principles of the teaching they represent and with the scientific discoveries of the time."* ('Abdu'l-Baha: *Paris Talks.* Page 43)

10. Universal education for every child on the planet.

Today, in lesser-developed countries, only about one third of the children receive anything approaching basic education. When you consider female children in the poorest of the developing countries, nearly sixty per-cent have inadequate or no education. Baha'u'llah says that unity and peace cannot possibly occur until and unless we change the education level of females and also guarantee a basic education to every child on the planet. Baha'i communities, wherever they are, are moving in this direction, teaching that all children must be educated and emphasizing the education of female children, which is often not carried out adequately in many developing countries. Indeed, it was not done to an appropriate extent in the culture of the United States just two or three generations ago!

11. Every man woman and child on this planet must utilize their minds in what Baha'u'llah called 'Independent Investigation' to seek out the truth for their lives.

This is last in the list, but certainly not least, and it should be first in one sense, as Baha'u'llah talked of it so often and also because it is so crucial to the way in which we collect, receive, and use information. It is Baha'u'llah's teaching, His injunction, that we must honor teachers, priests, ministers, parents, but not let them or anyone in authority interfere with our right and obligation to find out for ourselves the truth of any matter.

We can and should get advice, opinion, guidance, especially from parents and teachers, but in the end, Baha'u'llah says, it is up to us to decide the truth for ourselves and to make decisions from within, rather than on the basis of some form of external coercion. This is a quote from Baha'u'llah's Son, 'Abdu'l-Baha on this subject:

"Furthermore, know ye that God has created in man the power of reason, whereby man is enabled to investigate reality. God has not intended man to imitate blindly his fathers and ancestors. He has endowed him with mind, or the faculty of reasoning, by the exercise of which he is to investigate and discover the truth, and that which he finds real and true he must accept. He must not be an imitator or blind follower of any soul. He must not rely implicitly upon the opinion of any man without investigation; nay, each soul must seek intelligently and independently, arriving at a real conclusion and bound only by that reality." ('Abdu'l-Baha. *Promulgation of Universal Peace*, Page 291)

There are other social teachings, but this is a good sampling and, as you can see, all of Baha'u'llah's teachings—Baha'is believe them to be the Will of God—center around the idea of the oneness of mankind and flow out of the idea that God has again Manifested Himself in the Person of Baha'u'llah, appearing in our current time as *"The Father"* of all mankind, to draw us together into a unity and oneness that has been the dream of prophet and poet alike.

QUESTION: You said there were also 'laws' that Baha'u'llah gave? I guess you realize as we talked once before that Christianity is not a religion of laws. I do remember that you pointed out that Jesus did give several laws, including one regarding divorce and, of course, He gave the Great Commandment and a commandment is a law. And, now that we have had that discussion, I do remember that Jesus said: *"If you love Me, keep My commandments."* (John 14:15) But for the most part, the Christian Faith does not have many laws. What are the laws of Baha'u'llah?

RESPONSE: Yes, Baha'u'llah actually gave a complete code of laws, but said this about these laws: *"Think not that We have revealed unto you a mere code of laws. Nay, rather, We have unsealed the choice Wine with the fingers of might and power."* (Baha'u'llah: *Gleanings,* Page: 332) He also said: *"O ye peoples of the world! Know assuredly that My commandments are the lamps of My loving providence among My servants, and the keys of My mercy for My creatures."* (Baha'u'llah: *Gleanings,* Page 331)

Among these laws are laws governing marriage, inheritance, abstinence from alcohol and drugs, means of burial and numerous others that you can learn about as you begin to study the Baha'i Faith and the Revelation that is seen and witnessed in the life and writings of Baha'u'llah. Just as Christians do not see the Great Commandment of Jesus as coming from a human person, but from God, likewise, Baha'is see these laws as coming from God and constituting God's plan not only for individuals but for newly transformed human communities as well as the regeneration and revitalization of the entire planet.

QUESTION: That's just my problem! You speak of 'the writings' of Baha'u'llah as if they were God speaking. I don't understand that and I certainly find it hard to accept.

RESPONSE: We've spoken about this before, but in the time of Jesus, it must have been difficult, even for the disciples, to realize that when Jesus spoke, they were, in effect, listening to God. Later, after one of them made the discovery that all but Judas would acknowledge, that Jesus was the 'Son of God,' all of them realized that they were hearing the Will of God spoken to them through Jesus.

Likewise, there will be an evolution here for the people of the world, person by person, to realize first that the ideas being set forth by Baha'u'llah are, in fact, the very concepts needed to bring the world into unity. Then, as they—and you—begin the task to decide Who Baha'u'llah is, they will slowly, I believe surely, begin to realize that when Baha'u'llah speaks, one is hearing, as He said: *"The Voice of God."* It still comes back to that question, doesn't it? Who is Baha'u'llah? Madman, charlatan, or, just perhaps–He is Who He said He Is, the Return of Christ and the *'Father'* of all mankind.

In this regard, remember that earlier quote from Jesus where He says that He only taught what the Father had given to Him. He had innate divine knowledge. It is the same with Baha'u'llah, Who often spoke of Himself as a *'Pen'* in the Hand of God, so as to say that it was God Who was doing the writing while He was no more than the *'Pen'* of God. *"Thus biddeth you the Lord of creation, the movement of Whose Pen hath revolutionized the soul of mankind. Know ye from what heights your Lord, the All-Glorious is calling?"* (Baha'u'llah: *Gleanings*, Page: 139) We have no knowledge of Jesus having ever attended school. In the case of Baha'u'llah, we know most certainly that He did not attend school, at any age, as a child or as an adult.

QUESTION: Let me think about that one. I need to understand what Baha'u'llah is saying on several levels. It will take me some time. Meanwhile, what about the final category of teachings you spoke of? Teachings about prayer and meditation and fasting? I guess you know that not all Christians fast?

RESPONSE: Many Protestant Churches do not emphasize fasting, but some do. Most Catholics and Eastern Orthodox Christians fast, as you know. Some Protestants fast. Some Evangelicals and others. As far as I can figure it out, the only reason many Protestants don't fast is that early Protestants were simply trying to distinguish themselves from Catholics in their de-emphasis of fasting.

In my Methodist upbringing, fasting was almost never mentioned. I learned later that many other denominations and branches of Christianity *do* fast. In the case of the Baha'i Faith, fasting is practiced and required by Baha'u'llah as part of the code of laws He gave to the world.

All Baha'is who are not too young, too old or too ill or who must work in extremely demanding physical occupations, fast every year just prior to the Baha'i New Year, which falls on the first day of Spring, March 21. During the period of fasting, which lasts 19 days, Baha'is fast between sunrise and sunset each day. This means, of course, that they can take food and water before sunrise and after sunset. This fasting period serves the same purpose that it serves in Christianity, Islam, or Judaism, namely, for spiritual deepening and renewal. It may also have a beneficial physical effect as well, but is mainly for growth of the spirit.

Finally, this is how Jesus instructed His disciples to fast: *"But you, when you fast, anoint your head and wash your face, so that you do not appear to men to be fasting, but to your Father who is in the secret place; and your Father who sees in secret will reward you openly."* (Matt 6:17-19)

Baha'u'llah also spoke many times about prayer, the need to pray, and the rewards of prayer and how necessary prayer is to our spiritual growth. I hope you have been enjoying the prayers of Baha'u'llah and His Son, 'Abdu'l-Baha, that I have placed at the end of each chapter. The ones at the end of this chapter will be two prayers about the nature of prayer.

Baha'u'llah did give a commandment to His followers that they pray at least once each day and revealed special prayers for this purpose. All Baha'is are obliged to pray one of these several prayers each day and are strongly encouraged to develop a life of devotion, meditation and prayer as part of their spiritual discipline and life plan.

QUESTION: Any other teachings of Baha'u'llah?

RESPONSE: Do you remember me telling you that there are many thousands of documents, notes, letters, epistles, and books from the *'Pen'* of Baha'u'llah? I could not begin to give you the wealth of what Baha'u'llah called *"the ocean of my words."* I believe I have hit only the 'high spots' of Baha'u'llah's teachings. For the rest, you have a glorious opportunity to investigate and to discover for yourself.

I remember how beautiful the moment was in my life when I first found Christ for myself and accepted Him into my life. And I can remember very well, too, when I realized that, for me, Baha'u'llah was the Return of my Jesus. To quote a hymn of my youth: 'How precious did that Grace appear, when first I did believe.'

A new, never before seen English translation of Baha'u'llah's letters will be published early in the Twenty-First Century. Baha'is are very eager to see this, as you can imagine.

I believe there are very many other teachings, mostly of a spiritual nature, *"pearls"* as Baha'u'llah called them, from that *"ocean."* You can discover these 'pearls' for yourself and if it happens as it happened with me, it will be the discovery of your lifetime and a surprise beyond description.

Here is a summary of the teachings of Baha'u'llah, which I have offered to you for your thought, reflection, prayer and study:

1. The teachings about His own coming as the Return of Jesus Christ and also as *"The Father"* of all mankind and the 'Promise of All Ages.'
2. Teachings about the Oneness of God and the Oneness of the Manifestations of God.
3. Teachings about 'progressive revelation' and the way in which God 'manifests His own Being' into history.
4. Teachings about the oneness of humankind.
5. Teachings about social issues, such as elimination of prejudices, equality of men and women, the agreement of science and religion; economic justice, and many others.
6. Teachings about personal life areas, such as marriage,

burial, inheritance, abstinence from alcohol and drugs, and others.
7. Teachings about prayer, fasting, meditation, and the spiritual life.

Let's go on to the next chapter where we will discuss the 'similarities' and 'differences' between the Christian and Baha'i Faiths. You are in for something interesting here, I believe, especially if you feel that the Baha'i Faith is going to be seen as 'very different.'

But let me end, as we always do, with several prayers. Both these prayers, as you will see, are about 'prayer.' I hope you find them as moving and interesting as I did when I first heard them.

"Intone, O My servant, the verses of God that have been received by thee, as intoned by them who have drawn nigh unto Him, that the sweetness of thy melody may kindle thine own soul, and attract the hearts of all men. Whoso reciteth, in the privacy of his chamber, the verses revealed by God, the scattering angels of the Almighty shall scatter abroad the fragrance of the words uttered by his mouth, and shall cause the heart of every righteous man to throb.

"Though he may, at first, remain unaware of its effect, yet the virtue of the grace vouchsafed unto him must needs sooner or later exercise its influence upon his soul. Thus have the mysteries of the Revelation of God been decreed by virtue of the Will of Him Who is the Source of power and wisdom."
(Baha'u'llah: *Gleanings*, Page: 295)

And another prayer, about the subject of prayer, but from 'Abdu'l-Baha, the Son of Baha'u'llah:

"Make firm our steps, O Lord, in Thy path and strengthen Thou our hearts in Thine obedience. Turn our faces toward the beauty of Thy oneness, and gladden our bosoms with the signs of Thy divine unity. Adorn our bodies with the robe of Thy bounty, and remove from our eyes the veil of sinfulness,

and give us the chalice of Thy grace; that the essence of all beings may sing Thy praise before the vision of Thy grandeur.

"Reveal then Thyself, O Lord, by Thy merciful utterance and the mystery of Thy divine being, that the holy ecstasy of prayer may fill our souls—a prayer that shall rise above words and letters and transcend the murmur of syllables and sounds—that all things may be merged into nothingness before the revelation of Thy splendor.

"Lord! These are servants that have remained fast and firm in Thy Covenant and Thy Testament, that have held fast unto the cord of constancy in Thy Cause and clung unto the hem of the robe of Thy grandeur. Assist them, O Lord, with Thy grace, confirm with Thy power and strengthen their loins in obedience to Thee.

"Thou art the Pardoner, the Gracious." ('Abdu'l-Baha: *Baha'i Prayers* (US edition), Pages: 70-71)

CHAPTER NINE

SIMILARITIES AND DIFFERENCES
OF THE CHRISTIAN AND BAHA'I FAITHS

QUESTION: Sometimes when you are helping me to understand about Baha'u'llah and the Baha'i Faith, I think the two Faiths are very different. At other times, they seem quite similar. I'm not sure why that is so.

RESPONSE: Many people say the same thing. Others say: "I've always believed somewhat as you Baha'is believe." My belief and my personal experience is that a dedicated Christian can rather easily and quickly find a 'spiritual home' in the Baha'i Faith.

Once a Christian takes Baha'u'llah seriously, studies His claims, His teachings, His Person and, in particular, when they study His words, His Revelation, they find that Baha'u'llah is making a serious statement when He says that Christ has *"once more, in My person, been made mani-*

fest unto you. " (Baha'u'llah: *Gleanings,* Page: 101) At that point, coming to believe in Baha'u'llah is not so much a transformation as a kind of maturation, a metamorphosis into a fuller understanding of God's Plan for humanity and one's part in that Plan. When Peter suddenly realized, in a burst of spiritual insight Who Christ was, he was immediately transformed from a simple, uneducated blue-collar worker into a spiritual giant.

Just as Christians would say that a Jew, like St. Peter, could normally and naturally mature into a Christian in Christ's day or any time since, likewise, a Christian can naturally 'mature' into a Baha'i. Baha'u'llah once said: *"Thou art but one step away from the glorious heights above and from the celestial tree of love. Take thou one pace and with the next advance into the immortal realm and enter the pavilion of eternity. Give ear then to that which hath been revealed by the pen of glory."* (Baha'u'llah: *Hidden Words,* Page: 7)

QUESTION: Tell me about the similarities first. There seem to be many similarities and yet you say that the Baha'i Faith isn't a Christian denomination but a separate world religion.

RESPONSE: It probably sounds paradoxical, although I think it will make more sense as we go along, but the Baha'i Faith is a separate world religion; nevertheless, one with a very vibrant, central belief in Jesus as the *'Son of God.'*

When a Christian first looks at the Baha'i Faith, he or she finds many similarities. Here are only some of them: (1) Belief in one God; (2) Belief in Jesus as the 'Son of God'; (3) Belief in the Bible as the Word of God; (4) Belief in Heaven, Hell, and an afterlife; (5) Belief in a similar and nearly identical moral code (which all the religions believe in. You don't find a major religion which says steal, lie, murder, and commit adultery, do you?); (6) Belief in a social structure based on home, family, marriage; There are *many* other similarities, but these will do for a start.

QUESTION: Belief in God is held by most of the people of the world. I will admit that a century ago, many Christians thought other people believed in 'false' Gods, but in recent times, I and other thoughtful Christians understand that God as understood and believed in by other religions is the same God as the one we know in the Old and New Testaments. But, Christians would remind you quickly that there is also only one Jesus Christ, Alpha and Omega. That means 'first and last,' as you have always known.

RESPONSE: There can only be one Christ, only one 'Only Begotten' *'Son,'* just as there can be only one *'Father.'* But as to your other subject of 'One God': Yes, the God worshipped all over the world is the very same God, not a different or a false God. The God of Abraham, who is holy to Jews, is the same God worshipped by people of the Christian Faith and, in turn, the same God, not a different God, worshipped by followers of the Muslim Faith. Likewise, the God of Native Americans, Buddhists, Hindus, Zoroastrians and others is the one God that is called by many different names and, to be sure, understood in slightly different ways by different peoples.

But, there is more unity than diversity in this area of belief in God. In particular, believers who are Jews, Christians, Baha'is and Moslems are all spiritually descended from Abraham, whose *three* wives bore children from whom Christ, Muhammad and Baha'u'llah were literally, genetically descended. The entire Arabian peoples, from the midst of whom came Muhammad, also are descended from Abraham.

QUESTION: You say Abraham had three wives. I'm sure you are mistaken. He had only two that I remember.

RESPONSE: You are in for a little shock here, as was I when Baha'is first pointed out to me the third wife in the Bible. Her name is Keturah. The first wife, Sarah, was the ancestor of Jesus.

The New Testament says Jesus is descended from Abraham, through Sarah. The second wife, Hagar, who actually had Abraham's first child, Ishmael, is the ancestor of Muhammad and the Arab peoples. The third wife is the direct ancestor of Baha'u'llah. Look it up to check me out. I wish you would! Keturah is mentioned in Gen. 25:1.

Thus, Abraham is the great ancestor, along with His three wives, of Jesus, Muhammad, and Baha'u'llah. It looks as if God's promise to Abraham that His descendants would be *'multiplied'* greatly and that *'in Thee shall all families of earth be blessed'* (Gen. 12:3) was a true promise, literally as well as physically.

QUESTION: Even though I said what I did about Christian belief changing somewhat and even though Christians have always believed there is only one God, many Christians still do think that the believers of those other religions are worshipping false Gods.

RESPONSE: Yes, that's true. But, that could hardly be true of the Jews, could it? Jesus was a Jew, born to a Jewish mother and father and was a typical Jew in His boyhood and most of His adulthood. He was thirty years old before beginning His mission. In fact, He continued to be a practicing Jew throughout His Ministry.

Even in the several days before His death, He celebrated a major Jewish Festival—Passover. Of course, Christians call this the Last Supper, but it clearly was a Passover celebration that Jesus charged with new, expanded meaning. Jesus is often called 'Rabbi' in the New Testament, which is how people saw Him—as a religious teacher—not yet realizing His true and full reality as the *'Son of God.'*

If you read the Qur'an, the Holy Book of Islam, you quickly see that the God the Qur'an speaks of is the God of Abraham, Moses and Christ (Yes, Christ is frequently spoken of as the 'Spirit of God' and as 'The Son' in the Qur'an).

QUESTION: You are trying to tell me that all mankind worships the same God? In a way, that seems preposterous!

RESPONSE: Not everyone. Devil worshipers aren't worshipping the same God and not every little cult in the world is worshipping the same God. But, I am talking about the world's great, high religions. The God they all worship is one God, not many Gods. Jews, Christians and Moslems and Baha'is, to make it short, are all worshipping the same God. They even have that interesting connection to each other through Abraham.

Buddhists, Hindus, Zoroastrians and many others, together with Christians and Baha'is, Jews and Moslems all worship the same God, not different Gods. This is a new idea that is growing all over the earth and people will very soon realize that this idea has been a central teaching of Baha'u'llah for more than a century, dating back to the 1860's. They will begin to see that it is the power resident in His coming, His Person, His teachings, and the community that bears His name, which is bringing this reality into a global awareness. Why a global reality? Because there are Baha'is all over the earth and they are all working to spread this teaching of unity, in this case the unity of God.

So, yes, people all over the world worship the same God; it's just that they don't know it yet. This concept, this idea of the 'oneness of God' is a central Baha'i teaching and Baha'u'llah tells us that the women and men of earth will finally recognize that they have a common Father. When they realize that this common Father sent His *'only begotten Son'* to save and redeem them, and when they realize that this same *'Father'* has now come Himself to gather them together in oneness, these realizations will allow them to make great and quick strides toward unity and peace.

When people begin to accept this new reality, there will truly be a new day. Baha'u'llah said: *"Great indeed is this Day! The allusions made to it in all the sacred Scriptures as the Day of God attest its greatness. The soul of every Prophet of God, of every Divine Messenger, hath thirsted for this wondrous Day. All the divers kindreds of the earth have, likewise, yearned to attain it."* (Baha'u'llah: *Gleanings*, Page: 11)

Continuing to talk about this 'new Day,' He says: *"This is the Day in which God's most excellent favours have been poured out upon men, the Day in which His most mighty grace hath been infused into all created things."* (Baha'u'llah: *Proclamation of Baha'u'llah*, Page: 121) Also: *"Verily I say, this is the Day in which mankind can behold the Face, and hear the Voice, of the Promised One."* (Baha'u'llah: *Gleanings*, Page 10)

Baha'u'llah states that *"the hour hath now come"* and invites mankind to turn to Him (using the symbol of 'choice wine' to refer to His Coming and to His Revelation): *"The seal of the choice Wine of His Revelation hath, in this Day and in His Name, the Self-Sufficing, been broken. Its grace is being poured out upon men. Fill thy cup, and drink in, in His Name, the Most Holy, the All-Praised."* (Baha'u'llah: *Gleanings*, Page: 12)

In summary, Baha'is, Christians and all of the people of the world believe that one God, not many Gods, created the universe, our world and everything in it, as well as man and woman. Baha'is believe that this one God has been constantly at work in human history, progressively revealing Himself, sending His Manifestations, one of them His *'Son.'* This same God, only one God, has all along been guiding man, protecting, providing, shepherding mankind, leading the people of earth toward a great day of fulfillment and consummation. This great new Day has now been ushered in, Baha'u'llah teaches, by the appearance of *'the Father.'*

QUESTION: You said that Baha'is share a belief in Jesus Christ, but I'm sure Christian belief in Christ and Baha'i belief in Christ are quite different, aren't they?

RESPONSE: Not really. Please remember what we discussed in chapter six, where we talked about how Baha'is view the place of Christ in history and how they see the person of Christ. I don't want to repeat everything here, so you might want to refresh yourself on that discussion. But let me say this much: Christ is described in Baha'i Scriptures as the 'Word of God,' the 'Son of God,' the 'Spirit of God.' He is described as 'Savior' and as 'The Lord of All Being'.

Baha'u'llah wrote a most moving tribute to Christ, as strong as anything found anywhere in Christian writing; it is quoted in entirety in chapter six, but I'll repeat a portion of it here.

"Know thou that when the Son of Man yielded up His breath to God, the whole creation wept with a great weeping. By sacrificing Himself, however, a fresh capacity was infused into all created things. Its evidences, as witnessed in all the peoples of the earth, are now manifest before thee. The deepest wisdom which the sages have uttered, the profoundest learning which any mind hath unfolded, the arts which the ablest hands have produced, the influence exerted by the most potent of rulers, are but manifestations of the quickening power released by His transcendent, His all-pervasive, and resplendent Spirit." (Baha'u'llah: *Gleanings,* Pages: 85-86)

Make no mistake about it. Baha'is believe in Jesus Christ as the Son of God. Not another Christ, but the same Jesus of Nazareth that you believe in. The key and significant difference is that Christians have been taught to believe that the Christ Spirit, the 'Word of God' would and could only appear twice on earth, at His first and second Coming. Baha'is, on the other hand, have been taught by Baha'u'llah that this 'Christ Spirit,' this pre-existent 'Word of God' is the essence and reality of all the Manifestations that the one God caused to appear.

To review, you know by now that Baha'is have been taught by Baha'u'llah to call these many appearances of the 'Word of God' by the name of 'Manifestations' of God. Thus, as we have discussed before, Baha'is believe in what could be called a 'larger' Christ, as compared to the Christ as usually understood in history. This Christ with a larger, more encompassing historical presence and mission is the Christ Spirit, the 'Word of God' that appeared in, and was the reality of, Buddha, Krishna, Moses, Zoroaster, Moses, and Muhammad, as well as of Christ Himself. Today, this same 'Word of God' has appeared again, in our own time, in Baha'u'llah, *"the Father"* who told us that Jesus Christ has *"once more, in My person, been made manifest unto you.* " (Baha'u'llah: *Gleanings*, Page: 101)

QUESTION: You have to understand me. This is very challenging to hear. Sometimes confusing. Sometimes, I have to admit to you, it is infuriating! But wait—I'm going to say it before you do this time. Jews of the time of Jesus would have been infuriated and confused and also challenged by Jesus and His disciples. Jesus brought new teachings, *'New Wine'* that could not, He said, be put into *'old bottles.'* He brought a new religion, He 'broke' the Sabbath law (really, we Christians believe He was changing it) and other laws. They thought He was a blasphemer or even an agent of Satan. I really didn't want to hear that argument from you again, so I thought I would beat you to the punch.

.

RESPONSE: It may be true that I have belabored this point and I may have to bring it up again. If I do, please realize that Christians have been using this line of argument to Jews for twenty centuries. Allow me just a few cracks at bat to pose the same reasoning to you that Jews have had to endure for a very long time. I notice that you don't say the argument is wrong, just infuriating? Well, I'm actually trying to keep from confusing or infuriating you, so help me out and correct me if I 'beat a dead horse.' But if this argument, this line of thought, makes you ponder whether you can easily turn away from Baha'u'llah, maybe it is worth the unease you sometimes feel.

Baha'i House of Worship in Frankfurt, Germany.

QUESTION: Please, get back to those similarities you mentioned. Give me some details, if you will. The Baha'i Faith sounded so strange to me the first time I heard it, I am fascinated to find out that there are apparently so many similarities.

RESPONSE: Let's take those similarities up, one by one:

1. Similar belief in God:

Baha'is, like Christians, believe in the God Who made earth, heavens and the universe. We both believe that there are not many Gods, but one God. Both of us believe that God has been at work in human history. Both of us believe He has revealed Himself progressively (of course, Christians only see the 'progress' of God's Revelation beginning in the Old Testament with Abraham and Moses and ending with Christ's Second coming, while Baha'is have a view that is only slightly different.

It will be discussed later in the 'differences' part of this chapter).

Both Christians and Baha'is believe in a version (somewhat different) of what will happen in the 'last days,' but both believe God's Kingdom will, in fact, finally be set up on earth. Both of us believe in a time of fulfillment, of consummation, of peace and human unity.

2. Similar belief in Jesus Christ:

Baha'is, like Christians, believe in Jesus Christ as the 'pre-existent Word of God,' the 'Son of God,' as Savior and Redeemer. Both of us believe He will come again (of course, Baha'is believe He has already come again, in the person of Baha'u'llah), but both of us have shared this belief or expectation, that Christ will Return. I will not repeat everything we talked about just two or three pages ago, nor everything in chapter six, where we talked about how a Baha'i views the place of Christ in history, but I believe you are getting a strong feeling that there is great similarity and some (but not very much) difference in the way we both view Jesus.

QUESTION: The Bible. What about the Bible? Are there any similarities here? Is it or is it not the Word of God?

RESPONSE: It is the Word of God. Baha'u'llah and His Son 'Abdu'l-Baha both say so. When 'Abdu'l-Baha traveled in London at the turn of the century, He wrote in a famous Bible this inscription: *"This book is the Holy Book of God, of celestial Inspiration. It is the Bible of Salvation, the Noble Gospel. It is the mystery of the Kingdom and its* *light. It is the Divine Bounty, the sign of the guidance of God."* ('Abdu'l-Baha: *'Abdu'l-Baha in London,* Page: 18)

He also said: *"surely the Bible is the Book of God"* ('Abdu'l-Baha: *Paris Talks,* Page: 47)

Both 'Abdu'l-Baha and Baha'u'llah frequently quote the Bible. However, Baha'u'llah reminds us: The Pharisees often tried to 'trap' Jesus by quoting the Bible (the Old Testament). Baha'u'llah says that the Bible must never be used in this way.

Baha'u'llah was once speaking with a Christian clergyman who clearly wanted to use passages from the Bible to argue with Baha'u'llah (like the Pharisees did with Jesus). In reply to the cleric, Baha'u'llah said: *"What proof did the Jewish doctors adduce wherewith to condemn Him Who was the Spirit of God (Jesus Christ), when He came unto them with truth?"* He continued: *"Indeed thou hast produced, in this day, the same proofs which the foolish divines advanced in that age."* (Baha'u'llah: *Tablets of Baha'u'llah,* Page: 206)

Thus, Baha'u'llah warns us to be careful not to copy the behavior of the Pharisees.

Baha'u'llah also cautions us that the Manifestation of the very 'Self' of God, His presence in history in Jesus and in Baha'u'llah, is not to be questioned at all, but rather obeyed. Who was right in the time of Jesus, those who argued with Him, questioned Him or those who followed Him quickly and with very little argument or questions?

I guess you and I feel that some questions are O.K., but we probably wouldn't like to see someone arguing and questioning Jesus day after day, would we? Something seems wrong with that and Baha'u'llah tells us that even though He appealed to the people of God's earth to use His teaching of 'independent investigation of truth,' that we should remember that the Manifestation of God, whenever He appears, should not be tested, nor put in the balance. Rather, Baha'u'llah said that the Manifestation of God is the 'tester,' the 'assayer,' what He called *"The true balance"* for all men. He, the Manifestation, is the One who tests men, not the other way around.

After making this point forcefully, Baha'u'llah said He allowed men to question Him but warned that the questioning process was to lead to belief, rather than to be a means of putting the Manifestation 'on trial' as to His knowledge or as to His identity, whether He is Who He says He is. There is the sincere questioner, who is to be welcomed. Then, there are the Pharisees, who wish only to refute and reject or discredit the new Manifestation of God.

So, let's add another similarity:

3. Similar belief in the Bible:

Both Christians and Baha'is believe in the Bible as the revealed Word of God, both Old and New Testaments. The difference, as will be discussed later, is that while Christians adopted the scriptures of another religion—Judaism—and saw them as being divinely revealed, they do not see the scriptures of other religions as being divinely revealed, while Baha'is do.

QUESTION: I believe I heard you say that Baha'is believe in Heaven, Hell and an afterlife. Can you explain?

RESPONSE: Let's add another category of similarity:

4. Similar belief in heaven, hell and an afterlife.

This is a long and involved subject. I'm sure I won't be able to cover it adequately and short answers just won't work. You can, if you wish, read, study and explore, but when you do you will find a richness of belief about these subjects. Baha'u'llah clearly speaks of Heaven and Hell. (I just looked up the number of times Baha'u'llah mentions the word 'Heaven' in a concordance of Baha'u'llah's writings and it appears to be mentioned over four hundred times!) Be sure to consult the reading list in chapter sixteen.

The 'short version' of what Baha'u'llah teaches about Heaven and Hell is that He tells us that Heaven is nearness to God and Hell is the condition of being far away from or being separated from God. Baha'u'llah uses the imagery of Hell in His writings quite a few times, but He constantly brings us back to an understanding that is so very similar to that of Jesus, that Heaven is a condition of nearness to God and obedience to God; Hell, the opposite.

Both Jesus and Baha'u'llah, when talking of this subject, seem to be saying that Heaven and Hell are here right now, as well as conditions in an afterlife.

With regard to the next world, Baha'u'llah indicated that there are *"many worlds of God,"* and He said that our souls, after quitting this life, are to progress through all of these worlds. While both Baha'is and Christians believe in an afterlife, a difference could be that Christian belief seems mostly to be that one is in a 'static' condition after death, either in Hell or in Heaven for eternity (Catholics believe in an in-between condition, Purgatory, where progress is possible, as I understand it). In contrast, Baha'is believe that we are not in a 'fixed' condition after death, but may reach the next life in an undeveloped state or a state of 'unbelief.' Even so, these souls are destined to grow ever closer to the Divine Being, as they continue to progress through God's Mercy and their own understanding.

So, as Baha'u'llah teaches, Heaven is no static, resting place but rather a place of growth, of new understanding, of amplification and application of one's spiritual being. He also teaches that those in the afterlife can pray for those left behind. Though it isn't entirely clear, one gathers from reading Baha'i scriptural writings, that there is work to be done and divine plans for us to accomplish in these 'spiritual worlds' beyond our own.

Here are some statements from the Revelation of God through Baha'u'llah. Speaking about the 'True Believer,' one who has expressed belief in Him as the latest *Manifestation of God, Baha'u'llah says:*

" *If such be the blessings conferred on all created things, how superior must be the destiny of the true believer, whose existence and life are to be regarded as the originating purpose of all creation. Just as the conception of faith hath existed from the beginning that hath no beginning, and will endure till the end that hath no end, in like manner will the true believer eternally live and endure.*

"His spirit will everlastingly circle round the Will of God. He will last as long as God, Himself, will last. He is revealed through the Revelation of God, and is hidden at His bidding.

It is evident that the loftiest mansions in the Realm of Immortality have been ordained as the habitation of them that have truly believed in God and in His signs. Death can never invade that holy seat." (Baha'u'llah: *Gleanings*, Page: 141)

And here is Baha'u'llah's most famous and oft-quoted statement about death and the afterlife: *"O Son of the Supreme! I have made death a messenger of joy to thee. Wherefore dost thou grieve? I made the light to shed on thee its splendor. Why dost thou veil thyself therefrom?"* (Baha'u'llah: *Hidden Words,* Page: 32)

The following quotation from Baha'u'llah on the afterlife is, in my opinion, one of the most interesting and engaging statements of a Manifestation of God on the subject of the afterlife:

"And now concerning thy question regarding the soul of man and its survival after death. Know thou of a truth that the soul, after its separation from the body, will continue to progress until it attaineth the presence of God, in a state and condition which neither the revolution of ages and centuries, nor the changes and chances of this world, can alter. It will endure as long as the Kingdom of God, His sovereignty, His dominion and power will endure. It will manifest the signs of God and His attributes, and will reveal His loving-kindness and bounty.

"The movement of My Pen is stilled when it attempteth to befittingly describe the loftiness and glory of so exalted a station. The honor with which the Hand of Mercy will invest the soul is such as no tongue can adequately reveal, nor any other earthly agency describe. Blessed is the soul which, at the hour of its separation from the body, is sanctified from the vain imaginings of the peoples of the world. Such a soul liveth and moveth in accordance with the Will of its Creator, and entereth the all-highest Paradise.

Baha'u'llah continues to say that the *"inmates"* of heaven and even the *"prophets of God"* will *"seek its companionship. With them that soul will freely converse, and will recount unto them that which it hath been made to endure in the path of God, the Lord of all worlds. If any man be told that which hath been ordained for such a soul in the worlds of God, the Lord of the throne on high and of earth below, his whole being will instantly blaze out in his great longing to attain that most exalted, that sanctified and resplendent station . . . . The nature of the soul after death can never be described, nor is it meet and permissible to reveal its whole character to the eyes of men. The Prophets and Messengers of God have been sent down for the sole purpose of guiding mankind to the straight Path of Truth. The purpose underlying Their revelation hath been to educate all men, that they may, at the hour of death, ascend, in the utmost purity and sanctity and with absolute detachment, to the throne of the Most High.*

"The light which these souls radiate is responsible for the progress of the world and the advancement of its peoples. They are like unto leaven which leaveneth the world of being, and constitute the animating force through which the arts and wonders of the world are made manifest. Through them the clouds rain their bounty upon men, and the earth bringeth forth its fruits.

"All things must needs have a cause, a motive power, an animating principle. These souls and symbols of detachment have provided, and will continue to provide, the supreme moving impulse in the world of being. The world beyond is as different from this world as this world is different from that of the child while still in the womb of its mother. When the soul attaineth the Presence of God, it will assume the form that best befitteth its immortality and is worthy of its celestial habitation." (Baha'u'llah: *Gleanings,* Pages: 155-157)

There is much material on the afterlife in Baha'u'llah's Revelation. I will leave this to your personal investigation, but here is a prayer of Baha'u'llah's Son, 'Abdu'l-Baha, that is often read at Baha'i funerals:

"O my God! O Thou forgiver of sins, bestower of gifts, dispeller of afflictions! Verily, I beseech Thee to forgive the sins of such as have abandoned the physical garment and have ascended to the spiritual world.

"O my Lord! Purify them from trespasses, dispel their sorrows, and change their darkness into light. Cause them to enter the garden of happiness, cleanse them with the most pure water, and grant them to behold Thy splendors on the loftiest

mount. " ('Abdu'l-Baha: *Baha'i Prayers* (US edition), Pages: 44-46)

QUESTION: Do Baha'is believe in some new and different moral code?

RESPONSE: Yes, and no. First, Baha'is believe in the same general moral code as Christians, including the Ten Commandments (Baha'is believe Moses was a Manifestation of God, don't forget), and the Golden Rule (which is in every religion's moral code), just for two examples. Baha'u'llah's statement of the Golden Rule is given in at least two places. I will quote them both for you: *"Lay not on any soul a load which ye would not wish to be laid upon you, and desire not for any one the things ye would not desire for yourselves. This is My best counsel unto you, did ye but observe it."* (Baha'u'llah: Gleanings, Page: 128) and also: *"And if thine eyes be turned towards justice, choose thou for thy neighbor that which thou choosest for thyself."* (Baha'u'llah: *Epistle to the Son of the Wolf*, Page: 30)

However, just as Christians tried to follow every law or wish that Jesus set forth . . . .

QUESTION: Stop right there! Once before, I tried to tell you—Jesus gave no laws! His religion, as St. Paul often points out, was a religion to replace 'law' with the 'grace of God.'

RESPONSE: Well, I think you are mostly right, but not entirely right. Remember that Jesus said: *"A new commandment I give to you, that you love one another; as I have loved you, that you also love one another."* (John 13:34) He also said: *"But if you want to enter into life, keep the commandments."* (Matt 19:17) Finally, He said: *"If you love Me, keep My commandments."* (John 14:15) A commandment is, by definition, a law. But you are still mostly right. Jesus did give a few laws, including one about marriage and divorce, although I realize that many Christians don't look on them as laws. But when the Manifestation, be it Buddha, Christ or Baha'u'llah, gives laws or commandments or new understandings, their followers are duty-bound to follow those laws or new understandings. Jesus did give few laws and Christianity, as you say, is not primarily a religion of laws.

In the case of Baha'u'llah, He did reveal a code of laws to govern and guide the new world society that will emerge as a result of His Coming. He asked His followers—the Baha'is—to lead and inspire all humanity to build that new, united world. Let me repeat what He said about that code of laws: *"Think not that We have revealed unto you a mere code of laws. Nay, rather, We have unsealed the choice Wine with the fingers of might and power."* (Baha'u'llah: The *Kitab-i-Aqdas*, Page: 21)

Baha'u'llah gave us laws about marriage, inheritance, family life, burial and some (but only a few) laws governing personal behavior, including the fact that no Baha'i may use drugs or alcohol nor engage in prejudicial thinking or behavior toward a person of any other ethnic group or culture. There is a strong statement from Baha'u'llah on forbidding backbiting or gossip. You can learn more about the small group of what Jesus called *"commandments"* contained in this code of laws as you study the Baha'i Faith. So let's add another category of similarity:

5. Similar belief in a moral code of conduct:

To summarize, the Baha'i moral and social code is strongly similar to the code subscribed to by Christians. It is different only in serving to strengthen and codify certain of Christianity's best ideals, such as the explicit forbidding of racial prejudice, which Christian teaching only forbids by implication.

QUESTION: Just a minute. We've been through this before. Don't you realize that true Christians, the ones who are following Biblical teaching, will not be prejudiced? That they will deal fairly and equitably with others?

RESPONSE: I want you to know that I do know that, and I agree. My parents were excellent examples of that, even though they were born and raised in the Southern United States in the early Twentieth Century. The problem is that some Christians *do* deny racial oneness. Some Christians (by manipulating the meaning of the scriptures) can deny equality between men and women. Some Christians say drinking is permitted. In each of these cases, they cite biblical verses to back their stand (you and I would probably agree that they are twisting the meaning pretty hard when they do the above or when a terribly racist, terrorist group in Idaho calls itself 'Christian Identity').

The point I want to share is that the Baha'i lifestyle does not permit these behaviors because Baha'u'llah spoke so clearly about racial unity and the equality of men and women. No Baha'i would be likely to think this way, talk this way or act this way and would be immediately confronted by his or her fellow Baha'is if he or she did. People aren't perfect, but the Revelations of Christ and Baha'u'llah do represent perfection to those who believe in them. Baha'u'llah's Son 'Abdu'l-Baha reinforced these ideas of racial unity and gender equality strongly. To take another example, no Baha'i who comes from a Jewish or Buddhist or Hindu background can fail to express belief in Jesus Christ as the Son of God. It just wouldn't happen.

Several more examples: Because of ambiguity in Biblical quotations, Christians can choose whether or not to believe in the unity of mankind and the desirability of a united global civilization, while Baha'is believe strongly in these values. Of course, I know that many Christians do support that 'oneness of mankind' view, which I, for example, did before becoming a Baha'i. A Christian can honestly, sincerely decide to be against interracial marriage. A Baha'i cannot, since the Baha'i Faith strongly supports and encourages such marriages. Again, I realize that some Christians support racial unity and interracial marriages, though no Church takes a stand on this, to my knowledge. The Baha'is have taken a very clear stand, based on Baha'u'llah's direct and forceful words.

Christians can choose whether to believe that the races are one, or to believe that there are important differences between the races, sometimes (during the pre-civil war era) even important enough to allow for slavery, or for discrimination or to prevent the idea of interracial marriage. No Baha'i would be able to choose to believe anything other than that there is only one race on this planet, since the oneness of the races and therefore of mankind is a central teaching of Baha'u'llah.

Oh, almost forgot another one: Some Christians are pacifist; some are not. All Baha'is are told by Baha'u'llah to obey the government; therefore, they must serve in the armed forces, if drafted. However, they must serve in a non-combatant capacity. 'Abdu'l-Baha, Baha'u'llah's Son, said (based on the words of His Father): *"It is better for you to be killed than to kill"* ('Abdu'l-Baha: *Memorials of the Faithful*, Pages: 199-200)

No one should interpret this as a pacifist sentiment, however. 'Abdu'l-Baha said that Baha'is are simply fol-

lowing Baha'u'llah's explicit teaching about not killing.
Nor, said 'Abdu'l-Baha, should that teaching of
Baha'u'llah be interpreted that one cannot defend one-
self, one's family, a neighbor or even a stranger.

QUESTION: You mentioned a 'social structure' as
being a similarity of the Christian and Baha'i Faiths?

RESPONSE: Yes, Baha'u'llah says that God, through
the sending of His Manifestations, puts men and women
who witness the coming of that Manifestation on an entirely new foundation for renewal and growth and the
establishment of a new society. By turning fully to the
new Manifestation of God for the day in which they live,
they are in touch with new spiritual power, new purpose
and a sense of direction guiding them as they work to
establish new, vibrant communities and nations. The difference today is that Baha'is and everyone else for that
matter, are called upon not just to establish a new religion, a new culture, but to establish and build the first
international, unified, 'world society.'

Renewal starts with the salvation that each Manifestation brings, changing and transforming individual lives.
Then, when those transformed, spiritually renewed men
and women marry, as Baha'u'llah charges them to do,
that marriage becomes what Baha'u'llah called *"a fortress for well-being."* Such a strong marriage is clearly
viewed by Jews, Christians, Moslems and Baha'is as the
strong center of a well-functioning family. Baha'u'llah's
comments on the family and marriage as institutions with
a sacred foundation are numerous. Family, based upon
marriage, based in turn upon strong, spiritually renewed,
aware individuals.

QUESTION: So far this doesn't sound like anything

new. All religions, as far as I know, and certainly Christianity would say almost the same thing as you have said.

RESPONSE: True enough. What Baha'u'llah adds is the part of the social structure from the level of nationhood on up to the level of the oneness of humanity and the necessity of the entire world becoming united in thought, purpose and deed. When that can happen, the amount spent on armaments, for example, will be applied to hunger, health, housing, employment, and education. Education is especially important, Baha'u'llah says, for the renewing and rebuilding of the world.

The amount spent by the entire world on armaments in less than a ten-year period is in excess of four trillions of dollars. The amount spent by the entire world in about one human generation—say thirty years—is nearing fifteen trillion dollars (about .5 trillion per year or 3% of WGP (Gross World Product) at the turn of the millennium. In material terms, this would be enough to begin to house, feed, heal and educate every child and adult on the planet, though author John Huddleston warns that this task will not be an easy one, even with adequate funds. Transformation of the world will require not only material means but also a spiritual renewal and for both of these we need unity and peace. (See the reading list in chapter sixteen that includes Huddleston's fine book: *The Earth is but One Country.*)

A world at peace would be a greatly changed world. That needed change can only occur with the unification of mankind, which is Baha'u'llah's central teaching and, He tells us, God's Will for humanity today. One of the fascinating elements of His Revelation is that He tells us that the unity of mankind is not just a beautiful ideal, not just something that could or should happen; rather, He tells us that it is in process of happening in this very period of history. In fact, He tells us that nothing whatever can stop this process.

Thus, let's add another similarity:

6. Similar belief in a desirable social structure:

QUESTION: Whoa! I just have to stop you again. There's that 'pie in the sky' kind of thinking coming out in you again. Surely you don't believe in this 'world unity' business. That's just not going to happen. Only dreamers and the naive could believe in such a thing. I know I'm kind of pushing you, but all I can say is: 'Get real!'

RESPONSE: Really, I can't blame you for thinking of me as naive, or as a dreamer, but if I am, then there are six million Baha'is (the number of Baha'is in the year 2000) that are right there in this dream with me, and they aren't just dreaming. They are building and creating the kind of world we are talking about in their communities. This is happening today, not in some distant future. Those transformed individual lives we talked about and those new communities with new ideas, new energy, new sense of purpose, new direction, are all here, today. And, getting stronger day by day. And, inviting any and all of the people of the world to come aboard, to aid us in the creation of that united world.

When Martin Luther King, Jr. stood on the steps of the Lincoln Memorial in Washington in the summer of 1963, he gave his famous 'I have a dream' speech. Except for those who believed in the dream, everyone else heard this speech as 'pie in the sky' and as 'unreal.' It appears that 'dreamers' are the ones who finally do change the world. But dreams alone won't do it; we all know that.

In the case of the Baha'i Faith, the original dreamer

is God, Who has 'dreamed a new dream' of what we can become, a Divine Plan for our future. He charged Baha'u'llah to manifest His Presence in the world, providing salvation to individuals and to a sick, dying world. Baha'u'llah empowers individuals to lead radically new lives transformed with spiritual knowledge and direction; those individuals are building from the level of the individual, through marriage and the family, on up to community, nation and the international level of a united humanity. Some dream, isn't it? And often, we are so disheartened as to say: 'It can't happen'!

How could Christ have asked us to pray for something that can't happen? He told us to pray *"Thy Kingdom come, Thy Will be done, on earth, as it is in heaven"*. Surely Christ's prayer was not 'pie in the sky.' Surely He meant exactly what He said, that a Kingdom would be built *"on earth."*

All I ask of you is this: Don't tell the Baha'is that it can't happen, because we are too busy making it happen to listen. If you would like to be with us, so much the better! If you cannot be with us, cheer us on, or be a partner, as we try to fulfill not only the vision and the Divine Plan of Baha'u'llah, but of Jesus Christ.

There is a second reason I believe in this dream. Baha'u'llah said that He had been sent by God, had been Manifested by God to accomplish just this very thing— the bringing together of all the varied races, religions, cultures, all the children of humanity, into unity and oneness. He said that He came: *" . . . in the clouds of light"* to *"quicken all created things with the breezes of His Name, the Most Merciful, and unify the world, and gather all men around this Table which hath been sent down from heaven."* (Baha'u'llah: *Epistle to the Son of the Wolf*, Page: 46)

Also He described Himself as: *"He Who hath come to*

build anew the whole world . . . " (Baha'u'llah: *Gleanings*, Page: 100)

A third reason I can believe in this dream without dishing out 'pie in the sky' or seeming otherwise naive is that what I am talking about is already happening. This unity of mankind and the Baha'i community is already being built worldwide, both inside the Baha'i Faith and outside. Let's begin with world unity developments outside the Baha'i Faith. Postal service, telephone lines, satellite linkups, space cooperation, police cooperation, currency, the world economy, world wide health connections are just several examples of the 'internationalization' of the modern world. The Internet, steadily improving computer translation of languages, and the hundreds of international organizations all testify to the move in the direction of world unity.

Baha'u'llah called for nearly all of this in the 1860's and predicted most of it. You might want to read a book called *The Challenge of Baha'u'llah* written by Gary Matthews to get an idea of how much Baha'u'llah prophesied a hundred years before it happened. Baha'is believe that when a Manifestation appears in history, the centuries following His appearance are a period of special creativity, discovery and growth. Do you remember the statement of Baha'u'llah about the influence of Jesus Christ on history (chapter six)? Think of all the art, the discovery, the creativity, the radical new directions that history displayed after the appearance of Christ!

Baha'is believe that such a period of world-wide discovery and forward movement is now occurring, centered around our discovery of our human oneness and the possibility of our unity and based upon the appearance of a new Manifestation of God, *"The Father"* of all mankind and the Return of Jesus Christ.

Then, considering what is happening inside Baha'i

communities worldwide, we need to recall that Baha'u'llah told us exactly what the Baha'i internal structures should be like. He directed that wherever there are nine or more Baha'is in any locality, city, county or other governmental jurisdiction, a Local Spiritual Assembly be elected, which would govern the affairs of the Faith in that locality. National Spiritual Assemblies would be elected at the national level and there would be an assembly called the Universal House of Justice elected at the international level.

The Universal House of Justice was first elected in 1963, one hundred years after Baha'u'llah's proclamation to the world of His Revelation of God's new 'Testament' of His Will. It has been re-elected every five years since that date. Delegates, who are members of the National Spiritual Assemblies, gather from throughout the world in the Holy Land (in Haifa, Israel) to carry out the election. When Baha'u'llah laid out this institution in detail, He said it would act to extend His Revelation, that its decisions should be looked upon as if they were His own words. His Son, 'Abdu'l-Baha said: *"Whatsoever they decide is of God."* (Quoted in Shoghi Effendi: *Baha'i Administration*, Page: 7)

Because of these words of Baha'u'llah and His Son, Baha'is see the Universal House of Justice as continuing to reveal God's Will for us as we go about the task of helping to build that united world.

It is this structure of a new social order that Baha'is believe is the foundation for the long promised, long awaited *"Kingdom of God on earth."*

QUESTION: Sometimes you Baha'is seem to be so 'inflated' as to what you can achieve. You seem over-confident, sometimes almost fanatic. Do you ever just stop and listen to what you are saying?

RESPONSE: All I can suggest to you is to re-read the Book of Acts in the New Testament, to see how the early Christians felt and how they were perceived. If you've forgotten, it will be an eye-opener! The Christians in the months following the Resurrection of Christ were supremely confident and were seen as almost fanatic in their belief and their actions. Someone could certainly have called them 'dreamers' and could easily have said their ideas of what they could accomplish were inflated far beyond reality.

Baha'is of today are only two and three generations away from Baha'u'llah being on this earth. Once, when I was in my twenties (I reached my mid-sixties as the millennium turned), I met a very old woman who had met Baha'u'llah. We are *that* close to the Dawn of this Revelation of God. If you think about those early Christians as described in the book of Acts, you will understand us Baha'is much better, I think. Or, think of it this way: We Baha'is are currently living our own 'Book of Acts'!

Then, listen to some of the statements of Baha'u'llah that you will find in chapter fourteen and maybe you will be able to better understand our enthusiasm (the root of that word 'enthusiasm' means, as I suspect you know, to be 'filled with the spirit of God'). Just listen to Baha'u'llah, not to us, and you will not wonder at our confidence, our energy or our belief in what is about to happen in the world.

QUESTION: You've told me about similarities between the Christian and Baha'i Faiths. What about any differences?

RESPONSE: As we went along, I attempted to point out some of the small differences that exist alongside the main similarities. Now I will list some things that are somewhat or even quite different when you contrast the two faiths. There aren't many differences, but those that exist are important. The very first difference is the idea, which we've already discussed, that the Christ Spirit, the pre-existent Word of God has appeared many times in human history. I have referred to this (and I am trying hard to take your feelings into account as I say this) as the idea of a 'larger Christ.'

QUESTION: But I certainly hope you aren't trying to say my Christ is too small! That would be insulting and degrading and my understanding is that you Baha'is are trying to create unity, not discord.

RESPONSE: You really are beginning to understand me and, I hope, to trust me not to insult or degrade. I'm only saying what a Christian theologian, J. B. Phillips, observed several decades ago, when he said that most Christians had a God that was 'too small.' In reality, Christ cannot be any smaller or any larger than He is. The *"Son of God"* doesn't come in small, medium and large sizes, so maybe my saying that we, all of us, need a 'larger Christ' isn't such a good idea. But I said it in this context, namely, that your idea or my idea of Christ may limit Christ from being seen by us and by others as having played a larger role in history than ever imagined.

A Christ, as the pre-existent 'Word,' Who has been the energizing force within Buddha, Muhammad and Krishna, as well as Moses, the Bab and Baha'u'llah and who will appear yet again, numerous times in the tens of thousands of years ahead is indeed a 'larger Christ' than has ever before been described, couldn't you agree?

QUESTION: I cannot agree to that, at least not yet.

Let me hear more about the differences between Christian and Baha'i Faiths.

RESPONSE: The scriptures of the Baha'i Faith are an area with an interesting similarity, in that they are seen as the 'revealed Word of God,' just as the scriptures of the Jews, Christians and Moslems (for examples) are seen. The followers of all these religions believe that God sent His Will to them in these revealed messages that constitute their writings, whether Torah, Bible or Qur'an.

One difference between the Christian and Baha'i Faiths is that scriptures of the Christian Faith were not written down until decades after the Manifestation (that is, Christ) spoke them. By contrast, the scriptures of the Baha'i Faith, the writings of Baha'u'llah, are all in our possession in His own Hand or with His seal on them, *in the originals.*

I know this sounds incredible, but there they are, all of them, more than 10,000 documents, letters, papers and books. No scholar or skeptic can ever say (as they have said about Christian scripture), that Baha'u'llah did not say what He said, nor can they argue about the origin of Baha'i scripture. As you certainly know, this area has been one of sharp division and disagreement for Christians.

QUESTION: You aren't trying to undermine the authority of the Bible, are you?

RESPONSE: Not at all. We've already discussed that Baha'u'llah often quoted the Bible, and frequently stated it was God's Word. I'm only saying what every Christian scholar says, that the collection of the scripture that was formed into the New Testament, took over two hundred years after Christ to be completed. The 'canon,' as it was called, or the 'official' New Testament was the subject of intense disagreement and disunity, which was finally settled only by voting on it at several Church Councils.

There is a fascinating story about how the New Testament came into existence. Any good dictionary of the Bible will tell you the complete story. It seems as clear to Baha'is as to Christians that the Hand of God was involved in the construction of the entire Bible and that it has been Divinely inspired. Therefore, there is no attempt to undermine the Bible's authority, even though no originals exist and even though it was written down many decades after Christ ascended. Baha'u'llah and His Son 'Abdu'l-Baha both strongly certify the Bible as the revealed Word of God.

Here is a statement of Baha'u'llah that asserts Bible authenticity more strongly than I have ever heard: *"We have also heard a number of the foolish of the earth assert that the genuine text of the heavenly Gospel doth not exist amongst the Christians, that it hath ascended unto heaven. How grievously they have erred! How oblivious of the fact that such a statement imputeth the gravest injustice and tyranny to a gracious and loving Providence! How could God, when once the Day-star of the beauty of Jesus had disappeared from the sight of His people, and ascended unto the fourth heaven, cause His holy Book, His most great testimony amongst His creatures, to disappear also?"* (Baha'u'llah: The *Kitab-i-Iqan*, Page: 89)

QUESTION: What about a ministry or priesthood? I have heard that the Baha'i Faith doesn't have either priesthood or ministers. Is that correct? And, if so, how do you operate without it?

RESPONSE: Yes, this is a difference and a big difference, since Baha'is, as you say, do not have a ministry or priests and never will have, according to the express Will of Baha'u'llah.

QUESTION: But, you must have leaders of some kind?

RESPONSE: Of course, but the power of leadership in the Baha'i is never vested in one individual alone, but in a Local or National Spiritual Assembly or (as mentioned earlier) in the Universal House of Justice at the Baha'i World Center in Haifa, Israel. Each of the institutions just mentioned has nine individuals and it is the nine, acting as a body, that has authority, not any individual.

In Baha'u'llah's time and up to the present, a smaller number of individuals who served the Baha'i Cause faithfully and long were appointed 'Hands of the Cause' or 'Counselors,' but these persons are not paid a salary and have no power or authority of their own. They function under the guidance of the Universal House of Justice.

QUESTION: You have to have some kind of leaders, some people who are paid salaries, don't you? You have told me that there is a United States Baha'i National Center in Evanston, Illinois. People working there must earn a salary. What about that?

RESPONSE: At the national level, we pay a national 'Secretary General,' but this person is selected by election and may or may not be selected in the following year. This person also has no individual authority, because the authority is vested in the body of nine—the National Spiritual Assembly.

Finally, yes, we pay full-time salaries to administrators, secretaries, computer specialists and workers of all kinds, but none of these are 'leaders' and none of them represents anything like a priesthood or ministry.

QUESTION: What about rituals? You have said there are no rituals? That would be a pretty big difference.

RESPONSE: The Baha'i Faith has almost no rituals, nor will it have. This is by the express guidance of Baha'u'llah. There are two exceptions: The Bride and Groom at a Baha'i Wedding, which is remarkably free of form and ritual, are required to exchange a vow given them by Baha'u'llah, in which they say *"Verily, we will all abide by the will of God."* The other exception is a prayer to be said at funerals.

Although it is hard to believe, the Baha'i Faith neither has ministry nor rituals (with the exceptions just noted).

QUESTION: You already said that there was a similarity in the belief of the reality of sin in human lives, but you also said there was a difference?

RESPONSE: Yes. Both Christians and Baha'is believe in 'sin' as a corrupting influence in human lives. Christians believe in something called 'original sin' which, as taught by most Christians, is something 'inherited' from one's parents and originally, from Adam and Eve, the first parents. Baha'is do not believe, based upon Baha'u'llah's Revelation, that sin is inherited like a genetic disease, even though He makes it clear that sin is a very real force in individual human lives and in society at large.

Instead, Baha'u'llah taught that sin is the result of a man's or a woman's 'lower animal nature' being expressed with no guidance and control by our higher, spiritual nature. The ideas of 'original sin' versus 'sin' as the result of an unfettered, uncontrolled lower, animal nature are probably not that different in practical terms. However, 'original sin' as a concept doesn't seem to explain well enough (at least, to me) the true nature of men and women. The Baha'i concept of 'sin' gives a rational and meaningful explanation showing how men and women can lead lives transformed by the Salvation and the teachings of the Manifestation, to the point where their higher, spiritual natures are more in control and the 'energy' of the animal nature is channeled and more wisely used.

So, belief in 'sin' as the condition of turning away from God, failing to recognize and follow the guidance of the Manifestation, is something that Christians and Baha'is share. We also share the idea that our lower animal natures will instinctively involve themselves in sinful behavior unless human individuals experience salvation and follow the teachings of the Manifestation.

The difference is in the explanation of how that sinful inclination got there. Is it a 'genetic disease' that is inherited from our parents (the Jewish and Christian explanation) or rather, can it be explained by understanding the way our natures work? The clear understanding from Baha'u'llah is that our higher nature, our spiritual nature, must, with God's salvation and grace, be in charge of and in control of, our lower, animal nature, with all its energy (the Baha'i explanation).

QUESTION: But Christians, you must understand, believe that sin is the cause of all man's problems and flows from that deep 'original,' embedded, sinful nature that was installed in man in the Garden of Eden. This 'stain' upon man's nature can only be cleansed by salvation found exclusively in Jesus Christ.

RESPONSE: Baha'is and Christians aren't really that far apart on this issue, it seems to me. We've already stated the difference as being between 'original sin' as man's sinfully prone nature being inherited, on the one hand, contrasted with the Baha'i view of man's sinfully prone nature arising out of our lower, animal-like nature. In both cases, Christians and Baha'is believe in a lower, 'sinful' nature that we as humans are prone to give in to if we are not in a state of 'salvation' and if we do not make choices that allow our higher, spiritual nature to take control over our lower nature. But we do need God's forgiveness, always so plentiful and ready, as in Jesus' story about the Prodigal Son or as in 'Abdu'l-Baha's comment *"with one wave from the ocean of Thy forgiveness, all those encompassed by sin will be set free."* ('Abdu'l-Baha: *Baha'i Prayers* (US edition), Page: 47)

The two Faiths agree that only the power of God, as expressed in the appearance of a Manifestation such as Christ or Baha'u'llah, must assist man and enable man, through salvation, to change and control his 'sinfully' prone nature. Whether this nature was 'put there' from Adam and Eve's act in the Garden of Eden or whether we have finally simply discovered what man's nature is really like doesn't seem to me to make a practical difference. And we should remember that both Faiths teach that the soul of man is at the center of his being. Baha'u'llah said that God had 'invested' man with the ability to know Him: **"From among all created things He hath singled out for His special favor the pure, the gem-like reality of man, and invested it with a unique capacity of knowing Him and of reflecting the greatness of His glory."** (Baha'u'llah: *Gleanings*, Page: 77)

So in the final analysis, the two Faiths seem to have a great deal of agreement on this issue. While it is true that nearly every Christian denomination has as part of its creed a statement on 'original sin,' most Christians today don't believe human beings are 'inherently' genetically evil. What they seem to believe today is very close to what the Baha'i Faith teaches, namely, that the lower, animal nature of human beings is inherently prone to selfishness and sin, but that individual men and women can be best understood as being potentially good, needing only the assistance of God, through salvation and divine guidance, combined with their own commitment and their continual struggle over their lower, animal natures.

What is important to remember is that God created man as a good and 'noble' being. Baha'u'llah's Revelation says: **"O SON OF SPIRIT! Noble have I created thee, yet thou hast abased thyself. Rise then unto that for which thou wast created."** (Baha'u'llah: *Hidden Words*, Page: 22)

Both Faiths agree that God's salvation is necessary for the individual to be able to win this battle of his higher, spiritual nature over his lower, animal nature. Christians teach that this can come only through Jesus Christ. Here is a difference, in that Baha'u'llah taught that the salvation, which comes from God, is attained by human individuals through recognition of the Manifestation of God's own Being, whenever He appears in human history, *"in the form of a human temple."* He teaches that this has happened more than once, in fact, an untold number of times throughout humankind's long history.

This is why the Manifestations of God have been sent, says 'Abdu'l-Baha: *"so that man may be made free. Just as he is born into this world of imperfection from the womb of his earthly mother, so is he born into the world of spirit through divine education. When a man is born into the world of phe-*

nomena he finds the universe; when he is born from this world to the world of the spirit, he finds the Kingdom." ('Abdu'l-Baha: *Paris Talks*, Page: 178)

Thus, Baha'i teaching is that whenever a Manifestation appears, all must recognize and follow Him, since He is from God. Baha'u'llah teaches that each new Manifestation represents a fresh expression of the pre-existent Word of God. Through this recognition of the Manifestation, be it Jesus, or Muhammad or Buddha, and through responding to Him, following Him, obeying Him, one experiences 'salvation.' Baha'u'llah explains what happens when one recognizes the Manifestation, and also what occurs when one ignores or rejects Him.

"The first duty prescribed by God for His servants is the recognition of Him Who is the Dayspring of His Revelation and the Fountain of His laws, Who representeth the Godhead in both the Kingdom of His Cause and the world of creation. Whoso achieveth this duty hath attained unto all good; and whoso is deprived thereof hath gone astray, though he be the author of every righteous deed." (Baha'u'llah: The *Kitab-i-Aqdas*, Page: 19)

In this day, Baha'u'llah clearly announces to the world that He is the Return of Christ *"in My Person"* and that mankind should realize that *"The Father hath come."* Because of this re-introduction into history of the Person of Christ and because *"the Father"* has come, humankind will now enter the historical period of ingathering, unity, fulfillment and the building of the Kingdom of God *"on earth as it is in heaven."*

QUESTION: You mentioned earlier that the views of the two Faiths are similar in that they both view the Bible as God's revealed Word. But I'm still concerned that there is a difference in how both Faiths view their own scriptures.

RESPONSE: Baha'is do believe in the Bible as God's revealed Word as stated earlier, primarily because Baha'u'llah and His Son 'Abdu'l-Baha saw the Bible as a valid, divinely inspired expression of God's Manifestation of Himself to men. As I told you, both of them often quoted the Bible when they spoke or wrote. The Bible is mentioned and quoted in the Baha'i Scriptures many hundreds of times.

Baha'u'llah as a Manifestation would hardly be quoting a scriptural source that He did not believe represented the Will of God and His Revealed Word. As I have mentioned before, Jesus Christ frequently quoted the scriptures of another religion, the scriptures of the Jewish Faith. They were, of course, the scriptures of His boyhood. Christ, even though He was the 'Word of God,' nevertheless chose to quote from Jewish scriptures.

Where the difference appears, as astounding as it may seem, is that all, literally all the Baha'i scriptures exist in their originals. Every book, every prayer, every letter from Baha'u'llah is held in a temperature-controlled vault at the Baha'i World Center in Haifa, Israel in a special building constructed in the last several years of the Twentieth Century.

The building is called 'The Center for the Study of the Texts' and any scholar who applies can go to Haifa to study or do research. By contrast, the scriptures of all other Faiths, including Christianity, have been slowly collected over a period of years, sometimes many years, with not even one original document written by the Founder of that religion in existence anywhere. This, 'Abdu'l-Baha tells us, is why it important to realize God's Inspiration in the creation of all Holy Scriptures of all religions. Therefore, if anyone would ask, "Does all this make the Bible less than the Revealed Word of God?" a

Baha'i would reply: "It does *not*, as witnessed by both Baha'u'llah and 'Abdu'l-Baha."

They both tell us to be most careful here, however. Though historically important, the existence of these original Baha'i materials are not to lead us to the conclusion that this makes the Bible or the Qur'an or the scriptures of other religions any less than what they are, namely, the 'Word of God.' We have Baha'u'llah's word for that and that is why selections from the Bible and from other scriptures are read in Baha'i gatherings called 'Feasts' along with Baha'i scriptures. Baha'u'llah prayed: *"Praise be unto Thee, O our God, that Thou hast sent down unto us that which draweth us nigh unto Thee, and supplieth us with every good thing sent down by Thee in Thy Books and Thy Scriptures."* (Baha'u'llah: *Kitab-i-Aqdas*: Other Sections, Pages: 97-98) He included in those 'scriptures' the *'Torah'* (the Old Testament) and the *'Evangel'* (the New Testament).

QUESTION: Feasts! That's what early Christian meetings were called!

RESPONSE: Yes. A remarkable coincidence that apparently has no other significance. Baha'i meetings around the world, since it is a 'young' religion (only 157 years old at the turn of the century) are often held in Baha'i homes, as were early Christian 'Feasts.' Baha'i meetings probably greatly resemble the 'Feasts of love' that early Christians experienced when their Faith was, likewise, a 'young' Faith. While Christians usually don't call their worship services 'Feasts' any longer, Baha'is will always call them that, because it is the name given them by Baha'u'llah.

QUESTION: What about the Devil or Satan? I real-

ize that Christians themselves are very divided in opinion on this topic, since Catholics, Methodists, Pentecostals and Presbyterians (and the many thousands of Christian denominations) all seem to believe something different. What do Baha'is believe? Do they believe in Satan?

RESPONSE: The word 'Satan' appears many times
in Baha'u'llah's writings. Here are some examples: *"Watch
over yourselves, for the Evil One is lying in wait, ready to
entrap you. Gird yourselves against his wicked devices, and,
led by the light of the name of the All-Seeing God, make your
escape from the darkness that surroundeth you. Let your vision be world-embracing, rather than confined to your own
self. The Evil One is he that hindereth the rise and obstructeth
the spiritual progress of the children of men."* (Baha'u'llah:
Gleanings, Page: 94)

And Baha'u'llah speaks of those individuals who follow in *"the ways of those abject manifestations of the Prince
of Darkness."* (Baha'u'llah: The *Kitab-i-Iqan*, Page: 122)
Also: *"Keep us safe, then, through Thine unfailing protection, O Thou the Beloved of the entire creation and the Desire
of the whole universe, from them whom Thou hast made to be
the manifestations of the Evil Whisperer, who whisper in men's
breasts. Potent art Thou to do Thy pleasure."* (Baha'u'llah:
Prayers and Meditations, Page: 233)

Baha'u'llah, as you see, speaks of the *'Prince of Darkness'* (Baha'u'llah: *Kitab-i-Iqan*, Page 122), *'the Evil One'*
who is *"lying in wait, ready to entrap you."* Also, He speaks
of the *"whisperings of the Evil One,"* of *"the Evil One who
has stirred up mischief in their* [that is, men's] *hearts"*
(Baha'u'llah: *Gleanings*, Page 41) and says that this *"Evil
One"* is *"He that hindereth the spiritual progress of men."*
(Baha'u'llah: *Gleanings*, Page 94)

However, as one reads Baha'u'llah in a thorough

way and as one listens to His Son, 'Abdu'l-Baha (appointed in writing by Baha'u'llah as His official interpreter of the meaning of His words) you find that Baha'u'llah, in speaking of *"Satan," "the Evil One'* and *"The Prince of Darkness"* is using these phrases to symbolize our own lower animal natures, which must be brought under control, first, by the salvation that only the Manifestation of God can provide and second, by recognizing and obeying the commands and teachings of God's Manifestation of Himself. Even as Jesus said: *"If you love Me, keep My commandments.* (John 14:15)

What Baha'u'llah calls our *"evil and corrupt desires"* represents that lower, animal nature and He prays in many prayers that we may be *"purged"* from our *"evil inclinations."* He clarifies this even more when He refers to the *"Satan of self"* and *"the whisperings of selfish desire."* In fact, Baha'u'llah seems to be saying that *"Satanic knowledge"* comes about when man allows his lower self to rule and *"evil passions and corrupt desires"* to take strong control. This is, I would say, a very good definition of sin, whether thought of as 'original sin' or simply seen as the deeper, truer understanding of man's lower, animal nature.

In an earlier age of humankind, we referred to a being outside ourselves, a 'devil' who could be blamed for all our problems. Now, Baha'u'llah teaches us that the 'devil' and *"the Evil Whisperer who whispers in men's hearts"* is not an outside force but an aspect of our nature which must be brought under control through salvation, which comes through the Manifestation of God and by obedience to God through following the teachings of the Manifestation.

In another prayer, Baha'u'llah asks God to *"cleanse our hearts from the stain of evil desire."* Baha'u'llah remarked that a society that allowed this evil desire of man's lower nature to run free would be regarded as *"the me-tropolis of Satan."*

In that regard, there is a really good booklet you could read with that same title, *The Metropolis of Satan*, written by Baha'i author Gary Matthews. If you are interested in this topic of Satan, the Devil and the role of evil in the world from the Baha'i point of view, there is no better book or reference. Any Baha'i friend can get it for you, or you can order it from the Baha'i Publishing Trust. (See chapter sixteen for information on how to contact the Trust.) See chapter fifteen for an 800 number and various web sites.

Baha'u'llah said that it was His task, and one that we now share as human beings, to convert *"satanic strength into heavenly power."* This is exactly what happens in a life that is transformed by salvation and by the power that is experienced when individuals and a newly empowered society recognize and follow the Manifestation of God.

QUESTION: I can certainly see that Baha'u'llah believed in the reality of sin and the presence of evil in the world, but is there some other difference here as well?

RESPONSE: Yes, and no. Baha'u'llah does refer often to *"sin,"* to *"evil passions and corrupt desires,"* to *"satanic knowledge"* and the role they play in our lives, individually and collectively. Baha'u'llah's Son, 'Abdu'l-Baha (often referred to by the Baha'is as 'The Master') once said . . .

QUESTION: Wait a minute! Don't you realize that Christians refer to Christ as 'The Master'? I don't think I like hearing that a Baha'i leader is called by that same title.

RESPONSE: Well, let's remember that the title 'Master' is simply a title of honor in the middle and far east, given to a wise and honorable man or someone of special skill, and in religion, usually one who is seen to possess deep spiritual knowledge and truth. 'Abdu'l-Baha was not a Manifestation and therefore cannot be compared with Christ.

However, he has a unique place in Baha'i history. Why? Because Baha'u'llah said of him: *"Whoso turneth towards Him hath turned towards God"* (Quoted in Shoghi Effendi: *God Passes By*, Page: 242) and called him *"a shelter for all mankind."* (Quoted in Shoghi Effendi: *God Passes By*, Page: 243) Baha'u'llah asked all of His followers to turn to 'Abdu'l-Baha after His death, for leadership and interpretation of the meaning of Baha'u'llah's words and His Revelation.

This is probably why there is so little, in fact nearly none, of disagreement or argument as to what Baha'u'llah meant by what He said or wrote. By contrast, as we all know, the body of Christianity has at times been torn apart by differences of interpretation as to what Christ meant. Over and over, throughout the centuries, this has been decided by Church Councils, voting as a means of deciding scriptural meaning.

'Abdu'l-Baha's name is actually a self-chosen title and means 'Servant of Baha,' signifying that He wished to be a servant of His father, Baha'u'llah. The Master is significant and special to the Baha'is for two other reasons: First, Baha'u'llah told His followers and the world to look upon 'Abdu'l-Baha to see what men and women could be like at their best.

Baha'i writings call 'Abdu'l-Baha the 'Exemplar' of

the pattern of life taught by His Father. They see him as described by the Universal House of Justice: "This unique figure is at once the Exemplar of the pattern of life taught by His Father, the divinely inspired authoritative Interpreter of His Teachings and the Centre and Pivot of the Covenant which the Author of the Baha'i Revelation made with all who recognize Him." (Baha'u'llah: *Kitab-i-Aqdas*: Other Sections, Page: 3)

Come to think of it, here is a small difference between our Faiths. Christians are striving to be 'Christlike' while Baha'is, though they would try in a general way to show forth the characteristics of the person of Baha'u'llah, seek, rather, to be like 'Abdu'l-Baha, the 'Perfect Exemplar' of His father's teachings and the example of what a man or woman could be like at their best. Of course, a Baha'i from a Christian background, like myself, still strives to be 'Christlike,' while at the same time, attempting to be like 'Abdu'l-Baha, the 'Perfect Exemplar' of His Father's teachings. I have found that there is no difficulty in this, since the personal qualities of both of them are so much alike.

The second reason that 'Abdu'l-Baha has central importance in the Baha'i Faith is that His Father, Baha'u'llah, said that God was today setting forth another installment of the Covenant that God has always had with the people of the world. Baha'i writings say that 'Abdu'l-Baha is "the appointed Successor of Baha'u'llah and Center of His Covenant," (Quoted in Shoghi Effendi: *God Passes By*, Page: 233) This Covenant is a 'new covenant' that God had established with mankind in the coming of Baha'u'llah.

So, as you can see, although 'Abdu'l-Baha is not a Manifestation of God, he is very precious to the Baha'is of the world and one cannot really even fully grasp the Baha'i Faith without understanding the 'Covenant' and the role and the person of 'The Master,' 'Abdu'l-Baha. As you might realize, since I come from a Christian background, I, like you, will also always think of Christ as 'The Master', my father's favorite word for Jesus.

But weren't we discussing something else, before we went off on this important discussion of 'the Center of the Covenant,' 'Abdu'l-Baha?

QUESTION: Yes. The problem of evil. What is the Baha'i idea of evil? Do Baha'is believe in evil?

RESPONSE: Well, this is one of the thorny problems of all time, isn't it? All religions and all philosophies have struggled to understand the role of evil in human history. As best as I can understand what the Baha'i Faith teaches, and remembering the discussion we had not long ago about Satan and man's *"evil passions and corrupt desires,"* Baha'u'llah seems to be telling us (you should read and investigate for yourself, as I keep encouraging you to do) that 'evil' is really the outward manifestation of our own lower, corrupt, animal nature.

When an individual, a group or society lets their corrupt, sinful nature run out of control, we get a collective evil, like the Nazi party in Hitler's Germany, or, as Baha'u'llah put it so succinctly, a society that could be called *"the metropolis of Satan."* Evil can take such form, He says, that it can manifest *"satanic strength."* The world saw what Baha'u'llah meant when mankind was plunged into a Second World War, where over sixty million people were killed.

Or, consider the Holocaust, where six million or more Jews and other minorities were put to death in an unspeakably evil genocide dishonoring of man's higher, truer nature. Or consider Stalin's bestial behavior or Cambodia's 'Killing Fields.' No wonder Baha'u'llah prayed to God to *"Keep us safe from them whom Thou has made to be the manifestations of the Evil Whisperer, who whisper in men's breasts."* It's probably worth noting that the words 'Evil' or 'Satan' are usually capitalized in translations of Baha'u'llah's writings.

Finally, there is this important point. 'Abdu'l-Baha said that the evil we see in the world is the evil that exists and is manifested in man only when men and women are not trained, not given a spiritual education, not strengthened in the ways of the teachings of the Manifestation of God and when they are not transformed by salvation and the power that only the Manifestation of God can provide.

QUESTION: You know, when I consider the 'differences' between the two Faiths and I remember our discussion about 'similarities,' I do see that there are some real differences, but I'm struck by one fact, that the differences are not so great. Here is my question that remains, however. If there are so many similarities and when the differences aren't so great, why did you begin to follow this Faith? Why should I follow Baha'u'llah? Why shouldn't I just stick with Christ, with Christianity, and with my Church? I suspect you are going to talk to me about Jesus and the Jews, but please don't avoid answering my question!

RESPONSE: The reason I refer to Christ and His interaction with the Jews He taught is this: I believe that Jesus is the most authoritative source I can use to attempt to respond to your question.

When Jesus was asked almost an identical question, namely, 'Why can't I just take your new teachings, Jesus, but stick with Moses, with Judaism and my Synagogue?' you know what He replied, don't you? He said: *"Ye can-*

not put new wine in old wineskins. "You and I have to ask, could the Faith of Christianity have made its contribution to the world if its followers had stayed within the Synagogue? And, we must ask: What could a Jew do, what should he or she have done when Jesus looked them in the eye and said: *"Follow me"*?

Could they say: 'Well yes, I'd be glad to follow you, but only if I can stay in the Synagogue, or only if you don't ask too much of me'? Of course, we know this would not have worked. You probably know that there was quite a battle going on after Jesus' death and Resurrection (recorded in the book of Acts) as to whether to 'remain Jewish' or to realize that a new Faith had begun and that they must leave the Synagogue and Jewish practices and follow this new Faith. This struggle, largely between Peter and Paul, was resolved as Christians realized they were not just a sect or offshoot of Judaism but a new Faith.

Now, it is a New Day similar to the New Day in the time of Jesus. In the same way today, Baha'u'llah's Revelation and teachings, constitute a 'new wine' that cannot be held in 'old wineskins' of Christian institutions and Churches. Baha'u'llah said that God's greatest desire in this Day is to see the world of humanity united to the extent that they would see themselves as *"one soul and one body."* The Christian Church, by its own admission, is sadly and almost incredibly divided into literally a thousand sects, groups and denominations.

Christ wanted His followers to be *"the leaven"* that would leaven the whole world. However, just as Christ said, His teachings— *"the new wine"*—had to be put in *"new wineskins."* Likewise, it appears that the *"new wine"* of Baha'u'llah's teachings must also be put into the *"new wineskins"* of Baha'i institutions, which have been specifically set up by Baha'u'llah for the purpose of bringing

humanity into salvation, unity, peace and the age of fulfillment.

QUESTION: Christians are still striving to create
that unity themselves and especially among their own
ranks. If only Christians would focus on Christ, the Savior, and not on their own beliefs and desires, they would
begin to represent and to create the very unity you Baha'is
are talking about.

RESPONSE: I can't disagree. But now, in this new
Day, Baha'u'llah tells us that Christ has returned *"in my
person,"* appearing *"in the glory of the Father."* He tells us,
Christians in particular, that they can and should turn to
Baha'u'llah, *"the Father"* as the new Manifestation of God,
in the same way that, two-thousand years ago, Jesus told
Jews that they should turn to the new Manifestation of
God, Jesus Himself, *"The Son."*

To summarize, there are many similarities and some
differences between the two Faiths, Christian and Baha'i.
There is one thing that is both the strongest similarity
and, at the same time, the strongest difference. This one
thing is what I call the 'twin facts' of Christ and
Baha'u'llah.

Fact one is the set of differences. First, Christ came
two—thousand years ago, and Baha'u'llah came within
the time of your great or great, great Grandfather (if
you are reading this at twenty years of age around the
turn of the millennium). As to their teachings, different
somewhat, but not very much. Different in that while
Christ spoke primarily about individual salvation,
Baha'u'llah and His followers are primarily concerned
with bringing humankind into unity and actually building the 'Kingdom of God on earth' that Christ asked us
to pray for. Of course, it is true that Christians also want

a better world. Likewise, it is true that Baha'is recognize that salvation of individuals is vital to this task.

Fact two is that even with the differences, these two Faiths are strikingly similar. In both Faiths, the central figures, Christ and Baha'u'llah, are considered to come from one God. Both are considered Manifestations of God. Both are taken as examples of the brightness and power of God's 'pre-existent Word' that existed before the world began and through whom the world came into being. Both share a 'divinity' with God, Jesus as *'The Son'* and Baha'u'llah as *'The Father.'*

Sometimes it seems to me that Christians could easily see that Baha'u'llah represents a Return to the world of the Person of Christ and Christ's Spirit, with a fullness and brightness that allows them to feel 'at home,' even as they become followers of Baha'u'llah. At other times, I realize how difficult this thought is for some and I can only reflect on how incredibly difficult it was for a Jew to begin to follow Jesus.

QUESTION: You are right to see that what you are saying is hard to hear and it is very difficult to think seriously about following Baha'u'llah. I don't even feel that I am close to such a decision. But I now know that, having heard what you have told me, I need to make a decision for or against Baha'u'llah. I'm sure of that much, but I'm not sure how the decision will go. I am starting to realize that I will have to get major assistance from the Holy Spirit and strong guidance from the Master, my Jesus.

RESPONSE: Your statement is good enough for me. I can remember when I was somewhat at the same point in my thinking about Baha'u'llah. I commend you for 'hanging in there' on something that is, as you say, so important. In the next chapter, let's go on to contrast Jesus' statement about being *"fishers of men"* with Baha'u'llah's command to His followers to be *"quickeners of mankind."* I think you will find the discussion interesting, and that you will see that these two commands are actually complementary. And I want to close, as we often do, with two prayers from the Baha'i writings.

"O Thou Whose nearness is my wish, Whose presence is my hope, Whose remembrance is my desire, Whose court of glory is my goal, Whose abode is my aim, Whose name is my healing, Whose love is the radiance of my heart, Whose service is my highest aspiration! I beseech Thee by Thy Name, through which Thou hast enabled them that have recognized Thee to soar to the sublimest heights of the knowledge of Thee and empowered such as devoutly worship Thee to ascend into the precincts of the court of Thy holy favors, to aid me to turn my face towards Thy face, to fix mine eyes upon Thee, and to speak of Thy glory.

"I am the one, O my Lord, who hath forgotten all else but Thee, and turned towards the Day-Spring of Thy grace, who hath forsaken all save Thyself in the hope of drawing nigh unto Thy court. Behold me, then, with mine eyes lifted up towards the Seat that shineth with the splendors of the light of Thy Face. Send down, then, upon me, O my Beloved, that which will enable me to be steadfast in Thy Cause, so that the doubts of the infidels may not hinder me from turning towards Thee.

"Thou art, verily, the God of Power, the Help in Peril, the All-Glorious, the Almighty. " (Baha'u'llah: *Prayers and Meditations*, Pages: 174-175)

And a prayer from 'Abdu'l-Baha:

"O God! Refresh and gladden my spirit. Purify my heart. Illumine my powers. I lay all my affairs in Thy hand. Thou art my Guide and my Refuge. I will no longer be sorrowful and grieved; I will be a happy and joyful being. O God! I will

no longer be full of anxiety, nor will I let trouble harass me. I will not dwell on the unpleasant things of life.

"O God! Thou art more friend to me than I am to myself. I dedicate myself to Thee, O Lord." ('Abdu'l-Baha: *Baha'i Prayers* (US edition), Page: 152)

CHAPTER TEN

'FISHERS OF MEN' AND 'QUICKENERS OF MANKIND': MOVING HUMANKIND TOWARD UNITY AND PEACE

QUESTION: From what we just discussed in the last chapter, the Christian and Baha'i Faiths have great similarity. The differences are relatively minor.

RESPONSE: Well, I think you are right. And, the relationship between the two Faiths is very strong, as seen in that quote from Baha'u'llah: *"If ye be intent on crucifying once again Jesus, the Spirit of God, put Me to death, for He hath once more, in My person, been made manifest unto you."* (Baha'u'llah: *Gleanings*, Page: 101)

QUESTION: That certainly is a direct and forceful claim. Did Baha'u'llah make that claim in relation to any of the other Manifestations, such as Buddha, Muhammad or Moses?

RESPONSE: An interesting question! No, He did not, at least not as directly as in that quote. However, He did point out that the *'Word of God'* or the *'Light of God'* has been the same within the appearance of every Manifestation of God throughout history. He said that the *'Lamps'* (the physical person of the Manifestation) may be different, but the *'Light of God'* (the inner reality of the Presence of God among men, the 'Word of God') is the same in all of the Manifestations.

So, yes, there does seem to be an especially strong connection between Jesus Christ, *"The Son"* and Baha'u'llah, *"The Father."*

QUESTION: I've brought this up before, but I have to say again that I'm still having difficulty hearing Baha'u'llah called *'the Father.'* It seems so strange, almost as if Baha'u'llah is claiming to be God?

RESPONSE: Earlier, we discussed that both Jesus and Baha'u'llah seemed at some times to claim to be God, or one with God, or to claim that seeing them was seeing God. Then, at other times, both of them deny being God. Let's look again: Jesus said both of the following things: (1) *"The Father and I are One,"* [which seems to be saying, in effect, "I am God"]; and (2) Jesus also said: *"Why do you call Me good? No one is good but One, that is, God."* (Luke 18:19) [which seems to be saying: "I am not God"].

QUESTION: Wait a minute. Christians don't see a contradiction there, because the problem is resolved by the concept of the Trinity, with God, the Father, God the Son and God the Holy Spirit.

RESPONSE: That's right, even though the word 'Trinity' isn't even mentioned in the New Testament, because the concept and the word was only established by the Church Fathers several decades or more after the death of St. Paul and all the disciples. It was not a concept set forth by either Jesus or St. Paul, even though Baha'is understand and accept it. As you say, Christians resolved this apparent contradiction with the idea of the Trinity.

QUESTION: What did Baha'u'llah say about this?

RESPONSE: He said that He and Christ and all the other divinely sent Manifestations of God have a two-fold nature. First, they have a physical nature, in which they can be seen to be *"a man like you,"* as Baha'u'llah put it. Christ made a similar statement, as we have said. Those who were around Christ and Baha'u'llah saw this physical man-like nature. Christians fought a bitter battle for almost four centuries during which some Christians tried to deny that Jesus was a man.

A Church council resolved this with a vote that said that the Church would regard Jesus as 'fully man and fully God.' Whether one is listening to this Church Council or if one is listening to Baha'u'llah speak of the *"double station"* of the Manifestations, one still sees some difference, but practically speaking, it sounds very similar, doesn't it?

Those around Christ and Baha'u'llah also saw another, spiritual 'nature' which, Baha'u'llah says, is *"born of the substance of God Himself."* (Baha'u'llah: *Gleanings*, Page: 66) This is why Jesus could say *"the Father and I are one"* and both Christ and Baha'u'llah could say that if people saw them, they were seeing God. Also, Baha'u'llah said that all the Manifestations, including Christ and Himself, had a *"double station." "The first station, which is related to His innermost reality, representeth Him as One Whose voice is the voice of God Himself."* (Baha'u'llah: *Gleanings,* Page: 66)

The other 'station' is one in which Baha'u'llah suggested that any Manifestation might say: *"I am but a man like you."* (Baha'u'llah: *Kitab-i-Aqdas*: Notes, Page: 233) and where Christ similarly said *"Why do you call Me good? No one is good but One, that is, God."* (Luke 18:19), both of them focusing for the moment on this human side, the station of humanness.

So, you see from this discussion that the idea of the Trinity and the 'fully man, fully God' Church council solutions are not far from the Baha'i understanding of Manifestation. I am not saying that the two explanations are identical; they are not. What I am saying is that, upon a closer look, they are not that different. One rather large difference is that in the case of Christians, these formulations were made by votes in Church councils several centuries later, whereas in the Baha'i Revelation, these points were spelled out in writing by Baha'u'llah Himself in direct, unequivocal terms that cannot be easily misunderstood (and with His own Son appointed as the interpreter of the meaning of His words).

Summarizing, Jesus might say, *"The Father and I are One,"* and Baha'u'llah might say, *"my face is, verily, Thy face, and my call is Thy call, and my Revelation Thy Revelation, and my self Thy Self, and my Cause Thy Cause, and my behest Thy behest, and my Being Thy Being"* (Baha'u'llah: *Prayers and Meditations,* Page: 231). Jesus said: *"If you have seen Me, you have seen the Father"* and Baha'u'llah referred to Himself as *"Him in Whom Thou Thyself art manifest.*" (Baha'u'llah: *Prayers and Meditations*, Page: 235).

The point, I think, is that if we remember that Christ and Baha'u'llah and all the other Manifestations of God have 'two natures' and a 'two-fold station' we will understand what could otherwise be seen as a strange contradiction.

Whether it is resolved as the Christians did with their Church Councils and the concept of 'Trinity' or whether it is resolved from the direct words of Baha'u'llah, there is not as much difference between the two explanations as one might at first think, especially if we look at the actual words of Christ and the actual words of Baha'u'llah.

QUESTION: You called this chapter "Fishers of Men and Quickeners of Mankind." I recognize Christ's request for us to become *"Fishers of Men,"* but what do you mean by *"Quickeners of Mankind"?*

RESPONSE: Yes, Jesus did tell His disciples to become *"Fishers of Men"* and His message and teachings were strongly aimed at individual salvation and personal transformation. Christians have done an admirable work of following Christ's instructions: *"Go into all the world and preach the gospel to every creature."* (Mark 16:15)

Baha'u'llah's Revelation and message, or as He called it *"The Cause of God,"* is also concerned with individual salvation and the transformation of individual character that will be necessary to build a world described by Christ as the *"Kingdom"* right here *"on earth as it is in Heaven."* However, Baha'u'llah tells us that for this to be accomplished, the whole world must be brought from its nearly *"dead"* state into new life and new unity.

Also, for this to happen, regeneration must not only

take place in every individual, but it must also affect the whole world, all the religions, all the cultures and peoples of every tribe and nation who must be *"quickened."* The word 'quickened' means 'brought into life.' That is why Baha'u'llah asked His followers to be the *"Quickeners of Mankind."*

QUESTION: It sounds as if Baha'u'llah is saying that the world needs more than individual salvation. I'm not sure I can agree with that, even though I know true Christians want a better world and work hard always to achieve it.

RESPONSE: Yes they do. But transformed lives are only the start of what both Christ and Baha'u'llah wanted, as I see it. Christ's teachings do start to describe, at least in ideal terms and, by implication, the kind of world that ought to exist. When a believer in either Christ or Baha'u'llah experiences salvation through responding to them in the Day of Their Manifestation, this important personal event does change their life to such a degree that their thoughts and actions are greatly changed.

And, in Christian history, Christians have always tried to transform not only individual lives, but also they have tried and often succeeded in changing the world. Christ clearly taught His disciples to pray, as in the Lord's Prayer for the coming of a Kingdom and of the expression of God's Will *"on earth as it is in Heaven."*

The point is, and it seems clear when we focus on it, that Jesus wanted this Kingdom to be here *"on earth."* Otherwise, He would not have taught His disciples to pray in this way.

In Baha'u'llah's teaching . . .

QUESTION: May I just stop you right there! I know

I'm interrupting, but when Jesus Christ speaks, we Christians believe God is speaking. I don't know that I could ever feel the same way about Baha'u'llah's 'teachings.'

RESPONSE: Well, Jesus said: *"The words that I say unto you, I speak not from Myself, but the Father in Me doeth His works."* (John 14:10) So, I think you should feel exactly as you do about the words of Jesus, that when He speaks, it is God speaking. It will interest you to know that Baha'u'llah stated: *"I can utter no word, O my God, unless I be permitted by Thee, and can move in no direction until I obtain Thy sanction. It is Thou, O my God, Who hast called me into being through the power of Thy might, and hast endued me with Thy grace to manifest Thy Cause."* (Baha'u'llah: *Prayers and Meditations*, Page: 208)

Speaking of Himself, Baha'u'llah said: *"While in His presence, thou hast heard the Voice of the One true God."* (Baha'u'llah: *Tablets of Baha'u'llah*, Page: 240) Finally, Baha'u'llah said that when He spoke to His followers (and to you!) that God was *"calling thee from His seat of glory."* (Baha'u'llah: *Gleanings*, Page: 291).

QUESTION: I feel confused at what you are saying, or maybe you are confused? If God is speaking to us through Christ and, as you claim, God is speaking to us through Baha'u'llah, to whom do we listen?

RESPONSE: We listen to the Voice of God. In the time of Jesus, the Voice of God was speaking through Jesus, the *'Son of God.'* In this new day, that same 'Voice of God' (not a different one) is speaking through Baha'u'llah, *'The Father.'* And, all of the Manifestations of God, Buddha, Muhammad, Krishna, Moses and others (compare them to 'lamps' of different shapes and colors) all have the very same light of God in them, the 'pre-existent' Word of God.

The same Voice of God is heard from each and every one of them. Baha'u'llah says that they *"step forth out of the realm of the invisible into the visible world."* (Baha'u'llah: The *Kitab-i-Iqan*, Page: 25) and that these *"Beings* [the Manifestations] *though delivered from the womb of their mother, have in reality descended from the heaven of the will of God."* (Baha'u'llah: The *Kitab-i-Iqan*, Page: 67)

The Voice of God in this new day is again offering salvation, but the emphasis is not only on individual salvation and personal transformation, but also upon the unity of all mankind. That is why *"fishers of men"* and *"quickeners of mankind"* are both important. The men and women of earth must now learn that they are one people and that their very future, even their very existence depends upon the realization of their oneness and the construction, with Divine help, of their unity.

For a person such as myself, who grew up with Christian ideals and who received the priceless gift of salvation from Jesus Christ, the *"Son of God,"* it is doubly meaningful to experience the Spirit of Jesus returned in Baha'u'llah and to recognize Baha'u'llah as the long-awaited 'Promised One' and *"The Father"* of all mankind.

My discipleship is now two-fold: I can never forget the role that salvation played in my life, anymore than I can forget from Whom it first came—Jesus. Salvation must play a role in the lives of hundreds of millions of men and women if the world is to be renewed and resurrected from its 'dead' state. Baha'u'llah said that the purpose of His Revelation was *"the regeneration of the whole world, and the establishment of the unity of its peoples, and the salvation of all them that dwell therein."* (Baha'u'llah: *Gleanings*, Page: 243)

At another time, He said that God had *"sent down"* through His Revelation *"That which is conducive to the regeneration of the world and the salvation of the peoples and kindreds of the earth."* (Baha'u'llah: *Tablets of Baha'u'llah,* Page: 223)

He also stated the following, which is reminiscent of a verse from the New Testament: *"Say, O ye who are as dead! The Hand of Divine bounty proffereth unto you the Water of Life. Hasten and drink your fill. Whoso hath been re-born in this Day, shall never die; whoso remaineth dead, shall never live."* (Baha'u'llah: *Gleanings,* Page: 213)

In addition to my continuing task of urging individual men and women to seek the salvation that can only be obtained by recognizing the Manifestation of God in the Day in which He appears, I also must be a messenger of God's Will for this day, which is: that the people of the world may be brought back from the 'dead,' literally 'quickened,' to recognize their oneness, to claim their unity and to enter into a phase of building on earth that Kingdom of God, as prayed for by Christ.

Individual Salvation—all-important. Spiritual Resurrection and quickening of all mankind—equally important. And, it needs to be seen that the quickening cannot really happen without salvation; likewise the salvation of individuals must bear fruit, by leading to the realization of a united humanity.

QUESTION: A moment ago, you spoke of salvation as coming through recognizing the Manifestation of God. Christians believe that salvation was offered once and for all time by the death of Christ on the Cross. And, that believing in Jesus and giving your life over to Him provides that salvation.

RESPONSE: As I shared with you, I'm from a Christian background, so I'm well aware of Christian belief and I agree with what you said. The only thing that Baha'u'llah adds to these beliefs you have just stated is that the suffering of all of the Manifestations have provided the means of salvation to humanity and that when they appear, belief in them, following them, obeying them, connects a person to an experience of salvation that can only come from the Manifestation, in the day in which that Manifestation appears.

But, in any case, if Baha'u'llah is the Return of Christ and the Father of all mankind, no Christian would want to turn away from Him or deny that salvation is dependent upon recognizing Christ Returned. I do understand that the 'big issue' is whether or not Baha'u'llah is Who He said He is. When He tells us that Jesus, our Jesus, has come again to the world *"in my person,"* we are left with only two choices, either to find a way to disbelieve Him or to believe Him.

QUESTION: What you have just said still doesn't make sense to me. Christ and Baha'u'llah—you call them both Manifestations of God—were two different people. Everyone knows that Jesus was an historical person; so was Buddha, so was Baha'u'llah. To say that Baha'u'llah is the Return of Christ makes me feel that you are somewhat twisting the meaning of words.

RESPONSE: Let me go back to your original question. Every so often, I can't help but remind you that although I believe these things that may be troublesome or confusing to you, it is not really me talking: It is Baha'u'llah Who is saying these words. Maybe this will help: When Baha'u'llah says that the Manifestations of God are to be regarded as *"the same person,"* He is referring to the *"essential unity"* of these Manifestations.

Baha'u'llah says that in this 'station' of 'essential unity', they may, so to speak, be wearing a different suit of clothes, but says Baha'u'llah, *"If thou wilt observe with discriminating eyes, thou wilt behold Them all abiding in the same tabernacle, soaring in the same heaven, seated upon the same throne, uttering the same speech, and proclaiming the same Faith."* (Baha'u'llah: *Gleanings*, Page: 52)

And as for being the 'same person,' Baha'u'llah also says there is a 'second station' that the Manifestations have, of 'distinction'. *"In this respect each Manifestation of God hath a distinct individuality, a definitely prescribed mission, a predestined revelation, and specially designated limitations. Each one of them is known by a different name, is characterized by a special attribute, fulfils a definite mission, and is entrusted with a particular Revelation."* (Baha'u'llah: *Gleanings*, Page: 52)

Of special interest to Christians, Baha'u'llah says that God sent and empowered all the Manifestations: *"And to Jesus, Son of Mary, We gave manifest signs, and We strengthened Him with the Holy Spirit."* (Baha'u'llah: *Gleanings*, Page: 52)

QUESTION: I just have to follow up. Here's my problem. Yes, the explanation from Baha'u'llah you just gave about the two 'stations' of 'oneness' and 'distinction' helped, but you still seem to be 'playing around' with historical figures, almost ignoring reality.

RESPONSE: I truly hope I'm not doing that; at least, I'm not trying to. I must admit that I did feel somewhat the way you are feeling when I first heard about the Baha'is. However, I can think of something else that may help. I have done no more, or rather Baha'u'llah has said no more than Christ did when He told the multitudes that they should have understood that John the

Baptist was the return of Elijah (Matt 11:15), even though John the Baptist had said that he wasn't Elijah. (John 1:21)

We know that Jesus knew that John was the 'return' of Elijah, even though John did not recognize it, and neither you nor I would refute Him when He said that John the Baptist was the return of Elijah, who was an historical figure from centuries before. Would you say that Jesus was being careless or 'playing around' with historical figures? I'll bet you wouldn't!

QUESTION: You're right, I wouldn't. For a moment, I didn't believe you were right in your quotation of the Bible, so I looked it up. Jesus did say that. Interesting! However, haven't we drifted away from our discussion of 'fishers of men' and 'quickeners' of mankind?

RESPONSE: True enough, but I hope you will accept some of the responsibility for the 'drift.' That's the way conversations go, I guess. Well, we have already established that both the Christian Faith and the Baha'i Faith are primarily interested in the personal salvation and transformation of individual lives. We agree that both Faiths wish to establish 'good works' in the world. Changed lives should lead to changed, newly directed marriages, families, communities and, we hope, nations.

In the case of the Baha'i Faith, that change extends even out to the whole world, where we expect the world to be transformed for the better, in fact united, and not just in spirit but in practical reality. Both our Faiths want therefore to transform not only individuals but also the larger society itself, to make it nobler, more in line with the ideals and teachings of our two Faiths.

A difference between the two faiths may be that in the Baha'i teachings humanity is clearly called upon by

God to unify, to actually create the 'Kingdom of God on earth' that Christ prayed for. This unification cannot occur unless and until humankind discovers its essential oneness, until it realizes there is, actually, only one race on earth, the human race.

QUESTION: This is where I begin to have trouble again. There *are* many different races here on earth and also many other kinds of divisions and this idea of 'unification of the human race' sometimes seems either grandiose and unattainable, hopeless, or just plain silly.

RESPONSE: Believe it or not, I can understand you on this, because first of all, this is what most people believe. They have 'given up' and do not believe that the world could become united. The situation of the world does look 'hopeless' sometimes, but even you believe that if the principles of Jesus Christ had been or were now to be followed, this would be a changed world. Didn't you say that a while ago?

QUESTION: Well, yes I did. But just as you say, the situation of the world seems hopeless and I and many other Christians believe that it will not improve or get better until Christ Returns. Well, I guess that is exactly what you believe has happened?

RESPONSE: Yes, that's what Baha'is believe, because it's what Baha'u'llah said. Before we go on, I do want to say that some Christians and nearly all scientists believe what Baha'u'llah taught, that there is only one human group, one race here on planet earth, one species, not many. Where the confusion may come in is that there certainly are many ethnic groups, but only one race.

It is becoming more and more scientifically clear

that our species, our one race came from an original group in Africa. So the teaching of Baha'u'llah is completely in line with scientific opinion, and saying that there is only one race does not deny or ignore that many ethnic groups exist.

But let's go back to that idea that things seem hopeless. It is an idea that is widespread, so I'm not shocked you feel that way. It is as if nothing and no one can bring us from being 'dead' to life, that no one can 'quicken' us and lead our world into Resurrection. But that is precisely what Baha'u'llah says over and again that God sent Him into the world to do.

Baha'i House of Worship in Panama, Central America.

Let's do this for a moment. Let's play the game of 'What if?'

What if . . . just think with me for a moment, what if the people of the world heard and began to believe that they were really one? What if . . . the following statement from Baha'u'llah came to be deeply understood and believed? ***"Blessed and happy is he that ariseth to pro-***

*mote the best interests of the peoples and kindreds of the earth
. . . It is not for him to pride himself who loveth his own
country, but rather for him who loveth the whole world. The
earth is but one country, and mankind its citizens.*"
(Baha'u'llah: *Gleanings*, Page: 250)

What if . . . Baha'u'llah's teachings about humanity
were taken to heart when He said: *"O well-beloved ones!
The tabernacle of unity hath been raised; regard ye not one
another as strangers. Ye are the fruits of one tree, and the
leaves of one branch."* (Baha'u'llah: *Tablets of Baha'u'llah*,
Page: 164) 'Abdu'l-Baha, Baha'u'llah's Son said: *"mankind has been created from one single origin, has branched off
from one family. Thus in reality all mankind represents one
family. God has not created any difference. He has created all
as one that thus this family might live in perfect happiness
and well-being."* ('Abdu'l-Baha: *Foundations of World Unity*,
Page: 38)

Interestingly, as I said above, science has been slowly
moving toward the same conclusion.

What if . . . the believers of every religion and culture heard and believed that the 'Promised One' had
appeared, the one they had awaited, the one they had
been told would appear (or re-appear, as in the case of
the Second Coming of Christ). Buddhists, Hindus, Moslems, Jews and others also speak of a time in history
when a 'Promised One' would appear, though they may
use different names to name that 'Promised One.'

What if . . . the people of the world believed this
had happened? What if . . . they heard and believed
what Baha'u'llah said: *"He that was hidden from the eyes of
men is revealed, girded with sovereignty and power! . . . O
ye that inhabit the heavens and the earth! There hath appeared what hath never previously appeared. He Who, from
everlasting, had concealed His Face from the sight of creation
is now come."* (Baha'u'llah: *Gleanings*, Page: 31) What

would the world be like if they began to believe these things and acted on them, moving toward peace and unity?

QUESTION: Why are we playing this 'game'? None of this is true, nor is it likely to be true, as I see it. I'm not trying to be negative or cynical, nor without hope for the future. It's just that the world is nowhere near to what you are dreaming about, is it?

RESPONSE: My response is that it depends entirely on the source of your dream. If it came out of my own head, I would be truly 'crazy,' I agree. When one looks at the condition of the world, then the Baha'i hopes, beliefs and dreams are just 'way out of line,' on the surface. No question.

However, if Baha'u'llah is Who He said He is, if His coming represents the reappearance of Christ into history and if He is *'the Father,'* the *'Promised One,'* then all bets are off, aren't they? Everything is possible, if He is the one Who came, as He said: *"to build anew the whole world."* (Baha'u'llah: *Gleanings*, Page: 100)

When Baha'u'llah begins to do His work in history through changed, transformed individuals, living in new, vitalized communities that are modeled after His teachings and infused with His power, we will then be able to assess whether the world is being 'built anew.' The Jew who followed Christ was 'betting his life' that Jesus was Who He said He was, wasn't he?

Well, today I'm betting my life with a growing number of millions (six million at the turn of the millennium) who believe in Baha'u'llah, who follow Him, who are committed to enacting His teachings and doing their part to move the world toward unity and peace. I don't ever pretend that only Baha'is believe in the ideas, values and teachings put forth by Baha'u'llah. Many Christians, Jews and Moslems, Hindus, Buddhists and others also hold these ideals.

It was probably true that many Jews believed what Jesus said without following Him. But you don't believe, do you, that it would have been the same, for that Jew to simply follow the teachings of Jesus, but not Jesus? Nevertheless, today, Baha'is who have made a commitment to follow Baha'u'llah, are very willing and eager to share the task of *"building the world anew"* with committed Christians, Moslems, Hindus and anyone else who will work to unite humanity.

So, let me return to what you call a 'game,' but just for a minute, I promise. And in a moment, you will see why I believe it is not a game at all. I have a surprise for you.

What if . . . humankind woke up one day to the truth of Baha'u'llah's message: *"The Father hath come"*?

Finally, what if . . . all people everywhere recognized not only that they are one, but also that God is one and even the Manifestations of God, all of them, are one?

What then . . . ? I said that I had a surprise for you. Let's go back a moment to the first two, even three centuries after Christ. The Roman world took very little notice of the Christians or their Faith for a long time. Finally, more than a century later, they regarded them as a dangerous atheistic 'cult.' It wasn't until a full three centuries and more went by that they 'woke up' to the beauty, the reality and the healing message of Christ. They probably then said to themselves: 'Hey, where have I been while all this was going on?'

Something similar is going on right now. Remember all those 'crazy' 'what ifs' I just told you about? Here's the surprise. Erase the 'what ifs' because the worldwide Baha'i community is already practicing these beliefs and teachings, not tomorrow, but today. Not pie in the sky by and by, but a reality that can be seen, touched, and experienced in our communities today.

There is no 'what if' within the Baha'i community. The Baha'is, through their connections with the United Nations and many other international organizations, are speeding the transmission of knowledge of Baha'u'llah's healing message and its practical means and measures of uniting the world. I repeat, this is not just being dreamed of, as if happening in some distant tomorrow; it is happening today.

You may say it is on a small scale, but remember this: Christianity started with only eleven faithful disciples and a few others. One hundred fifty years later, it certainly had no more adherents than the Baha'i Faith now has and it was spread only into the near Middle East, the Mediterranean and perhaps to India. Even in the third century, the Christian Faith was still relatively small, represented in few countries, and anyone not knowing the truth of the matter would have said it was lacking in the power to bring about change

But look what happened in the Fourth Century! It suddenly became powerful in its ability to influence whole communities and nations with a new spiritual power, a new ethic, a new sense of purpose and new ideals and practices. It is the same story that we have been talking about: Transformed individuals forming into newly organized communities with a sense of purpose, direction and spiritual power that comes from the appearance of the new Manifestation. The Baha'is long ago took a page from the early Christians and forgot 'What if' and went on to 'Let's do it now'!

As to whether these things can actually come to pass, there is a passage from Baha'u'llah's Revelation that is utterly fascinating. I want to share it with you. It indicates that many 'bounties' have been recently placed into history and hints that something big is about to happen in our world. Here it is: *"The universe is pregnant with these manifold bounties, awaiting the hour when the effects of Its unseen gifts will be made manifest in this world."* (Baha'u'llah: The *Kitab-i-Iqan*, Page: 60)

QUESTION: That sounds very good indeed, but it still seems a little like a dream to me. You Baha'is are admirable in what you are doing, but I still can't see how mankind will ever unify. There is just too much strong division.

RESPONSE: All I can do until you read the writings of Baha'u'llah for yourself is to admit that you are right. There is great, terrible strength in the things that divide us. However, Baha'u'llah said that God had sent Him to the world with a 'task': *"the task of converting satanic strength into heavenly power is one that We have been empowered to accomplish."* (Baha'u'llah: *Gleanings*, Page: 200) And His Son, 'Abdu'l-Baha, said that God has given the Baha'is of the world a mission to *"reorient the minds of men."* ('Abdu'l-Baha: *Selections from 'Abdu'l-Baha*, Page 3)

Clearly, if that *"heavenly power"* Baha'u'llah describes is not available to us, the world is heading toward a downward spiral that could only be described as a 'catastrophe.' Several popular movies of the late 1990's had as their plot that a world-killing meteor was headed toward earth. This could, of course, happen, but it's very unlikely. The real 'world-killer' is not a meteor, but our own lack of unity and our inability to see and believe in our oneness and our unwillingness to go about the task of creating and building world unity.

QUESTION: So the 'quickening of mankind' that

Baha'u'llah talks about refers to the unification of the whole human race? Yes, it would be wonderful. I guess anyone would agree with that, but it still seems as unlikely to me as that meteor you spoke of. Of course, I don't have the vision of what those existing Baha'i communities are doing, or what they are like, but I plan to take a look. It's not that I doubt you; I just have to see for myself. If they believe and do what you say, it would be interesting, and it would be hopeful.

RESPONSE: I hope you will take a look at us and, I might add, go anywhere in the world, literally anywhere, to test whether Baha'i communities are living this 'dream' today, not tomorrow, turning the 'dream' into a 'reality.' And, remember that the word 'quickening' refers to reviving someone from death or bringing her or him to life. Baha'u'llah teaches that there must be individuals who are transformed by salvation, and then those individuals must work very diligently within communities to bring about the kind of world the Baha'i Teachings (and most of Christian Teachings) reflect.

What kind of world? A world where there is an end to war, and where 'peace' is not just an end to war, but a condition of discovery of our oneness and the pursuit of building a new 'kingdom of God,' a new world, free of the corrosive prejudices of gender, class, race and culture. A world where each culture and ethnic group would be seen to be valuable and unique, but not ever superior to that of any other.

A world where one God is worshipped by all, where all the Manifestations are recognized as being of and from that same God, where all history starts to make sense, as we begin, dimly at first, then brightly to understand history as a slow, steady unfolding of a vast and meaningful divine plan.

A world where every promise and prophecy laid down in the thousands of years of earth's history begins to be fulfilled as the 'Promised One,' the Return of Christ, the *'Father'* of all mankind guides us into an era of fulfillment and discovery of our individual and collective destiny, as defined by God's Will, as seen in the Scriptures of all religions and as seen today in the writings and the Revelation of Baha'u'llah.

So someone may say: "What if?" "What then?" But the Baha'is are saying: "Why wait?" "We are doing it now!"

QUESTION: You have just painted a beautiful picture, to which most Christians would probably subscribe, and probably most Jews and Moslems and others, now that I think about it. Christians have always wanted to contribute to the building of that kind of world and they have, to a degree, been quite successful in building such a world. We have also had our failures; probably the Baha'is will also have successes and failures, too, if history is any guide. But I'm beginning to see that you are offering Baha'u'llah to the world just as we offer Christ; is that it?

RESPONSE: We are indeed offering Baha'u'llah, but we are offering Christ, too, and Buddha, Moses, Krishna, Zoroaster, Muhammad, the Bab, plus all the unnamed Manifestations Who came in the dim reaches of past time and, as well, the Manifestations that God will send in the future, now that we know how He works to guide us.

Christians have been quite successful, I agree. As the Baha'is work to build that united world, we are well aware that Christians, if they do not decide to follow Baha'u'llah, will at least support many, if not most of His teachings. Be a follower of Baha'u'llah if you can, we say. Be a friend, supporter and fellow builder at the very least. Believer or partner, we all have work to do.

QUESTION: I'm never perfectly able to get a key question across to you, so I will state it as directly as I can: We have Jesus Christ! Why do we need Baha'u'llah? Many of His teachings are extremely helpful, but why do we need to believe in Him, personally?

RESPONSE: Everything, as we have said often in this conversation, everything depends and rests upon the question of 'Who is Baha'u'llah?' If He is, as He said, the One in Whom Christ has *"once more, in My person, been made manifest unto you,"* (Baha'u'llah: *Gleanings*, Page: 101) then committed Christians would certainly wish to become His followers. They would realize that if He was right and they turned away, they wouldn't have Baha'u'llah nor would they any longer have Jesus, for if they turned away from Baha'u'llah, they would also be turning away from Jesus.

QUESTION: You know…you are going 'right up to the line' in saying that. It's one thing to be challenging, but why do you think you have the right to make such an observation? I'm trying to stay with you in this conversation, but I don't want to be pushed, or patronized.

RESPONSE: Let me immediately apologize if you think I have pushed or patronized you. I don't want to do that. Actually, my authority for saying what I said is from Jesus Christ, Himself. Do you remember when Jesus told the Pharisees and others: *"For if you believed Moses, you would believe Me; for he wrote about Me."* (John 5:46)

Jesus is clearly telling them, is He not, that if they do not believe in Him, they never believed in Moses, either.

The only observation I'm making is that just as denial of
Jesus of Nazareth was denial of Moses, then the danger
today is that (*if* what Baha'u'llah says is true) denial of
Baha'u'llah may be denial of Jesus.

In fact, it may be even worse than that, according to
Baha'u'llah, since He says in a famous letter to a man
named Ahmad: *"Be thou assured in thyself that verily, he
who turns away from this Beauty* [the Person of the Manifestation in this Day—Baha'u'llah] *hath also turned away
from the Messengers of the past and showeth pride towards
God from all eternity to all eternity."* (Baha'u'llah: *Baha'i
Prayers*, Page: 213)

No, I certainly do not want to patronize you, insult
you, nor push in any way. On the other hand, I do want
to give you the full, true message that Baha'u'llah asked
me to give to the people of the world with whom I come
in contact. If you have a problem with this message, please
(a little humor, if you will) don't 'beat me up' about it.
Take it up at its source; talk to Baha'u'llah about it. Talk
to Christ about it. The answer will come, I am sure.

So, as I was saying before, if a Christian did come to
believe that Baha'u'llah was the Return of Christ, the
Promised One and the 'Father' of all mankind, that Christian or any Christian would certainly bow before
Baha'u'llah, seeing in Him the fulfillment not only of
their fondest, highest hopes and dreams of the Return of
Christ, but also the realization of their own and all
humanity's long awaited era of peace and unity.

QUESTION: You said earlier several times that
Christ said that He wanted to teach His disciples other
things, but told them: *"you cannot bear them now. However, when He, the Spirit of truth, has come, He will guide
you into all truth"* (John 16:12-13). Are you saying that
Baha'u'llah is that 'Spirit of Truth'?

RESPONSE: Please bear with me when I tell you once again that I am only 'delivering the message' of what Baha'u'llah said. I've tried very hard in this conversation not to inject so much of my own opinion and, instead, to give a true, full statement of Baha'u'llah's actual words. Yes, He did say His coming represented the promised appearance of the *"Spirit of Truth."*

I think that, in some ways, you are not going to be satisfied, and you shouldn't be, until you read Baha'u'llah's writings for yourself. I encourage you to do so. There is a reading list in Chapter Sixteen and other Baha'i friends can suggest books to read. I know I'm not misquoting Him, but what you get out of what He says will surely and undoubtedly be different from what I have gleaned.

Baha'u'llah not only said that He was the *"Spirit of Truth"* that Jesus promised to send, but pointed out that this 'Spirit of Truth' was really the reappearance or Second Coming of Christ. Baha'u'llah also said that when Christ came the first time, He came with the 'station' and name of *'the Son.'* This time, at Jesus' Second Coming, even though it is the same Jesus (*"once more, in My person, been made manifest unto you"*), Baha'u'llah's name and station today is that of *"The Father."*

QUESTION: I guess you know what I'm going to say. I've said it before but I feel compelled to say again that I have a problem, a big one, with Baha'u'llah calling Himself *"The Father."* In some ways, it is the hardest thing for me to deal with. I suppose if I did agree that Baha'u'llah was Christ Returned in the name of *'The Father,'* I would have no choice and no other desire, really, but to turn to Him and follow Him, but this would turn my whole life and much of my previous thinking completely upside-down!

RESPONSE: You know, come to think of it, the biggest problem of Jews as they listened to Jesus was that His disciples called him the *"Son of God."* This seemed blasphemous to them. You must be noticing the similarity of your trouble to theirs. Instead of *"Son of God"* being the problem, it is the title that Baha'u'llah tells us to understand Him by: *"The Father."*

I suppose what you have said about a life being turned 'upside-down' is true. Actually, I went through that, and things did seem upside down for a short time, but when I realized Who Baha'u'llah was and committed myself thoroughly to Him as Christ Returned, it didn't seem disorienting at all, just amazing and joyous, like a homecoming, as if I were where I always wanted to be, but never did quite understand.

Just imagine a Jew in the time of Jesus. Imagine him going home from meeting Jesus to tell his family and friends that He was going to follow a new 'teacher' Who said He was the *"Son of God"*, Who stated *"No man cometh unto the Father but by Me,"* *"Before Abraham was, I am"* and *"I am the Way, the Truth and the Life."* Just imagine!

What could that Jew expect to hear from family, friends, his Rabbi, his teachers? Can we imagine? Yes, you are right. Those who followed Jesus had their lives turned upside down. Some were even killed, martyred (Stephen comes to mind and later, even Peter and Paul, and many others). Those who were not martyred were told by family, friends, Rabbis and teachers (and probably everyone else) that they were betraying their precious Faith to follow a 'Sabbath breaker,' a person who hung out with drunkards and prostitutes, someone who in their view was even perhaps a mouthpiece for Satan, himself. (Of course, you recognize all these statements are taken from the New Testament record.)

We know Jesus was none of these things, but imagine the abuse and scorn, even the threat of death, heaped upon anyone who followed Jesus in those early days. It was the same, we learn, with any of the Manifestations, with Zoroaster, with Moses, with Buddha, Muhammad and in this new day, with the Bab (Baha'u'llah's predecessor) and Baha'u'llah Himself.

QUESTION: I'm not about ready to make such a decision, but I have begun to wonder how I would be able to deal with my own family and friends if I were to make such a commitment?

RESPONSE: How would that Jew in Jesus' time have answered that question? Jesus Himself was, a strong proponent of family and marriage. He attended and blessed a marriage, as you recall, but He was rather severe when disciples seemed to waiver in their commitment. He told one disciple who wanted to have 'leave' to go bury a relative (a seemingly reasonable request) *"Let the dead bury the dead."* (Luke 9:60)

On another occasion, He actually said: *"He who loves father or mother more than Me is not worthy of Me. And he who loves son or daughter more than Me is not worthy of Me. And he who does not take his cross and follow after Me is not worthy of Me. He who finds his life will lose it, and he who loses his life for My sake will find it."* (Matt 10:37-39)

So, it appears that Jesus expected discipleship in Him to come before all else, even before family, and expected His disciples to go to any length, including torture and death, if necessary, in commitment to that decision to follow Him.

It would be no less in the case of Christ Returned in

the name of *"The Father,"* that is, Baha'u'llah. Several tens of thousands of followers of the Bab and of Baha'u'llah have been cruelly martyred, including being tied to mouths of cannon and hacked to death with shovels and hoes, when one word of denial would have saved their lives. So, we have the examples of St. Stephen, who was stoned rather than deny Christ and of a sixteen-year-old girl, Mona, in Iran in the 1980's, who was hanged by the Iranian authorities rather than deny her Faith. Baha'is continue to be martyred in Iran, throughout the 1990's and as late as 1999.

QUESTION: I need time to think. Let's change the subject. Don't you think it's time for me to see that letter that you say Baha'u'llah wrote specifically to Christians? If you don't mind, I think I've waited long enough! I'd like to see it now and, if you don't mind, with as little comment from you as possible, while I read it.

RESPONSE: Yes, I agree. It's time you saw the letter. It is a letter that, as you say, Baha'u'llah wrote directly to Christians and I maintain that, therefore, the letter was written...to you. I'm just the postman.

Before we close, here are two prayers, one from Baha'u'llah and the other from His Son, 'Abdu'l-Baha. The first is from Baha'u'llah:

"O God, Who art the Author of all Manifestations, the Source of all Sources, the Fountain-Head of all Revelations, and the Well-Spring of all Lights! I testify that by Thy Name the heaven of understanding hath been adorned, and the ocean of utterance hath surged, and the dispensations of Thy providence have been promulgated unto the followers of all religions.

"I beseech Thee so to enrich me as to dispense with all save Thee, and be made independent of any one except Thy-

self. Rain down, then, upon me out of the clouds of Thy bounty that which shall profit me in every world of Thy worlds. Assist me, then, through Thy strengthening grace, so to serve Thy Cause amidst Thy servants that I may show forth what will cause me to be remembered as long as Thine own kingdom endureth and Thy dominion will last.

"This is Thy servant, O my Lord, who with his whole being hath turned unto the horizon of Thy bounty, and the ocean of Thy grace, and the heaven of Thy gifts. Do with me then as becometh Thy majesty, and Thy glory, and Thy bounteousness, and Thy grace.

"Thou, in truth, art the God of strength and power, Who art meet to answer them that pray Thee. There is no God save Thee, the All-Knowing, the All-Wise." (Baha'u'llah: *Prayers and Meditations*, Pages: 59-61)

And a prayer from 'Abdu'l-Baha:

"O my God! O my God! Verily, I invoke Thee and supplicate before Thy threshold, asking Thee that all Thy mercies may descend upon these souls. Specialize them for Thy favor and Thy truth.

"O Lord! Unite and bind together the hearts, join in accord all the souls, and exhilarate the spirits through the signs of Thy sanctity and oneness. O Lord! Make these faces radiant through the light of Thy oneness. Strengthen the loins of Thy servants in the service of Thy kingdom.

"O Lord, Thou possessor of infinite mercy! O Lord of forgiveness and pardon! Forgive our sins, pardon our shortcomings, and cause us to turn to the kingdom of Thy clemency, invoking the kingdom of might and power, humble at Thy shrine and submissive before the glory of Thine evidences.

"O Lord God! Make us as waves of the sea, as flowers of the garden, united, agreed through the bounties of Thy love. O Lord! Dilate the breasts through the signs of Thy oneness, and make all mankind as stars shining from the same height of glory, as perfect fruits growing upon Thy tree of life.

"Verily, Thou art the Almighty, the Self-Subsistent, the Giver, the Forgiving, the Pardoner, the Omniscient, the One Creator.

('Abdu'l-Baha: *Baha'i Prayers* (US edition), Pages: 204-205)

CHAPTER ELEVEN

BAHA'U'LLAH CALLS TO CHRISTIANS: A NEW DISCIPLESHIP FROM 'THE FATHER'

QUESTION: You have told me several times that Baha'u'llah wrote a letter specifically to Christians. And, you have said that you think I should regard it as a letter written from Baha'u'llah, to me personally. Please show me that letter.

RESPONSE: I will. But let me give a short preface, a story that I think is fascinating. It is the story of how and to whom this letter was written. Though I think each Christian should regard it as a personal letter written to her or him, it was originally written to an individual Christian. Later, the letter was regarded by Baha'u'llah and all the Baha'is as a letter written to all Christians, which is why it is sometimes called: 'The Letter to the Christians.'

QUESTION: Do we actually know the person who was the recipient of the letter?

RESPONSE: Well, let me put it this way: We *think* we know who the letter was written to. However, the evidence isn't fully conclusive. Here is what I believe and the greatest modern scholar of Baha'u'llah's writings, Dr. Adib Taherzadeh, says that the following story is probably true and he indicates his own belief that the events I will now describe are the probable true story of the first Christian to become a follower of Baha'u'llah. Of only two things are we certain: that this man was the first person of Christian background to become a Baha'i and that He sent a letter to Baha'u'llah and probably did receive a letter from Baha'u'llah. Many people believe the letter you will see, *or some portion of it*, is the letter written to this person.

Though the document that you will see below is usually dated later than the story you will now hear, it could still be that portions of this letter were written to the person we will describe in the story. The reason for this is that Baha'u'llah often quoted Himself from earlier writings. We think He may have quoted from the letter to this particular person when He later wrote a famous letter, the title of which is 'The Most Holy Tablet,' but which is most often called, 'Letter to the Christians.'

Here is the story of the first Christian to realize that Baha'u'llah was the long-promised, long awaited *"Father"* of all mankind Who had finally appeared to gather all the people of earth into a new realization of unity and peace.

His name was Faris Effendi, a Syrian physician and clergyman. He had been thrown into prison in Alexandria, Egypt, where his cellmate was a well-known Baha'i teacher, writer and poet—Nabil. Nabil had been sent to Egypt by Baha'u'llah to teach His Faith and because of persecution, was put in prison in Cairo, then transferred to a prison in Alexandria. Nabil's frequent experience with persecution was similar to that of Peter and Paul in Christ's time.

Faris Effendi had come to Egypt to teach the Christian Faith, no more popular with Muslims at that time than the new, strange Faith called Baha'i. Faris began immediately to attempt to convert Nabil to a belief in Christ. He was shocked to learn that Nabil already believed in Christ (as every Baha'i does) and to learn that Nabil's belief was as strong as his own. Finally, Nabil began to tell Faris Effendi about Baha'u'llah and His claim to be the Return of Christ. Within a short time Faris Effendi became a fervent believer in Baha'u'llah.

Then, one of those mysterious moments in history occurred. One day, Nabil was on the roof of the prison, where prisoners were allowed. He was praying, when he looked down to the street and saw a man he knew! It was the person who prepared meals not only for Baha'u'llah and His family, but for His followers who were in exile with Him. Nabil had been out of touch because of being imprisoned and believed Baha'u'llah to be under 'house arrest,' hundreds of miles away, in Adrianople. (modern Edirne, Turkey)

Nabil and the cook were equally astounded to see each other and carried out a shouted rooftop to street conversation, the cook explaining that Baha'u'llah was on a steamship in the harbor, a ship which was taking Baha'u'llah to one of the worst prisons in the Ottoman Empire, in the whole world, for that matter. He had been sent by the Sultan into deep exile to a prison city called Akka, in what was then called Palestine, now called Israel.

Looking up and out into the harbor, Nabil could see the ship, several hundred yards away. The ship that carried his Lord! So close, but far beyond his reach, because of his imprisonment. He rushed downstairs to tell Faris Effendi. Neither of them could sleep that night, excited at being so near to Baha'u'llah and frustrated at not being able to see and speak with Him. They decided to write letters to Baha'u'llah. Here is a portion of Faris Effendi's letter.

Note that Faris Effendi becomes poetical in a middle-eastern way in the last paragraph, where he addresses cities Baha'u'llah passes through, as if they were people. This is common in Arabic literature.

"O Thou the Glory of the Most Glorious and the Exalted of the Most Exalted! I write this letter and present it to the One Who has been subjected to the same sufferings as Jesus Christ . . . It is incumbent upon us to offer praise and thanksgiving to God, the All-Glorious, the All-Bountiful. And now, I beseech Thee to grant me and my kindred a portion of the ocean of Thy bounty, O Thou who art the Ever-Living, the Self-subsisting and the Well-spring of Purity and Sanctity.

"I entreat Thee by the mystery of Thy most joyful Being, by Thy Prophet who conversed with Thee (Moses), by Thy Son (Jesus), by Thy Friend (Muhammad) and by Thy Herald (The Bab) who for the love of Thee offered up His life in Thy path, not to deprive me and my family, these poor ones, from beholding the glory of Thy countenance.

"O Thou who hast endured for our sake sufferings and tribulations. Strengthen our faith, choose us for Thy service and accept us as martyrs in Thy path so that our blood may be shed for the love of Thee. We are weak and ignorant, confer upon us Thy glory so that we may not be among the losers. Grant us the distinction of love and faith, and cleanse our hearts from whatsoever runs counter to Thy good pleasure. Aid us to forget our own selves so that we may seek no rest in Thy service except by Thy leave and pleasure.

"O Thou who knowest the secrets of the hearts! Art Thou sailing in an ark made of wood? O how I long to be a part of that vessel, for it is blessed to be a carrier of the Lord. O, the surging sea! is thy restlessness because of the fear of the glorious Lord? O Alexandria! Art thou grief-stricken because He who is the Ever-Living, the All-Wise, is leaving thy shores? O, the desolate city of Akka! Thou art clapping thy hands in fervent joy and art in a state of rapture and ecstasy, for the Lord in His great glory will bless thy land with His footsteps . . . "

Faris and Nabil asked a Christian friend named Constantine the Clockmaker, to take the letter to Baha'u'llah's ship. Both of them went up to the rooftop again to watch Constantine row a small boat out to the ship. To their horror, the steamship started pulling away, leaving Constantine far behind in the rowboat. Grief-stricken and deeply disappointed, they dropped to their knees in tears and fervent prayer for divine assistance.

Which came! When they looked up, they were amazed to see that the large steamship had slowed to a stop and, presently, Constantine's small boat caught up and he boarded the ship with their letters. When Faris Effendi's letter was delivered to Baha'u'llah, there was great rejoicing, because Baha'u'llah told them that Faris Effendi was the first Christian to become a Baha'i. Baha'u'llah read the letter aloud to the small crowd of followers who had chosen to go into exile and prison with Him. In years to come, Baha'u'llah often referred to Faris Effendi and to the day that He received the letter of Faris Effendi's declaration of faith.

Baha'u'llah wrote replies to both Nabil and Faris

Effendi and—this is the important part—Baha'u'llah wrote one of His most important books entitled 'Letter to the Christians' (It's known by this title, even though its exact title is 'The Most Holy Tablet'). You will understand when you read it why it got its name—'Letter to the Christians.'

The young Christian, Constantine, who delivered Faris Effendi's letter to Baha'u'llah, was awestruck by meeting Baha'u'llah, and when he brought Baha'u'llah's return letters to Nabil and Faris, Constantine exclaimed: "By God, I have seen the Face of the Heavenly Father!" Faris Effendi took the young man in his arms and kissed the eyes that had seen the face of his Lord. In Baha'u'llah's letter to Nabil, He promised that He would soon be released from prison and, three days later, that promise came true.

The story of Faris Effendi has now been duplicated tens of thousands of times, as many more Christians are declaring their Faith in Baha'u'llah, but we can remember this wonderful story of the first Christian to do so. Baha'u'llah told His followers as the ship steamed away from Alexandria that God had *"transformed"* the heart of Faris Effendi and *"created Him anew."* He further told them that (in the words of a Baha'i scholar, Dr. Adib Taherzadeh): "Such a creation is greater in the sight of God than the creation of heaven and earth."

So, here is the 'Letter to the Christians,' which I maintain, for all practical purposes, is to be read as a letter that Baha'u'llah wrote . . . *to you!*

This letter starts with a preface in the Arabic style of writing:

"This is the Most Holy Tablet sent down from the holy kingdom unto the one who hath set his face towards the Object of the adoration of the world, He Who hath come from the heaven of eternity, invested with transcendent glory

"In the name of the Lord, the Lord of great glory. This is an Epistle from Our presence unto him whom the veils of names have failed to keep back from God, the Creator of earth and heaven, that his eyes may be cheered in the days of his Lord, the Help in Peril, the Self-Subsisting.

"Say, O followers of the Son! [Baha'u'llah often calls Christians 'Followers of the Son' or 'Followers of the Spirit.'] *Have ye shut out yourselves from Me by reason of My Name? Wherefore ponder ye not in your hearts? Day and night ye have been calling upon your Lord, the Omnipotent, but when He came from the heaven of eternity in His great glory, ye turned aside from Him and remained sunk in heedlessness.*

"Consider those who rejected the Spirit [that is, Jesus] *when He came unto them with manifest dominion. How numerous the Pharisees who had secluded themselves in synagogues in His name, lamenting over their separation from Him, and yet when the portals of reunion were flung open and the divine Luminary shone resplendent from the Dayspring of Beauty, they disbelieved in God, the Exalted, the Mighty. They failed to attain His presence, notwithstanding that His advent had been promised them in the Book of Isaiah as well as in the Books of the Prophets and the Messengers.*

"No one from among them turned his face towards the Dayspring of divine bounty except such as were destitute of any power amongst men. And yet, today, every man endowed with power and invested with sovereignty prideth himself on His Name. Moreover, call thou to mind the one who sentenced Jesus to death. He was the most learned of his age in his own country, whilst he who was only a fisherman believed in Him. Take good heed and be of them that observe the warning.

"Consider likewise, how numerous at this time are the monks who have secluded themselves in their churches, calling upon the Spirit, [that is, Jesus] *but when He appeared through the power of Truth, they failed to draw nigh unto*

Him and are numbered with those that have gone far astray. Happy are they that have abandoned them and set their faces towards Him Who is the Desire of all that are in the heavens and all that are on the earth.

"They read the Evangel [the New Testament] *and yet refuse to acknowledge the All-Glorious Lord, notwithstanding that He hath come through the potency of His exalted, His mighty and gracious dominion. We, verily, have come for your sakes, and have borne the misfortunes of the world for your salvation. Flee ye the One Who hath sacrificed His life that ye may be quickened? Fear God, O followers of the Spirit, and walk not in the footsteps of every divine that hath gone far astray. Do ye imagine that He seeketh His own interests, when He hath, at all times, been threatened by the swords of the enemies; or that He seeketh the vanities of the world, after He hath been imprisoned in the most desolate of cities? Be fair in your judgement and follow not the footsteps of the unjust.*

"Open the doors of your hearts. He Who is the Spirit [that is, Jesus] *verily standeth before them. Wherefore banish ye Him Who hath purposed to draw you nigh unto a Resplendent Spot? Say: We, in truth, have opened unto you the gates of the Kingdom. Will ye bar the doors of your houses in My face? This indeed is naught but a grievous error. He, verily, hath again come down from heaven, even as He came down from it the first time. Beware lest ye dispute that which He proclaimeth, even as the people before you disputed His utterances. Thus instructeth you the True One, could ye but perceive it.*

"The river Jordan is joined to the Most Great Ocean, and the Son, [Jesus] *in the holy vale, crieth out: 'Here am I, here am I O Lord, my God!', whilst Sinai circleth round the House, and the Burning Bush calleth aloud: 'He Who is the Desired One is come in His transcendent majesty.' Say, Lo! The Father is come, and that which ye were promised in the King-*

dom is fulfilled! This is the Word which the Son concealed, when to those around Him He said: 'Ye cannot bear it now.' And when the appointed time was fulfilled and the Hour had struck, the Word shone forth above the horizon of the Will of God.

"Beware, O followers of the Son, that ye cast it not behind your backs. Take ye fast hold of it. Better is this for you than all that ye possess. Verily He is nigh unto them that do good. The Hour which We had concealed from the knowledge of the peoples of the earth and of the favoured angels hath come to pass. Say, verily, He hath testified of Me, and I do testify of Him. Indeed, He hath purposed no one other than Me. Unto this beareth witness every fair-minded and understanding soul.

"Though beset with countless afflictions, We summon the people unto God, the Lord of names. Say, strive ye to attain that which ye have been promised in the Books of God, and walk not in the way of the ignorant. My body hath endured imprisonment that ye may be released from the bondage of self. Set your faces then towards His countenance and follow not the footsteps of every hostile oppressor. Verily, He hath consented to be sorely abased that ye may attain unto glory, and yet, ye are disporting yourselves in the vale of heedlessness. He, in truth, liveth in the most desolate of abodes for your sakes, whilst ye dwell in your palaces.

"Say, did ye not hearken to the Voice of the Crier, [this refers to the Bab, the predecessor of Baha'u'llah] *calling aloud in the wilderness of the Bayan, bearing unto you the glad-tidings of the coming of your Lord, the All-Merciful? Lo! He is come in the sheltering shadow of Testimony, invested with conclusive proof and evidence, and those who truly believe in Him regard His presence as the embodiment of the Kingdom of God. Blessed is the man who turneth towards Him, and woe betide such as deny or doubt Him.*

"Announce thou unto the priests: Lo! He Who is the Ruler

is come. Step out from behind the veil in the name of thy Lord, He Who layeth low the necks of all men. Proclaim then unto all mankind the glad-tidings of this mighty, this glorious Revelation. Verily, He Who is the Spirit of Truth is come to guide you unto all truth. He speaketh not as prompted by His own self, but as bidden by Him Who is the All-Knowing, the All-Wise.

"Say, this is the One Who hath glorified the Son and hath exalted His Cause. Cast away, O peoples of the earth, that which ye have and take fast hold of that which ye are bidden by the All-Powerful, He Who is the Bearer of the Trust of God. Purge ye your ears and set your hearts towards Him that ye may hearken to the most wondrous Call which hath been raised from Sinai, the habitation of your Lord, the Most Glorious. It will, in truth, draw you nigh unto the Spot wherein ye will perceive the splendour of the light of His countenance which shineth above this luminous Horizon.

"O concourse of priests! Leave the bells, and come forth, then, from your churches. It behoveth you, in this day, to proclaim aloud the Most Great Name among the nations. Prefer ye to be silent, whilst every stone and every tree shouteth aloud: 'The Lord is come in His great glory!'? Well is it with the man who hasteneth unto Him. Verily, he is numbered among them whose names will be eternally recorded and who will be mentioned by the Concourse on High. Thus hath it been decreed by the Spirit in this wondrous Tablet. He that summoneth men in My name is, verily, of Me, and he will show forth that which is beyond the power of all that are on earth. Follow ye the Way of the Lord and walk not in the footsteps of them that are sunk in heedlessness. Well is it with the slumberer who is stirred by the Breeze of God and ariseth from amongst the dead, directing his steps towards the Way of the Lord. Verily, such a man is regarded, in the sight of God, the True One, as a jewel amongst men and is reckoned with the blissful.

"*Say: In the East the light of His Revelation hath broken; in the West have appeared the signs of His dominion. Ponder this in your hearts, O people, and be not of those who have turned a deaf ear to the admonitions of Him Who is the Al-mighty, the All-Praised. Let the Breeze of God awaken you. Verily, it hath wafted over the world. Well is it with him that hath discovered the fragrance thereof and been accounted among the well-assured.*

"*O concourse of bishops! Ye are the stars of the heaven of My knowledge. My mercy desireth not that ye should fall upon the earth. My justice, however, declareth: 'This is that which the Son hath decreed.' And whatsoever hath proceeded out of His blameless, His truth-speaking, trustworthy mouth, can never be altered. The bells, verily, peal out My Name, and lament over Me, but My spirit rejoiceth with evident glad-ness. The body of the Loved One yearneth for the cross, and His head is eager for the spear, in the path of the All-Merciful. The ascendancy of the oppressor can in no wise deter Him from His purpose. We have summoned all created things to attain the presence of thy Lord, the King of all names. Blessed is the man that hath set his face towards God, the Lord of the Day of Reckoning.*

"*O concourse of monks! If ye choose to follow Me, I will make you heirs of My Kingdom; and if ye transgress against Me, I will, in My long-suffering, endure it patiently, and I, verily, am the Ever-Forgiving, the All-Merciful.*

"*O land of Syria! What hath become of thy righteous-ness? Thou art, in truth, ennobled by the footsteps of thy Lord. Hast thou perceived the fragrance of heavenly reunion, or art thou to be accounted of the heedless?*

[In the following paragraphs, Baha'u'llah uses 'po-etic license,' as is the custom in Arabic literature, to have a city, and a mountain, speak as if with human voice. Bethlehem speaks to Baha'u'llah and He answers. They carry on a conversation. Mt. Sinai speaks also.]

"Bethlehem is astir with the Breeze of God. We hear her voice saying: 'O most generous Lord! Where is Thy great glory established? The sweet savours of Thy presence have quickened me, after I had melted in my separation from Thee. Praised be Thou in that Thou hast raised the veils, and come with power in evident glory.' We called unto her from behind the Tabernacle of Majesty and Grandeur: 'O Bethlehem! This Light hath risen in the orient, and travelled towards the occident, until it reached thee in the evening of its life. Tell Me then: Do the sons recognize the Father, and acknowledge Him, or do they deny Him, even as the people aforetime denied Him (Jesus)?' Whereupon she cried out saying: 'Thou art, in truth, the All-Knowing, the Best-Informed.' Verily, We behold all created things moved to bear witness unto Us. Some know Us and bear witness, while the majority bear witness, yet know Us not.

"Mount Sinai is astir with the joy of beholding Our countenance. She hath lifted her enthralling voice in glorification of her Lord, saying: 'O Lord! I sense the fragrance of Thy garment. Methinks Thou art near, invested with the signs of God. Thou hast ennobled these regions with Thy footsteps. Great is the blessedness of Thy people, could they but know Thee and inhale Thy sweet savours; and woe betide them that are fast asleep.'

"Happy art thou who hast turned thy face towards My countenance, inasmuch as thou hast rent the veils asunder, hast shattered the idols and recognized thine eternal Lord. The people of the Qur'an [that is, Moslems] *have risen up against Us without any clear proof or evidence, tormenting Us at every moment with a fresh torment. They idly imagine that tribulations can frustrate Our Purpose. Vain indeed is that which they have imagined. Verily, thy Lord is the One Who ordaineth whatsoever He pleaseth.*

[In the following paragraph, Baha'u'llah inserts a passage He had previously written to the King of Persia telling Him that He longed for crucifixion or martyr-dom.]

"I never passed a tree but Mine heart addressed it say-ing: 'O would that thou wert cut down in My name, and My body crucified upon thee.' We revealed this passage in the Epistle to the Shah that it might serve as a warning to the followers of religions. Verily, thy Lord is the All-Knowing, the All-Wise.

"Let not the things they have perpetrated grieve thee. Truly they are even as dead, and not living. Leave them unto the dead, then turn thy face towards Him Who is the Life-Giver of the world. Beware lest the sayings of the heedless sadden thee. Be thou steadfast in the Cause, and teach the people with consummate wisdom. Thus enjoineth thee the Ruler of earth and heaven. He is in truth the Almighty, the Most Generous. Ere long will God exalt thy remembrance and will inscribe with the Pen of Glory that which thou didst utter for the sake of His love. He is in truth the Protector of the doers of good.

"Give My remembrance to the one named Murad and say: 'Blessed art thou, O Murad, inasmuch as thou didst cast away the promptings of thine own desire and hast followed Him Who is the Desire of all mankind.'

[The following part of Baha'u'llah's 'Letter to the Christians' and to you, contains what are often referred to as the 'Baha'i Beatitudes.' It is one of several similar passages in the Baha'i Scriptures.]

"Say: Blessed the slumberer who is awakened by My Breeze. Blessed the lifeless one who is quickened through My reviving breaths. Blessed the eye that is solaced by gazing at My beauty. Blessed the wayfarer who directeth his steps to-wards the Tabernacle of My glory and majesty. Blessed the distressed one who seeketh refuge beneath the shadow of My canopy. Blessed the sore athirst who hasteneth to the soft-flowing waters of My loving-kindness.

"Blessed the insatiate soul who casteth away his selfish desires for love of Me and taketh his place at the banquet table which I have sent down from the heaven of divine bounty for My chosen ones. Blessed the abased one who layeth fast hold on the cord of My glory; and the needy one who entereth beneath the shadow of the Tabernacle of My wealth. Blessed the ignorant one who seeketh the fountain of My knowledge; and the heedless one who cleaveth to the cord of My remembrance. Blessed the soul that hath been raised to life through My quickening breath and hath gained admittance into My heavenly Kingdom.

"Blessed the man whom the sweet savours of reunion with Me have stirred and caused to draw nigh unto the Dayspring of My Revelation. Blessed the ear that hath heard and the tongue that hath borne witness and the eye that hath seen and recognized the Lord Himself, in His great glory and majesty, invested with grandeur and dominion. Blessed are they that have attained His presence. Blessed the man who hath sought enlightenment from the Day-Star of My Word. Blessed he who hath attired his head with the diadem of My love.

"Blessed is he who hath heard of My grief and hath arisen to aid Me among My people. Blessed is he who hath laid down his life in My path and hath borne manifold hardships for the sake of My Name. Blessed the man who, assured of My Word, hath arisen from among the dead to celebrate My praise. Blessed is he that hath been enraptured by My wondrous melodies and hath rent the veils asunder through the potency of My might. Blessed is he who hath remained faithful to My Covenant, and whom the things of the world have not kept back from attaining My Court of holiness.

"Blessed is the man who hath detached himself from all else but Me, hath soared in the atmosphere of My love, hath gained admittance into My Kingdom, gazed upon My realms of glory, quaffed the living waters of My bounty, hath drunk his fill from the heavenly river of My loving providence, ac-

quainted himself with My Cause, apprehended that which I concealed within the treasury of My Words, and hath shone forth from the horizon of divine knowledge engaged in My praise and glorification. Verily, he is of Me. Upon him rest My mercy, My loving-kindness, My bounty and My glory."
(Baha'u'llah: *Tablets of Baha'u'llah*, Pages: 9-19)

QUESTION: I feel a sense of shock in hearing that letter. I've never read anything quite like it! It only deepens my feeling and my resolve to make a decision about Who Baha'u'llah is, and especially, whether or not He is the Return of Christ, as He clearly states in this letter. I do see, also, that you have not been quoting things 'out of context'. As you said, the context even makes Baha'u'llah's statements stronger.

RESPONSE: I can recall my own sense of 'shock' when I first read Baha'u'llah's 'Letter to the Christians.' It definitely calls for deep thought on the part of almost anyone who reads it. The Christian cannot fail to recognize that Baha'u'llah is calling upon him to recognize Him and become His disciple. The next chapter spells out why I think Christians have compelling reasons to become disciples of Baha'u'llah.

Here is a short prayer of Baha'u'llah to close this chapter:

"Suffer me, O my God, to draw nigh unto Thee, and to abide within the precincts of Thy court, for remoteness from Thee hath well-nigh consumed me. Cause me to rest under the shadow of the wings of Thy grace, for the flame of my separation from Thee hath melted my heart within me. Draw me nearer unto the river that is life indeed, for my soul burneth with thirst in its ceaseless search after Thee. My sighs, O my God, proclaim the bitterness of mine anguish, and the tears I shed attest my love for Thee.

"I beseech Thee, by the praise wherewith Thou praisest Thyself and the glory wherewith Thou glorifiest Thine own Essence, to grant that we may be numbered among them that have recognized Thee and acknowledged Thy sovereignty in Thy days. Help us then to quaff, O my God, from the fingers of mercy the living waters of Thy loving-kindness, that we may utterly forget all else except Thee, and be occupied only with Thy Self. Powerful art Thou to do what Thou willest. No God is there beside Thee, the Mighty, the Help in Peril, the Self-Subsisting.

"Glorified be Thy name, O Thou Who art the King of all Kings!" (Baha'u'llah: *Prayers and Meditations*, Pages: 30-31)

And here are several short selections from my favorite part of the Revelation of Baha'u'llah, *The Hidden Words*:

"O SON OF BEING! Thy Paradise is My love; thy heavenly home, reunion with Me. Enter therein and tarry not. This is that which hath been destined for thee in Our kingdom above and Our exalted Dominion." (Baha'u'llah: (Arabic) *Hidden Words*, Pages: 5-6)

"O SON OF BEING! Thy heart is My home; sanctify it for My descent. Thy spirit is My place of revelation; cleanse it for My manifestation." Baha'u'llah: (Arabic) *Hidden Words*, Pages: 58-59)

"O SON OF LOVE! Thou art but one step away from the glorious heights above and from the celestial tree of love. Take thou one pace and with the next advance into the immortal realm and enter the pavilion of eternity. Give ear then to that which hath been revealed by the pen of glory." (Baha'u'llah: (Persian) Hidden *Words*, Page: 7)

"O OFFSPRING OF DUST! Be not content with the ease of a passing day, and deprive not thyself of everlasting rest. Barter not the garden of eternal delight for the dust-

heap of a mortal world. Up from thy prison ascend unto the glorious meads above, and from thy mortal cage wing thy flight unto the paradise of the Placeless. " (Baha'u'llah: (Persian) *Hidden Words*, Page: 39)

CHAPTER TWELVE

COMMITTED CHRISTIANS HAVE COMPELLING REASONS TO DEVELOP INTO FOLLOWERS OF BAHA'U'LLAH

QUESTION: The title of this chapter bothers me a little. You seem to be saying that Christians are not 'complete' unless they become followers of Baha'u'llah?

RESPONSE: Please don't take offense. But consider this: A Jew in Jesus' time 'completed' his faith by following Jesus, don't you think? And, in that same fashion, it may be likewise true that the decision of a Christian to become a Baha'i, that is, a follower of Baha'u'llah, may give that person a sense of 'completion' and natural growth from one phase of understanding and growth into another newly discovered era of spiritual life. I can remember having such feelings, and I imagine Faris

Effendi, the first Christian to become a Baha'i, felt that way.

QUESTION: It still sounds vaguely insulting, even though you say you don't mean it that way. I believe my Faith and my Christ are all I need. But, I can see the point that a Jew may have been insulted by the suggestions of Christ and His disciples that following Him would 'complete' their Faith. I think it was true in that case; in this case, I'm not convinced.

RESPONSE: First, I'm not trying to 'convince' you. All I want to do is to present Baha'u'llah to you. Then, it's up to you how you respond. Second, I agree with you that your Christ is all you need. Your understanding of what to do about all of this hinges entirely, in my opinion, on who you decide Baha'u'llah is. If He is the return of Christ *"once more, in My person made manifest unto you,"* (Baha'u'llah: *Gleanings*, Page: 101) then, as you say, your Christ is all you need. You would now see Christ not only in Baha'u'llah, but as the 'Word of God' that was the reality in all the other Manifestations of God.

The big question is: Who is Baha'u'llah? Is He a madman, just a wise man, a philosopher, or only a prophetic voice? If so, you can easily walk away, and you should. Or is He *"The Voice and Face of God"*? If that is Who Baha'u'llah is, if He is *"The Father"* of all mankind, then the question for you becomes, I suggest: Is this 'my Christ' speaking to me through Baha'u'llah?

If Baha'u'llah is Christ returned, if He is the Promised One, the *"Spirit of Truth,"* if He is *"The Father"* come *"in all His Glory,"* then you can hardly turn away, as you yourself said.

QUESTION: Yes, but I'm not at the point of believing all those things. Nevertheless, I am interested in investigating and thinking about all of this. But, I'm troubled by what I'm hearing at times. It is so challenging. As you say, everything rests on Who Baha'u'llah is; on that, I agree. To follow Him or to turn away—either response could be a huge mistake, or the most important positive spiritual decision I have ever made in my life. What if I make the wrong decision? Surely you don't expect me to make this decision quickly or easily?

RESPONSE: I couldn't agree more. When we talked about this once before, I recalled that when from the instant some people saw Christ, they became His follower. The same thing often happened with Baha'u'llah. Several people recognized Him immediately. They needed no words, no teachings, no miracles, but merely looked into His Face and instantly committed their lives, fate and spiritual fortune and future to their Lord.

But, this is not the pathway of most people, I agree. Baha'u'llah Himself spoke of a 'search' that people could go through in deciding Who He was. He even suggested some of the methods to be used in this 'search'. We talked about them in chapter seven and I'll remind you of them in the next chapter.

QUESTION: But, how can one go about such an important search? It seems so complex and daunting and almost impossible to sort it all out to the point of making a decision.

RESPONSE: Well, let me share something that may help. When Christians talk to Jews, they try to show that becoming a follower of Christ is not at all a betrayal of their Faith, but a natural progression, a recognition of a new chapter of God's Will, a 'New Testament.' The Christian points out to the Jewish believer who is considering becoming a follower of Christ that Jesus is the long-awaited Messiah that was promised in His faith, the 'Promised One,' if you will.

And, although the concept of the 'Son of God' is a difficult one for that Jewish person to hear and accept (it initially sounds blasphemous to them), the Christian lovingly and patiently explains, leads and assists His Jewish friend to understand that Jesus meant nothing blasphemous by His words, but rather, had been sent by the 'Heavenly Father' and was saying only what God told Him to say.

Isn't this what happens? The Christian in this conversation with a Jew explains that in becoming a Christian, this move is a natural development of His own Faith, a normally expected discovery that any Jew could themselves make by study of his own scriptures. The Christian would continue by telling the Jew that Jews should be the first to recognize Jesus, since Jesus was a Jew, appeared among and to Jews first, that Jesus was a rabbi, or teacher and one Who was raised in Jewish traditions.

Most importantly, the Christian would probably point out that Jesus brought His message *originally* to Jews and Jews alone . . .

QUESTION: That is very mistaken! You were raised in a Christian home and you of all people should know that Jesus brought His message to the whole world. Why did you say that?

RESPONSE: The key word in the sentence above that seemed to trouble you is 'originally.' It is true that Jesus ultimately wanted His message to be taken into the whole world, but He clearly wanted to present it to Jews first and foremost. In preparation for this book, I read the Gospels many times, consulting as many as seventeen different translations, even looking up the original Greek meanings of words.

Jesus was once approached by a non-Jewish woman who wanted Him to heal her daughter, but He answered, *"I was not sent except to the lost sheep of the house of Israel."* Then she implored Jesus, saying, *"Lord, help me!" But He answered and said, "It is not good to take the children's bread and throw it to the little dogs." And she said, "Yes, Lord, yet even the little dogs eat the crumbs which fall from their masters' table." Then Jesus answered and said to her, "O woman, great is your faith! Let it be to you as you desire." And her daughter was healed from that very hour."* (Matt 15:24-28)

This is certainly an interesting episode from the New Testament (that you almost never hear preached about in a sermon). While Jesus sounds almost cruel here, we know He wasn't being cruel, but was testing the faith of this woman. Also, we have to remember that Jesus was born a Jew, raised a Jew, practiced religion as a Jew for thirty years, and even in His ministry frequented the Temple and celebrated Jewish Holidays, including a Jewish holiday (Passover) within days of His crucifixion.

But back to the argument that a Christian might make to a Jew, I ask you again, don't I have this argument right? Isn't this what a Christian would say to a Jew?

QUESTION: Yes, I've heard Christian ministers and missionaries make exactly that line of argument to Jews and I certainly do see where you are going with this.

RESPONSE: Of course you do. I am going to make the same appeal to you about Baha'u'llah that the Christian would make to a Jew about Christ. Christians, whom Baha'u'llah called *"the People of the Son,"* should not be the last but the first to recognize *"the Father."* Recall the last chapter, in the letter that Baha'u'llah wrote to all Christians (and therefore to you!), He said: *"Tell Me then, do the Sons recognize the Father?"* (That is, do the Christians recognize Baha'u'llah?)

Becoming a follower of Baha'u'llah would be quite another thing if He had not said that Jesus Christ had once more been made manifest *"in my Person."* It would be a different question entirely if Baha'u'llah had not said to you that He is the *"Spirit of Truth,"* if He had not said that His coming represented not only the Return of Christ, but the appearance in history of the 'Promised One' of all ages, and *"The Father"* of all mankind.

So, it seems to me, of the followers of all the religions, it is the Christians, who would be the first to recognize Baha'u'llah, to understand and adore Him, to follow Him with love and commitment and a strong sense of connection, fulfillment and purpose.

QUESTION: Yes, I suppose these are the same arguments, in both cases, in terms of what the Christian would say to a Jew and what the Baha'i might now be saying to a Christian, but I'm still wondering if you are saying that becoming a Baha'i fulfills and completes commitment to Christ?

RESPONSE: It was true in my case, but you must discover for yourself what you believe. You can't and shouldn't take my word for it. I can give my testimony, my 'witness,' but then the task and the discovery process is yours entirely. This is your search and your challenge. It belongs to you and you alone. I can give you information and I can assist you, pray with you, suggest further pathways of study and things to read, but finally, this momentous decision is entirely up to you.

What I can tell you is that, yes, I felt that way, that

becoming a Baha'i gave me a sense of completion, of deeper connection to Jesus, of moving further along the path that I had already been on for my entire life. In my home and in my life, there was never a time I didn't know Jesus and feel close to Him. A hymn of my youth says it so well: 'Jesus is all the world to me, my life, my joy, my all.' So, yes, I felt fulfilled when I made a decision to follow Baha'u'llah. At one point in my study, I realized that, for me, Baha'u'llah's Voice was indeed a voice I recognized; it was, for me, the Voice of Jesus Christ.

I knew that Voice. I was familiar with it. I had the personal experience of 'walking with Jesus in the Garden.' I found that as I read the Writings and Prayers of Baha'u'llah, it was the familiar Voice of Christ that I was hearing. When Baha'u'llah told me that Christ had appeared again *"in My Person"* I felt challenged until I made the decision to follow Baha'u'llah. And when I did, I felt now that I had a 'double discipleship' to Christ and to Christ Returned—Baha'u'llah.

QUESTION: You sure do bring up that quote a lot, about Christ being again manifested in Baha'u'llah *"in My Person,"* as He puts it.

RESPONSE: Yes, and for a reason: It was this short sentence that became both my stumbling block and (later) my means of entering into discipleship with Baha'u'llah as Christ Returned. When I read that sentence, it was so direct, so unmistakable, that I knew I would have to make a decision as to whether Baha'u'llah was telling the truth about His identity.

If He was not, then my decision was clear and the path easy. I would just forget it and go on to the next class, unbothered. (I was in seminary at the time study-

ing for the ministry,) But, on the other hand, if
Baha'u'llah meant what He said and if He was What and
Who He said He was, if He was telling the truth, if this
was spiritual reality, then I had no choice. I realized I
would have to follow my Jesus wherever He led me, even
though the road ahead would be difficult and hard.

If I were to follow Baha'u'llah, then I would have to
face my professors, fellow divinity school students, my
dear parents (my Father a Minister), other friends, and
the world at large.

QUESTION: Did you have any misgivings, second
thoughts?

RESPONSE: Lots of them. Once my decision was
made, I didn't ever doubt that Baha'u'llah was the 'Promised One.' I never doubted that He was the Return of
Christ to the World. Never doubted that *"The Father hath
come."* But, I wondered how I would make it in a world
where I would be regarded as one who had joined what
was widely regarded as a strange 'sect,' or even a 'cult'.
What, I wondered, would they think of me?

Then, I remembered that Paul and Peter were regarded in exactly this way by the citizens of Rome. They
were seen in Rome as believers in 'an eastern cult,' a
Jewish 'sect,' as atheists, as believers in a strange or weird
set of beliefs that merited rejection and punishment, even
death. Peter and Paul were crucified like their Master
for their faith in the 'eastern sect' of Christianity.

Permit me some humor. I sort of hoped at the time
that crucifixion wouldn't be my fate although now (forty
years later) I realize that Peter probably was happy beyond measure to lay down his life for Jesus, just as Paul
was happy to be, as he put it so well, 'a fool for Christ' in
the eyes of the people of Rome.

QUESTION: Well, speaking of 'foolishness,' some of the things that you have told me in this conversation, especially about 'uniting the world' have made you sound naive, if not foolish, in the light of today's facts and reality.

RESPONSE: I can't argue. I know it sounds that way. Apparently, that's the way it always is, when a new Manifestation of God appears and His teachings are set forth. These teachings are shocking or they seem 'too hopeful' or, as you said, they sound like 'pie in the sky.' They can even seem 'satanic' or 'blasphemous', as we have discussed. In any case, they never fit current reality or the 'facts of today.' So, it seems to me that the believers in any new Faith must always go through a period of seeming foolish, uninformed, or naive.

But then . . . as decades roll by, then centuries, what originally seemed foolish or crazy, uninformed or naive suddenly seems to be the new standard for truth. Suddenly, everyone says:

'Of course this is true!'

Strange, isn't it!

QUESTION: Very strange! And I'm still struggling with the question of Who Baha'u'llah is, whether He is someone Who can just be dismissed as a wise man, even a powerful prophetic voice, but not the Return of Christ in the Glory of the Father. I remember you telling me that a Christian theologian said Jesus had to be one of three things; a madman, a charlatan and trickster or (the only other choice) He had to be Who He said He was.

RESPONSE: And I'm sure you remember that the New Testament tells us that some people who heard

Christ even thought He was the Devil, or in league with the Devil. Christians have to contend with these same four choices in deciding about Baha'u'llah, including one other choice, that He might be the Antichrist. As I said before when we discussed this, I'm quite sure that if you investigate, study, read and pray, if you fully investigate the life and teachings of Baha'u'llah, you will quickly discover that He isn't the Antichrist, nor is He any more the Devil than Christ was.

You will have a hard time seeing him as a madman and He won't fit in easily into the category of charlatan or trickster, since few of that kind of folk are willing to undergo the torture, beatings, loss of all belongings, the death of His son, banishment from His native land and forty years of imprisonment and house arrest that was the lot of Baha'u'llah. These deprivations and tortures were lifelong. Charlatans and con men wouldn't last through such deprivations.

From the time of His full recognition of being the new Manifestation of God in the 1850's until His Ascension in 1892, Baha'u'llah remained true to the Mission that God had commanded Him to carry out. He said: *"This Wronged One, rid of all attachment to the world, hath striven with utmost endeavour to quench the fire of animosity and hatred which burneth fiercely in the hearts of the peoples of the earth."*

Then Baha'u'llah called upon us all to assist Him in turning *"fire into light"* and *"hatred into love."* The full quote: *"It behoveth every just and fair-minded person to render thanks unto God—exalted be His glory—and to arise to promote this pre-eminent Cause, that fire may turn into light, and hatred may give way to fellowship and love."* (Baha'u'llah: *Tablets of Baha'u'llah*, Page: 44)

QUESTION: What do you mean, a few moments

ago, by using the word 'ascension'? Did Baha'u'llah ascend? That doesn't sound right!

RESPONSE: Baha'u'llah taught that all the Manifestations come from an *'invisible heaven.'* This was true,
He said, even though they apparently appear in the world
from the womb of their mother. When the Manifestations experience what we call 'death,' it really refers,
Baha'u'llah says, to the death of their physical bodies. At
'death,' their Spirit returns to God or 'ascends,' returning to the *'invisible heaven'* from which it came.

QUESTION: Well, when Christians say 'ascend,' they
believe the physical body of the risen Christ ascended
into heaven. What do Baha'is believe about that?

RESPONSE: Baha'u'llah taught that the Resurrection and Ascension of the Manifestations are spiritual
events rather than material events. To treat them as material events poses two problems.

First, it causes us to miss the beautiful, spiritual truth
about the Resurrection and Ascension.

Second, seeing these two events as material events
causes us to put our religion in conflict with what we
know to be true about the findings of science. You remember that one of the central Baha'i teachings is that
science and religion are like two wings of a bird. They
should not conflict but should support each other. Just
as a bird needs not one but two wings to fly, knowledge
and faith function in their fullness only when applied
together.

When the Gospels were written, it was possible to
believe that a material body could float up into the air,
rising to a material heaven. Almost no thoughtful Christian who has elementary scientific knowledge believes

this, but it doesn't stop them from realizing that there was a spiritual event in Christ's departing this life, when His Spirit returned to the place He described as *"at the right Hand of God."*

QUESTION: Well, this makes me wonder if the Baha'is believe in the Resurrection of Christ, a central belief of Christianity?

RESPONSE: Sometimes Baha'is have been accused of not believing in the Resurrection. This is not true. Baha'is do believe in the Resurrection of Christ, but what they believe is, again, that it was a spiritual event, not a material event, and needs to be understood and interpreted in a spiritual way.

Certainly, the Christian beliefs of the empty tomb, the Risen Christ, His appearance to His disciples have to be seen as central to Christian belief and nothing in Baha'i teaching denies that the disciples experienced very fully the reality of the Risen Christ. If you want to hear what 'Abdu'l-Baha said about the Resurrection, turn to the back of this book (Chapter 16), where various subjects are listed alphabetically with brief explanations of Baha'i teaching on them.

Yes, the Resurrection did occur. Yes, the disciples did experience the Risen Christ. However, we must be sure not to interpret this wonderful and vitally important event in a materialistic way, for if we do, we miss the spiritual and inner meaning of this central event of early Christian history. A Baha'i, Dr. Kavian Milani, is working on a clear, rational statement on the Resurrection, based both upon the Bible and the Baha'i Revelation. When it is available, it will be included in an edition of this book/conversation. And I am especially awaiting the publication of a book on the Resurrection by Gary Matthews, author of The *Challenge of Baha'u'llah* and *He Cometh With Clouds.*

A careful reading of the Gospels makes it clear (and many Christians agree on this), that the events of the Resurrection and Ascension are indeed spiritual events, rather than materialistic and anti-scientific. Even St. Paul describes the body that Christians will have when they, too, 'rise,' as being a 'spiritual body,' not a material one. (I Cor. 15: 44)

QUESTION: Surely you realize, though, that many Christians interpret the Resurrection as entirely physical and material and that their Faith is founded on this event as a 'miracle.'

RESPONSE: Yes, I do. The Resurrection of Christ was a 'spiritual miracle.' I can only tell you that when I and many other Christians as well as Baha'is think deeply and long about both the Resurrection and the Ascension of Christ, it actually makes more sense and is more spiritually satisfying to think of these events as primarily spiritual in nature, not material.

If the Ascension is material, then we have a material heaven, something that few Christians today believe in. If the Ascension was spiritual in nature, as Baha'u'llah taught, then the Resurrection as well can be seen as spiritual, in its most real, deep meaning. Be sure to turn to the back of the book, to get the full quote on this subject. I point out there that the disciples certainly did experience some new vision of the 'Risen Christ.'

QUESTION: Perhaps I will, later. Right now, I still want help on this central decision that I feel forced to make . . .

RESPONSE: I hope you aren't feeling any 'force' coming from me!

QUESTION: Sometimes a little 'push' but nothing I can't handle. No, the pressure to make a decision is coming from me, not from you. It's my own internal need to have this resolved, as to Who Baha'u'llah is. Is He just a man, or is he what Baha'u'llah called Himself, a Manifestation of the *"Self of God"*? And, especially, whether He does or doesn't represent the Return of Christ. If Christ is here again in the *"Person"* of Baha'u'llah, it would mean everything to me. I have to know the truth of this. No, the 'push' is coming right from inside me to make this decision.

RESPONSE: I'm trying to be helpful, as I said before, without being 'too helpful.' I know that I would resent any 'pushing' on a question so sensitive. Like you, I realized early upon hearing of Baha'u'llah, that I had to make a decision about Him. Others could help me, but the decision was mine and mine alone. The best thing I can do for you was what was done for me, to give you information and to point you in a direction to find Baha'u'llah's Writings.

QUESTION: Please do just that. My decision needs to be on what Baha'u'llah says—I mean no offense—not on what you or anyone else says.

RESPONSE: No offense taken. You are doing exactly what Baha'u'llah urged the people of the world to do, to investigate His claims and His person fairly and, above all, with an independent mind and spirit. As I have pointed out, one of His central teachings is the 'independent investigation of truth.'

Here are some statements of Baha'u'llah that I believe may be helpful in this decision. They are very challenging, but keep in mind as you hear them that a Jew in the time of Jesus would have been constantly challenged by what Jesus said.

For example, Baha'u'llah, speaking of Himself, described what God had done: *"Thou hast called into being Him Who speaketh in Thy name before all who are in Thy heaven and on Thy earth, and hast bidden Him cry out amongst Thy creatures."* (Baha'u'llah: *Prayers and Meditations*, Page: 152)

As to His Mission, Baha'u'llah said: *"Neither the hosts of the earth nor those of heaven can keep me back from revealing the things I am commanded to manifest. I have no will before Thy will, and can cherish no desire in the face of Thy desire."* (Baha'u'llah: *Prayers and Meditations*, Page: 184) And also: *"I can utter no word, O my God, unless I be permitted by Thee, and can move in no direction until I obtain Thy sanction. It is Thou, O my God, Who hast called me into being through the power of Thy might, and hast endued me with Thy grace to manifest Thy Cause."* (Baha'u'llah: *Prayers and Meditations*, Page: 208)

QUESTION: That sounds very similar to a statement of Christ.

RESPONSE: Yes, the quote from Jesus is: *"I do nothing of myself, but as the Father taught me, I speak these things."* (John 8:29) This quote from Jesus and several others like it in the New Testament are particularly challenging when one thinks of Baha'u'llah appearing in the 'station' of *'The Father.'*

QUESTION: That is still hard to swallow: Baha'u'llah being called *'The Father'*?

RESPONSE: I always feel compelled to remind you that it isn't me or any other Baha'i who called Him that; it is Baha'u'llah Himself Who says He is *'The Father.'* Let's revisit that quotation: *"Lo! The Father is come, and that which ye were promised in the Kingdom is fulfilled!"* (Baha'u'llah: *Tablets of Baha'u'llah*, Page: 11)

" *In Thy holy Books, in Thy Scriptures and Thy Scrolls Thou hast promised all the peoples of the world that Thou Thyself shalt appear and shalt remove the veils of glory from Thy face . . . I bear witness that Thou hast in truth fulfilled Thy pledge and hast made manifest the One Whose advent was foretold by Thy Prophets . . .* " (Baha'u'llah: *Tablets of Baha'u'llah*, Page: 115)

Baha'u'llah also addresses Christians in particular (referring to them as 'Sons': *"Tell Me then: Do the sons recognize the Father, and acknowledge Him, or do they deny Him, even as the people aforetime denied Him (Jesus)?"* (Baha'u'llah: *Proclamation of Baha'u'llah*, Page: 97)

A Christian echo to that statement is Jesus' lament: *"I am come in my Father's name and ye receive me not"* and *"If ye believed Moses, ye would believe me."* (John 5: 43-46) Just as Jesus was clearly implying that lack of belief in Him showed lack of belief in Moses, so Baha'u'llah seems to be saying in a powerful way that lack of belief in Him indicates lack of belief in Jesus.

In the early days as I was hearing about Baha'u'llah, I began to realize that if a young Jew in Jesus' time rejected Christ, he would be losing not only Christ but Moses as well. This added to my conviction that I must make a decision, and a good, thoughtful decision at that, in order that I would not be in the same position to lose not only Baha'u'llah, but Jesus as well.

And Baha'u'llah also appealed to us to tear away the 'veils' that keep us from seeing Him: *"Rend the veils asun-*

der. He Who is the Lord of Lords is come overshadowed with clouds, and the decree hath been fulfilled by God, the Almighty, the Unrestrained . . . He, verily, hath again come down from Heaven even as He came down from it the first time. Beware that thou dispute not with Him even as the Pharisees disputed with Him (Jesus) without a clear token or proof."

(Baha'u'llah: *Proclamation of Baha'u'llah*, Page: 83)

In His unique appeal to Christians, Baha'u'llah says that Jesus stands at our heart's door: *"Open the doors of your hearts. He Who is the Spirit (Jesus) verily, standeth before them. Wherefore keep ye afar from Him Who hath purposed to draw you nigh unto a Resplendent Spot? Say: We, in truth, have opened unto you the gates of the Kingdom. Will ye bar the doors of your houses in My face? . . . Beware, O followers of the Son* [Jesus], *that ye cast it not behind your backs."* (Baha'u'llah: *Proclamation of Baha'u'llah*, Page: 92)

Baha'u'llah tells us that in this New Day of Revelation, there is 'great rejoicing' in Heaven: *"In this Day a great festival is taking place in the Realm above; for whatsoever was promised in the sacred Scriptures hath been fulfilled. This is the Day of great rejoicing. It behoveth everyone to hasten towards the court of His nearness with exceeding joy, gladness, exultation and delight and to deliver himself from the fire of remoteness."* (Baha'u'llah: *Tablets of Baha'u'llah*, Pages: 78-79)

QUESTION: Well, you warned me. These statements are indeed very strong and forceful and call for a decision. I was glad to learn that you went through a similar torment when you first heard about Baha'u'llah. I'm confused though. Baha'u'llah seems to be claiming to be the Return of Christ, while at other times to be *'The Father.'* Which is He?

RESPONSE: Baha'u'llah clearly did say both these things. The quote that you and I are both struck with is where Baha'u'llah says that Christ is now again present in the world *'in My person.'* In another quote, He says: *"Lo, the Father hath come."* These quotes often appear in the same passage in Baha'u'llah's Writings. In these quotes and in many other places Baha'u'llah does indeed present Himself as both the Return of Christ and as *"The Father"* and even as the *"Lord of all mankind."* (Baha'u'llah: *Epistle to the Son of the Wolf,* Page: 59)

QUESTION: The *"Lord of all mankind"*? Did He really say that?!

RESPONSE: Yes, and more than one time. And did Jesus really say: *"All authority hath been given to me in heaven and on earth"*? Did Jesus say: *"I am the Way, the Truth, and the life"*?

Yes, of course, Jesus and Baha'u'llah did say these things. In the case of Jesus, we accept them quickly because we have hindsight and we know Who He was and is. In the case of Baha'u'llah, we must make our decision on Who He *is* and Who He *will be* for us and for the world, without knowing what future centuries will reveal. These sayings of Jesus and Baha'u'llah can only be explained, as we have often said, as one of the following: (1) The sayings of a madman; (2) The sayings of a charlatan, trickster or even the devil in disguise or 3) The sayings of One Who is what and Who He says He is (in the case of Christ, the *"Son"* of God; in the case of Baha'u'llah, the *"Father"* and *"Lord of all mankind."*)

That quote about *"The Lord of all Mankind"* is especially interesting because it comes from a letter Baha'u'llah wrote to Queen Victoria of England. I men-

tioned to you earlier that Baha'u'llah wrote letters to all
the western rulers and *"Kings of the earth"* announcing
His coming. Here is the full quote, calling upon Queen
Victoria to 'cast away' all her possessions and recognize
and follow Him. Doesn't it remind you, as it does me, of
the 'Rich Young Ruler'? (Luke 18: 18)

*"O Queen in London! Incline thine ear unto the voice of
thy Lord, the Lord of all mankind, calling from the Divine
Lote-Tree: Verily, no God is there but Me, the Almighty, the
All-Wise! Cast away all that is on earth, and attire the head
of thy kingdom with the crown of the remembrance of Thy
Lord, the All-Glorious. He, in truth, hath come unto the world
in His most great glory, and all that hath been mentioned in
the Gospel hath been fulfilled."* [This would, I think, be a
good place for us to remember the saying of Jesus: *"The
Father and I are One."*]

*"The land of Syria hath been honored by the footsteps of
its Lord,* [that is, Baha'u'llah] *the Lord of all men, and
North and South are both inebriated with the wine of His
presence. Blessed is the man that hath inhaled the fragrance
of the Most Merciful, and turned unto the Dawning-Place of
His beauty, in this resplendent Dawn."* (Baha'u'llah: *Epistle
to the Son of the Wolf*, Pages: 59-60)

QUESTION: I'm ready to hear more, although to
tell you the truth, some of these quotes are almost overwhelming. I've never heard anything like them and I
have to drop my previous idea that Baha'u'llah is just a
saintly figure like Mother Teresa or Martin Luther King,
Jr. or a prophetic voice like Elijah or Jeremiah.

RESPONSE: Yes, because people like Mother Teresa
or Jeremiah would never have said the things that
Baha'u'llah or Jesus said. They wouldn't have said, as
Baha'u'llah did, about His coming: *"The Ancient of Days*

is come in His great glory!" (Baha'u'llah: *Epistle to the Son of the Wolf,* Page: 47)

Nor would Martin Luther King, Jr. or Elijah say, as Baha'u'llah did: *"Call out to Zion, O Carmel, and announce the joyful tidings: He that was hidden from mortal eyes is come! His all-conquering sovereignty is manifest; His all-encompassing splendor is revealed."* (Baha'u'llah: *Gleanings,* Page: 16)

Baha'u'llah said He was the *"Lord of creation, the movement of Whose Pen hath revolutionized the soul of mankind."* (Baha'u'llah: The *Kitab-i-Aqdas,* Page: 39) Also, He spoke of Himself as *"He, for Whose sake the world was called into being."* (Baha'u'llah: *Epistle to the Son of the Wolf,* Page: 56) Finally, He calls upon us to 'proclaim' this new announcement: *"Behold, your Well-Beloved hath come among men! . . . Lo, the Adored One hath appeared arrayed in the fullness of His glory!"* (Baha'u'llah: *Gleanings,* Page: 320) and *"The Promised Day is come and the Lord of Hosts hath appeared."* (Baha'u'llah: *Tablets of Baha'u'llah,* Page: 239)

In the next chapter of this conversation, let's discuss how one might actually go about this important decision of finding out Who Baha'u'llah is. But first, here are prayers from Baha'u'llah and 'Abdu'l-Baha that I think match the tone of our current shared thoughts.

First a prayer from Baha'u'llah, Who mentions not only that He is the Manifestation of God's *'Self,'* but also refers to His banishment from His native land and His lengthy imprisonment in what He called *'The Most Great Prison,'* which was the prison city of Akka, in Israel. The worst criminals of the Ottoman Empire were sent there.

Here is the prayer:

"Thou seest, O my God, how Thy servants have been cleaving fast to Thy names, and have been calling on them in the daytime and in the night season. No sooner, however, had He been made manifest through Whose word the kingdom of

names and the heaven of eternity were created, than they broke away from Him and disbelieved in the greatest of Thy signs. They finally banished Him from the land of His birth, and caused Him to dwell within the most desolate of cities, though all the world had been built up for His sake. Within this, the Most Great Prison, He hath established His seat. Though sore tried by trials, the like to which the eye of creation hath not seen, He summoneth the people unto Thee, O Thou Who art the fashioner of the universe!

"I beseech Thee, O Thou the Shaper of all the nations and the Quickener of every mouldering bone, to graciously enable Thy servants to recognize Him Who is the Manifestation of Thy Self and the Revealer of Thy transcendent might, that they may cut down, by Thy power, all the idols of their corrupt inclinations, and enter beneath the shadow of Thine all-encompassing mercy, which, by virtue of Thy name, the Most Exalted, the All-Glorious, hath surpassed the entire creation.

"I know not, O my God, how long will Thy creatures continue to slumber on the bed of forgetfulness and evil desires, and remain far removed from Thee and shut out from Thy presence. Draw them nearer, O my God, unto the scene of Thine effulgent glory, and enrapture their hearts with the sweet savours of Thine inspiration, through which they who adore Thy unity have soared on the wings of desire towards Thee, and they who are devoted to Thee have reached unto Him Who is the Dawning Place of the Day-Star of Thy creation.

"Cleave asunder, O my Lord, the veils that shut them out from Thee, that they may behold Thee shining above the horizon of Thy oneness and shedding Thy radiance from the dawning-place of Thy Sovereignty. By Thy glory! Were they to discover the sweetness of Thy remembrance and apprehend the excellence of the things that are sent down upon them from the right hand of the throne of Thy majesty, they would cast away all that they possess, and would rush forth into the wilderness

of their longing after Thee, that the glance of Thy loving-kindness may be directed towards them and the radiance of the Day-Star of Thy beauty may be shed upon them.

"Let their hearts, O my Lord, be carried away by Thy remembrance, and their souls enriched by Thy riches, and their wills strengthened to proclaim Thy Cause amidst Thy creatures. Thou art, verily, the Great Giver, the Ever-Forgiving, the Most Compassionate."(Baha'u'llah: Prayers and Meditations, Page 202)

And a prayer from 'Abdul'-Baha:

"O Thou compassionate Lord, Thou Who art generous and able! We are servants of Thine sheltered beneath Thy providence. Cast Thy glance of favor upon us. Give light to our eyes, hearing to our ears, and understanding and love to our hearts. Render our souls joyous and happy through Thy glad tidings. O Lord! Point out to us the pathway of Thy kingdom and resuscitate all of us through the breaths of the Holy Spirit.

"Bestow upon us life everlasting and confer upon us never-ending honor. Unify mankind and illumine the world of humanity. May we all follow Thy pathway, long for Thy good pleasure and seek the mysteries of Thy kingdom. O God! Unite us and connect our hearts with Thine indissoluble bond. Verily, Thou art the Giver, Thou art the Kind One and Thou art the Almighty." ('Abdu'l-Baha: Promulgation of Universal Peace, Page: 397)

CHAPTER THIRTEEN

MAKING YOUR DECISION
ABOUT BAHA'U'LLAH

QUESTION: You aren't going to try to urge me into making a decision, are you?

RESPONSE: There does seem to be a decision to be made. I will probably urge you to investigate, to pray, to study and read. The rest is up to you. Baha'u'llah Himself challenged the people of the world to use the greatest gift of God, namely, the power of one's own mind, to make this decision. He said that each individual person should use her or his God-given power of 'independent investigation of truth' to arrive at a conclusion. Even children and people with minor mental limitations have some degree of ability to 'figure things out' for themselves. Baha'u'llah encouraged every human individual to use the powers they possess as a God-given right.

His Great-grandson, Shoghi Effendi, leader of the Baha'i Faith in the first half of the Twentieth Century, said that one of the leading principles of the Baha'i Faith was "The independent search after truth, unfettered by superstition or tradition." (Quoted in Shoghi Effendi: *God Passes By*, Page: 281) The 'independent investigation of truth' is a central Baha'i principle. However, Baha'u'llah did warn mankind that individuals should not attempt to test the Manifestation when He appears, as, for example, the Pharisees did with Jesus. Baha'u'llah said that *"God should test His creatures, and they should not test God."* (Quoted in Shoghi Effendi: *God Passes By*, Page: 144)

An interesting story: When Baha'u'llah was in exile from His native land, residing in Baghdad, the Islamic Clergy came to Him, asking for a miracle to be performed, so that He could 'prove' who He was. After reminding them that man should not 'test' God, Baha'u'llah nevertheless wrote these clergymen, telling them to pick a specific miracle that all of them agreed upon. Further, that they sign a public pledge to become His followers if the miracle was performed. After their receipt of this letter Baha'u'llah never heard from them again.

QUESTION: This reminds me, though, that I wanted to say to you that Christ's miracles do seem to be a proof of His Mission, don't they? Where are Baha'u'llah's miracles?

RESPONSE: Those around Baha'u'llah said they saw miraculous acts often, but were expressly forbidden by Baha'u'llah from talking about them. We probably ought to be reminded that Christ often told those whom He healed not to tell anyone. His reason may have been the same one that Baha'u'llah told His followers, namely, that He wished people to believe in Him for the 'right' reason.

Here again, we see the difference between a materialistic and a spiritual definition of reality. Let's ask: What did Jesus and Baha'u'llah want? Did They want people to believe in them because of miracles, many of which magicians or charlatans could do or pretend to do, *or* did Jesus and Baha'u'llah want to be believed in for the right reason, namely, that people would realize and recognized the truth, beauty and power of God in Their Persons?

QUESTION: I agree with that, but still the fact of no miracles bothers me.

RESPONSE: The other thing to remember is that miracles only work perfectly well for those who see them. Later on, others can only take the word of those who saw the miracle. Therefore, miracles are not convincing to many people. In fact, the miracles reported in the New Testament, so meaningful to you and me from our Christian background, are actually stumbling blocks in this scientific age for many sincere people who are working from a rational base.

Another story: A man who was constantly around Baha'u'llah collected a lengthy book of miraculous acts he had seen Baha'u'llah perform. When he showed the book, Baha'u'llah took Him for a walk along the Tigris River in Baghdad. As they walked, Baha'u'llah tore out page after page and threw them into the river, as He lovingly but firmly explained that the reason for belief should not be miracles, or a magic show, but true, sincere recognition of the voice of God in the person of the

Manifestation, whether He be the *"Son"* [Jesus] or *"the Father"* [Baha'u'llah].

QUESTION: No miracles at all then?

RESPONSE: Not in the material sense. Baha'u'llah said that the 'biggest miracle of all' is the miracle of Faith, which changes individual people in a dramatic way for the better. When others see this kind of change, it is something that can easily be understood and believed in–a true spiritual (and practical) miracle. It is the miracle of lives that are transformed and redirected by faith in Jesus or, in this case, faith in Baha'u'llah, as Jesus Returned.

The following is one of the ways that *you* can use to decide if Baha'u'llah is Who He said He was. Look at the Baha'is to see if their individual lives and their communities represent transformed lives devoted to the establishment of human unity through the strong attempt to eradicate prejudices of all kinds. Check them out closely to see if they *really* believe in the equality of men and women. This isn't to indicate that Baha'is are perfect, but rather, that they are perfectly, strongly motivated to follow Baha'u'llah and to fulfill His teachings, which we believe are God's Will for today's world.

Changed, transformed lives and new human communities leading toward human unity are the only true miracles that can and must be believed. In the case of the Baha'i Community, these are not events in the distant past. There are changed lives and transformed communities right here, right now, in our present world; and they are right before your eyes!

Oh, and that miracle of the kind you are looking for? I'm not going to tell you about it, because of Baha'u'llah's injunction not to focus on miracles, but I'll tell you where to find it. Pull down the *Encyclopedia*

Britannica and find 'Babi Faith' (this is what the Baha'i Faith was called before Baha'u'llah's declaration) and read the story of the execution of the Bab (Baha'u'llah's predecessor, as John the Baptist was the predecessor of Jesus). This execution was observed in 1850 by almost ten thousand people, including several Western visitors, who happened to be in the city of Tabriz, Persia (Iran) at the time. The Britannica tells the story well. What it won't tell you is the role played by a Christian, who resisted the killing of the Bab.

You will be proud of this person. His name was Sam Khan; he was the officer in charge of the Bab's execution. Apparently Sam Khan realized the Bab was a good and holy man, so he told the Bab he saw no reason He should be killed. The Bab looked at him and told Sam Khan *"Follow your instructions, and if your intention be sincere, the Almighty is surely able to relieve you of your perplexity."* (Quoted in Shoghi Effendi: *God Passes By*, Page: 52) I'm not going to tell you the end of the story, but I will tell you that although the Bab was finally executed that terrible day, it was not at Sam Khan's hands. And, when you read the article in the Britannica, you may think it was a 'miracle.'

QUESTION: I still feel some sense of 'pressure.' I don't believe it is coming from you, not deliberately, at any rate. But I still want to know why you call this chapter: 'Making Your Decision About Baha'u'llah'?

RESPONSE: Partially because I feel now about Baha'u'llah the same way I felt about Christ before I knew about the Baha'i Faith. Back then, I realized that somehow, without merit, I possessed what Jesus called a *"pearl of great price"* (Matt 13:46) in knowing and following Christ, my Lord and Savior. It was unthinkable that I would fail to let others know about the one who was *"the way, the truth, and the life,"* one who offered a new redeemed life through personal salvation, one who was the *"Son of God"* and who said: *"No man cometh unto the Father but by me."* (John 14:6)

Now that I (again) somehow, and (again) without merit have found, or been found by Baha'u'llah, how can I do any less than before? How can I fail to tell people about Him, especially when He says that Jesus, my Savior *"hath once more, in My person, been made manifest unto you."* (Baha'u'llah: *Gleanings,* Page: 101)

How can I fail to tell all people, but *especially* Christians about one who represents the appearance of the *"Spirit of Truth,"* the Return of Christ and, in Baha'u'llah's words, *"Him Who is the Manifestation of Thine own Self"* and Whose face is *"the face of God Himself."* (Baha'u'llah: The *Kitab-i-Iqan,* Page: 4)

How can I keep silent when I have experienced Christ Returned, as the Gospel of Mark says, *"in the glory of His Father,"* (Mark 8:38) if that verse refers, as I believe it does, to Baha'u'llah, the 'Father of all mankind'?

QUESTION: Surely you remember that statements like those you just made sound very strange to me. I've even told you several times that ideas like Baha'u'llah being the 'Father' and being 'the Face of God' and 'the Voice of God' sound almost crazy and certainly blasphemous from a point of view of historic Christian doctrine.

RESPONSE: Yes, I do remember and I know you remember my analogy to a Jew in Jesus' time and how he would have felt as he heard the comments of Jesus, such as that His hearers would soon see Him sitting *"at the right hand of the Power* [that is, God]*"* (Matt 26:64) and *"I and my Father are one"*(John 10:30) or *"Before Abraham was, I am."* (John 8:58)

But another thing you could remember is that I'm not the one saying these things. It is Baha'u'llah saying them. Please don't blame me as the messenger. Go to the source, that is, to Baha'u'llah and argue with Him, so to speak. I can tell you that I would *never* have thought to say such things and, had I said them, you could properly use the words 'crazy' and 'blasphemous.' That's what the Jews said about Jesus (and even worse) and that's what some people are going to say about Baha'u'llah. But I hope in your case that you will investigate first, rather than walk away without looking into the matter, because: Isn't that what most Jews did?

Now, to get back to why I can't be quiet: How can I fail to shout out that the Kingdom *"on earth, as it is in Heaven"* that Christ prayed for is going to be built, is in progress of being built right now? Shouldn't I have been out on the rooftops shouting the glad tidings of Christ when I was twenty years old? Shouldn't I be out there now on those same rooftops proclaiming that the era of fulfillment of prophecy, of unity and peace is upon us? I'm sure you would agree that if that is what I believe, then it should be proclaimed. One of the favorite hymns of my youth sums it all up: 'I love to tell the story, it did so much for me and that is just the reason, I tell it now to thee.' I always did love to tell the story of Christ and now I can tell the story of Christ . . . and Christ Returned.

And, especially, shouldn't I be inviting Christians to become the *'quickeners of mankind"* that Baha'u'llah asked His followers to be? By 'quickeners,' He meant what the Bible meant by 'quickened,' that is, to be brought to life from a state of 'spiritual' death. Several times both Christ and Baha'u'llah spoke of those who did not follow them as among the 'dead' and those who recognized the new

Manifestation, whether Christ or Baha'u'llah, to now be 'alive.' Remember Jesus refusing one of His disciples 'time off' to bury his father, saying: *"Let the dead bury the dead"*?

QUESTION: But this is what I don't understand. Why don't you go to the unbelievers, the unchurched, the spiritually 'dead'? Why bring this message to true, practicing Christians who are happy with their Faith and aren't looking for anything new?

RESPONSE: I'd say there are three reasons. First, Baha'u'llah said this message, this revelation, was to be taken to every person in the world. Second, it was Baha'u'llah's decision, not mine, to single out Christians in a special way to receive His message. Though He appealed to all humankind, every individual in the world, of every culture, religion and nation, I am not aware that He had such high expectation of anyone becoming His followers as He had for Christians. The third reason is from Jesus Christ. When He brought His message, His Revelation, He did not take it to the Romans or the Greeks, but to His own people, the Jews. I am trying to follow His example, to take the Baha'i Revelation first to the Christians, whom I know best, then to the entire world.

Remember what Baha'u'llah said in that letter that He wrote to Christians and therefore, to *you* (take another look at that letter in chapter Eleven). He described anyone as *"Blessed"* who *"hath detached himself from all else but Me, hath soared in the atmosphere of My love, hath gained admittance into My Kingdom, gazed upon My realms of glory, quaffed the living waters of My bounty, hath drunk his fill from the heavenly river of My loving providence, acquainted himself with My Cause, apprehended that which I concealed within the treasury of My Words, and hath shone*

forth from the horizon of divine knowledge engaged in My praise and glorification. Verily, he is of Me. Upon him rest My mercy, My loving-kindness, My bounty and My glory."
(Baha'u'llah: *Tablets of Baha'u'llah*, Page: 17)

QUESTION: Baha'u'llah does seem to appeal very directly to Christians, I agree. That is one of the reasons that I am beginning to be convinced that I will have to make a decision to be either for or against him. His claim to be the Return of my Jesus doesn't leave me room to be 'neutral.'

RESPONSE: I understand. That was the same feeling I had when first hearing of Baha'u'llah, especially after reading the "Letter to the Christians." I knew from the content of that letter that I would certainly have to make a decision, if for no other reason, to be able to explain to other Christians why Baha'u'llah was *not* who He said He was.

Are the words of Jesus ringing in your ears? Jesus seemed to indicate, if you remember, that you couldn't just walk away from Him and be 'neutral.' You couldn't be luke-warm, wishy-washy-indecisive, since not being 'for' Him was like being 'against' Him. I'm sure you remember the quote. In another place in the Gospel, however, one Gospel writer has Him saying it a little differently, a little softer, namely: *"he that is not against us is for us."* (Luke 9:50) I suppose that you could apply this to Baha'u'llah to say that not being for Him is dangerously close to being against Him, but at the very least, it wouldn't be a good thing to be against either Jesus or Baha'u'llah, *if* they were who they said they were.

In any case, I'm just agreeing with what you seem to be concluding. I am understanding you to say that this decision you want to make about whether or not to recognize and follow Baha'u'llah as the Returned Christ is all important. And that the decision may lead you to devote your life to Him, to His teachings and to the task of *"quickening"* humankind. I can only agree with you that this decision seems fateful and important beyond words and life-changing in many ways. It certainly was for me, over forty years ago, and continues to be.

QUESTION: So, are you actually inviting me to become a follower of Baha'u'llah?

RESPONSE: I'm first inviting you to read, study and pray and then, but only then, to turn away from Baha'u'llah if you do not hear the clear voice of Jesus in His Words. If you do not come to believe He is Christ returned, and if you do not come to recognize Baha'u'llah as *"the Father,"* the long awaited, 'Promised One of all ages,' then you should walk away.

QUESTION: Do you really mean that? Sounds dangerous!

RESPONSE: Either the presence of God is in Baha'u'llah or it isn't. If it is, you will recognize that through study, reading and prayer. If not, you'll certainly recognize that too. Either Baha'u'llah is the Return or Christ, or He isn't. But I'll go even further. Baha'u'llah warns that it is not right for man to test God; rather, it is God Who tests man. Thus, when the Pharisees continually tried to test Jesus with trick questions, they were doing the wrong thing entirely.

Nevertheless, I believe that while it's not good to test God, you *can* test the situation you are in by asking Christ in prayer to show you the truth. At the same time, you can ask Baha'u'llah to reveal Himself to you, if He is the *"spirit of Truth"* and the Return of Christ that He claims to be. This is not so much a test as a plea to be shown what you need to know. As I said before, pray, read and study, look at the Baha'i Writings, the prayers, re-read Baha'u'llah's letter to you, pray some more, then wait for results, for some kind of unveiling, some inner or outer message, some knocking on the door of your heart and mind.

What I say with confidence is this: If you have done all this and nothing at all happens, walk away. But on the other hand, if you hear that knock on the door and you open it to find Jesus returned, standing there in the *"Glory of the Father,"* and if it is Baha'u'llah Who is standing at the door, then I believe you will know what to do.

QUESTION: You are beginning to sound like a preacher calling people to the altar at the end of a service, inviting them to give their lives to Jesus.

RESPONSE: I suppose I must plead 'Guilty.' I come by this honestly, since I made that 'invitation' hundreds of times as a student Christian minister of two country churches in Iowa in the 1950's. Seldom did I fail to invite those in the congregation to give their lives to Christ for the first time or more fully and to accept salvation. Though just a student minister, I preached and ministered at these two churches for three years. What I did then, I do now, but with a difference.

Now, I am asking you to renew your faith in Christ Jesus, by recognizing Him Who is the return of that same Jesus. I am bringing you His message that *"the Father hath come"* and I bring you as well His appeal to Christians: *"Tell Me then: Do the sons recognize the Father, and acknowledge Him, or do they deny Him, even as the people aforetime denied Him (Jesus)?"* (Baha'u'llah: *Proclamation of Baha'u'llah,* Page: 97) *"Open the doors of your hearts. He Who is the Spirit (Jesus) verily, standeth before them."*

QUESTION: I'm really confused, or, I wonder, is it you that's confused? You seem to be ready to wait for me to make a rational, reasoned decision based on prayer and study of Baha'u'llah's writings. Then, you seem to become evangelistic, urging me to declare my faith in Baha'u'llah, as Christ returned, as you call it, *"in the Glory of the Father."*

RESPONSE: What can I say? You are right. I suppose my evangelistic Christian background keeps coming out. I spent twenty-one years in the Church and that impulse to challenge and invite people to declare their belief and to follow Jesus must be causing me now to urge you and others to follow Baha'u'llah. Baha'is are forbidden by Baha'u'llah to 'proselytize' in the sense of pressuring people to consider His Faith, but He also told His followers to 'teach' His Faith throughout the world.

My own progress into the Baha'i Faith as a follower of Christ Returned in the *"Glory of the Father"*— Baha'u'llah—was through study and prayer. My prayers were, as usual, to God through His Son Jesus, to give me a sign, to show me the way. I read everything I could find about Baha'u'llah and everything I could find that He revealed. Of greatest help to me were the writings of His Son, 'Abdu'l-Baha and His great-grandson, Shoghi Effendi. I also read and reread the words of Jesus. In addition to earnest prayers to Jesus for guidance, I asked Baha'u'llah to reveal Himself to me in a way that I would understand, the only way that I would understand, as Jesus Returned.

Actually, I would have to say, with reflection, that there are many paths that a Jew could have taken in Jesus' day or a Christian can take in this day of Baha'u'llah, to be able to decide whether or not to be a follower. The question becomes whether or not to recognize the new Manifestation, and to accept the *"new wine"* (new teachings) along with the *"new wineskins"* (new institutions) that can properly contain the wine of new teachings.

QUESTION: What do you mean by "many paths" that could be taken?

RESPONSE: Well, people are coming to believe in Baha'u'llah, the 'Promised One of all ages' from all kinds of backgrounds. In addition to Christians believers are emerging from such backgrounds as Judaism, Islam, Zoroastrianism (the 'Three Wise Men' were Zoroastrian priests), Buddhism, Hinduism, the Mormon Faith, even agnostics and atheists.

QUESTION: Wait a minute! How in the world could an atheist become a follower of Baha'u'llah—a Baha'i?

RESPONSE: Probably what helps a person from this kind of background is that the Baha'i Faith is profoundly rational, while, at the same time, deeply spiritual and sometimes mystical and poetic. In the Baha'i writings, God is called *"an unknowable essence."* These are the words of Baha'u'llah, Who says that nevertheless, God and His will *can* be known through His Manifestations, the Ones who bring to mankind the 'Word of God' and God's very presence into history. A central teaching of the Baha'i Faith is the unity of science and religion. Miracles are de-emphasized and the Baha'i teachings portray a realistic and practical path for humankind to take toward fulfillment of unity and peace.

A Baha'i friend of mine brought up by atheist parents who were militant in their disbelief in God told me that the Baha'i Faith was a 'breath of fresh air' to her, something she had been looking for all her life—a combination of something rational and reasonable, together with something that was deeply spiritual and emotional. Something with mysticism and poetry, that at the same time did not require her to 'turn off her mind.' Rather, the opposite: that her mind and human spirit could *both* be fully turned on, fully integrated and fully devoted to Baha'u'llah as God's latest Manifestation and as the One Who would gather together all the people of earth.

QUESTION: A question just occurred to me. It has always bothered me somewhat, just as you said in Chapter Two it bothered you too. Some Christians believe that you have to consider other religions as 'false.' While many of my friends feel this way, I never did. However, I do think that Christ and Christianity represent the highest expression of the Will of God and that Jesus, in His Oneness with God, is far above any other 'persons' or 'messengers' of other religions. But, I don't have to think of them as 'false.'

RESPONSE: You and I share an opinion on that, at least in part. When I was a Christian, my belief in Christ was strong and central in my life. I definitely saw Jesus as the *'Son of God,'* but I was aware of the 'truth' in other religions. I believed in Christ but always wanted a way to understand and appreciate that God had worked His Will in other ways, other places, other times.

So, that was a major attraction for me, when I considered the Baha'i Faith. The Baha'i Faith doesn't require disbelief in other religions, but the opposite: To see all the religions as one, in the sense that they have all been revealed by one God, who Manifested Himself not once but many times in human history, Who cared enough to send His *'only begotten Son'* and Who finally, in a time of fullness and fulfillment, stepped forward as Baha'u'llah said, *"out of the realm of the invisible into the visible world"* (Baha'u'llah: The *Kitab-i-Iqan*, Page: 25) to finally allow all humankind *"to behold the Face, and hear the Voice, of the Promised One."* (Baha'u'llah: *Gleanings*, Page: 10)

The idea that one could, by becoming a Baha'i, believe in all the Manifestations, Moses, Buddha, Zoroaster, Jesus, Muhammad, Krishna, the Bab and Baha'u'llah is, to many people, like a joyous homecoming, an embrace of all history and of all humanity. It is to understand, for the first time, what has been happening in history and where we are headed, by the Grace of God.

QUESTION: This is not a question and please don't take offense, but you Baha'is have got to be either the greatest fools or just maybe you are 'on to something.'

RESPONSE: Well, I don't feel 'on to something.' I am just a disciple of Christ and now also of Christ Returned—Baha'u'llah. I didn't make this up. It didn't come out of a committee, a council, a conference, or a meeting of wise men. It came from Baha'u'llah—all of it—written down by His Pen. Actually, Baha'u'llah often referred to Himself as the *"Pen"* of God, Who allowed Him to write or speak only what God wished Him to express. He expressly said in one place that He was a *"Pen"* held in the Hands of God.

Remember that Jesus said that He only spoke what God told Him to speak. *"The words that I speak to you I do not speak on My own authority; but the Father who dwells in Me does the works."* (John 14:10) Apparently it was the same with Baha'u'llah, who said: *"I have no will but Thy will, O my Lord, and cherish no desire except Thy desire. "* (Baha'u'llah: *Prayers and Meditations*, Page: 108) and *"I can utter no word, O my God, unless I be permitted by Thee, and can move in no direction until I obtain Thy sanction. It is Thou, O my God, Who hast called me into being through the power of Thy might, and hast endued me with Thy grace to manifest Thy Cause. "* (Baha'u'llah: *Prayers and Meditations*, Page: 208)

As for Baha'is being 'on to something,' most Baha'is do feel very excited to be living in this day. Imagine for a moment you were alive just four or five generations after Jesus lived. Imagine how you would feel if you had actually met someone who had met Jesus. That is how I feel, since I did meet in the 1960's a very elderly person, who as a small child had met Baha'u'llah. The feeling of being around someone who had been in the presence of Baha'u'llah was overwhelming to me.

Are Baha'is excited? Yes! You will find this to be true wherever you may meet them, spread around the whole world as they are. There is a saying that there aren't many Baha'is anywhere but there are some Baha'is everywhere. Actually, that's not true anymore, since there are over a million and a half Baha'is in India alone, as of the turn of the Christian millennium.

QUESTION: You know, I have this feeling that Baha'is are mostly located in the United States, maybe in California, and that most of them are, so to speak, 'intellectuals.' Is that the case?

RESPONSE: It isn't the case at all. However, I have heard this before. Maybe it's because people think new religions begin on the west coast of the United States! You'll be interested, I think, to learn that the Baha'i Community in the United States and all of Europe numbers less than five percent of the Baha'is of the world.

The other ninety-five or so percent are not intellectuals, are largely poor, many cannot read or write, they are dispossessed of power; in other words, they greatly resemble early Christians! If you have studied the religions (some of your questions indicate that you have), especially how they began, you must have noticed new religions never immediately attract the glamorous people, the powerful, the rich, the intellectuals, the religious, the educated elite, or even any of the 'leading lights' of the day.

Jesus once said: *"I thank You, Father, Lord of heaven and earth, that You have hidden these things from the wise and prudent and have revealed them to babes."* (Matt 11:25) Apparently, this is the way God wishes to work. I'm sure a very few of the early Christians in Rome were aristocrats and of the learned, but this would not have been true until several hundred years after Christ's Ascension. In the beginning, new religions are started out not with the wise and the powerful, but with 'babes,' just as Jesus said.

New religions, as in the case of Jesus and His message, attract the simple, pure-minded, poor, dispossessed people whom the establishment despises or has cast aside. It is only several centuries later that the intellectuals, the powerful and the wealthy begin to respond. There was not one 'intellectual' among Jesus' disciples. Yes, after a short time, there was Paul—quite an intellect—but few of that kind for many decades, even for several hundred years.

I just had a thought. This may explain something you have brought up several times, namely, why you have not heard so much about the Baha'is. According to what we have just said, if you were living in Rome in 157 AD, no one of the 'intelligentsia' would have been talking about Christ, or would ever have heard of Him. If they *had* heard, the information they would have gotten would be what was said in Rome in the second century after Christ, that these Christians were an 'atheistic eastern cult.' No, the rich, the powerful, the educated are always 'trumped' in the *"Day of God"* by the poor, the powerless, and those without formal education.

Yes, Baha'is are happy and excited to be living in this Day of God, a day in which God has not only revealed Himself again, not only a day in which, as Baha'is believe, Jesus has returned, but also a day in which, as Baha'u'llah said: *"The Flower, thus far hidden from the sight of men, is unveiled to your eyes. In the open radiance of His glory He standeth before you."*(Baha'u'llah: *Gleanings*, Page: 322)

And: *"It is the Beloved Himself Who now is calling His lovers and is inviting them to attain His presence."* (Baha'u'llah: *Gleanings*, Page: 320) Finally, He said: *"He Who is the King of Kings hath appeared, arrayed in His most wondrous glory, and is summoning you unto Himself."* (Baha'u'llah: The *Kitab-i-Aqdas*, Page: 49)

QUESTION: Wait a minute! Jesus Christ has been known for over twenty centuries as the 'King of Kings.'

RESPONSE: And that title can never be taken from Christ, nor should it, but it should be remembered that Christ never once said He was the King of Kings nor would He allow His disciples to call Him that. (The references to 'King of Kings' are found in the book of Timothy and in Revelations. One of the references in Revelations seems to refer to Baha'u'llah, according to some Baha'i scholars.) But, nevertheless, you are right. Jesus has been known in scripture, poetry and song as, in one hymn of my youth: "King of Kings and Lord of Lords."

In the case of Baha'u'llah, He *did* call Himself the King of Kings and even more striking, He wrote epistles or letters to the major Rulers and Kings of the West to tell them very directly that they were His vassals or subjects. I sometimes wonder how Pilate felt, standing before one that was thought of as the 'King of the Jews.' Jesus wouldn't even encourage Pilate to call Him that, though He didn't deny it. And, in the same way, I wonder what the Kings felt and thought when they received Baha'u'llah's epistles? Czar Nicholas or Napoleon III or Queen Victoria? What must it have been like for them to be addressed as 'vassals' by Baha'u'llah? How did they feel when He told them they were His 'subjects'? Kings and Queens don't usually get addressed in this way!

When Napoleon III received His letter, he threw it down and stepped on it, saying: "If this man is God, then I am two Gods!" Baha'u'llah wrote him again, saying, as one might imagine the 'King of Kings' speaking: *"Exultest thou over the treasures thou dost possess, knowing they shall perish? Rejoicest thou in that thou rulest a span of earth? . . . Abandon it unto such as have set their affections upon it, and turn thou unto Him Who is the Desire of the world."* (Quoted in Shoghi Effendi: The *Promised Day is Come,* Page: 30)

Baha'u'llah also told Napoleon III: *"For what thou hast done, thy kingdom shall be thrown into confusion, and thine empire shall pass from thine hands, as a punishment for that which thou hast wrought. Then wilt thou know how thou hast plainly erred."* (Quoted in Shoghi Effendi: The *Promised Day is Come,* Page: 30) In a very short time, Napoleon III's kingdom was overthrown.

QUESTION: You spoke a moment ago that the 'Day' in which we are living is a special 'Day of God.' We Christians believe that the supreme Day of God that was so special was the 'Day' that He sent His *'only begotten son'* to earth to save mankind.

RESPONSE: That was indeed a special 'Day of Days.' Baha'u'llah refers to it often. He tells us, though, that every day in which the 'Christ Spirit' or 'Word of God' reappears in human history in the form of a *"human Temple"* or Manifestation of God, is a special Day. And, today is the Day of Baha'u'llah manifest as *"the Father"* of all mankind, as Jesus returning, appearing *"in the Glory of the Father."*

Other statements about this special 'Day of God' in which Baha'u'llah has appeared are these: *"Verily I say, this is the Day in which mankind can behold the Face, and hear the Voice, of the Promised One. The Call of God hath been raised, and the light of His countenance hath been lifted up upon men."* (Baha'u'llah: *Gleanings,* Pages: 10-11)

"Great indeed is this Day! The allusions made to it in all the sacred Scriptures as the Day of God attest its greatness. The soul of every Prophet of God, of every Divine Messenger, hath thirsted for this wondrous Day. All the divers kindreds of the earth have, likewise, yearned to attain it." (Baha'u'llah: *Gleanings,* Page: 11)

"All glory be to this Day, the Day in which the fragrances of mercy have been wafted over all created things, a Day so blest that past ages and centuries can never hope to rival it, a Day in which the countenance of the Ancient of Days hath turned towards His holy seat." (Baha'u'llah: *Gleanings,* Page: 14) Further: Referring to Mt. Carmel, the 'Mountain of the Lord, mentioned so often in the Old Testament, Baha'u'llah says: *"Call out to Zion, O Carmel, and announce the joyful tidings: He that was hidden from mortal eyes is come!"* (Baha'u'llah: *Gleanings,* Page: 16)

Mt. Carmel, the 'Mountain of the Lord,' where Elijah engaged in contest with the priests of Baal, is the seat of the Baha'i International Center. The building on the left is the Universal House of Justice. On the extreme right is the Archives Building.

Further, speaking about this special Day of God, Baha'u'llah said: *"Bestir yourselves, O people, in anticipation of the days of Divine justice, for the promised hour is now come."* (Baha'u'llah: *Gleanings*, Page: 17). And: *"The Divine Springtime is come . . . Bestir thyself, and magnify, before the entire creation, the name of God, and celebrate His praise, in such wise that all created things may be regenerated and made new. Speak, and hold not thy peace . . . Arise before the nations of the earth, and arm thyself with the power of this Most Great Name, and be not of those who tarry."* (Baha'u'llah: *Gleanings*, Pages: 27-28)

"Take heed lest anything deter thee from extolling the greatness of this Day—the Day whereon the Finger of majesty and power hath opened the seal of the Wine of Reunion,

and called all who are in the heavens and all who are on the earth." (Baha'u'llah: *Gleanings*, Page: 28) And: *"Great is thy blessedness, O earth, for thou hast been made the footstool of thy God, and been chosen as the seat of His mighty throne."* (Baha'u'llah: *Gleanings*, Page: 30)

QUESTION: I'm especially interested in these particular statements from Baha'u'llah. They sharpen my need to know whether Baha'u'llah was a madman, a trickster or—Who He said He was. I want to hear more, even though Baha'u'llah's words are very challenging to me.

RESPONSE: These quotes from Baha'u'llah are indeed very challenging, I agree. I can remember having some of the same thoughts you've just mentioned. I thought: "Is this person mad?" But I read on and I listened, I prayed and I pondered, until I came to my own decision that Baha'u'llah was the 'Promise of all Ages' and, more important to me, that He represented the return of my Lord, my Savior, Jesus.

Several other quotations that you asked for are about the 'Day of God' that we spoke about: Baha'u'llah said this is a *"matchless Day . . . The whole human race hath longed for this Day, that perchance it may fulfil that which well beseemeth its station, and is worthy of its destiny."* (Baha'u'llah: *Gleanings*, Page: 39)

Baha'u'llah invites us all, and this includes you, to partake *"in this spiritual Springtime, of the outpourings of His grace . . . Arise in the name of Him Who is the Object of all knowledge, and, with absolute detachment from the learning of men, lift up your voices and proclaim His Cause. I swear by the Day Star of Divine Revelation! The very moment ye arise, ye will witness how a flood of Divine knowledge will gush out of your heart."* (Baha'u'llah: *Gleanings*, Page: 84)

Baha'u'llah counsels us: *"refresh and revive your souls through the gracious favors which in this Divine, this soul-stirring Springtime are being showered upon you."* (Baha'u'llah: *Gleanings,* Page: 94) And: *"Say: O people! The Day, promised unto you in all the Scriptures, is now come. Fear ye God, and withhold not yourselves from recognizing the One Who is the Object of your creation. Hasten ye unto Him. Better is this for you than the world and all that is therein. Would that ye could perceive it!"* (Baha'u'llah: *Gleanings,* Page: 314)

Finally, here are several more quotations from Baha'u'llah that I think will sharpen even more your dilemma of what to make of Him, how to decide Who He is: He said: *"This is the day whereon every man endued with perception hath discovered the fragrance of the breeze of the All-Merciful in the world of creation, and every man of insight hath hastened unto the living waters of the mercy of His Lord."* (Baha'u'llah: *Tablets of Baha'u'llah,* Page: 214)

Also: *"The Promised Day is come and the Lord of Hosts hath appeared."* (Baha'u'llah: *Tablets of Baha'u'llah,* Page: 239) and *"Say: This is the Day of God Himself."* (Baha'u'llah: *Tablets of Baha'u'llah,* Page: 241) Finally, Baha'u'llah said that He was calling aloud *"betwixt earth and heaven, saying: The Promised Day is come. The Lord of creation proclaimeth: Verily, there is no God besides Me, the Almighty, the All-Bountiful."* (Baha'u'llah: *Tablets of Baha'u'llah,* Pages: 243-244)

QUESTION: How dare you! Have you lost all your senses? In the last few sentences, you have called Baha'u'llah 'God Himself,' 'the Lord of Hosts' and the 'Ancient of Days.' This sounds crazy! It's madness, isn't it?

RESPONSE: You know, I really don't want to frustrate you and I won't patronize you, but I must remind you that these are not my words, nor from my opinion. They are the exact words of Baha'u'llah.

QUESTION: They must be taken out of context. Surely, He didn't say exactly what you are quoting. It's just too strange!

RESPONSE: I assure you, they are not taken out of their context. If anything, the context would make them stronger and clearer, more striking and more challenging. But, you can check for yourself. Get two books: (1) *Gleanings* (from the writings of Baha'u'llah) and (2) *Tablets of Baha'u'llah* and check the page references I have supplied.

Yes, these statements were certainly made by Baha'u'llah and I have supplied them to you in their true, intended meaning. I agree that it does lead us back to what we agreed on earlier in our conversation. That is, Baha'u'llah must be either (1) A madman or crazy; (2) A charlatan or trickster, or (3) He must be Who He said He was. And now, I am going to ask you: "What do you think about Baha'u'llah?" Jesus asked His disciples: *"Who do men say that I am?"* (Mark 8:27) and later: *"But who do you say that I am?"* (Matt 16:15-16)

Imagine yourself being with Jesus and being asked these questions. How would you have answered? Only one of the disciples knew how to answer. It was a tough question, wasn't it? A real test of faith?

Now, try an experiment. Imagine you are with Baha'u'llah in 1863. He has been in a foul dungeon, banished even further from His native land, His feet are damaged from the Persian torture of being beaten with rods. Deep scars from heavy chains are on His wrists, neck and ankles. He is ill from having been deliberately poisoned. He is on His way to being sent to the Middle East's worst Prison (in Akka, in the country then called Palestine, now called Israel). In this imagined event, you are in a garden with Him, an actual garden just outside Baghdad, called 'Paradise.' He turns to you and says what Christ said: "Who do *you* say that I am?" What is your answer?

QUESTION: I don't know. I just don't know. It will take some time, I believe, to decide this. It's too important. Don't you understand that?

RESPONSE: Yes, I believe I do, because it took me some time to decide. But, you and I should remember that while several disciples of Christ gave poor or incorrect answers to the question Christ asked: *"Who do men say that I am?"* that nevertheless, Simon Peter answered directly, immediately and strongly: *"Thou art the Christ, the Son of the living God."* (Matt 16:16) Other disciples answered incorrectly or didn't answer at all. They hesitated, or maybe they were just like you and me; they wanted time to think, to decide.

QUESTION: To tell the truth, I sometimes wonder what I would have said if I *had* been with Jesus. It would have been a great test, I'm sure of that! Would I have been a Simon Peter, or would I have given a weak, incorrect answer, such as: "Some say that you are Elijah." Or, would I have just been silent, preferring to wait? I hate to think that I might have wanted more time, that I might have played it safe. And, before you say it, I will say it myself and beat you to it. I'm 'playing it safe' right now on Baha'u'llah.

RESPONSE: It's not a crime to be thoughtful. If so,

you and I are both guilty of wanting time to think things over carefully. But, as you say, it is a daunting, almost threatening thought to wonder what we would have done, had Christ asked that question not of Matthew or John or Peter, but if He had turned to us and had put the question straight in our direction, asking no one else but us what *we* thought about who He was. The scariest thing to me, and probably to you, is that we might have been asked that question by Jesus and we could have said: "Can I get back to you, Jesus. I have to think this over at more length."

What I say to you is this: If you think that you would have answered like St. Peter, boldly, passionately, then if you do know Who Baha'u'llah is, don't hesitate to declare your faith in Him immediately in what He called *"this blessed, this glorious Day."* He further said, and maybe He is talking to you: *"Deprive not yourselves of the liberal effusions of bounty which the Lord of abounding grace hath vouchsafed unto you. In this Day showers of wisdom and utterance are pouring down from the clouds of divine mercy."* (Baha'u'llah: *Tablets of Baha'u'llah*, Page: 85)

But, if you need time, as I did, if you need reflection, study and prayer, then I am sure that Jesus *"the Son"* and Baha'u'llah *"the Father"* will understand. However, don't forget that both Jesus and Baha'u'llah admonished Their followers not to tarry, not to take too long. Do you remember the parable Jesus told about this? The Wise and Foolish Virgins? You may want to take a look at in the twenty-fifth chapter of Matthew. Jesus praises the Wise Virgins for being ready with oil for their lamps, so that they will be prepared for the appearance of the *"Son of Man."* How much more important that a wise person today be ready, fully ready, for the appearance of one who is *"the Father"* of all mankind.

In closing here is a prayer of Baha'u'llah that speaks

about this Day as the *"King of Days."*

"Magnified be Thy name, O my God, for that Thou hast manifested the Day which is the King of Days, the Day which Thou didst announce unto Thy chosen Ones and Thy Prophets in Thy most excellent Tablets, the Day whereon Thou didst shed the splendor of the glory of all Thy names upon all created things. Great is his blessedness whosoever hath set himself towards Thee, and entered Thy presence, and caught the accents of Thy voice.

"I beseech Thee, O my Lord, by the name of Him round Whom circleth in adoration the kingdom of Thy names, that Thou wilt graciously assist them that are dear to Thee to glorify Thy word among Thy servants, and to shed abroad Thy praise amidst Thy creatures, so that the ecstasies of Thy revelation may fill the souls of all the dwellers of Thine earth.

"Since Thou hast guided them, O my Lord, unto the living waters of Thy grace, grant, by Thy bounty, that they may not be kept back from Thee; and since Thou hast summoned them to the habitation of Thy throne, drive them not out from Thy presence, through Thy loving-kindness. Send down upon them what shall wholly detach them from aught else except Thee, and make them able to soar in the atmosphere of Thy nearness, in such wise that neither the ascendancy of the oppressor nor the suggestions of them that have disbelieved in Thy most august and most mighty Self shall be capable of keeping them back from Thee." (Baha'u'llah: *Prayers and Meditations*, Pages: 117-118)

And because you have told me that you are a 'seeker,' one who feels they must 'make a decision,' here is a famous letter Baha'u'llah wrote to just such a person, advising them about how to make a spiritual decision. It is often called 'The Tablet to the True Seeker':

"O My brother! When a true seeker determineth to take the step of search in the path leading unto the knowledge of the Ancient of Days, he must, before all else, cleanse his heart,

which is the seat of the revelation of the inner mysteries of God, from the obscuring dust of all acquired knowledge, and the allusions of the embodiments of satanic fancy. He must purge his breast, which is the sanctuary of the abiding love of the Beloved, of every defilement, and sanctify his soul from all that pertaineth to water and clay, from all shadowy and ephemeral attachments.

"He must so cleanse his heart that no remnant of either love or hate may linger therein, lest that love blindly incline him to error, or that hate repel him away from the truth. Even as thou dost witness in this Day how most of the people, because of such love and hate, are bereft of the immortal Face, have strayed far from the Embodiments of the Divine mysteries, and, shepherdless, are roaming through the wilderness of oblivion and error.

"That seeker must, at all times, put his trust in God, must renounce the peoples of the earth, must detach himself from the world of dust, and cleave unto Him Who is the Lord of Lords. He must never seek to exalt himself above any one, must wash away from the tablet of his heart every trace of pride and vain-glory, must cling unto patience and resignation, observe silence and refrain from idle talk. For the tongue is a smoldering fire, and excess of speech a deadly poison. Material fire consumeth the body, whereas the fire of the tongue devoureth both heart and soul. The force of the former lasteth but for a time, whilst the effects of the latter endureth a century.

"That seeker should, also, regard backbiting as grievous error, and keep himself aloof from its dominion, inasmuch as backbiting quencheth the light of the heart, and extinguisheth the life of the soul. He should be content with little, and be freed from all inordinate desire. He should treasure the companionship of them that have renounced the world, and regard avoidance of boastful and worldly people a precious benefit.

"At the dawn of every day he should commune with God, and, with all his soul, persevere in the quest of his Beloved. He should consume every wayward thought with the flame of His loving mention, and, with the swiftness of lightning, pass by all else save Him. He should succor the dispossessed, and never withhold his favor from the destitute. He should show kindness to animals, how much more unto his fellow-man, to him who is endowed with the power of utterance.

"He should not hesitate to offer up his life for his Beloved, nor allow the censure of the people to turn him away from the Truth. He should not wish for others that which he doth not wish for himself, nor promise that which he doth not fulfil. With all his heart he should avoid fellowship with evil-doers, and pray for the remission of their sins. He should forgive the sinful, and never despise his low estate, for none knoweth what his own end shall be. How often hath a sinner attained, at the hour of death, to the essence of faith, and, quaffing the immortal draught, hath taken his flight unto the Concourse on high! And how often hath a devout believer, at the hour of his soul's ascension, been so changed as to fall into the nethermost fire!

"Our purpose in revealing these convincing and weighty utterances is to impress upon the seeker that he should regard all else beside God as transient, and count all things save Him, Who is the Object of all adoration, as utter nothingness.

"These are among the attributes of the exalted, and constitute the hall-mark of the spiritually-minded. They have already been mentioned in connection with the requirements of the wayfarers that tread the path of Positive Knowledge. When the detached wayfarer and sincere seeker hath fulfilled these essential conditions, then and only then can he be called a true seeker. Whensoever he hath fulfilled the conditions implied in the verse: 'Whoso maketh efforts for Us', he shall enjoy the blessings conferred by the words: 'in Our Ways shall We assuredly guide him.'

"Only when the lamp of search, of earnest striving, of longing desire, of passionate devotion, of fervid love, of rapture, and ecstasy, is kindled within the seeker's heart, and the breeze of His loving-kindness is wafted upon his soul, will the darkness of error be dispelled, the mists of doubts and misgivings be dissipated, and the lights of knowledge and certitude envelop his being. At that hour will the Mystic Herald, bearing the joyful tidings of the Spirit, shine forth from the City of God resplendent as the morn, and, through the trumpet-blast of knowledge, will awaken the heart, the soul, and the spirit from the slumber of heedlessness.

"Then will the manifold favors and outpouring grace of the holy and everlasting Spirit confer such new life upon the seeker that he will find himself endowed with a new eye, a new ear, a new heart, and a new mind. He will contemplate the manifest signs of the universe, and will penetrate the hidden mysteries of the soul. Gazing with the eye of God, he will perceive within every atom a door that leadeth him to the stations of absolute certitude. He will discover in all things the mysteries of Divine Revelation, and the evidences of an everlasting Manifestation.

"I swear by God! Were he that treadeth the path of guidance and seeketh to scale the heights of righteousness to attain unto this glorious and exalted station, he would inhale, at a distance of a thousand leagues, the fragrance of God, and would perceive the resplendent morn of a Divine guidance rising above the Day Spring of all things. Each and every thing, however small, would be to him a revelation, leading him to his Beloved, the Object of his quest. So great shall be the discernment of this seeker that he will discriminate between truth and falsehood, even as he doth distinguish the sun from shadow.

"If in the uttermost corners of the East the sweet savors of God be wafted, he will assuredly recognize and inhale their fragrance, even though he be dwelling in the uttermost ends of the West. He will, likewise, clearly distinguish all the signs of God—His wondrous utterances, His great works, and mighty

*deeds—from the doings, the words and ways of men, even as
the jeweler who knoweth the gem from the stone, or the man
who distinguisheth the spring from autumn, and heat from
cold. When the channel of the human soul is cleansed of all
worldly and impeding attachments, it will unfailingly perceive the breath of the Beloved across immeasurable distances,
and will, led by its perfume, attain and enter the City of
Certitude.*

*"Therein he will discern the wonders of His ancient Wis-
dom, and will perceive all the hidden teachings from the rustling leaves of the Tree that flourisheth in that City. With both
his inner and outer ear, he will hear from its dust the hymns of
glory and praise ascending unto the Lord of Lords, and with
his inner eye will he discover the mysteries of 'return' and
'revival'.*

*"How unspeakably glorious are the signs, the tokens, the
revelations, and splendors which He, Who is the King of Names
and Attributes, hath destined for that City! The attainment
unto this City quencheth thirst without water, and kindleth
the love of God without fire. Within every blade of grass are
enshrined the mysteries of an inscrutable Wisdom, and upon
every rose-bush a myriad nightingales pour out, in blissful
rapture, their melody. Its wondrous tulips unfold the mystery
of the undying Fire in the Burning Bush, and its sweet savors
of holiness breathe the perfume of the Messianic Spirit. It
bestoweth wealth without gold, and conferreth immortality
without death. In each one of its leaves ineffable delights are
treasured, and within every chamber unnumbered mysteries
lie hidden.*

*"They that valiantly labor in quest of God, will, when
once they have renounced all else but Him, be so attached
and wedded unto that City, that a moment's separation from
it would to them be unthinkable. They will hearken unto infallible proofs from the Hyacinth of that assembly, and will
receive the surest testimonies from the beauty of its Rose, and*

the melody of its Nightingale. Once in about a thousand years shall this City be renewed and readorned . . . .

"That City is none other than the Word of God revealed in every age and dispensation. In the days of Moses it was the Pentateuch; in the days of Jesus, the Gospel; in the days of Muhammad, the Messenger of God, the Qur'an; in this day, the Bayan; [the Revelation of Baha'u'llah's predecessor, the Bab] *and in the Dispensation of Him Whom God will make manifest,* [Baha'u'llah Himself] *His own Book—the Book unto which all the Books of former Dispensations must needs be referred, the Book that standeth amongst them all transcendent and supreme."*

(Baha'u'llah: *Gleanings*, Pages: 264-270)

CHAPTER FOURTEEN

REBIRTH AND RENEWAL: MY NEW RESPONSIBILITY AS A DISCIPLE OF BAHA'U'LLAH

QUESTION: I'm not sure why you gave this chapter the title: 'My New Responsibility as a Disciple of Baha'u'llah.' I just got through telling you that I'm not ready to take that step.

RESPONSE: Yes, I did hear you. The only reason this chapter has this name is that I have no idea exactly who will be reading this book, or at what time and in what state of decision. Therefore, I have no idea how a given individual reader will respond. I have hopes that this book/ conversation will be read by thousands of persons. One person may recognize Baha'u'llah immediately as Christ returned in *"the Glory of the Father"* while another person may be partly interested (as you seem to say at times) but not entirely ready. Still another third person may reject Baha'u'llah outright and strongly, as some rejected Christ at His first Coming.

QUESTION: But you are talking to me now, and I wish you would deal more directly with *my* particular concerns!

RESPONSE: You are right, and I will, but permit me to say something to those other two categories, the ones who are immediately ready to accept the appearance of *"The Father"* of all mankind and also the ones who feel compelled to reject Baha'u'llah as in impostor, a madman, as the Devil or even Anti-Christ. After I talk to them, I promise we will get back to discussing what you might do to further your spiritual quest of seeking the fuller truth that you would need and deserve to have before recommitting to Christ by committing to Baha'u'llah.

QUESTION: Fair enough, but I do want you to get back to me. For now, though, what would you say to those who reject?

RESPONSE: I would say: "You are in great company!" The biggest, strongest rejecter of Jesus Christ in history was, let us remember, St. Paul himself! I'm sure we both recall that Paul was very angry when he, a devout Jew, heard about the Christian Faith. He saw this new Faith as a cult, its teachings a devilish, blasphemous, confused perversion of his own Faith, and he devoted himself full time to a personal crusade to combat Christian teachers.

He was very serious about this. So much so, that when he could, he killed Christians or had them killed. Paul, or Saul as he was known before his conversion, murdered many Christians. He sincerely felt that Christian teachings were a terrible betrayal of all that his Jewish Faith stood for and wanted literally to exterminate this new 'heresy' even if it meant putting Christians to death, usually by stoning.

Read again in the book of Acts about the stoning of Stephen, an early Christian believer and martyr. Just as an aside, and for something that is truly amazing, read the book of Acts in the New Testament where the 'stoning of Stephen' is chronicled. Note what Stephen saw in the heavens, as he was being stoned to death by the crowd, and while St. Paul watched and perhaps participated.

Just before his death, Stephen looked up to the heavens and beheld, "the Glory of God." You had better get ready for this one! In the original New Testament language of Aramaic—the language that Jesus spoke–the book of Acts reports that Stephen beheld "Baha–allah," which means 'Glory of God.' (I thank Dr. Kendrick Grobel, a Vanderbilt University School of Divinity Professor of mine, for supplying this interesting information. Dr. Grobel was an internationally recognized expert in the Greek language and other languages related to the Bible. Interestingly, Dr. Grobel had studied with an even more famous New Testament scholar, T. K. Cheney, who declared his belief in Baha'u'llah.)

So, if you sincerely believe that Baha'u'llah and the Baha'i Faith and Baha'i teachings are wrong or blasphemous or of the devil or an invention of Antichrist, it would seem to me to be inconceivable that you would not oppose it—even strongly (but hopefully not with the 'killer' zeal of Saul of Tarsus!)

QUESTION: This seems to be a very strange thing for you to say. It's almost as if you are 'egging someone on'!

RESPONSE: Not really. Only God knows what is in

the hearts of men and women. If they are sincere, He will not only understand, but He may choose to do the same thing that He did with Saul of Tarsus. He obviously looked at the zealous, very real and deep belief of Saul and saw someone whose energy, intelligence and faith He wanted in a believer.

What did God do? He 'struck down' Saul on the road to Damascus, where he had been headed for more persecution and more killing of Christians. God blinded Saul and then led him to Christians who cared for him, brought him back to physical and spiritual health and into Christian belief and into a new identity as Paul. Now, we know him as the writer of most of the New Testament and as St. Paul.

QUESTION: So you don't worry about those who oppose?

RESPONSE: Oh, I could worry if I felt Baha'is were again going to be killed. More than 20,000 Baha'is died terrible deaths of martyrdom (just as St. Stephen did) in the 1840's and 1850's and beyond when just a word of denial of their faith would have saved their lives. In the 1980's, hundreds of Baha'is died because of their belief. Even as late as the year 2000, Baha'is were dying for their Faith. They laid down their lives as modern martyrs, rather than utter one life-saving word of denial of their lord— Baha'u'llah.

QUESTION: Well, I guess you realize that many Christians have been willing to die for their faith, including Jesus Himself, St. Peter, and the one you were just talking about, St. Paul, not to mention literally thousands of others, some of whom are being martyred in Africa, South America and in China in the 1990's.

RESPONSE: Yes, I do know and respect that. Actually, whenever a Manifestation appears in human history (for our purposes and from the perspective of our conversation, we can think of these Manifestations as the 'Christ-Spirit' or the pre-existent Word of God, appearing in Moses, Buddha, Jesus, Zoroaster, Muhammad or Baha'u'llah), whenever these Manifestations of God appear, they gather together disciples or believers who are always willing to go even to their deaths to defend their belief in, say, Buddha, Baha'u'llah or Jesus.

This teen-aged Baha'i, Ruhullah (whose name means the Spirit of God), was martyred in Iran in the mid-nineteenth century. This picture was taken just before his martyrdom. Notice the heavy chain about his neck.

QUESTION: You mentioned a moment ago that Baha'i believers have even been martyred in Iran as recently as 1999?

RESPONSE: It's true. Both Houses of the United States Congress have held numerous hearings in Washington, DC in the 1980's and the 1990's to let the world know of the plight of the Iranian (Persian) Baha'is. After the arrival of the Iranian revolution in the late 1970's, hundreds of Baha'is were systematically slaughtered, including several teen-aged girls and women, who chose to be martyrs to their Faith rather than to deny Baha'u'llah. Many thousands were driven from their homes, hounded out of their employment, removed from taking part in university studies.

One girl, aged sixteen, named 'Mona' went to her death by hanging, in the 1980's. Others fell before firing squads. Others were beaten to death, some strangled. In every case, had they been willing to utter one single word of denial of their faith in their Lord—Baha'u'llah—their lives would have been spared.

It is this kind of strength of faith that is seen in early Christian history, early Islamic history and now, even in the 1990's, among Baha'is and, as you say, some Christians in China, Africa and South America.

QUESTION: Christians still give their lives for the Gospel and for Christ.

RESPONSE: As do sincere Muslims, Buddhists and Baha'is. Tibetan Buddhists and Chinese Christians, as you say, have met their deaths through martyrdom. There is no sense of competition here. Faith is Faith, and those who believe deeply, while not wishing to lose their lives, would be ready to give up their lives to defend their faith, wouldn't they?

Baha'i belief speaks of only one God, Who has sent all the Manifestations of God, every one of them, and Who even sent His only-begotten *"Son"* and in this Day, this great Day, has fulfilled His long-standing promise to mankind to appear *"Himself"* in the 'station' of *"The Father"* of all mankind.

As I've told you, there can be no spirit of competition for Baha'is, whose belief in Christ and in all the Manifestations of God is as strong as their belief in Baha'u'llah.

QUESTION: But surely you must realize that if the Baha'i Faith is attacked, it will be put to a very severe test?

RESPONSE: I'm hoping you will read a little of Baha'i history. You will see that those 'tests' and persecutions you speak of have already happened numerous times. We are under no illusions, though, and realize that other attacks may happen. Christians were being persecuted by the Roman Empire well into the fourth century after Christ. This is only the second century after Baha'u'llah, whom we believe is Christ Returned. So, yes, I realize that Baha'is may be put through what you call 'severe tests,' but consider this: Faiths, when they are attacked, either die or start to grow very rapidly, depending on whether or not they are 'true' faiths. If false, they are immediately or soon crushed or put on the sidelines and margins of history, or disappear entirely.

But, if true, the attack itself becomes a form of energy. Isn't that what happened with Christianity? This 'energy' causes the new faith to burst forth with dynamic growth. Again, remember Saul of Tarsus. His vehement attack on the faith of Jesus was quite literally the very best thing that ever happened to Christianity. For, out of that attack was born the greatest of Christian teachers— St. Paul. It has always been this way, that persecution and attack energizes a faith and causes it to grow rapidly.

Even if attacks don't bring forth a St. Paul, they tend to prune the new faith of weak and uncertain disciples and also focus the attention of the world on that faith, causing people to make their own decisions based upon Baha'u'llah's suggestion of 'independent investigation.' Finally, most of the people of the world are going to be alerted when they realize that there is a group of believers who are ready not only to build and act and live by their beliefs, but also to die for them, if necessary.

Baha'u'llah did not permit 'fanatic' behavior, but like Christ, He did expect His disciples to *"take up the cross."* Just as Christ did, Baha'u'llah expected His disciples to make a convincing witness to the world, and if it became a necessity, to be willing to die in order to help to bring humanity into unity and peace.

Baha'u'llah says in the *Hidden Words* that if the men and women of the world can do so, they should take to heart all that He has revealed, writing it down with "ink" made of "light" or of the "essence" of the heart. But He says if this is not possible, men and women should write with "crimson ink," that is, they should be ready to shed their blood, giving their lives for their faith. Here is the actual quote:

"O SON OF MAN! Write all that We have revealed unto thee with the ink of light upon the tablet of thy spirit. Should this not be in thy power, then make thine ink of the essence of thy heart. If this thou canst not do, then write with that crimson ink that hath been shed in My path. Sweeter indeed is

this to Me than all else, that its light may endure for ever. "
(Baha'u'llah: (Arabic) *Hidden Words*, Page: 71)

One final word to the person who chooses to oppose
and reject Baha'u'llah. Let me suggest that you pray to
Jesus Christ to continue to guide you in your understanding. Pray that He will give you strength to resist
Baha'u'llah if that be His Will, but pray also that He will
give you the spiritual vigor and power to accept
Baha'u'llah if you are mistaken about Him.

Remember Saul of Tarsus, whatever you do. You
might call this suggestion I have made to you the 'Saul of
Tarsus Insurance Policy.' If God wants you badly enough,
He has the power to call you into discipleship, even
against your own plans and powers. Even if He has to
'strike you down' as He did Saul.

QUESTION: What would you say to someone who
is immediately ready to declare his or her faith in
Baha'u'llah? You know I'm not in that category, but I
would like to hear what you would say to them, anyway.

RESPONSE: What I, personally, would say is: 'Welcome to the world!' Welcome to a more fully understood
history of humankind. Welcome to humanity with its
entire story, the good and the bad. Welcome to a new
understanding of history, in which a Plan of God can be
seen to have been laid out, then enacted through the
centuries and is now entering a consummation phase of
the building of the Kingdom of God *"on earth as it is in
heaven."*

I would say: Welcome, welcome, to the knowledge
of Baha'u'llah and to discipleship with Him, where you
will not only be a builder of the *'Kingdom'* and of the
unity of mankind, but also someone who works to bring
a dying and dead world into life, new birth and renewal.

Baha'u'llah charged His disciples and followers to be the *"quickeners of mankind,"* which means to bring a renewing, life-giving message to a spiritually 'dead' world.

For someone like me—and perhaps you—belief in Christ and a renewed, rekindled belief in Christ Returned in *"the glory of the Father"* makes us the possessors of a 'double-discipleship.' We can be both *"fishers of men"* as Christ asked us to be and *"quickeners of mankind"* as Baha'u'llah commanded. And, we can do both at the same time! In our 'double discipleship' to both Christ and Baha'u'llah, Christ Returned, our sense of commitment is very full and broad.

QUESTION: What kind of person is it that hears Baha'u'llah and immediately believes and quite literally–like some disciples of Jesus–gives up everything to follow Him? Are there, or were there such persons?

RESPONSE: There were and there are. There were numerous instances of that in the early days of the Baha'i Faith. One of my favorites is a man who said that he knew Who Baha'u'llah was even before He spoke. Many others then and even today hear one prayer of Baha'u'llah and experience instant, strong belief.

QUESTION: Do you trust that?

RESPONSE: Do you trust what happened to St. Paul in a short period of time? Do you trust what millions of Christians have experienced in an immediate conversion experience? Do you trust being suddenly 'born again'? Do you trust, in a Christian context that—in some persons—faith can blaze into full reality in an instant?

I believe you do, if I may be presumptuous. And if you ask me if I believe this can happen in a Christian context, my answer is 'Yes.' And, yes again, I believe it can happen when someone simply is told Who Baha'u'llah is, that they can express instant faith. I do not understand it, but I have seen it as a Christian and I have seen it as a Baha'i. Yes, I do trust it, even without understanding.

What I think is that there are many different paths that different kinds of people walk along toward their experience of recognition of a Manifestation of God. Some will recognize Baha'u'llah instantly; I have seen it. Some, I believe like you and me, will take some time to reflect and choose. Some others still, will go through a phase (like St. Paul) of active disbelief and even rejection before experiencing belief. A famous African-American phrase fits here very well: 'Diffrent strokes for diffrent folks.'

So, I don't try to criticize or second-guess anyone for their 'method' or 'pathway' of their experience of recognizing the Manifestation of God, whether Jesus or Baha'u'llah. But, to that person who instantly believes, I do have four suggestions:

1. Put yourself in strong touch with a really active Baha'i community. Think how lucky a new Christian believer would have been to live in Ephesus, Corinth, Galatia, Thessaly or Rome. He or she would have had the guidance and strong teaching of experienced, born-again Christians (and letters and visits now and then from none other than St. Paul!). I had a 'St. Paul' type figure in my early Baha'i life. His name was Winston Evans.

As a new Baha'i, you need the same thing, namely, the guidance and teaching of spiritually deep Baha'i believers.

2. Read! Read! Read! Baha'u'llah, as I have mentioned, wrote some ten thousand or more documents. Read, I say, and this is so important, do more than read. Read for spiritual deepening, not just intellectual understanding. Read not only Baha'u'llah's books such as the *Book of Certitude*, but His *Prayers and Meditations*. Read a book by Baha'u'llah called *The Hidden Words*. Baha'u'llah said *The Hidden Words* was a distillation and abbreviation of all of scriptures of all the world's religions. Yes, He did say that. You may want to take a look at this extremely interesting book. It is like no other.

3. Pray! Pray! Pray! I've just suggested you read for spiritual Deepening. This new path you are on is a spiritual path and will require spiritual discipline and readiness for spiritual growth. The best and, in fact, only real way to ensure this growth is through prayer and meditation, as well as reading. There is an amazing wealth of prayers revealed by Baha'u'llah. You have been reading some of them at the end of each chapter of this conversation.

4. You could also attend a Baha'i Summer or Winter School, which would give you a chance not only to learn, but also to observe the Baha'is, to see them in the terms of their community life and interaction.

To the person reading this book, youth or adult, who responds immediately or quickly to the Call of Baha'u'llah. Let me give you words of 'Abdu'l-Baha and Baha'u'llah which I believe will mean more to you than anything I could say.

"O Lord, I have turned my face unto Thy kingdom of

oneness and am immersed in the sea of Thy mercy. O Lord, enlighten my sight by beholding Thy lights in this dark night, and make me happy by the wine of Thy love in this wonderful age. O Lord, make me hear Thy call, and open before my face the doors of Thy heaven, so that I may see the light of Thy glory and become attracted to Thy beauty.

"Verily, Thou art the Giver, the Generous, the Merciful, the Forgiving."

('Abdu'l-Baha: *Baha'i Prayers* (US edition), Pages: 61-62)

The following is a prayer from Baha'u'llah:

"Create in me a pure heart, O my God, and renew a tranquil conscience within me, O my Hope! Through the spirit of power confirm Thou me in Thy Cause, O my Best-Beloved, and by the light of Thy glory reveal unto me Thy path, O Thou the Goal of my desire! Through the power of Thy transcendent might lift me up unto the heaven of Thy holiness, O Source of my being, and by the breezes of Thine eternity gladden me, O Thou Who art my God! Let Thine everlasting melodies breathe tranquillity on me, O my Companion, and let the riches of Thine ancient countenance deliver me from all except Thee, O my Master, and let the tidings of the revelation of Thine incorruptible Essence bring me joy, O Thou Who art the most manifest of the manifest and the most hidden of the hidden! (Baha'u'llah: *Prayers and Meditations*, Pages: 248-249)

The following passage is from the writings of the Bab, Baha'u'llah's predecessor, and Himself a Manifestation of God, according to Baha'u'llah. The Bab prays to God that He will recognize the new Manifestation of Baha'u'llah (much the same, I suppose, as John the Baptist must have prayed to recognize the Messiah, Jesus).

"Abandon me not to myself, O my Lord, nor deprive me of recognizing Him Who is the Manifestation of Thine Own Self, nor account me with such as have turned away from Thy holy

presence. Number me, O my God, with those who are privileged to fix their gaze upon Thy Beauty and who take such delight therein that they would not exchange a single moment thereof with the sovereignty of the kingdom of heavens and earth or with the entire realm of creation.

"Deliver me, O Lord, from the fire of ignorance and of selfish desire, suffer me to be admitted into the precincts of Thy transcendent mercy and send down upon me that which Thou hast ordained for Thy chosen ones. Potent art Thou to do what Thou willest."

(The Bab: *Selections from the Bab,* Page: 216)

Again from Baha'u'llah, who speaks to a believer, who Baha'u'llah says will be *"enraptured by the vitalizing breaths of the revealed verses and art carried away by the pure, life-giving water proffered by the hand of the bounty of thy Lord, the sovereign Ruler of the Day of Resurrection, lift up thy voice and say: O my God! O my God! I yield Thee thanks that Thou hast directed me towards Thyself, hast guided me unto Thy horizon, hast clearly set forth for me Thy Path, hast revealed to me Thy testimony and enabled me to set my face towards Thee while most of the doctors and divines among Thy servants together with such as follow them have, without the least proof or evidence from Thee, turned away from Thee.*

"Blessing be unto Thee, O Lord of Names, and glory be unto Thee, O Creator of the heavens, inasmuch as Thou hast, through the power of Thy Name, the Self-Subsisting, given me to drink of Thy sealed wine, hast caused me to draw nigh unto Thee and hast enabled me to recognize the Dayspring of Thine utterance, the Manifestation of Thy signs, the Fountainhead of Thy laws and commandments and the Source of Thy wisdom and bestowals." (Baha'u'llah: *Tablets of Baha'u'llah,* Pages: 110-111)

Baha'u'llah speaks of the 'bounty' of the new believer, and how God has chosen him and caused him to be a 'shower of bounty' for mankind. He further tells that believer that he has been given to 'drink' of the 'choice wine' of the words of the 'Nightingale' (one of the titles of Baha'u'llah):

"Yield thou praise unto God for having graciously chosen thee to be a shower of bounty for that which We have sown in the pure and blessed soil and enabled thee to serve as a springtime of tender mercy for the wondrous and sublime trees We have planted. Indeed so great is this favour that of all created things in the world of existence, none can ever hope to rival it.

We have moreover given thee to drink the choice wine of utterance from the chalice of the heavenly bestowals of thy merciful Lord, which is none other than this Tongue of holiness—a Tongue that, as soon as it was unloosed, quickened the entire creation, set in motion all beings and caused the Nightingale to pour forth its melodies. This is the Fountain of living water for all that dwell in the realm of being."
(Baha'u'llah: *Tablets of Baha'u'llah*, Page: 195)

Baha'u'llah tells that same new believer *to "invite thou the receptive souls unto God's holy court, that perchance they may not remain deprived of the heavenly Fountain of living water"*. (Baha'u'llah: *Tablets of Baha'u'llah*, Pages: 236-237) Baha'u'llah assures him: *"We make mention of him who hath been attracted by Our Call when it was raised from the summit of transcendent glory and hath set his face towards God, the Lord of creation"*. (Baha'u'llah: *Tablets of Baha'u'llah*, Page: 238)

In a passage that is nothing short of amazing, especially in the light of our division of response into (1) Those who reject; (2) Those who respond immediately and (3) Those who need to take their time to read study and pray, Baha'u'llah lists the different ways that human beings have responded to Him, but speaks especially about the person who 'immediately' responds:

"We have raised the Call unto all that dwell in the realm of creation. Amongst men there are those who have been car-

ried away by the fragrance of the utterance of their Lord in such manner that they have forsaken everything which pertaineth unto men in their eagerness to attain the court of the presence of God, the Lord of the mighty throne. There are also those who are sore perplexed and wavering. Others have made haste, winged their way to answer the Call of their Lord, the Ancient of Days. Still others have turned aside, rejected the truth and eventually disbelieved in God, the Almighty, the All-Praised.

Baha'u'llah further says about all these 'categories of response': *"We have graciously summoned them unto the river that is life indeed . . . We have revealed Ourself unto men, have unveiled the Cause, guided all mankind towards God's Straight Path".* (Baha'u'llah: *Tablets of Baha'u'llah,* Page: 251)

Baha'u'llah advises the one who has responded 'immediately,' His new follower and believer to *"drink deep from the life-giving waters of Our gracious providence that he may be enabled to draw nigh unto My Horizon, be adorned with Mine attributes, soar in Mine atmosphere, be confirmed in that which will cause the sanctity of My Cause to be manifested amongst My people and to celebrate My praise in a manner that will cause every hesitating soul to hasten, every motionless creature to wing its flight, every mortal frame to be consumed, every chilled heart to be stirred with life and every dejected spirit to surge with delight. Thus doth it behove him who hath turned his face to Mine, hath entered beneath the shadow of My loving-kindness and received My verses which have pervaded the whole world."* (Baha'u'llah: Tablets of Baha'u'llah, Pages: 262-263)

He continues to advise: *"Grieve thou not at men's failure to apprehend the Truth. Ere long thou shalt find them turning towards God, the Lord of all mankind."* (Baha'u'llah: *Tablets of Baha'u'llah,* Pages: 263-264) Baha'u'llah is in prison as He writes a letter to a believer, but refers to that same prison as *"a Scene of incomparable glory."* Baha'u'llah mentions the believer's mother, who has just recognized Him. This is what He tells the new believer that has immediately responded to Him:

"O friend! The Best-Beloved is calling thee from His Most Great Prison and exhorteth thee to observe that which Mine exalted Pen hath revealed . . . that thou mayest hold fast unto it with such resolve and power as is born of Me; and I verily am the Ordainer, the All-Wise.

"Great is indeed your blessedness inasmuch as His unfailing grace hath been vouchsafed unto you and ye have been aided to recognize this Cause—a Cause through whose potency the heavens have been folded together and every lofty and towering mountain hath been scattered in dust.

"Moreover through Our boundless grace We make mention of your mother who hath been privileged to recognize God. We send her Our greetings from this glorious station. We remember every one of you, men and women, and from this Spot—the Scene of incomparable glory—regard you all as one soul and send you the joyous tidings of divine blessings which have preceded all created things, and of My remembrance that pervadeth everyone, whether young or old. The glory of God rest upon you, O people of Baha. Rejoice with exceeding gladness through My remembrance, for He is indeed with you at all times." (Baha'u'llah: *Tablets of Baha'u'llah*, Page: 264)

Baha'u'llah, in writing to a woman believer, tells her how favored she is over 'kings and queens' who have been 'debarred' from recognizing Him and then encourages her to accomplish a 'deed' that will endure forever:

"Well is it with thee inasmuch as thou hast forsaken idle imaginings and taken fast hold of the Cord of God that no man can sever. Consider the gracious favour of God—exalted be His glory. How numerous are the kings and queens on earth who, despite much yearning, anticipation and waiting,

*have been debarred from Him Who is the Desire of the world,
whilst thou didst attain. God willing, thou mayest accomplish
a deed whose fragrance shall endure as long as the Names of
God—exalted be His glory—will endure. By the righteousness of God!* . . . [He gives her a prediction]: *"Ere long the
eyes of mankind shall be illumined and cheered by recognizing that which Our Pen of Glory hath revealed."* (Baha'u'llah:
Tablets of Baha'u'llah, Page: 252)

Baha'u'llah indicates that the new believer has entered a new 'Ark' that God has provided and promises
that if the believer recognizes Him, he will gain admittance into 'God's Paradise':

*"Blessed art thou, O My name, inasmuch as thou hast
entered Mine Ark, and art speeding, through the power of My
sovereign and most exalted might, on the ocean of grandeur,
and art numbered with My favored ones whose names the
Finger of God hath inscribed. Thou hast quaffed the cup which
is life indeed from the hands of this Youth, around Whom
revolve the Manifestations of the All-Glorious, and the brightness of Whose presence they Who are the Day Springs of Mercy
extol in the day time and in the night season.*

*"His glory be with thee, inasmuch as thou hast journeyed
from God unto God, and entered within the borders of the
Court of unfading splendor—the Spot which mortal man can
never describe. Therein hath the breeze of holiness, laden
with the love of thy Lord, stirred thy spirit within thee, and
the waters of understanding have washed from thee the stains
of remoteness and ungodliness. Thou hast gained admittance
into the Paradise of God's Remembrance, through thy recognition of Him Who is the Embodiment of that Remembrance
amongst men.* [that is, Baha'u'llah].

*"Wherefore, be thankful to God, for having strengthened
thee to aid His Cause, for having made the flowers of knowledge and understanding to spring forth in the garden of thine
heart. Thus hath His grace encompassed thee, and encom-*

*passed the whole of creation. Beware, lest thou allow any-
thing whatsoever to grieve thee. Rid thyself of all attachment
to the vain allusions of men, and cast behind thy back the idle
and subtle disputations of them that are veiled from God.
Proclaim, then, that which the Most Great Spirit will inspire
thee to utter in the service of the Cause of thy Lord, that thou
mayest stir up the souls of all men and incline their hearts
unto this most blessed and all-glorious Court . . .   "*
(Baha'u'llah: *Gleanings*, Pages: 302-303)

My final word to the person who has accepted
Baha'u'llah is to quote Baha'u'llah Himself in saying *"take
up thy life in thine hand, and with infinite longing, cast it
before the new Beloved One."*

QUESTION: I'm very glad you have shared so much
of the writings of Baha'u'llah. They are very helpful, even
if very challenging. He certainly is no mere Elijah, or
Jeremiah or just a wise man. The situation is getting
clearer, in terms of the decision that I think must be
made. But, have you at last set aside some time for me?
I'm the one who is not yet decided on acceptance of
Baha'u'llah. How can you help me? Or can you help?

RESPONSE: I hope I can help, but this decision
belongs to you. It is yours, yours alone. Your search.
Your spiritual struggle. I will stand beside you, but you
must do the important work of decision-making and spiritual commitment. In other words, yes, I will do everything to help but the 'heavy lifting' is yours. You have not
only my friendship, but my strong personal and heart-
felt encouragement and my prayers. After all, don't forget that I went through a similar period as the one you
are describing.

QUESTION: Thanks a lot, but I don't just want 'encouragement.' I need something practical, some down to earth advice on how to proceed. You are almost lecturing me on the fact that the struggle and the decision are mine. Please! I already understand that and I accept the challenge, which as I've told you, is not coming from you or from anyone else. In a way, I'm realizing for the first time that the challenge to me is coming from none other than Baha'u'llah!

RESPONSE: Well, here's something that may help. Let's use our imaginations: Imagine you are back in early Christian times, but about a century and a half after Jesus' death and Resurrection.

You have accepted Jesus and you travel to Corinth for a meeting with the vibrant community of Christians there. St. Paul had visited Corinth from time to time and wrote two famous letters to the Corinthians, key books of the New Testament. You are surprised to meet a boyhood friend, a Jew, who lives there. He asks you about Jesus and the Christian Faith and you begin teaching him. He seems somewhat interested, but then he says to you: 'I'm just uncertain. I'm not sure and I'm not ready to make a decision on this. How can you help me to make this decision?'

QUESTION: That's not fair!

RESPONSE: Oh, yes it is! Very fair, in fact, because it is the identical situation to the two of us (except for being childhood friends). But just go along with me for a moment. It is now (at the turn of the millennium) one hundred fifty-seven years after the Baha'i Faith began. So, in our example, it is now one hundred fifty-seven years after Christ. What will you say to your boyhood Jewish friend in Corinth? I want to know what you will say, because as you suspect, I am then going to say to you that you, yourself should follow whatever advice you would give to him

QUESTION: You are 'copping out'!

RESPONSE: Well maybe it seems that way, but I will redeem myself. After you tell me what you would say, I will 'step up to the plate' and tell you what I think may help you. First, I just want to see what you will say?

But wait, I can see you think I'm being unfair, so how about this? Let me speculate on what I 'think' you would say to that boyhood Jewish friend in Corinth who is interested in the Christian Faith, but reluctant to accept Jesus. As I take a 'crack' at imagining what you would say, please see if I am right or not. I'm ready to be wrong and you may tell me so, but I think I have a very good idea of what you would say, at least in part.

Remembering that the date is 157 AD, similar to the amount of time between the start of the Baha'i Faith and the year 2000, this is what I think you might say to this Jewish friend of yours: "Well, you have taken the first step already by listening to me and to others about Jesus' life and teachings. Now, all I can advise you to do is to pray for enlightenment. Pray to discover the truth. In your prayers, ask Jesus to show you a sign of some kind, to make the way clear for you, for what you should decide. Study your own scriptures for prophecies and portents of Jesus' coming. Read the sayings of Jesus, His sermons, especially the Sermon on the Mount, read His prayers, read His predictions and promises of His Return. Read Paul's letters to Christians, especially the two he wrote to the Christians right here in Corinth."

I think you would say to him (am I getting this right?): "Spend time around the Christians here in

Corinth. If you like, go to Ephesus or Thessaly to see if Christians there are also living a new kind of life. If you go to Rome, look up the Christians there. Talk to them, pray and worship with them. Watch them carefully to see if they really do lead lives that have been 'saved' and transformed by being 'born again.'

"Then, if your reading, your prayer and your association with disciples of Christ do not lead you closer to a decision to follow Jesus, you should turn away with a clear, clean conscience and a feeling that you have honestly investigated and found nothing and no one in whom to believe."

Finally, I think you might say to him: "If you feel your heart and mind experiencing a warmth, a change, if you feel yourself drawn to Jesus, do not hesitate to commit your life to Him, to give up anything and everything, to follow Him."

Did I get this at all right? Is this close to what you would have said?

QUESTION: Very close. Maybe I would have chosen some different words, but yes, it is exactly the message I would have given to my Jewish friend. And I see what is coming. You want me to do, in my search and my decision about Baha'u'llah, what I told him to do in his search and decision about Christ. You want me to: 1. Read the writings of Baha'u'llah; 2. Pray; 3. Associate with Baha'is, to worship, discuss, and pray with them. But I have a question: How did you pray when you had to make this decision? And to Whom?

RESPONSE: It seems to me that a Christian is first and foremost going to pray to his Lord, Jesus Christ, or to God, in the name of Jesus. At least, that's what I did. I asked God in the name of His Son, Jesus, to show me the way. Because my minister father had taught me to know Jesus in an 'intimate' personal way, I 'had a little talk with Jesus,' in the words of the revival song. Another hymn was ringing in my ears: 'Open my eyes that I may see', with the verse: 'Silently now, I wait for Thee, ready my God, Thy Will to see. Open my eyes, illumine me, Spirit divine.'

I expected and wanted Jesus to 'give me a sign' until I remembered that Jesus was somewhat disgusted with people always asking Him for a sign, as if He were a court magician instead of the Son of God. Baha'u'llah felt the same way, that people were not to accept Him or reject Him on the basis of performing some convincing 'magic trick' or even a true miracle; rather, they were to recognize, using faith as well as reason, that *"the Father hath come"* and if they were Christians, He expected them to recognize the Return of Christ *"in my person."*

But there came a time that I was very close to believing in Baha'u'llah, but still 'not quite there.' I was then that I began to pray some Baha'i prayers that were marked in the Baha'i prayer book for 'Tests and Difficulties.' I prayed to God, still in the name of Christ (that was all I knew) but also in the name of Baha'u'llah, based on His claim to be the Return of Christ. I asked my Jesus to help me, show me, if not a sign, some form of 'guidance', something, anything, that would help me in my decision. And, I asked Baha'u'llah to show Himself somehow to me, as Jesus Returned.

The answer to my prayers came in an unusual way. The year was 1957. Baha'i meetings in Nashville, Tennessee were often held in the home of Georgia and Roy Miller. They were a middle aged, Black couple, neither of them very well educated in the formal sense, but they had become Baha'is in the early 1940's. I looked at them with amazement, noticing that they had become transformed into what seemed to me to be 'spiritual giants,' who without that formal education had surged ahead of their world and the world of Nashville to become 'citizens of the world.'

I remember sitting in their home one evening and marveling at what the Revelation of Baha'u'llah had done in their lives. It was all the answer I needed. If Baha'u'llah could do this very complete work in their lives, I reasoned, He was very certainly Who He said He was, the Return of my Jesus.

Baha'u'llah had done in the lives of these simple people the same miracle that Jesus had worked in the totally uneducated Simon Peter. Suddenly, I realized my prayer had been answered, my test and my questions ended. I believed in Baha'u'llah as Christ Returned. I often think of Roy and Georgia Miller and even named one of my daughters—Georgine—after Mrs. Miller.

Let me share another story with you about a Baha'i friend from a Christian background who set out to 'challenge' Baha'u'llah when he first heard about the Baha'i Faith. We should remember, as I've said before, that Baha'u'llah said that we should never test the Manifestations of God; rather, that they will test us, to see if we are wanting in courage and understanding.

Nevertheless, Baha'u'llah several times surprised persons who came into His presence planning to 'test' Him by having a question that He would have to answer. In many of these cases, they 'forgot' their question and were doubly surprised, even shocked, when Baha'u'llah reminded them of their question by giving them the answer they sought. They were stunned. Even though the question had not been asked, even though they had literally forgotten the question entirely, He had brought forth the answer as He talked with them.

Well, back to my friend. He read in a prayer of

Baha'u'llah called 'The Tablet of Ahmad' that Baha'u'llah revealed: *"By God! Should one who is in affliction or grief read this Tablet with absolute sincerity, God will dispel his sadness, solve his difficulties and remove his afflictions."* (Baha'u'llah: *Baha'i Prayers* (US), Page: 213) My friend didn't have sadness or affliction, but he reasoned that he certainly did have 'difficulties' in making his decision about Who Baha'u'llah was.

So, to test Baha'u'llah (remembering that it is not the best thing to do, to test the Manifestation of God), my friend told several of his Baha'i friends that he was going to pray this prayer, with all the sincerity he could muster, once a day, for one month. Then, he reasoned, if nothing happened, if there was no sign of anything, not even some indication of guidance, if nothing was in any way revealed to him personally, he would walk away.

His point, he told me, was that Baha'u'llah's promise in this prayer was, to him, the perfect 'test' of the truth of this Faith. The promise was so direct, so definite, so literal, that my friend felt (whether he was right or wrong, I do not say) that he could find the truth, make his decision one way or the other, and move on. He even felt that it was not so much 'testing God' as just taking Baha'u'llah completely at His word. After all, my friend said, it was Baha'u'llah Who made this promise. My friend just decided to see if the promise could be relied upon.

When he told me the story years later, he said that on the eleventh day of this 'test', he was kneeling in prayer and felt overwhelmed with an experience of 'spiritual presence.' He could not move, not a muscle. He could not speak, nor open his eyes. He remained in this position for several hours, until he heard one word: 'Arise!' He told me that he had the overwhelming conviction that he had been reborn and that it was Baha'u'llah Who had spoken that word 'Arise' to him. From that day to this, he told me, he has not doubted the truth of Baha'u'llah being the Return of Christ and the appearance in the world of *"The Father"* of all mankind.

QUESTION: I'm sure you realize that there are many such stories of Christians who have experienced similar rebirth, similar confirmation of belief?

RESPONSE: Thousands of them, both in the Christian Faith and in the Baha'i Faith. And, I have now learned from my readings and study into the history of other faiths that many Moslems, Hindus, Buddhists, Jews, Zoroastrians and others report this kind of experience within their faiths. It really is helpful to learn about other faiths, because we quickly learn the truth of what Baha'u'llah teaches, that God has been 'at work' more often and in more places, with more Manifestations of Himself than we ever knew, or could imagine.

But, let's get back to you. When you asked me Who I prayed to, I said I prayed to God in the name of Jesus, to Jesus directly and then, very near to my decision, I prayed to Jesus and to Baha'u'llah, to show me the way. I realized at about this point that if Baha'u'llah was Jesus returned, I wasn't even praying to two people, but to the same person. I felt that I was going to receive confirmation and that is what happened. I think it may be possible that you could feel that same thing. But, it is up to you to choose your path, as we have agreed.

I believe you would be most likely, as I was, to pray to Jesus, but if along the way, you begin to pray Baha'u'llah's prayers or prayers of your own, but directed not just to Jesus, but to Baha'u'llah as Christ Returned, you are going to get an answer either way. If your prayer is sincere, I believe an answer will come. My Jesus (and your Jesus) told me, from as early in my life as I can remember: *"And I say unto you, Ask, and it shall be given you; seek, and ye shall find; knock, and it shall be opened unto you."* (Luke 11:9)

I asked, even pleaded to Jesus for an answer and for the 'door' to be opened. Finally, I was asking Baha'u'llah, as well. The door opened, as you can see, and the answer came, and the Person standing on the other side of the door was—my Jesus, in the person of Baha'u'llah!

QUESTION: But what I'm looking for exactly is how you managed to make this decision. What did you do? I'm still looking for practical advice.

RESPONSE: It wasn't very remarkable. I don't have as good a story as the one I told you about my friend who prayed the 'Tablet of Ahmad'. However, this is what happened. I learned about the Baha'i Faith and about Baha'u'llah from reading a book in a clergyman friend's library. The book was Stanwood Cobb's *Security for a Failing World.* Then, I heard more in a lecture by a Baha'i, Winston Evans, in my comparative religion class in seminary at Vanderbilt University School of Divinity, where I was preparing to become a Methodist minister.

Following that, I began to read everything I could find about the Faith and I began to spend time around the Baha'is. I really wanted to look them over. I realized that you don't test the Manifestations of God but I definitely wanted to 'test' the Baha'is to find out what they were made of, and whether they would represent to me the kind of changed, transformed lives that would be, according to Jesus, the best 'proof' of the new Manifestation of God.

Jesus did say, (we talked about this earlier, I believe) that His disciples would be able to distinguish His true

Return from a false prophet by, among other things, the *"fruits"* that they would see in the followers of this person. *"Ye will know them by their fruits. Do men gather grapes from thornbushes or figs from thistles?"* (Matt 7:16) I wanted to see these Baha'is, the *"fruits"* of the Tree of Baha'u'llah's Manifestation of God. That, I thought, would be the real proof. If, as Jesus taught me, I found thorns or thistles, then I would have a quick answer that this was a 'false prophet.' On the other hand, if I found grapes and figs, I would have to begin to take Baha'u'llah seriously.

And that proof came! I decided that it wasn't going to be so much what the Baha'is said as who they were, the way they were, how they thought and how they acted and, especially, how their communities functioned that would impress me. And I was impressed. I saw grapes and figs! And I saw one thing that had me absolutely convinced. As I have told you, the year of my becoming a follower of Baha'u'llah was 1957. It happened that about half of the small Nashville community was White, the other half Black. Several of the White members were elderly, so would have to have been born in the late 1800's.

Aha, I said. This would be my test of the Baha'is. I knew that you don't test God, but you sure can test His followers, I reasoned. These elderly White individuals were born in the 1890's, a time when there was not even a smidgen of the idea of equality between Blacks and Whites. How would these White Baha'is come off on this test? For that matter, how would the Black Baha'is come off on the test of dropping resentments and hatreds towards Whites for what had been done to them?

And, there was an even better test. The Baha'i Faith not only had an absolutely uncompromising stand on the oneness of humanity and the equality of the races,

but it also actually promoted the idea of interracial marriage. I have to tell you that I strongly believed that these
older White ladies would fail miserably on this test.

They did not! I literally reeled back in amazement,
then realized that there must be some new kind of force
at work and I realized it was the 'salvation' and 'quickening' power of the new Manifestation of God—
Baha'u'llah—that could take Southern Whites raised in
that strictly segregated era and completely transform
them, then take the Black Baha'is and transform them
too, so that there could be love, harmony, fellowship
and unity in the 1930's in the South, when this community of Baha'is was formed. This was proof enough for
me!

As I continued to look and observe, no longer testing the Baha'is but just wanting to see more, I realized
that these people really acted out the Baha'i teachings,
including the equality of men and women, the reverse of
what those Baha'is in their 50's, 60's and 70's and older
were raised to believe. These people actually believed in
the oneness of mankind! In world citizenship! They actually held and practiced a belief system that encompassed
Moses, Jesus, Muhammad, Buddha, Krishna, Zoroaster
and others, and they believed in Baha'u'llah.

I was, at first, unbelieving, but there it was in front of
me. I felt as if I had gone back in a time machine and
had stumbled into a Christian meeting in 113 AD in
Corinth or Ephesus, Thessaly or Rome, where I would
have met a small group of people who not only believed
new beliefs, but acted out those beliefs in transformed
lives and communities. Simple and often uneducated
people, who at first seemed to have no power that the
world would respect, but who then revealed that they
possessed a spiritual power that would not only inspire
them to live a new kind of life, but which would em-

power them to go to their death rather than deny their faith.

Here was such a community! This really pushed me to a decision, but made that decision much easier. I was compelled. One night, I lay awake for many hours, thinking about the need for a decision. I got out of bed, went downstairs to the study and prayed a Baha'i prayer that has remained my favorite for forty-two years, a prayer that said: 'I lay all my affairs in Thy hand.' Here is that prayer, given to us by 'Abdu'l-Baha:

"O my God! O my God! Refresh and gladden my spirit. Purify my heart. Illumine my powers. I lay all my affairs in Thy hand. Thou art my Guide and my Refuge. I will no longer be sorrowful and grieved; I will be a happy and joyful being. O God! I will no longer be full of anxiety, nor will I let trouble harass me. I will not dwell on the unpleasant things of life.

"O God! Thou art more friend to me than I am to myself. I dedicate myself to Thee, O Lord." 'Abdu'l-Baha: *Baha'i Prayers,* US Edition, P. 152.

The next morning, I awoke with the full knowledge that Baha'u'llah was, for me, Christ Returned in the Name of *"The Father."* That was over forty years ago. As I, with others, enter the new millennium, my discipleship in Jesus and Baha'u'llah has been re-energized.

My commitment to Jesus had always been strong. Now, it seemed even more compelling as I realized and practiced my 'double discipleship' to Jesus and to Baha'u'llah—Jesus Returned. I am today a *"fisher of men"* and now a *"quickener of mankind"* as well. I know that whenever I lead a human soul to belief in Baha'u'llah that I am also leading him or her to deeper belief in Christ.

When that person coming to belief in Baha'u'llah is a Christian, I am offering an opportunity to realize what he or she has always prayed for and expected, the Return of Christ, and an opportunity to experience what I call 'double discipleship.'

As always, I continue to believe in and to work toward the building of the Kingdom of God on earth, as Jesus prayed for it: *"Thy kingdom come. Thy will be done in earth, as it is in heaven."* (Matt 6:10) It still echoes in my ears, even as Baha'u'llah says: *"The earth is but one country, and mankind its citizens."* (Baha'u'llah: *Gleanings*, Page: 250)

QUESTION: It's getting more and more clear that the time is coming when I, too, will have to make a decision about Baha'u'llah. I've listened carefully to your thoughts and ideas, and now I'm listening with even greater care to Baha'u'llah. But as I told you once before, I'd like to hear more of what Baha'u'llah says about making this decision. Did He say anything about this process of decision that might help me?

RESPONSE: Oh, yes. Plenty. I do believe it will help you but I must warn you again . . .

QUESTION: Stop with the warnings, already! I'm ready to hear whatever Baha'u'llah has to say. I'm even eager to hear it. I don't need to be pampered or warned away from things that Baha'u'llah may say that are very challenging. If that were the case, if I were that tender, that weak in my Faith in Jesus Christ, I would have stopped listening long ago.

RESPONSE: I will not again issue any more 'warnings.' I only wanted you to have the best and the most complete opportunity to see Baha'u'llah in a way that would allow you to approach this decision without any unnecessary blockages getting in your way.

Here are, as you asked for them, some of the statements of Baha'u'llah that speak directly to your task of decision. He first tells you, interestingly enough, to go to Jesus for advice: *"Give ear unto that which the Spirit* [Baha'u'llah often calls Jesus 'the Spirit'] *imparteth unto thee from the verses of God, the Help in Peril, the Self-Subsisting, that His Call may attract thee to the Summit of transcendent glory and draw thee nigh unto the Station where thou shalt behold thine entire being set ablaze with the fire of the love of God"* (Baha'u'llah: *Tablets of Baha'u'llah*, Pages: 264-265)

He then pleads with God *"graciously to aid Thy creatures to accomplish that which is pleasing and acceptable unto Thee, that they may arise to serve Thy Cause amidst Thy creatures, and to speak forth Thy praise before all who are in heaven and on earth."* (Baha'u'llah: *Prayers and Meditations*, Page: 244)

He quotes Jesus as saying: *"Unless a man be born of water and spirit, he cannot enter the Kingdom of God."* Baha'u'llah then says: *"whosoever in every dispensation is born of the Spirit and is quickened by the breath of the Manifestation of Holiness, he verily is of those that have attained unto 'life' and 'resurrection' and have entered into the 'paradise' of the love of God. And whosoever is not of them, is condemned to 'death' and 'deprivation.' to the 'fire' of unbelief, and to the 'wrath' of God."* (Baha'u'llah: The *Kitab-i-Iqan*, Page: 118)

QUESTION: Baha'u'llah almost sounds in this passage like a revival preacher scaring people with a 'fire and brimstone' sermon, offering paradise and threatening hell, and it doesn't sound like Jesus, does it, or like the loving Father that Jesus told us about?

RESPONSE: Well, if you read and study Baha'u'llah

at some length, you will find that His approach to humankind and to you as an individual is not threatening at all, but in places He is 'plainspoken' and direct, just as Jesus was. Remember, Jesus could be exceptionally 'plainspoken', as when He refused to release a disciple to bury his father, telling him *"Let the dead bury the dead"*. Or, when Jesus said: *"It is easier for a camel to go through the eye of a needle, than for a rich man to enter into the kingdom of God."* (Matt 19:24) or, very similar to the passage above from Baha'u'llah, Jesus says: *"if ye believe not that I am he, ye shall die in your sins."* (John 8:24)

QUESTION: I guess the Manifestations of God don't 'mince words'! And, I'm just realizing that it is easier for me to hear such things from Jesus, Whom I regard as the *"Son of God,"* than it is for me to hear similar things said by someone Who was a contemporary of my Great, Great Grandfather, someone Who walked the earth in the nineteenth century!

RESPONSE: Probably that's it, all right. If you were a Jew and had been around Jesus, as He spoke, the Jewish scriptures, the Torah, the Prophets and the Law would have been comforting, authoritative, well known and deeply accepted, while the words of Jesus would have been challenging and disturbing at best, but sounding blasphemous and almost devilish at worst.

QUESTION: I want to hear more from Baha'u'llah.

RESPONSE: You mentioned a moment ago that Baha'u'llah almost sounded like a 'revivalist preacher.' As I told you, Baha'u'llah isn't at all like that, but neither does he 'pull punches.' He spoke, just like Jesus did, directly and forcefully.

He tells us of the seriousness of this decision about Him and tells us to make it before it is *"too late"*: He says: *"Beware lest the transitory things of human life withhold you from turning unto God"*. (Baha'u'llah: *Tablets of Baha'u'llah*, Page: 267) *"The day is approaching when everything now discernible will have faded away and ye shall weep for having failed in your duty towards God"*. (Baha'u'llah: *Tablets of Baha'u'llah*, Page: 245)

Baha'u'llah says that it is *"regrettable indeed that man should debar himself from the fruits of the tree of wisdom while his days and hours pass swiftly away."* (Baha'u'llah: *Tablets of Baha'u'llah*, Page: 174) and that man will only have life *"till of a sudden the fowler Death throws it upon the dust"*. (Baha'u'llah: (Persian) *Hidden Words*, Page: 75)

And this: *"Hear Me, ye mortal birds! In the Rose Garden of changeless splendor a Flower hath begun to bloom, compared to which every other flower is but a thorn, and before the brightness of Whose glory the very essence of beauty must pale and wither. Arise, therefore, and, with the whole enthusiasm of your hearts, with all the eagerness of your souls, the full fervor of your will, and the concentrated efforts of your entire being, strive to attain the paradise of His presence, and endeavor to inhale the fragrance of the incorruptible Flower, to breathe the sweet savors of holiness, and to obtain a portion of this perfume of celestial glory.*

"Whoso followeth this counsel will break his chains asunder, will taste the abandonment of enraptured love, will attain unto his heart's desire, and will surrender his soul into the hands of his Beloved. Bursting through his cage, he will, even as the bird of the spirit, wing his flight to his holy and everlasting nest.

"Night hath succeeded day, and day hath succeeded night, and the hours and moments of your lives have come and gone, and yet none of you hath, for one instant, consented to detach himself from that which perisheth. Bestir yourselves, that the

brief moments that are still yours may not be dissipated and lost. Even as the swiftness of lightning your days shall pass, and your bodies shall be laid to rest beneath a canopy of dust. What can ye then achieve? How can ye atone for your past failure?" (Baha'u'llah: *Gleanings*, Pages: 320-321)

Here is more from Baha'u'llah: *"O SON OF BEING! Thy Paradise is My love; thy heavenly home, reunion with Me. Enter therein and tarry not. This is that which hath been destined for thee in Our kingdom above and Our exalted Dominion."* (Baha'u'llah: (Arabic) *Hidden Words*, Page: 6)

And He counsels: *"Take heed that ye do not vacillate in your determination to embrace the truth of this Cause—a Cause through which the potentialities of the might of God have been revealed, and His sovereignty established. With faces beaming with joy, hasten ye unto Him. This is the changeless Faith of God, eternal in the past, eternal in the future."* (Baha'u'llah: *Proclamation of Baha'u'llah*, Page: 119)

A passage from Baha'u'llah that has always meant much to me: *"Know ye from what heights your Lord, the All-Glorious, is calling? Think ye that ye have recognized the Pen wherewith your Lord, the Lord of all names, commandeth you? Nay, by My life! Did ye but know it, ye would renounce the world, and would hasten with your whole hearts to the presence of the Well-Beloved".* (Baha'u'llah: The *Kitab-i-Aqdas*, Page: 39)

He also said: *"Fear ye God, O ye servants of God, and suffer not yourselves to be kept back from this pure Wine that hath flowed from the right hand of the throne of the mercy of your Lord, the Most Merciful. I swear by God! Better for you is what He possesseth than the things ye yourselves possess and the things ye have sought and are now seeking in this vain and empty life.*

"Forsake the world, and set your faces towards the all-glorious Horizon. Whoso hath partaken of the wine of His remembrance will forget every other remembrance, and whoso

hath recognized Him will rid himself of all attachment to this
life and to all that pertaineth unto it." (Baha'u'llah: *Prayers*
and Meditations, Page: 188)

QUESTION: Those passages do begin to sound more
like the Jesus that I know, I have to admit. Let me hear
more. I'll tell you when to stop. I don't want anything
held back. I want to hear it all.

RESPONSE: O. K. You asked for it, as they say.
Baha'u'llah prays to God (Keep in mind that Jesus prayed
to God, as we have discussed) asking God to enable humanity to *"haste to the river that is life indeed"* and further
asks God to enable them to *"drink of the river that is life*
indeed" that their *"eyes may be opened,* and He teaches
His followers to pray that: *"my face be illumined, and my*
heart be assured, and my soul be enlightened, and my steps
be made firm" (Baha'u'llah: *Prayers and Meditations,* Page:
4)

"The Divine Springtime is come . . . Bestir thyself, and
magnify, before the entire creation, the name of God, and
celebrate His praise, in such wise that all created things may
be regenerated and made new. Speak, and hold not thy peace
. . . Arise before the nations of the earth, and arm thyself
with the power of this Most Great Name, [a title of
Baha'u'llah] *and be not of those who tarry."* (Baha'u'llah:
Gleanings, Pages: 27-28)

QUESTION: What Baha'u'llah just said puts me in
mind of a parable about the Foolish Virgins who tar-
ried, as was previously mentioned.

RESPONSE: Yes, a favorite of mine. Another parable that I always loved is the one about the owner of a
Vineyard, where the workers have revolted. The owner

sends overseers, who are stoned and chased away by the workers. He then sends His only son, because he cannot believe the workers will kill him, but they do exactly that, they kill the son. Jesus goes on to say that the owner of the vineyard realizes that things will only be set right by making a personal appearance. He then decides to go himself to the vineyard. Remember that one?

QUESTION: Are you suggesting that the owner of the Vineyard is Baha'u'llah?

RESPONSE: Remember that both Christian and Baha'i teachings tells us to regard the Manifestations of God as identical with God. They are the only God that we will ever see or hear. When Jesus speaks, we hear God speak. When Baha'u'llah speaks, Baha'is likewise hear God speaking. Baha'u'llah taught His followers to regard God and the Manifestation of God as *"one and the same."* (Baha'u'llah: *Gleanings*, Page 78)

He said that God "manifested Himself" many times in history. Here is how He put it: *"He hath manifested unto men the Day Stars of His divine guidance, the Symbols of His divine unity, and hath ordained the knowledge of these sanctified Beings to be identical with the knowledge of His own Self. Whoso recognizeth them hath recognized God. Whoso hearkeneth to their call, hath hearkened to the Voice of God, and whoso testifieth to the truth of their Revelation, hath testified to the truth of God Himself.*

"Whoso turneth away from them, hath turned away from God, and whoso disbelieveth in them, hath disbelieved in God. Every one of them is the Way of God that connecteth this world with the realms above, and the Standard of His Truth unto every one in the kingdoms of earth and heaven. They are the Manifestations of God amidst men, the evidences of His

Truth, and the signs of His glory. " (Baha'u'llah: *Gleanings*, Page: 50)

So, yes, I see the owner of the Vineyard as Baha'u'llah. Here are a few more statements of Baha'u'llah's that I think might aid you in making your decision. *"O SON OF SPIRIT! Burst thy cage asunder, and even as the phoenix of love soar into the firmament of holiness. Renounce thyself and, filled with the spirit of mercy, abide in the realm of celestial sanctity.* " (Baha'u'llah: (Persian) *Hidden Words*, Page: 38)

And: *"O MY SERVANT! Abandon not for that which perisheth an everlasting dominion, and cast not away celestial sovereignty for a worldly desire. This is the river of everlasting life that hath flowed from the well-spring of the pen of the merciful; well is it with them that drink!"* (Baha'u'llah: (Persian) *Hidden Words*, Page: 37)

Another favorite of mine: *"O SON OF LOVE! Thou art but one step away from the glorious heights above and from the celestial tree of love. Take thou one pace and with the next advance into the immortal realm and enter the pavilion of eternity. Give ear then to that which hath been revealed by the pen of glory.* " (Baha'u'llah: (Persian) *Hidden Words*, Page: 7)

Finally: *"Purge and sanctify your breasts, and your hearts, and your ears, and your eyes with the living waters of the utterance of the All-Merciful, and set, then, your faces towards Him. By the righteousness of God! Ye shall hear all things proclaim: 'Verily, He the True One is come. Blessed are they that judge with fairness, and blessed they that turn towards Him!'"* (Baha'u'llah: *Epistle to the Son of the Wolf*, Page: 65)

Baha'u'llah rhetorically says that if we turn to Him and are spiritually sensitive, we will hear the entire creation, birds and trees, streams, the wind, even the rocks, proclaiming His Coming and His Presence. In the quote just above, He says we would hear this proclamation from *"all things."* One of the most beautiful and poetic of Baha'u'llah's prayers is the following, which speaks of what we may hear, if we are attuned to the Presence of God in the creation:

"By Thy glory! Every time I lift up mine eyes unto Thy heaven, I call to mind Thy highness and Thy loftiness, and Thine incomparable glory and greatness; and every time I turn my gaze to Thine earth, I am made to recognize the evidences of Thy power and the tokens of Thy bounty. And when I behold the sea, I find that it speaketh to me of Thy majesty, and of the potency of Thy might, and of Thy sovereignty and Thy grandeur. And at whatever time I contemplate the mountains, I am led to discover the ensigns of Thy victory and the standards of Thine omnipotence.

"I swear by Thy might, O Thou in Whose grasp are the reins of all mankind, and the destinies of the nations! I am so inflamed by my love for Thee, and so inebriated with the wine of Thy oneness, that I can hear from the whisper of the winds the sound of Thy glorification and praise, and can recognize in the murmur of the waters the voice that proclaimeth Thy virtues and Thine attributes, and can apprehend from the rustling of the leaves the mysteries that have been irrevocably ordained by Thee in Thy realm.

"Glorified art Thou, O God of all names and Creator of the heavens! I render Thee thanks that Thou hast made known unto Thy servants this Day whereon the river that is life indeed hath flowed forth from the fingers of Thy bounty, and the springtime of Thy revelation and Thy presence hath appeared through Thy manifestation unto all who are in Thy heaven and all who are on Thy earth." (Baha'u'llah: *Prayers and Meditations*, Pages: 272-273)

As I told you before, Baha'u'llah wrote letters to all the kings and rulers of the earth, including one to the Presidents of the Republics of the American continent.

(Baha'u'llah: *Kitab-i-Aqdas*: Other Sections, Page: 15) Since these letters were written in the late 1800's, President Ulysses Grant would have received one of these letters. Some letters were to individuals, such as Queen Victoria and Czar Nicholas, while other letters were collectively addressed to world rulers, to the Presidents of the American Republics, to the Christian clergy, or to the Christians of the world.

To Napoleon III of France, He wrote with a claim of being the Return of Christ. He tells Napoleon to follow Him (that is, Baha'u'llah). He also tells Napoleon III to follow *"Him Who is the Spirit of God (Jesus Christ) in this, the Straight Path. Hath thy pomp made thee proud? By My Life! It shall not endure; nay, it shall soon pass away, unless thou holdest fast by this firm Cord. We see abasement hastening after thee, whilst thou art of the heedless. It behooveth thee when thou hearest His Voice calling from the seat of glory to cast away all that thou possessest, and cry out: `Here am I, O Lord of all that is in heaven and all that is on earth!'* " (Baha'u'llah: *Epistle to the Son of the Wolf*, Page: 51)

QUESTION: Baha'u'llah sounds very presumptuous, talking this way to a King! And to tell him, the King, to give away everything sounds a little strange. Oh, wait; I won't let you catch me on this one. Jesus said the very same thing to a 'rich young ruler' who expressed interest in discipleship, didn't He?

RESPONSE: I was tempted to 'pounce' on you for that one, so I'm glad you remembered it. As for presumptuousness, when Jesus is in the presence of earthly rulers, as with Pilate or Annas or Caiaphas, He speaks to them as a Ruler would speak to subjects. His power, wouldn't we both agree, was far greater than theirs, even beyond compare? Remember that Jesus said to His disciples: *"All power is given unto me in heaven and in earth."* (Matt 28:18) Certainly, this is power far beyond the power of any King; it is true power, the kind that Kings would desire, but never have.

If Christ was not Who He said He was (but He was!) He was being presumptuous. But if Jesus was indeed Who He said He was, it is quite a different story, isn't it?

If Baha'u'llah is not Who He says He is (but I testify to you that He is!) he is presumptuous; but if He is Who He said He is, he is the 'True King' talking to the Kings of the earth, who are His servants. Likewise, when Baha'u'llah sends messages to Queen Victoria or Czar Nicholas of Russia or President Grant, He is speaking, as did Jesus, with the power of the 'King of Kings.'

In fact, Baha'u'llah said in a collective letter to the Kings of the earth: *"Ye are but vassals, O kings of the earth! He Who is the King of Kings hath appeared, arrayed in His most wondrous glory, and is summoning you unto Himself, the Help in Peril, the Self-Subsisting. Take heed lest pride deter you from recognizing the Source of Revelation, lest the things of this world shut you out as by a veil from Him Who is the Creator of heaven. Arise, and serve Him Who is the Desire of all nations, Who hath created you through a word from Him, and ordained you to be, for all time, the emblems of His sovereignty."* (Baha'u'llah: The *Kitab-i-Aqdas*, Page: 49)

QUESTION: Next, you're probably going to say that Baha'u'llah warned of the 'fires of hell'?

RESPONSE: I see you are still on that comparison to a revivalist preacher. You know, Jesus could speak very plainly, bluntly and severely. I'm thinking of His calling the wise, the religious leaders and the unbelievers: *"Ye serpents, ye generation of vipers, how can ye escape the damnation of hell?"* (Matt 23:33) or *"I thank thee, O Father,*

Lord of heaven and earth, because thou hast hid these things from the wise and prudent, and hast revealed them unto babes." (Matt 11:25) Or, again, how about this one: *"for if ye believe not that I am he, ye shall die in your sins."* (John 8:24)

Jesus was 'plainspoken' when He said: *"He that is not with me is against me."* Matt 12:30 Try this one: *"he that believeth not the Son shall not see life; but the wrath of God abideth on him."* (John 3:36) As we discussed before, when Jesus says the unbeliever will face the *"wrath of God"* it doesn't seem to upset us as much as when Baha'u'llah says the very same thing; but we also came to an understanding on that, as I recall.

QUESTION: O.K., O.K. I guess I won't call Baha'u'llah a revivalist preacher anymore. I was just 'needling' you anyway. The things He is saying in this day are, I have to admit, very similar to what Jesus said.

RESPONSE: Maybe that's because it is the same Jesus, speaking now in Baha'u'llah, *"The Father"?* Jesus speaks of a time when He will come *"in the glory of his Father"* (Matt 16:27). Perhaps you are living in the day in which your Jesus has returned in *"the glory of his Father,"* keeping in mind that Baha'u'llah's very name means 'the Glory of God' and His title is *"The Father."*

QUESTION: I've heard enough for now. I really want to hear more, but not until I've had a chance to think and, as you suggested, to pray and meditate. I do want you to know that I have accepted your challenge to make my decision about Baha'u'llah. I know that a decision has to be made.

RESPONSE: I'm glad to hear that, but I'd like to

connect with you on one thing, if I may. I suppose you
have a right to say I have challenged you, but the real
challenge is not from me. The challenge you feel is from
Baha'u'llah Himself, directly to you, to your heart and
mind, to your soul. I'm only the messenger, the one who
has presented Baha'u'llah to you, but I will admit to 'inviting' you to consider Him as the Return of Christ, the
Promise of All Ages and the appearance of the 'Father
of all mankind'.

And, it may be that the challenge is not only from
Baha'u'llah, but from Jesus Himself, the one you know,
love and obey, if He is now speaking to you from the
person of Baha'u'llah.

In closing, I want to point out that Jesus said, while
teaching the multitudes about God:

*"Ye have neither heard his voice at any time, nor seen his
shape."* (John 5:37) In this day, Baha'u'llah tells us: *"He
that was hidden from the eyes of men is revealed, girded with
sovereignty and power!"* And: *"He Who, from everlasting,
had concealed His Face from the sight of creation is now come."*
(Baha'u'llah: *Gleanings*, Page: 31)

And finally: *"While in His presence,* [that is,
Baha'u'llah's presence] *thou hast heard the Voice of the
One true God"*. (Baha'u'llah: *Tablets of Baha'u'llah*, Page:
240)

I have enjoyed this 'conversation.' I have tried to
listen to your questions and I've also delivered a message to you, in a spirit of sharing and sincerity. I've done
it for several reasons, but one main reason, namely, because Baha'u'llah asked me to do so.

Earlier in this conversation I shared with you that in
becoming a Baha'i, I drew closer to Jesus. In the writing
this conversation/book, I have experienced a renewed
commitment to Jesus Christ. I now believe Jesus has again

been manifested; to me and to you and to all of humanity in the *"person"* of Baha'u'llah.

I hope I have carried out my task of presenting Baha'u'llah and the Baha'i Faith to you in a good enough way, but I rely on your implied promise to think, pray and investigate. I close my appeal to you with the words of Baha'u'llah, who instructed His followers to teach His Faith in the following way, a standard I know I can never reach, but to which I aspire with all my heart:

"If they arise to teach My Cause, they must let the breath of Him Who is the Unconstrained, stir them and must spread it abroad on the earth with high resolve, with minds that are wholly centered in Him, and with hearts that are completely detached from and independent of all things, and with souls that are sanctified from the world and its vanities. It behoveth them to choose as the best provision for their journey reliance upon God, and to clothe themselves with the love of their Lord, the Most Exalted, the All-Glorious. If they do so, their words shall influence their hearers." (Baha'u'llah: *Gleanings*, Page: 201)

And, in a passage that sounds like some advice Christ gave His disciples: *"Consort with all men, O people of Baha, in a spirit of friendliness and fellowship. If ye be aware of a certain truth, if ye possess a jewel, of which others are deprived, share it with them in a language of utmost kindliness and good-will. If it be accepted, if it fulfill its purpose, your object is attained. If anyone should refuse it, leave him unto himself, and beseech God to guide him."* (Baha'u'llah: *Epistle to the Son of the Wolf*, Page: 15)

In the next chapter, I invite you to 'join the conversation' in a different way, by actually writing or, preferably, emailing me, to suggest how this conversation/book can be improved in any future edition. If you have a question that didn't get raised, or treated sufficiently, let me know about it, please. By joining the conversation in that

way, I will be able to know what changes could be made
to achieve my goal of presenting Baha'u'llah in a way
that can best be understood by my many Christian friends.
And if you have declared your Faith in Baha'u'llah, please
let me know.

A hymn called 'Watch Night Song' that I found recently in the Methodist Hymnal contains this line, with
which I will end this conversation:

'The New Day dawns when Christ shall reign, all
power and mystery unsealed, in One Who comes to bring
new life, and God's full Glory to reveal.'

CHAPTER FIFTEEN

CONTACTING THE AUTHOR:
CONTINUING THE CONVERSATION

QUESTION: This is a little unusual, to have a chapter explaining how to contact the author. Why do that? And what makes you think that someone will want to contact you to continue this conversation?

RESPONSE: I'm sure that some will want to make a personal connection. At least, that would be my response if I had been reading this book. Whether I disagreed or agreed, I would be one to 'continue the conversation.' If I disagreed, I would want to put in my 'two cents worth,' to make a good faith argument of the facts or to put forth another interpretation.

If I agreed, I would probably want to respond, just to be in touch, to network and to suggest changes that would make the book clearer and better. I might want to suggest other topics that didn't get covered at all or didn't get covered in the depth or in the way that I thought they should be.

Anyway, while I explained in the first chapter that most of these questions are ones that came from Christian friends or were questions that I asked when I first encountered the Baha'i Faith, nevertheless, I acknowledge that I have chosen, selected and arranged the questions. Now, however, when others decide to respond to the book, they will actually become contributors to an effort to do a really good job of revising and enlarging 'Questions from Christians.'

So, yes, I do expect and I do want to get response. The book is meant as a 'conversation' between writer and reader and as such, I just don't think that the conversation has to or should end.

QUESTION: O.K. with me. I just thought it's a 'little different' but now that I have had a chance to think about it, I kind of like it. It will probably keep you more honest, to have real people asking real questions, maybe tougher questions than I have been able to ask.

RESPONSE: In thinking back, I believe that your questions were pretty tough and to the point. I have to remind you that all these questions were from 'real' people. I'm a real person, and all I had to do was to remember what I was thinking when I first learned about Baha'u'llah. However, the majority of the questions are from an actual file that I collected over forty years when I talked to Christian groups. Definitely real questions, from real people.

But, I can see what you mean. When people respond, and I strongly expect them to do so and I invite them to do so, those responses will include questions that will add a 'sharpness' and 'challenge' to the way this book is constructed. I promise you this: any and all responses will be read, noted and utilized to remake and revise this book. It should come out better than ever, once that has happened. I look forward to it.

QUESTION: How can you be contacted directly and how do you want to be contacted?

RESPONSE: For the foreseeable future, I can be reached at the following address:

Thom Thompson, Ste. L-101, 200 E. Joppa Road, Towson, MD 21286

HOWEVER:

Because it will not change, and because I check it every day, I greatly prefer to be contacted at my email address, which is: **daystarthom@yahoo.com**

Should I ever change my email address, you would be able to find my email address through checking my name, Thom Thompson, at: **bigfoot.com** on the Internet.

So, *please do use my email address listed above*–daystarthom@yahoo.com. You will get a reply, however brief, if you do. If you use regular mail, I will still try to reply, but I may be slower. With email, I can at least quickly acknowledge that I have received your entry into the conversation and perhaps give a brief response.

I would especially like to give you a warm response of welcome if you decide that you want to become a follower of Baha'u'llah because you believe, as I did and do, that Jesus has returned, as Baha'u'llah said, *"in my Person."*

QUESTION: Are you saying that you will respond

to everyone who emails and that you will try to incorporate their suggestions into a revision of this book? That sounds pretty ambitious and maybe not possible.

RESPONSE: You could be right about that. Here is my pledge, however: To the extent possible, and I will try very hard, I will read and respond, even if briefly, to every email or other mail that comes in. Further, I will think hard about any and all responses and especially new questions and will seriously consider including them in any future revision of this book. So, I am of good conscience in asking for response.

Remember too, that I have been a university professor for thirty-three years. I like response and I treat it seriously always. And, I know the value of different points of view and am willing to revise and even change my own thinking if new, important and challenging views and thoughts are presented to me. I invite all views, even those that are diametrically opposed to my thinking. I will treat them seriously and will learn from them; at least I hope so. That has been my life plan and I don't intend to depart from it at this late date.

So, please do contact me. Remember that you are much more likely to get a brief reply using email. Let me hear from you. 'Join the conversation!'

The email address again is: **daystarthom@yahoo.com**

(Let me repeat that if this email address does not work, look up Thom Thompson at: bigfoot.com)

To Declare your Faith in Baha'u'llah as Christ Returned:

If anyone reading this book has decided to recognize and follow Baha'u'llah as they have been taking part in this conversation, I want to know about it, of course.

Please email me. In fact, if you are of a mind to declare your belief in Baha'u'llah, then, in addition to emailing me (and if you live in the United States), you can call this national toll-free number:

1-800-22-UNITE

No one will call on you at your home, but if you request it, the Baha'is will mail you literature and tell you how to contact the Baha'is nearest to you. Finally, you can go to the following website, hosted by the Baha'i International Community: **www.bahai.org** Note: Other websites are listed in chapter sixteen.

The mailing address for the Baha'is of the United States is:

Baha'is of the United States, 536 Sheridan Road, Wilmette, IL 60091

POSTSCRIPT: Let me thank you for taking the time and effort to read this book, to take part in this 'conversation.' It has been one of those 'labors of love' and my fond hope is that it has been of some benefit to you and has stimulated your thinking. See that 'teacher' in me still coming out?! Please . . . join the conversation!

Oh, there is another section of the book, chapter sixteen, that follows this chapter, where you can look up, alphabetically, one-hundred Christian topics to get a short response on what Baha'is believe in relation to that topic.

Here, in closing, is one of my favorite inspirational passages from Baha'u'llah, from a letter written to one of His sons, offering advice on living a meaningful and ethical life:

"Be generous in prosperity, and thankful in adversity. Be

worthy of the trust of thy neighbor, and look upon him with a bright and friendly face. Be a treasure to the poor, an admonisher to the rich, an answerer to the cry of the needy, a preserver of the sanctity of thy pledge. Be fair in thy judgment, and guarded in thy speech. Be unjust to no man, and show all meekness to all men. Be as a lamp unto them that walk in darkness, a joy to the sorrowful, a sea for the thirsty, a haven for the distressed, an upholder and defender of the victim of oppression. Let integrity and uprightness distinguish all thine acts.

"Be a home for the stranger, a balm to the suffering, a tower of strength for the fugitive. Be eyes to the blind, and a guiding light unto the feet of the erring. Be an ornament to the countenance of truth, a crown to the brow of fidelity, a pillar of the temple of righteousness, a breath of life to the body of mankind, an ensign of the hosts of justice, a luminary above the horizon of virtue, a dew to the soil of the human heart, an ark on the ocean of knowledge, a sun in the heaven of bounty, a gem on the diadem of wisdom, a shining light in the firmament of thy generation, a fruit upon the tree of humility."

(Baha'u'llah: *Epistle to the Son of the Wolf*, Pages: 93-94)

Shrine of the Bab, at the center of Mt. Carmel, God's Holy Mountain.

CHAPTER SIXTEEN

A LIST: CHRISTIAN TOPICS, ALPHABETICALLY ARRANGED, WITH SHORT RESPONSES AND SUGGESTIONS FOR FURTHER READING

NOTE: These individual items below are designed to give only *short responses* to questions that have been asked of the author by Christian friends over the years. Upon learning of Baha'u'llah and the Baha'i Faith, they would inevitably ask: 'What do Baha'is believe about the Bible?' or 'What do Baha'is think about the Divinity of Christ?' 'What about salvation?' Or even, 'Do Baha'is believe in God?'

These responses are *not* given as full or complete responses or information. They are just 'nuggets' of information, hopefully inspiring you to investigate further.

For more detail, read the chapters in the book as indicated, or consult the further readings that are suggested.

SUGGESTED READINGS:

QUESTION: Since the Baha'i Writings are so large a body of literature, as you have been telling me, how does one make a start on picking books or sources to read? What do you suggest?

RESPONSE: Actually, it is somewhat hard to answer your question, only because there is such a 'richness' and large volume of these scriptures, and of the thousands of books that have now been written about Baha'u'llah and the Baha'i Faith.

If I am limited to a suggestion of four or five books, then the task becomes easier. The list would be as follows: Any Baha'i friend or Local Spiritual Assembly of Baha'is can supply you with these books or tell you how to get copies or they may be in your local library.

1. *Gleanings* (from the Writings of Baha'u'llah). This is the best book available to sample the writings of Baha'u'llah, gathered or 'gleaned' from the vast *"ocean"* (as He called it) of His writings. This particular selection of His Writings is the one put together by His Great-grandson, Shoghi Effendi, the Guardian of the Baha'i Faith and its leader until his death in 1957. Published by and available from the United States Baha'i Publishing Trust.
2. *Some Answered Questions.* This book is a recording of answers given by 'Abdu'l-Baha on a number of subjects, including many Christian topics, such as the

Virgin Birth, the Trinity, the Resurrection, etc. Baha'i
Publishing Trust.

3. *Baha'u'llah and the New Era.* By John Esslemont. This
book was written early in the Twentieth Century, but
has recently been revised and is one of the quickest
ways to learn the 'basics' of the Baha'i Faith, its history and teachings.

4. *The Baha'i Faith: The Emerging Global Religion,* by William Hatcher and Douglas Martin. This book contains a more intellectual presentation of the Faith. I
highly recommend it. Published by Harper and Row,
available through the Baha'i Publishing Trust.

5. *He Cometh With Clouds.* An excellent work by Gary
Matthews in paperback. It describes in interesting
detail why Baha'is believe Baha'u'llah to be the Return of Christ. Published by George Ronald and available through the Baha'i Publishing Trust. Gary
Matthews also has a monograph available through
the Trust describing very well the Baha'i beliefs about
evil, and Satan. The monograph is called: *The Metropolis of Satan.* It is informative and extremely interesting. Gary's other fine book is *The Challenge of
Baha'u'llah.*

6. *The Earth is But One Country.* By John Huddleston—an
excellent author of several books on the Baha'i Faith
and various international topics. Can be obtained
through the Baha'i Publishing Trust. John is an expert on the international scene, because of his lengthy
service in international financial institutions.

7. *The Hidden Words.* I saved the best till last. My favorite.
These are the '*Hidden Words*' of Baha'u'llah. He says
in the prologue to the '*Hidden Words*' that He has
taken all the scriptures of past history of all religions
and ***"clothed them in the garment of brevity."*** While that
seems at first glance an improbable claim, you can

take a look. You may agree. They certainly do constitute the most beautiful and poetic, brief statements
of deep spiritual truths ever gathered in one place,
in a book of just a few pages.

There are many more suggestions that I could make,
but this is a 'starter' program of readings. Talk to any
Baha'i and they can suggest other readings that may be
more suitable to your particular interests and your individual search. But, I am sure that the above books and
readings will get you started quite well.

Web Sites:

There are hundreds of websites on the Baha'i Faith,
but here are several to get started:

www.Bahai.org The official Baha'i World Faith site.
Lots of good information.

www.Bahai.com/ Use this one for good general information and look up something on this site called: Baha'i
Magazine.

www.promisedday.com One of my favorite sites. Lots
of good information for the seeker who is a Christian.
This site speaks the language of the Christian believer.

www.geocities.com/~quddus/ This one is slow to load
but it is worth it, if you are interested in what the Baha'i
Faith has to say about prophecy.

http://bounty.bcca.org/~cvoogt This site offers an opportunity to link to almost any important Baha'i site,
several thousand of them. It also has a 'find' feature so
that you will probably be able to find a particular item
of your special interest.

Call **1-800-22 UNITE** to reach Baha'is in your area,
if you need help finding books or accessing websites, or
you just want to meet and talk with the local Baha'is.
This 800 number works only in the United States.

NOW OTHER TOPICS:

Let me repeat that these are only **brief responses**, meant to whet your interest. To get a fuller and more complete treatment, read the appropriate chapters of this conversation/book and the readings that were suggested.

Here is the list of topics, in alphabetical form, except for the first four entries, which are 'Jesus Christ', 'Baha'u'llah', 'Baha'i Faith' and 'Baha'i teachings.' This list is not exhaustive, but covers, I hope, many of the topics that will readily come to mind. If you think of a topic that I have not included (there could be many) please email me (see chapter fifteen for the address) and I will attempt to include that topic in any revision of this book. The list begins below:

Jesus Christ
Baha'u'llah
Baha'i Faith
Baha'i Teachings
Alpha and Omega
Ancient of Days (See God)
Angels
Antichrist
Apocalypse (See also 'Last Days')
Ascension (See 'Resurrection')
Asceticism
Baptism
Bible
Body of Christ
Born Again
Clergy
Communion
Confession

Confirmation

Covenant

Creation

Day of God

Demon Possession

Devil

Divinity of Christ (See Jesus Christ at the top of this
    list)

Everlasting Life

Evil (See Devil)

Faith and Deeds

False Prophets

Family

Fasting

Forgiveness/Salvation

God

Grace

Guilt

Health and Healing

Heaven/Hell

Hell (See Heaven above)

Holy Ghost/Holy Spirit

Immaculate Conception (See 'Mary')

Incarnation

Infallibility

Jehovah (see God)

Jesus Christ (See the top of this list)

Judgment/Judgment Day

Kingdom of God

Last Days

Laying on of Hands

Life after Death

Limbo (See also 'Life After Death)

Lord and Savior (See 'Savior')

Lord of Hosts (See God)

Marriage/Divorce (See 'Family')
Mary/Immaculate Conception
Mercy
Miracles/Visions
Non-Believers
Original Sin (See 'Sin')
Penance
Prayer
Predestination
Prophecy
Psalms
Purgatory (See 'Limbo' and 'Life After Death')
Ransom (See Forgiveness)
Rapture
Redemption (See Forgiveness)
Relics
Resurrection/Ascension
Return of Christ
Revelation
Sacrifice
Salvation
Satan (See Devil)
Savior
Sin
Soul
Suffering (See Tribulation)
Time of the End (See Last Days)
Tithing
Tongues
Transfiguration
Tribulation
Trinity
Trumpet (See also Last Days)
Virgin Birth
Will of God

Word of God

JESUS CHRIST:

QUESTION: Do Baha'is believe in Jesus Christ and do they accept Him as their Lord and Savior, as Christians understand it?

RESPONSE: Baha'is do indeed believe in Jesus as the 'Son of God' and as God present in Christ in human history in all His fullness. They believe that Jesus offered salvation to humanity and that He is Lord. Jesus is very central in the Baha'i Faith, especially since Baha'u'llah claimed to be Jesus Returned. Baha'u'llah said: *"If ye be intent on crucifying once again Jesus, the Spirit of God, put Me to death, for He hath once more, in My person, been made manifest unto you."* (Baha'u'llah: *Gleanings*, Page: 101) Read chapter six of this conversation/book entitled: " 'Who Do Men say that I am?': A Baha'i considers the place of Jesus Christ in History."

QUESTION: Do Baha'is believe in the 'Divinity of Christ'?

RESPONSE: Yes. This is affirmed many times by Baha'u'llah and also by His Son, 'Abdu'l-Baha. Baha'u'llah teaches that when any Manifestation of God, such as Jesus, Buddha, or Baha'u'llah Himself (just to take three examples) appear in human history, men and women are to see them as if God is standing before them, to hear them as if God were speaking, to obey them as if obeying God.

Jesus said: *"I and My Father are one."* (John 10:30)

and Baha'u'llah, referring to Himself, said: *"The Father hath come"* even though both of them were born of a woman and had a human nature. Baha'u'llah tells us that they have a 'divine nature' as well, which is close or identical to Christian teaching. For more information, read chapter five of this conversation/book, where you will hear about 'Manifestation: A New Way of Understanding how God Reveals Himself' and chapter six.

BAHA'U'LLAH:

QUESTION: Who is Baha'u'llah and how do your pronounce His name?

RESPONSE: As Baha'u'llah teaches, from time to time, God 'Manifests' Himself in history, in what Baha'u'llah called *"the form of the human temple,"* in other words God manifesting Himself very fully in a human life. Jesus was such a 'Manifestation.' Baha'u'llah is another of the 'Manifestations' of God. In fact, 'Manifestation' is the name Baha'u'llah gave to those individuals in history who manifested God's full presence to men. He called them 'Manifestations of God.'

He said God sent Manifestations to the world, from time to time, calling them *"Gems of Holiness"* which God caused *"to appear out of the realm of the spirit, in the noble form of the human temple, and be made manifest unto all men, that they may impart unto the world the mysteries of the unchangeable Being, and tell of the subtleties of His imperishable Essence."* (Baha'u'llah: *Gleanings*, Page: 47)

As for pronouncing Baha'u'llah's name, it is accented on the second and last syllable, so that it is pronounced, phonetically, BAH-**HAH**-O-**LAH**. Jesus' given name was 'Jesus of Nazareth'; His title is Christ, which means 'The

Anointed One.' Baha'u'llah's given name was Mirza Husayn Ali; His title is Baha'u'llah, which means 'The Glory of God.' Baha'u'llah lived and suffered and taught, as a Manifestation of God, in about the lifetime (if you are reading this as a young person at start of the Twenty-First Century) of your Great, Great Grandfather, so God's presence in history is very recent.

Of most importance to Christians, Baha'u'llah announced that He was the Return of Christ, saying: *"If ye be intent on crucifying once again Jesus, the Spirit of God, put Me to death, for He hath once more, in My person, been made manifest unto you. Deal with Me as ye wish, for I have vowed to lay down My life in the path of God."* (Baha'u'llah: *Gleanings*, Page: 101)

For this reason, He expected Christians to be the first to be His followers. Saying that He was *"The Father"* of all mankind, He wrote, in a letter to Christians around the world: *"Do the sons* [that is, the Christians] *recognize the Father . . . ?"* and *"Open the doors of your hearts. He Who is the Spirit (Jesus) verily, standeth before them. Wherefore keep ye afar from Him Who hath purposed to draw you nigh unto a Resplendent Spot? Say: We, in truth, have opened unto you the gates of the Kingdom. Will ye bar the doors of your houses in My face?"* (Baha'u'llah: *Proclamation of Baha'u'llah*, Page: 92) This passage is taken from the letter that Baha'u'llah wrote to the Christians of the world, and therefore, to you! The letter is included in full in one of the chapters of this conversation/book.

This entire conversation is devoted to giving you a good answer to the question 'Who is Baha'u'llah' and 'what does His Coming mean to a Christian?' I recommend you start on Chapter One and 'join the conversation.'

BAHA'I FAITH:

QUESTION: Where does that name come from?

RESPONSE: Just as the name 'Christian' comes from the title 'Christ' with an ending—'ian'—meaning 'follower of,' likewise, Baha'i comes from a part of the name of Baha'u'llah. The shortened form of His name, which is also a title, 'Baha' is completed with an ending, in this case—'i'—but again meaning ' follower of.' So, Baha'i means: follower of Baha'u'llah. (You can pronounce Baha'i phonetically, accenting the second part of the word: Bah-**HIGH**)

QUESTION: Who are the Baha'is? I hate to ask so many questions, and so directly, but I've never heard of the Baha'is. Who are they, and where are they?

RESPONSE: It would be hard, indeed, to describe the Baha'is, but I'll try. They come from all over the world, every country, territory and island on the planet, from several thousand ethnic groups or races, all religions, all cultures. The Baha'i Faith is sometimes referred to as 'the world religion' or as described in the recommended readings above, 'the emerging global religion.' So, it's not far off the mark to say that Baha'is are the people of the entire world, beginning to come together, in response to Baha'u'llah, the 'Father' of all mankind, to recognize and enact their suspected, wished-for oneness and to begin to form their long promised unity.

But, maybe the best definition of Baha'is or followers of Baha'u'llah comes from Baha'u'llah Himself. He spoke of His followers in this way: *"The Book of God is wide open, and His Word is summoning mankind unto Him. No more than a mere handful, however, hath been found will-*

ing to cleave to His Cause, or to become the instruments for its promotion.

"These few have been endued with the Divine Elixir that can, alone, transmute into purest gold the dross of the world, and have been empowered to administer the infallible remedy for all the ills that afflict the children of men. No man can obtain everlasting life, unless he embraceth the truth of this inestimable, this wondrous, and sublime Revelation." (Baha'u'llah: *Gleanings,* Page: 183)

He asked those followers to *"Address yourselves to the promotion of the well-being and tranquillity of the children of men. Bend your minds and wills to the education of the peoples and kindreds of the earth, that haply the dissensions that divide it may, through the power of the Most Great Name,* [this is one of the titles of Baha'u'llah] *be blotted out from its face, and all mankind become the upholders of one Order, and the inhabitants of one City. Illumine and hallow your hearts; let them not be profaned by the thorns of hate or the thistles of malice. Ye dwell in one world, and have been created through the operation of one Will. Blessed is he who mingleth with all men in a spirit of utmost kindliness and love."* (Baha'u'llah: *Gleanings,* Page: 333)

Also, He said of the Baha'is: *"Methinks, the lamp of Thy love is burning in their hearts,"* (Baha'u'llah: *Prayers and Meditations,* Page: 3) and that *"neither doubts nor insinuations, nor swords, nor cannon could hold them back or deprive them of His* (that is, Baha'u'llah's) *presence"* (Baha'u'llah: *Tablets of Baha'u'llah,* Page: 123)

The reason Baha'u'llah mentioned 'sword and cannon' is that more than 20,000 early Baha'is were cruelly martyred for their Faith in the 1850's (See Chapter Three 'How it all Began' for more detail on the early history of the Baha'i Faith). Some were tied to the mouths of cannons and blown apart. One word of denial would have saved their lives, but like Christian martyrs, they refused to deny their Lord. Even today, as recently as the 1980's and late 1990's, Baha'is in Iran have been executed for their belief in Baha'u'llah. One was a sixteen-year-old girl, Mona, who was hanged for refusing to renounce her faith and belief in Baha'u'llah.

Baha'u'llah promised each of His followers that His *"heavenly Spirit shall descend upon him in the daytime and in the night season"* and would *"unloose his tongue"* and *"graciously assist him to glorify the Name of his Lord"*. (Baha'u'llah: *Tablets of Baha'u'llah*, Page: 181)

Be sure to read chapter three: 'How it All Began.'

BAHA'I TEACHINGS:

Chapter eight is devoted to the Teachings of Baha'u'llah. However, here is a *very brief* listing of those teachings. For greater detail, please see chapter eight, 'Baha'u'llah's Teachings: What they could mean for the Christian and for the World'.

BAHA'I TEACHINGS:

1. There is only one God.
2. This one God created humanity. .
3. Humanity is therefore one. One racial group. Many ethnic groups and cultures, but only one race, the human race.
4. God has sent many Messengers, or 'Manifestations of Himself' to humankind, including Krishna, Buddha, Moses, Jesus, Zoroaster, Muhammad, and in this day, the Bab and Baha'u'llah. Baha'is are taught by Baha'u'llah that they are not only 'from God' but that they are Divine, that they brought God's real and full Presence into human history.
5. Each and all of these 'Manifestations of God' having brought God's very Presence into human history,

have also brought God's Will to mankind, progressively unfolding and revealing this Will, guiding and leading the human race to a day of recognition of their oneness, the enactment of their unity and the establishment of peace.

6. That Baha'u'llah is the Return of Christ to Christians and the 'Promised One' of all religions and cultures, the One prophesied and awaited in the scriptures of all religions and by all the people of the world.

7. That Baha'u'llah also represents the appearance in history of *"The Father"* of all humankind, the One Who was prophesied and expected. And the One Who will now lead the people of earth into unity, a renewal, a homecoming, a bringing to new life that can truly be called a 'Resurrection' of humanity.

8. Based upon the above, that God is One, the Prophets are One, and humanity is One.

9. That therefore we must rid ourselves of all racial and religious and cultural prejudices. If humanity is truly one, we must 'enact' this oneness. The Baha'i Faith tell us that this includes marrying across ethnic, cultural, religious and so-called racial lines (the latter of which under Baha'u'llah's teachings, do not exist, though ethnic groups and cultures do exist).

10. That there must be absolute equality of women and men and that this must not simply be a beautiful ideal, but must be enacted and created. Baha'u'llah said: *"Women and men have been and will always be equal in the sight of God. The Dawning-Place of the Light of God sheddeth its radiance upon all with the same effulgence. Verily God created women for men, and men for women."* (Baha'u'llah: Women, p. 379).

11. That science and religion must agree.

12. That 'extremes' of poverty and riches must end. Baha'u'llah clearly stated that individuals would be

found at different class levels, based on individual effort. He nevertheless said that we must work to do away with both the extremes of grinding poverty and excessive wealth.

13. That every child on earth must receive a basic education and, interestingly, that girls should be given preference for education, since they are the 'first educators' of children.

14. That the people of the world should adopt a universal language, so that they would speak two languages. One would be their original, cultural language, the other the language of the entire world. Baha'u'llah said that, then, wherever a person went it would be *"as if he were entering his own home"* (Baha'u'llah: *Gleanings*, Page: 250).

15. That Peace must come to this world. To that end, Baha'u'llah called upon the peoples and legislatures of the world to meet to form a planetary government, which would involve agreement to disarm and to agree to put down any government that would attempt to start armed conflict. (Similar to what was done by the world in the 1990's to put down the current Iraqi ruler who was threatening the Middle East and the stability of the world.).

Here is the passage from Baha'u'llah, which speaks of what must be done. It is probably helpful for us to remember that this was revealed in the 1870's, long before any thought of anything such as the League of Nations or the United Nations. *"The time must come when the imperative necessity for the holding of a vast, an all-embracing assemblage of men will be universally realized. The rulers and kings of the earth must needs attend it, and, participating in its deliberations, must consider such ways and means as will lay the foundations of the world's Great Peace amongst men. Such a peace demandeth that the Great Powers should resolve, for the sake of the tranquillity of the peoples of the earth, to be fully reconciled among themselves.*

"Should any king take up arms against another, all should unitedly arise and prevent him. If this be done, the nations of the world will no longer require any armaments, except for the purpose of preserving the security of their realms and of maintaining internal order within their territories. This will ensure the peace and composure of every people, government and nation. We fain would hope that the kings and rulers of the earth, the mirrors of the gracious and almighty name of God, may attain unto this station, and shield mankind from the onslaught of tyranny." (Baha'u'llah: *Gleanings*, Page: 249)

16. That every man, woman and youth on the planet has the responsibility to investigate the truth of any question in an independent manner, accepting advice from parents and authority figures, but, in the end, basing their understanding and decision-making on their own independent judgment.

These are not the only teachings of Baha'u'llah. They do represent His key or central teachings and I again direct you to Chapter Eight: 'Baha'u'llah's teachings: What they Could Mean for the Christian and for the World'. You will find much more detail in that chapter.

ALPHA AND OMEGA:

Christ is referred to in the Christian Scriptures as 'Alpha and Omega.' Jesus is certainly the 'first and last' in the sense of being God's *"only begotten Son"* and likewise, there would not be another Manifestation that would be called *"the Father,"* as Baha'u'llah is called. Most Christians interpret 'Alpha and Omega" to mean that it is the first time and the last time that God has come to man in His Fullness. Baha'u'llah teaches that God has acted in Manifesting Himself many times in human history, in fulfillment of a Covenant that God has with man to continue to assist and guide him.

Read chapters four and five of this 'conversation book.' Chapter four is entitled: 'Progressive Revelation: A New Way of understanding history.' Chapter five: 'Manifestation: A New Way of Understanding How God Reveals Himself.'

ANCIENT OF DAYS (See 'God' below.)

ANGELS:

QUESTION: What does the Baha'i Faith say about angels, if anything?

RESPONSE: Baha'u'llah refers to Angels often. Let me quote His statements about angels. Baha'u'llah asked his followers to go into the entire world with His message of unity and with the Glad Tidings that *"The Father"* of all mankind had appeared. He said of those who left their homes to travel throughout the world with this 'healing' message: *"We behold you from Our realm of glory, and shall aid whosoever will arise for the triumph of Our Cause with the hosts of the Concourse on high and a company of Our favoured angels."* (Baha'u'llah: The *Kitab-i-Aqdas*, Page: 39)

He even defined 'Angels' in this way: *"By 'angels' is meant those who, reinforced by the power of the spirit, have consumed, with the fire of the love of God, all human traits and limitations, and have clothed themselves with the attributes of the most exalted Beings and of the Cherubim."* ('Cherubim' of course, referring, as in the Bible, to angels.) (Baha'u'llah: The *Kitab-i-Iqan*, Pages: 78-79) Jesus, of course, spoke frequently of 'angels', several dozen times, in my count.

Baha'u'llah said of those Baha'is who 'pioneer' ('Pioneers' are unpaid traveling teachers of His Faith) that these pioneers will have company, namely, *"A company of Our chosen angels shall go forth with them"*. (Baha'u'llah: *Gleanings*, Page: 334) And, once again, He prayed to God to *"aid us by Thine invisible hosts and by a company of the angels of Thy Cause"* (Baha'u'llah: *Prayers and Meditations*, Page: 173) Read for yourself in Baha'u'llah's writings and you will see, as with Jesus, many references to Angels.

QUESTION: Jesus made very similar promises to His followers.

RESPONSE: Indeed, you are right. Jesus kept those promises, and now Baha'is are beginning to testify all over the world that Baha'u'llah, Who claims to be the Return of Jesus Christ, is keeping His promises to them, as well.

QUESTION: The Return of Christ! Did He really say that?

RESPONSE: Yes. Read Chapters Four and Five of this book for more detail, but for now, what I'll leave you with is Baha'u'llah's words to a community of Jews in Hamadan, Persia (modern Iran): *"O Jews! If ye be intent on crucifying once again Jesus, the Spirit of God, put Me to death, for He hath once more, in My person, been made manifest unto you."* (Baha'u'llah: *Gleanings*, Page: 101) As an aside, I should mention that when this statement is read in the context of the entire letter, Baha'u'llah was not blaming Jews for Christ's death. This letter was very

loving and many of the Jews of Hamadan became followers of Baha'u'llah after they received it.

ANTICHRIST:

'Antichrist' is mentioned several times in the Baha'i
Scriptures. It refers to those who opposed either Christ,
when He came, or Baha'u'llah, when He appeared.
Baha'u'llah's Son, 'Abdu'l-Baha (whose name means 'Ser-
vant of Baha'u'llah') spoke of the 'Antichrist' in this way:
"... *these wars and cruelties* [speaking of the first World
War], *this bloodshed and sorrow are Antichrist, not Christ.
These are the forces of death and Satan, not the hosts of the
Supreme Concourse of heaven.*" ('Abdu'l Baha: *Promulga-
tion of Universal Peace*, Page 6)

And, speaking of the disunity among the thousands
of Christian denominations and sects, 'Abdu'l-Baha said:
"*No less bitter is the conflict between sects and denominations.
Christ was a divine Center of unity and love. Whenever discord prevails instead of unity, wherever hatred and antago-
nism take the place of love and spiritual fellowship, Antichrist
reigns instead of Christ.*" ('Abdu'l-Baha: *Promulgation of
Universal peace*, Page 6)

Therefore, from these several quotes, one can see
that in the Baha'i Scriptures, Antichrist can be viewed
either as a person, or as a 'force' in history. Read chapters four and five, where the question arises and is discussed, as to whether Baha'u'llah could be the 'Antichrist.'
Clearly He is not, but one thing is certain, both Christ
and Baha'u'llah are one of three things (as one Christian theologian said about Christ), either a madman, a
charlatan, or (the only other choice), He was, and is,
who He said He was.

Christ was accused several times of being the Devil,
or Satan, or Beelzebub (another name for Satan), so

Christ was accused of being what we today would call the 'Antichrist.' People who heard Christ had to decide whether to see Him as the Devil or as the *"Son of God."* Today, people have the same choice, whether to see Baha'u'llah as a false prophet or an Antichrist, or to see Him as the Return of Christ and as *"the Father"* of all mankind and the 'Promise of all Ages." For more information, see 'False Prophets' below in this list and read chapters four and five.

APOCALYPSE:
See also 'Last Days' below.

Baha'u'llah does not use the exact word 'Apocalypse' but speaks of it often, using the terms 'Last Days' and the 'Day of God' and the time of 'Resurrection' for all mankind. One of the first things we learn from Baha'u'llah is that our pessimistic and somewhat materialistic opinion of the apocalyptic period for mankind may be largely mistaken. While it will be a time of tests and trials, perhaps even of suffering, it will also be the time of 'New Birth' for humankind. The following quotation from Shoghi Effendi, the Guardian of the Baha'i Faith and its leader during the first half of the Twentieth Century, may do better than I can do to explain (read chapter three for some of the history of the Baha'i Faith and to learn more about Shoghi Effendi):

"The writer of the Apocalypse, prefiguring the millennial glory which a redeemed, a jubilant humanity must witness, has similarly testified: *'And I saw a new heaven and a new earth: for the first heaven and the first earth were passed away; and there was no more sea. And I, John, saw the holy city, new Jerusalem, coming down from God out of heaven, prepared as a bride adorned for her husband. And I heard a great voice out of heaven saying, 'Behold, the taber-*

nacle of God is with men, and he will dwell with them, and they shall be his people, and God himself shall be with them, and be their God. And God shall wipe away all tears from their eyes; and there shall be no more death, neither sorrow, nor crying, neither shall there be any more pain: for the former things are passed away.' (Rev. 21:1)

"Who can doubt that such a consummation—the coming of age of the human race—must signalize, in its turn, the inauguration of a world civilization such as no mortal eye hath ever beheld or human mind conceived? Who is it that can imagine the lofty standard that such a civilization, as it unfolds itself, is destined to attain? Who can measure the heights to which human intelligence, liberated from its shackles, will soar? Who can visualize the realms that the human spirit, vitalized by the outpouring light of Baha'u'llah, shining in the plenitude of its glory, will discover?

"What more fitting conclusion to this theme than these words of Baha'u'llah, written in anticipation of the golden age of His Faith—the age in which the face of the earth, from pole to pole, will mirror the ineffable splendors of the Abha Paradise? [author's note: 'Abha Paradise is a Baha'i name for Heaven]

"This is the Day whereon naught can be seen except the splendors of the Light that shineth from the face of thy Lord, the Gracious, the Most Bountiful. Verily, We have caused every soul to expire by virtue of Our irresistible and all-subduing sovereignty. We have then called into being a new creation, as a token of Our grace unto men. I am, verily, the All-Bountiful, the Ancient of Days. This is the Day whereon the unseen world crieth out: 'Great is thy blessedness, O earth, for thou hast been made the foot-stool of thy God, and been chosen as the seat of His mighty throne!'" (Quoted in Shoghi Effendi: *World Order of Baha'u'llah,* Pages: 205-206)

ASCENSION: (See 'Resurrection' below in this list)

ASCETICISM:

QUESTION: Does the Baha'i Faith promote asceticism, or withdrawing from the world? You say you have no priesthood or ministry. What about monks and nuns? What about fasting, self-denial and what some Christians would call 'mortification of the flesh'?

RESPONSE: He said several important things. First, that asceticism in any form is not allowed. This does not mean that Baha'is cannot sacrifice their own needs for others, but rather that they are not to lead lives of asceticism, apart from others. Baha'u'llah specifically wrote to Pope Pius IX, telling him to order the monks and nuns to come out of their monasteries and cloisters, to marry and to serve His Faith. Baha'u'llah clearly forbids asceticism but makes it clear that Baha'is are to live a life of service to humanity, to be earnestly concerned with the fate of the world and its peoples, to work for peace, to work for unity.

He tells His disciples to pray a prayer that includes the words: *"Waft, then, unto me, O my God and my Beloved, from the right hand of Thy mercy and Thy loving-kindness, the holy breaths of Thy favors, that they may draw me away from myself and from the world unto the courts of Thy nearness and Thy presence."* (Baha'u'llah: *Prayers and Meditations*, Page: 312)

That last phrase *"draw me away from the world"* does not refer to any ascetic practice, but to spiritual 'detachment' from *"the things of this world"* which could come between the believer and their God. Spiritual detachment from the pull of the material world is, in fact, a key concept in the Baha'i Faith (just as it is in Christianity). However, it needs to be understood in context, since Baha'u'llah charged Baha'is with the task of creating human unity, in essence bringing a dead world to life.

Baha'u'llah tells the people of the world, and this quote reminds us of many sayings of Christ: *"Wert thou to give ear to My voice, thou wouldst cast away all thy possessions, and wouldst set thy face towards the Spot wherein the ocean of wisdom and of utterance hath surged, and the sweet savors of the loving-kindness of thy Lord, the Compassionate, have wafted."* (Baha'u'llah: *Epistle to the Son of the Wolf*, Page: 19)

And from Baha'u'llah's memorable '*Hidden Words*', where one reads as if hearing not His voice, but God's: *"O MY SERVANT! Abandon not for that which perisheth an everlasting dominion, and cast not away celestial sovereignty for a worldly desire. This is the river of everlasting life that hath flowed from the well-spring of the pen of the merciful; well is it with them that drink!"* (Baha'u'llah: (Persian) *Hidden Words*, Page: 37)

And: *"O SON OF SPIRIT! Burst thy cage asunder, and even as the phoenix of love soar into the firmament of holiness. Renounce thyself and, filled with the spirit of mercy, abide in the realm of celestial sanctity."* (Baha'u'llah: (Persian) *Hidden Words*, Page: 38)

Finally: *"O SON OF SPIRIT! There is no peace for thee save by renouncing thyself and turning unto Me; for it behooveth thee to glory in My name, not in thine own; to put thy trust in Me and not in thyself, since I desire to be loved alone and above all that is."* (Baha'u'llah: (Arabic) *Hidden Words*, Page: 8)

So there is renunciation, sacrifice, detachment, but no ascetic practice is allowed and no withdrawing from the world in the sense of being unwilling or unavailable to work with all the people of the planet to bring about the oneness of humanity, unity of all peoples and the condition of peace.

BAHA'I FAITH AND BAHA'I TEACHINGS:

See items three and four in the list above. Also, see chapter eight for 'Baha'i Teachings.'

BAHA'U'LLAH:
See the second item in the list above.

BAPTISM:

QUESTION: Do Baha'is believe in Baptism?

RESPONSE: In the idea of being born again, yes. In the symbolism of 'water' as the sign of rebirth into a new life, yes. As a ritual, no. Baha'is have no rituals, or almost none. This is by the design and express written wish of Baha'u'llah. There is one congregational 'Prayer for the Dead' to be used at a funeral and a statement to be read by the bride and groom at weddings *"We will all, verily, abide by the Will of God."* (Baha'u'llah: *Kitab-i-Aqdas*: Questions and Answers, Page: 105)

Other than these, there are no rituals in the Baha'i Faith. What is present in our Faith is prayer, fasting (Jesus, we are reminded, fasted as well as prayed), meditation and certain laws to follow, such as abstinence from alcohol and drugs, freeing yourself from prejudices of all kinds, etc., but no other rituals exist.

QUESTION: What did you mean about the 'symbolism' of water as the sign of rebirth and entry into a new life?

RESPONSE: What is meant is that Baha'u'llah, in His Revelation . . .

QUESTION: Please! Stop right there! What do you mean, 'Revelation'? Aren't Baha'u'llah's writings just that, the writings of a wise and good man, but only a man? Why do you call them a 'Revelation,' as if they came from God?'

RESPONSE: It is Baha'u'llah Himself Who calls His writings 'Revelation.' All I'm doing is quoting Him. He said that His words and actions were from God, and told His followers that what He 'revealed' to them had been *"sent down from the Throne on high"*. (Baha'u'llah: *Gleanings*, Page: 105) He described His Revelation as *"the Bread which cometh down from Heaven."* (Baha'u'llah: *Gleanings*, Page: 195)

Finally, He said: *"My holy, My divinely ordained Revelation may be likened unto an ocean in whose depths are concealed innumerable pearls of great price, of surpassing luster. It is the duty of every seeker to bestir himself and strive to attain the shores of this ocean."* (Baha'u'llah: *Gleanings*, Page: 326) See 'Revelation' in the list below for more information.

QUESTION: Can you get back to baptism?

RESPONSE: Surely. You brought up revelation and I wanted to respond immediately to your question. Before returning to Baptism, do you remember that Jesus said something similar to what I've shared with you from Baha'u'llah? Jesus said: *"Do you not believe that I am in the*

*Father, and the Father in Me? The words that I speak to you
I do not speak on My own authority; but the Father who dwells
in Me does the works."* (John 14:9-10) and *"whatever I speak,
just as the Father has told Me, so I speak."* (John 12:50)

Apparently, both Jesus and Baha'u'llah felt that the
things they did and the words they spoke came not from
themselves, but from God. Both felt not that they were
delivering 'God's Word,' but that they *were* the 'Word of
God, and therefore, the 'Revelation of God.'

Now, baptism: Though there is no ritual, there are
many symbolic references in the Baha'i Revelation to
the life-giving 'water' of God that has a cleansing, life
changing effect on a person. Consider these words of
Baha'u'llah from some of the prayers that He taught us
to pray: *"Cleanse me with the waters of Thy mercy, O my
Lord, and make me wholly Thine,"* (Baha'u'llah: *Prayers
and Meditations*, Page: 139) or: *"Send down, also, upon
me, O my God, that which will wash me from anything that is
not of Thee."* (Baha'u'llah: *Prayers and Meditations*, Page:
207)

Or finally: *"...rain down upon us, and upon Thy servants, the overflowing rain of Thy mercy, that it may cleanse
us from the remembrance of all else but Thee, and draw us
nigh unto the shores of the ocean of Thy grace."* (Baha'u'llah:
Gleanings, Page: 301) and *"Wash away, then, my sins, O
my God, by Thy grace and bounty"* (Baha'u'llah: *Prayers
and Meditations*, Page: 212)

There are numerous quotations that have as their
theme being cleansed of sin and *"a corrupt inclination"* by
"life giving waters." I'll give you just one more from a
prayer that Baha'u'llah asked Baha'is to pray daily: *"Make
my prayer, O my Lord, a fountain of living waters whereby I
may live as long as Thy sovereignty endureth, and may make
mention of Thee in every world of Thy worlds."* (Baha'u'llah:
Prayers and Meditations, Page 318)

In summary, while the Baha'i Faith is a religion mostly free of rituals, the symbolism behind Christian rituals is still there and is richly represented in our Scriptures. One such example of the symbolism of water and baptism is:

O wayfarer in the path of God! Take thou thy portion of the ocean of His grace, and deprive not thyself of the things that lie hidden in its depths. Be thou of them that have partaken of its treasures. A dewdrop out of this ocean would, if shed upon all that are in the heavens and on the earth, suffice to enrich them with the bounty of God, the Almighty, the All-Knowing, the All-Wise.

"With the hands of renunciation draw forth from its life-giving waters, and sprinkle therewith all created things, that they may be cleansed from all man-made limitations and may approach the mighty seat of God, this hallowed and resplendent Spot." (Baha'u'llah: *Gleanings*, Pages: 279-280)

BIBLE:

QUESTION: Do Baha'is believe in the Bible? And do they believe it is the Word of God?

RESPONSE: They do indeed believe in the Bible, which is sometimes read along with Baha'i Scriptures at Baha'i religious meetings, which are called 'Feasts'.

QUESTION: Wait a minute! That's what early Christians called their meetings! Did you copy that from Christians?

RESPONSE: No, it's just a coincidence, I suppose, but an interesting one, I agree. There are many similarities between the two Faiths, Christianity and the Baha'i Faith. You may want to turn to Chapter Nine of this book that is entitled: 'Similarities and Differences of the Christian and Baha'i Faiths.'

Let me get back to the question of the Bible. Yes, beyond all doubt and from Baha'u'llah Himself, the idea of the Bible as divinely inspired is supported. Where you may find a challenging difference to what you believe is that Baha'u'llah teaches that *all* the scriptures of *all* the major religions were divinely inspired. Why? Because they all came from the appearance in human history of what Baha'is call 'Manifestations' of God. These 'Manifestations' represent the reality of God Himself present in human history. They bring a fresh outpouring of divine guidance and a spiritual power to change and renew individuals and the whole world.

These Manifestations, such as Krishna, Buddha, Moses, Jesus, Muhammad and Baha'u'llah all proceed from God or, as one might say, are sent from God. They ***"step forth out of the realm of the invisible into the visible world".*** (Baha'u'llah: The *Kitab-i-Iqan*, Page: 25) So, if all the Manifestations are from God, then all the religions are 'true' and the scriptures of each religion equally true and, in every case, divinely inspired.

QUESTION: Well, Christians, as you probably know, don't feel that way about other scriptures.

RESPONSE: I do realize that but, in one instance, Christians *do* feel that way about the Scriptures of another religion. The Jewish Scriptures existed a thousand years before the appearance of Jesus Christ. Jesus quoted from them liberally and frequently, as did the Gospel writers and St. Paul. The Jewish Scriptures were finally accepted by the Christian Church as divinely inspired, but only after a centuries long battle that went on within the Church.

Some early Church fathers wanted to do away with the Old Testament as being 'scriptures of another religion' (which they *were*). The reason they could not do this was, as I said, that Jesus had frequently quoted from the Old Testament, many times (the best example of which was the 'Great Commandment' that Jesus gave, cited below:)

"The first of all the commandments is: 'Hear, O Israel, the LORD our God, the LORD is one. And you shall love the LORD your God with all your heart, with all your soul, with all your mind, and with all your strength.' This is the first commandment. And the second, like it, is this: 'You shall love your neighbor as yourself.' There is no other commandment greater than these." (Mark 12:29-31)

Jesus was quoting, very literally, from the 'scriptures of another religion' (Deut. 6:4 and Lev. 19:18). The battle on whether to include the 'scriptures of another religion' was fought vigorously within the Church for over a century, but finally there was no choice but to accept them as valid and divinely inspired, particularly since not only had they been quoted by Jesus, but the Gospel writers had also quoted liberally from them, in proof of the station of Jesus.

There is another interesting connection between Christianity and another religion. The three wise men are now thought to have been Priests of the Zoroastrian religion, which means that God chose the Priests of another religion to discover the appearance of baby Jesus. And there is yet another fascinating 'connection' that the Baha'i Faith has to Christianity; you can read about it in chapter nine and has something to do with Abraham's 'third' wife, from whom Baha'u'llah is descended. Christians usually only focus on the first two wives, so this might be interesting to you. I can also give you more detail in chapters three and four of this conversation/book.

To summarize, Baha'u'llah teaches Baha'is to regard the Bible as divinely inspired and He often quotes the Bible. However, He teaches the people of the world to believe in what I call a 'Greater God,' a God that has been at work many times in many places in history, sending Manifestations of Himself many times (not just one time), then sending His *'Son'* and finally, appearing Himself as the *'Father'* of all mankind, in the name of the Glory of God, Baha'u'llah.

To understand this better, you may want to read chapters Four and Five of this book. Chapter Four explains 'Progressive Revelation: A New Way of Understanding History' while Chapter Five tells about: 'Manifestation: A New Way of Understanding How God Reveals Himself'.

Here is a strong statement of Baha'u'llah on the authenticity of the Bible: *"We have also heard a number of the foolish of the earth assert that the genuine text of the heavenly Gospel doth not exist amongst the Christians . . . How grievously they have erred! How oblivious of the fact that such a statement imputeth the gravest injustice and tyranny to a gracious and loving Providence! How could God, when once the Day-star of the beauty of Jesus had disappeared from the sight of His people, and ascended unto the fourth heaven, cause His holy Book, His most great testimony amongst His creatures, to disappear also?"* (Baha'u'llah: The *Kitab-i-Iqan*, Page: 89)

BODY OF CHRIST:

The understanding that Christians have of the Church being the 'Body of Christ' is very similar to the understanding of Baha'is, who are told often by Baha'u'llah that they are *"the people of Baha"* and that they are the Community of the 'Greatest Name' (one of the titles of

Baha'u'llah). Here is a quote from Baha'u'llah about this community: *"These are the ones, O my God, whom Thou hast graciously enabled to have fellowship with Thee and to commune with Him Who is the Revealer of Thyself. The winds of Thy will have scattered them abroad until Thou didst gather them together beneath Thy shadow, and didst cause them to enter into the precincts of Thy court.*

"Now that Thou hast made them to abide under the shade of the canopy of Thy mercy, do Thou assist them to attain what must befit so august a station. Suffer them not, O my Lord, to be numbered with them who, though enjoying near access to Thee, have been kept back from recognizing Thy face, and who, though meeting with Thee, are deprived of Thy presence. . . . Send down, therefore, upon them what will thoroughly purge them of all Thou abhorrest, that they may be wholly devoted to Thee, and may detach themselves entirely from all except Thyself.

"Rain down, then, upon us, O my God, that which beseemeth Thy grace and befitteth Thy bounty. Enable us, then, O my God, to live in remembrance of Thee and to die in love of Thee, and supply us with the gift of Thy presence in Thy worlds hereafter—worlds which are inscrutable to all except Thee. Thou art our Lord and the Lord of all worlds, and the God of all that are in heaven and all that are on earth." (Baha'u'llah: *Prayers and Meditations*, Pages: 144-145)

BORN AGAIN:

In researching Baha'u'llah's Writings for this conversation/book, I noted that there were many dozens of references to new birth, spiritual resurrection of individuals and the regeneration and rebirth of all mankind in general. It is a strong, frequent theme of Baha'u'llah's teachings. Below are three quotes; you can finish the research yourself by reading in *Gleanings* (see suggested readings above).

Before I give you the quotes, let me observe that in Jesus, God sacrificed His only begotten Son for the salvation of the world. Baha'u'llah teaches that when God sends Manifestations of Himself into the world, such as Jesus, Muhammad, Buddha, or Baha'u'llah, He always 'sacrifices' them for the salvation of individuals and for the regeneration of all mankind. In the following passage, Baha'u'llah, one of Whose titles is the 'Most Great Name,' speaks of His own sacrifice and says that one of the purposes of that sacrifice is that all the inhabitants of the earth may be 'born anew.'

"Praised be Thou, O Lord my God! I implore Thee by Thine Ancient Beauty and Most Great Name, [these are both titles for Baha'u'llah] *Whom Thou hast sacrificed that all the dwellers of Thine earth and heaven may be born anew, and Whom Thou hast cast into prison that mankind may, as a token of Thy bounty and of Thy sovereign might, be released from the bondage of evil passions and corrupt desires, to number me with those who have so deeply inhaled the fragrance of Thy mercy, and hastened with such speed unto the living waters of Thy grace . . . "* (Baha'u'llah: *Prayers and Meditations*, Page: 44)

Baha'u'llah says that *"We have, then, called into being a new creation"* (Baha'u'llah: *Gleanings*, Page: 29) and again refers to 'rebirth' in this passage: *"Whoso firmly believeth today in the rebirth of man and is fully conscious that God, the Most Exalted, wieldeth supreme ascendancy and absolute authority over this new creation, verily such a man is reckoned with them that are endued with insight in this most great Revelation."* (Baha'u'llah: *Tablets of Baha'u'llah*, Page: 142)

Finally, Baha'u'llah speaks of those who accept Him as *"endued with new life"* and says this is because, through

Baha'u'llah's appearance, God *"hast caused them to be born again."* (Baha'u'llah: *Prayers and Meditations*, Page: 42)

CLERGY:

QUESTION: Is there a clergy, priesthood or ministry in the Baha'i Faith?

RESPONSE: Although it's a little hard to believe at first, there is no clergy or ministry, nor will there ever be. This again is by the express, written wish of Baha'u'llah. Each believer is to read, pray, meditate and act without any intermediary person. This is the day, Baha'u'llah tells us, of 'independent investigation' of truth, which is one of His central teachings.

An annually elected body of nine persons called the 'Local Spiritual Assembly' runs the internal affairs of the Baha'i Faith in any locality. There are nationally elected bodies, which are called 'National Spiritual Assemblies'. An important and unusual international body called the 'Universal House of Justice' is elected every five years. The administration of the Baha'i Faith is described in chapter three: 'How it All Began'.

Baha'u'llah appealed often to the clergy of all Faiths, including the Christian Faith, asking them to listen to His claims and become His followers: He said to them: *"Who is there among you, O people, who will renounce the world, and draw nigh unto God, the Lord of all names? Where is he to be found who, through the power of My name that transcendeth all created things, will cast away the things that men possess, and cling, with all his might, to the things which God, the Knower of the unseen and of the seen, hath bidden him observe?"* (Baha'u'llah: *Gleanings*, Pages: 34-35)

Unfortunately, as in the case of Jesus, His greatest

enemies were the Jewish clergy. Similarly in the case of Baha'u'llah, His greatest enemies were the Islamic clergy (since He appeared in an Islamic culture—Iran). Finally, realizing that neither Kings nor clergy would recognize Him, He stated in His writings (in the 1870's) a prophetic announcement: *"From two ranks amongst men . . . power hath been seized: kings and ecclesiastics."* (Quoted in Shoghi Effendi: *God Passes By*, Page: 230)

Nevertheless, Baha'u'llah continued to make His appeal to any person, clergy or otherwise: *"Where is that fair-minded soul, O my God, who will judge equitably Thy Cause, and where is the man of insight to be found who will behold Thee with Thine own eyes? Is there any man of hearing who will hear Thee with Thine ears, or one endued with eloquence who will speak the truth in Thy days?"* (Baha'u'llah: *Prayers and Meditations*, Page: 285)

COMMUNION:

As discussed above in the section on 'Baptism', the Baha'i Faith does not have rituals. This was by the express wish of Baha'u'llah. So, there is nothing similar to the Christian ritual of communion. However, as far as 'communion' as we understand it spiritually, Baha'is do certainly 'commune' with God and with Baha'u'llah, in our prayers and meditations.

An interesting statement from 'Abdu'l-Baha about Baha'i 'Feasts' (the spiritual meeting Baha'is all over the world have every three weeks) speaks about a comparison of the 'Feast' to the 'Last Supper.' *"If the Feast is befittingly held, in the manner described, then this supper will verily be the Lord's Supper, for its fruits will be the very fruits of that Supper, and its influence the same."* ('Abdu'l-Baha: *The Nineteen Day Feast*, Page: 425)

CONFESSION:

Confession is permitted in the Baha'i Faith, but only to God, not to any man or priest. Here is what Baha'u'llah revealed: *"When the sinner findeth himself wholly detached and freed from all save God, he should beg forgiveness and pardon from Him. Confession of sins and transgressions before human beings is not permissible, as it hath never been nor will ever be conducive to divine forgiveness. Moreover such confession before people results in one's humiliation and abasement, and God—exalted be His glory—wisheth not the humiliation of His servants. Verily He is the Compassionate, the Merciful. The sinner should, between himself and God, implore mercy from the Ocean of mercy, beg forgiveness from the Heaven of generosity . . . "* (Baha'u'llah: *Tablets of Baha'u'llah*, Page: 24)

Baha'u'llah goes on in this scriptural passage to reveal a beautiful prayer that one can use to confess to God and receive forgiveness and pardon. See 'Forgiveness' in the list below. The Universal House of Justice has said that sharing one's life story, including listing one's wrongdoing in a therapeutic setting, either in therapy group or in a group like Alcoholics Anonymous, is quite acceptable.

Here is a portion of the 'forgiveness prayer' mentioned above: *"O Lord! Thou seest this essence of sinfulness turning unto the ocean of Thy favour and this feeble one seeking the kingdom of Thy divine power and this poor creature inclining himself towards the day-star of Thy wealth. By Thy mercy and Thy grace, disappoint him not, O Lord, nor debar him from the revelations of Thy bounty in Thy days, nor cast him away from Thy door which Thou hast opened wide to all that dwell in Thy heaven and on Thine earth.*

"Alas! Alas! My sins have prevented me from approaching the Court of Thy holiness and my trespasses have caused

me to stray far from the Tabernacle of Thy majesty. I have committed that which Thou didst forbid me to do and have put away what Thou didst order me to observe.

"I pray Thee by Him Who is the sovereign Lord of Names to write down for me with the Pen of Thy bounty that which will enable me to draw nigh unto Thee and will purge me from my trespasses which have intervened between me and Thy forgiveness and Thy pardon.

"Verily, Thou art the Potent, the Bountiful. No God is there but Thee, the Mighty, the Gracious." (Baha'u'llah: *Tablets of Baha'u'llah*, Page: 25)

CONFIRMATION:

Jews and Catholic Christians both have a 'ritual' of confirmation or coming of age, as do many of the religions and cultures of the world. Protestant Christians do not have a set ritual, but having a 'salvation' experience during the teen years is often similar to such a 'coming of age' ritual (as it was for me). For Baha'is, while there is no 'ritual' involved, Baha'u'llah stated that the age of the beginning of adulthood was fifteen and Baha'i youth are encouraged, after having independently investigated, to make a special 'declaration' and renewal of Faith in God and in Baha'u'llah.

COVENANT:

The topic of 'Covenant' is very strong in the Baha'i Revelation and is spoken of frequently. Baha'u'llah indicated that God has made a 'Covenant' with mankind that He would never leave them alone, but would always be with them and would assist them by sending Manifestations of Himself *"in the form of the human temple."* He further said that each Manifestation of God made a 'Covenant' with His followers that He would 'Return' to them, in a spiritual way, even if with a 'new Name.' Read chapter four: 'Progressive Revelation: A New Way of Understanding History.'

CREATION:

When I accessed an electronic concordance of Baha'u'llah's Writings, there were so many thousands of mentions of the words 'create,' 'creator,' and 'creation,' that it was hard to choose from among them. Baha'u'llah frequently mentions God as *"Fashioner of the heavens and the Creator of all things..."* (Baha'u'llah: Tablets of Baha'u'llah, Page: 227 and most often mentions God as *"your Lord, the Creator of earth and heaven."* Baha'u'llah: Kitab-i-Aqdas, Page: 48.

But man is God's supreme creation, says Baha'u'llah, as shown in this quotation: *"All praise and glory be to God Who, through the power of His might, hath delivered His creation from the nakedness of non-existence, and clothed it with the mantle of life. From among all created things He hath singled out for His special favor the pure, the gem-like reality of man, and invested it with a unique capacity of knowing Him and of reflecting the greatness of His glory."* (Baha'u'llah: *Gleanings*, Page: 77)

Baha'u'llah even refers to *"the Word"* through which creation came into being: *"Thy Word which was hidden in Thy wisdom and whereby Thou didst create Thy heaven and Thy earth..."*

(Baha'u'llah: *Prayers and Meditations*, Pages: 219-220) You can read more in chapter four of this conversation/ book about the *"Word"* that Christians believe was in Christ and, Baha'is believe, in every one of the other Manifestations of God, as well. Baha'is definitely believe that, as Baha'u'llah says, the earth and the heavens and all that is in them was created by God through this *"Word"* of God spoken of in the Gospel of John.

DAY OF GOD:

QUESTION: I attended a meeting at the home of some Baha'i Friends. I think they called it a 'Fireside,' though I don't know why, but anyway, they kept talking about this period of history being a 'special day of God.' What did they mean?

RESPONSE: As for the name 'Fireside,' it is simply a name that has been adopted for our informal method of teaching our Faith. We are a young, as yet small religion with few temples or buildings, so most worship and teaching takes place in private homes. To teach our faith, we invite friends into our homes to hear about Baha'u'llah and the Baha'i Faith. We may or may not be sitting 'beside the fire' but the phrase 'Fireside' indicates that the tone is informal and relaxed.

As to the 'Day of God,' the Baha'is were referring to something Baha'u'llah talked about frequently. Here are several quotations, from among many hundreds, to whet your interest: *"O people! The Day, promised unto you in all the Scriptures, is now come."* [Baha'u'llah explains elsewhere that He means the scriptures of *all* religions] *"Fear ye God, and withhold not yourselves from recognizing the One Who is the Object of your creation. Hasten ye unto Him. Better is this for you than the world and all that is therein. Would that ye could perceive it!"* (Baha'u'llah: *Gleanings*, Page: 314)

"This is the Day in which God's most excellent favours have been poured out upon men, the Day in which His most mighty grace hath been infused into all created things. It is incumbent upon all the peoples of the world to reconcile their

differences, and, with perfect unity and peace, abide beneath the shadow of the Tree of His care and loving-kindness . . . Beseech ye the one true God to grant that all men may be graciously assisted to fulfil that which is acceptable in Our sight. Soon will the present-day order be rolled up, and a new one spread out in its stead." (Baha'u'llah: *Proclamation of Baha'u'llah,* Pages: 121-122)

Finally: *"Verily I say, this is the Day in which mankind can behold the Face, and hear the Voice, of the Promised One. The Call of God hath been raised, and the light of His countenance hath been lifted up upon men."* (Baha'u'llah: *Gleanings,* Pages: 10-11) and *"Great indeed is this Day! The allusions made to it in all the sacred Scriptures as the Day of God attest its greatness. The soul of every Prophet of God, of every Divine Messenger, hath thirsted for this wondrous Day. All the divers kindreds of the earth have, likewise, yearned to attain it."* (Baha'u'llah: *Gleanings,* Page: 11)

Read more in *Gleanings* from the Writings of Baha'u'llah on this topic. See the reading list above.

DEMON POSSESSION:

Baha'u'llah's Son, 'Abdu'l-Baha said this: *"As to the question of evil spirits, demons and monsters, any references made to them in the Holy Books have symbolic meaning. What is currently known among the public is but sheer superstition."* (*Lights of Guidance,* Page: 513) Reading the Baha'i Scriptures attempting to understand the 'symbolic meaning' he speaks of, one comes to an understanding that 'demons' or 'evil spirits' refer to man's uncontrolled, untaught, unenlightened lower, animal nature that is in need of education, control and spiritual salvation. See the entry below on 'Devil, Evil and Satan.'

DEVIL/SATAN/EVIL:

QUESTION: Do Baha'is believe in the Devil, or Satan? Do they believe in the existence of evil?

RESPONSE: Baha'u'llah very frequently uses the term 'Satan' and uses other terms, too, such as *'the Evil One"* or *"the Prince of Darkness."* He encourages Baha'is to *"Walk not in the paths of the Evil One."* (Baha'u'llah: *Gleanings*, Page: 126) He speaks of that same 'Evil One' as *"lying in wait, ready to entrap you."* (Baha'u'llah: *Gleanings*, Page: 94) Finally, He speaks of the *"manifestations of the Evil Whisperer, who whisper in men's breasts."* (Baha'u'llah: *Prayers and Meditations*, Page: 233)

As one reads further, however, it is very clear (and this is confirmed by 'Abdu'l-Baha, chosen by Baha'u'llah as His main interpreter) that Baha'u'llah uses these terms, such as 'Satan' and 'the Evil One' or even 'Prince of Darkness' to dramatize His teaching that these 'Satanic' impulses come from within each of us. Baha'u'llah says that there is a *"Satan of self"* within us that must be conquered. (Baha'u'llah: The *Kitab-i-Iqan*, Page: 112).

Baha'u'llah asks us to cleanse our hearts *"from the stain of evil desire"* (Baha'u'llah: *Gleanings*, Page: 85) and to work to rid ourselves of *"evil or corrupt desire"* (Baha'u'llah: *Prayers and Meditations*, Page: 225) and that we must ask God's help to" purge" us from *"evil inclinations."* (Baha'u'llah: *Tablets of Baha'u'llah*, Page: 178)

As I told you before, He tells us that there are men who are ruled by the *"Satan of self"* and calls them 'The Manifestations of Satan.' He advises: *"Only those will attain to the knowledge of the Word of God that have turned unto Him, and repudiated the manifestations of Satan."* (Baha'u'llah: The *Kitab-i-Iqan*, Pages: 122-123) Baha'u'llah's Son 'Abdu'l-Baha said *"...Satan, or what-*

ever is interpreted as evil, refers to the lower nature in man." ('Abdu'l-Baha: Promulgation of Universal Peace, Page 294) He also said that ideas such as 'evil spirit' or 'Satan' are *"...symbols expressing the mere human or earthly nature of man."* ('Abdu'l-Baha: Promulgation of Universal Peace, page 295)

Some people have said that the Baha'is do not believe in the existence of Evil. Nothing could be further from the truth, as the quotations above show. This idea probably comes from a statement of 'Abdu'l-Baha in which he stated that evil does not have a philosophical existence of its own, apart from the very real existence that it has when the 'evil and corrupt desires' that are in every human heart take control of a person's life and 'the Satan of self' expresses itself with horrible consequences. Hitler, Stalin, Pol Pot, a murderous racist or a crazed homophobe come to mind,

But what was true of Hitler in the extreme is also true of every human being, namely, that each of us is fighting a 'spiritual battle,' trying to strengthen our God-given soul or higher self against our lower, animal nature, which is always beckoning for control. Baha'u'llah teaches that this 'evil' of 'selfish and corrupt desire' is there within every human heart. It must experience salvation, be cleansed and put under control of our higher spiritual natures.

This happens, He says, through responding to the Manifestation of God Who appears in the Day in which we live. Finally, Baha'u'llah said that God had given Him a special duty: *"The task of converting satanic strength into heavenly power is one that We have been empowered to accomplish. The Force capable of such a transformation transcendeth the potency of the Elixir itself. The Word of God, alone, can claim the distinction of being endowed with the*

capacity required for so great and far-reaching a change."
(Baha'u'llah: *Gleanings*, Page: 200)

For further reading on this topic of 'Satan' and 'Evil' you cannot do better than to obtain a copy of *The Metropolis of Satan*, written by Gary Matthews. It can be obtained through the Baha'i Publishing Trust or through Stonehaven Press. See the reading list above.

DIVINITY OF CHRIST:
(See Jesus Christ, at the top of this list).

EVERLASTING LIFE:

Both Jesus and Baha'u'llah told those who heard Them that 'everlasting life' began the moment they realized Who They were and recognized and accepted the new 'Manifestation of God.' Both Jesus and Baha'u'llah assured Their followers that this new 'Life' continued after death, but They both expected those who believed in Them to live a certain kind of life while still on this earth. As Jesus said: *"If you love Me, keep My commandments."* John 14:15

There is a striking quote from Baha'u'llah where He uses the metaphor of 'wine' to refer to the 'everlasting life' that He offers to men and women today and tells those who desire to follow Him that they must become the *'arteries'* in the *'body of mankind,'* to put forth efforts to achieve, in cooperation with other like minded people, the unity and peace that are mankind's new God-supplied goals. Here is the full quote:

"This day, it behoveth whoso hath quaffed the Mystic Wine of everlasting life from the Hands of the loving-kindness of the Lord his God, the Merciful, to pulsate even as the throbbing artery in the body of mankind, that through him may be

quickened the world and every crumbling bone. " (Baha'u'llah: The *Kitab-i-Aqdas*, Page: 82)

Baha'u'llah gave many teachings of assurance of 'Life after Death' and you may refer to that section below in this list. In this section, I want to share several quotes from Baha'u'llah about 'Everlasting Life,' but with the understanding, first, that this new 'Life' begins when one recognizes the new Manifestation, Jesus, as *"the Son"* in His day; Baha'u'llah as *"the Father"* in this day. The second understanding is that everlasting life means just that, a life that will continue beyond this earthly life. See the section on 'Life after Death' below, as suggested.

Here are the quotes from Baha'u'llah: *"The waters of everlasting life have, in their fullness, been proffered unto men. Every single cup hath been borne round by the hand of the Well-Beloved. Draw near, and tarry not, though it be for one short moment.*" Baha'u'llah: *Gleanings*, Page: 34) And: *"Death proffereth unto every confident believer the cup that is life indeed. It bestoweth joy, and is the bearer of gladness. It conferreth the gift of everlasting life.*" (Baha'u'llah: *Gleanings*, Page: 345)

Baha'u'llah talks of 'meditating' upon the necessity to 'surrender' one's will completely to God. He states that this 'surrender' is necessary to obtain 'everlasting life' and that this same 'everlasting life' reaches us by "flowing" through His words. Remembering that Jesus asked His disciples to follow His commandments, Baha'u'llah said that following His commandments causes *"complete surrender of one's will to the Will of God. Meditate on this, that thou mayest drink in the waters of everlasting life which flow through the words of the Lord of all mankind."* (Baha'u'llah: *Gleanings*, Page: 338)

Just as Jesus said: *"No one comes to the Father except through Me,"* (John 14:6) Baha'u'llah said: *"No man can obtain everlasting life, unless he embraceth the truth of this*

inestimable, this wondrous, and sublime Revelation."
(Baha'u'llah: *Gleanings*, Page: 183) Baha'u'llah teaches
that, whenever a new Manifestation of 'the Self' of God
appears in history, all must turn to Him, receive salvation from Him and through this recognition and obedience, one obtains 'everlasting life.'

Finally, Baha'u'llah tells of the purpose of His coming, the reason God caused Him to appear out of the
"invisible heaven": He says that " . . . *the purpose of Him
Who is the Eternal Truth hath been to confer everlasting life
upon all men, and ensure their security and peace . . .* "
(Baha'u'llah: *Gleanings*, Page: 116) He ends with an appeal to humankind to act in their best interests: *O MY
SERVANT! Abandon not for that which perisheth an everlasting dominion, and cast not away celestial sovereignty for a
worldly desire. This is the river of everlasting life that hath
flowed from the well-spring of the pen of the merciful; well is
it with them that drink!"* (Baha'u'llah: (Persian) *Hidden
Words*, Page: 37)

EVIL:
(See 'Devil' above on this list.)

FAITH AND DEEDS:

In the Christian Faith, the primary and very first duty
that a Christian has is to recognize Jesus. The second
duty is to follow Him. Jesus said: *"If you love Me, keep My
commandments."* (John 14:15) Likewise, in the Baha'i Faith,
Baha'u'llah speaks of *"twin duties"* that a person who
wishes to follow Him would have: *"The first duty prescribed
by God for His servants is the recognition of Him Who is the
Dayspring of His Revelation* [that is, Baha'u'llah] *and the
Fountain of His laws . . .* " Baha'u'llah describes that He

is the One *"Who representeth the Godhead in . . . the world of creation"*. (Baha'u'llah: *Kitab-i-Aqdas*, Page: 19)

He further states this about any person who has recognized Him" *"Whoso achieveth this duty hath attained unto all good; and whoso is deprived thereof hath gone astray, though he be the author of every righteous deed."* (Baha'u'llah: The *Kitab-i-Aqdas*, Page: 19)

The 'second duty' of man in this day, says Baha'u'llah, is to *"observe every ordinance* [teachings and laws] *of Him Who is the Desire of the World."* Baha'u'llah then says: *"These twin duties* [recognition of the Manifestation of God and following His teachings and laws] *"are inseparable. Neither is acceptable without the other."* (Baha'u'llah: *Gleanings*, Page 330)

Thus, it is clear that faith and deeds go together in Baha'i teaching. The first duty is believing, involving 'faith'; the second duty is 'doing,' or 'deeds.' As Baha'u'llah says, neither is acceptable without the other. Baha'u'llah says in another place, however, that the 'first duty' must, in fact, come first: *"Man's actions are acceptable after his having recognized"* the Manifestation of God when He appears in human history. (Baha'u'llah: *Epistle to the Son of the Wolf*, Page: 61) A final comment from Baha'u'llah: *"Let deeds, not words, be your adorning."* (Baha'u'llah: (Persian) *Hidden Words*, Page: 5)

FALSE PROPHETS:

This phrase comes from a talk Jesus had with His disciples. He was on the Mount of Olives, when He warned them against 'false prophets.' He had been talking with them about His Return, then speaks of 'false prophets': *"Take heed that no one deceives you. For many will come in My name, saying, 'I am the Christ,' and will deceive many."* (Matt 24:4-5)

Then, He speaks to them again, saying: *"Beware of false prophets, who come to you in sheep's clothing, but inwardly they are ravenous wolves. You will know them by their fruits. Do men gather grapes from thornbushes or figs from thistles? Even so, every good tree bears good fruit, but a bad tree bears bad fruit. A good tree cannot bear bad fruit, nor can a bad tree bear good fruit."* (Matt 7:15-18)

Christians, and for that matter, people of any religion, whether Jews or Moslems or Baha'is need to beware of 'false prophets.' Fortunately, Jesus gave the test for whether prophets are 'false' or 'true.' With great simplicity, He tells us that *"a bad tree cannot bear good fruit"* and makes the unforgettable, practical point that you cannot *"gather grapes from thornbushes or figs from thistles."*

Thus, for the Christian who is looking at Baha'u'llah to see whether He might be a 'false prophet' (and this thought immediately crossed my mind forty years ago before I became His follower), all that Christian must do is to observe the *"tree"* of Baha'u'llah and the Baha'i Faith. If it is a bad tree, it cannot bear good fruit; whereas, if it is a good tree, it cannot bear bad fruit.

So one must observe the Baha'i Community, the *"people of Baha"* to find whether or not this *"tree"* is a thornbush, a thistle, or whether it is a fig tree, and a true grape vine, bearing goodly fruits. It appears that Christ has given us not the answer, but the method we can use to find the answer. Baha'u'llah says, in the *Hidden Words*: *"O SON OF MAN! Upon the tree of effulgent glory I have hung for thee the choicest fruits, wherefore hast thou turned away and contented thyself with that which is less good? Return then unto that which is better for thee in the realm on high."* (Baha'u'llah: (Arabic) *Hidden Words*, Page: 21)

Baha'u'llah begins a letter to one of His followers in this way: *"Know thou, O fruit of My Tree."*(Baha'u'llah: *Gleanings*, Page: 133) He is indicating that those who follow Him are the 'fruits' of the *"Tree"* of His Person and of His Revelation.

So, as much as it may make me fearful that the Baha'is may not always 'measure up,' I am nevertheless confident in telling you that, using the standard method that Christ gave to us, you can decide if Baha'u'llah is 'false' or 'true' by looking carefully at the worldwide Baha'i Community, that bears His Name. Christ was clear: A *'bad tree'* bears *'bad'* fruit. A *"good tree"* will bear *"good fruit."* It cannot do otherwise. In chapter fourteen, I relate how I used Christ's 'test' of 'false and true' prophets to make my decision that Baha'u'llah was the Return of Christ.

FAMILY:

QUESTION: What does the Baha'i Faith teach about marriage and family?

RESPONSE: Baha'u'llah teaches that marriage is a *"fortress for well-being"* and encourages His followers to marry. There are numerous teachings and laws given to support strong marriage and healthy families. Two of the many of these teachings are these: First, Baha'is are not to marry without securing the understanding and permission of their parents, in order that family unity will be more likely maintained. However, parents may not interfere in advance with their child's choice of a mate. This law of Baha'u'llah serves to make families closer and more secure.

Dozens of books have been written in the late Twentieth Century concerning the numerous Baha'i scriptures and teachings that are in strong support of marriage and family. Ask a Baha'i friend to suggest several of them. Divorce is strongly disapproved, but finally permitted after a one-year period called the 'year of patience' during which every effort is to be made to renew the marriage. Let me stress that this is not simply a 'waiting period' but an active period of prayer and discovery, using professional help where possible.

The second example that I will tell you about is, I think you will agree, a most interesting one and one that is quite different from anything ever to exist in human history. Baha'u'llah teaches that all children must receive an education but that education of girls around the world, in every culture, is all-important. In much of the world, girls receive inadequate or no education. Both Baha'u'llah and His Son, 'Abdu'l-Baha, indicate that the peace and unity of the world are dependent upon girls becoming educated.

'Abdu'l-Baha said, men and women are like 'two wings of a bird' and humanity will not be able to fly and negotiate into the new world we seek with only 'one wing'. However, Baha'u'llah tells His followers that, if there are two children, one a boy and one a girl, and there are only the resources to educate one child of the two, then education of the girl must come first. One important reason for this is that 'Abdu'l-Baha said: "*the mother is the first educator of the child. It is she who must, at the very beginning, suckle the newborn at the breast of God's Faith and God's Law, that divine love may enter into him even with his mother's milk, and be with him till his final breath.*" ('Abdu'l-Baha: Selections from the writings of 'Abdu'l-Baha, P. 138) Read *Baha'u'llah and the New Era* by John Esslemont for more information. See the reading list at the beginning of this chapter.

Family unity is paramount among Baha'is. Baha'u'llah told His followers: *"Show honour to your parents and pay homage to them. This will cause blessings to descend upon you from the clouds of the bounty of your Lord, the Exalted, the Great"* and *"Beware lest ye commit that which would sadden the hearts of your fathers and mothers...Should anyone give you a choice between the opportunity to render a service to Me and a service to them, choose ye to serve them, and let such a service be a path leading you to Me. This is My exhortation and command unto thee. Observe therefore that which thy Lord, the Mighty, the Gracious, hath prescribed unto you."*

FASTING:

QUESTION: I have heard that the Baha'i Faith calls for 'Fasting.' Why is that necessary? Christians don't fast.

RESPONSE: I can see from your question that you must be of Protestant background, just as I am. Most Catholics and some Protestants *do* fast and it was always a little difficult, as I was growing up, for me to see why all Christians didn't fast, since Jesus expected that His disciples would fast, and even gave them instructions on the proper method of fasting.

QUESTION: I don't believe you are right about that. Where does that idea come from?

RESPONSE: From the New Testament. Jesus instructed His disciples how to fast (Matt. 6:17-18), telling them to anoint their heads, to wash their faces and to do this act in secret. He would not instruct His disciples to do something unless He expected they would be doing it, would He? On another occasion, Jesus told the disciples that a man could only be healed by *"prayer and fasting."* (Matt. 17:21)

Even though Jesus told His disciples that they would fast after His going away from them, even though the

Book of Acts mentions fasting several times and even though St. Paul recommends fasting, somewhere along the line, most Protestant denominations dropped or de-emphasized the practice of fasting.

In any case, with the Baha'is, it wasn't a committee or Church Council that prescribed fasting. It was Baha'u'llah Himself who, like Jesus, taught His followers to fast. In Baha'u'llah's Writings, fasting is a spiritual obligation, a law. For all adult Baha'is, who are not sick, pregnant, traveling or aged, fasting (from dawn to dusk) is prescribed once a year, for a period of several weeks. So, just as Jesus taught His disciples to fast, so did Baha'u'llah. You can ask a Baha'i friend to provide the details of the Baha'i Fast. Or, log onto Bahai.org—the official Baha'i Internet site—to get any information you need.

FORGIVENESS/REDEMPTION; also see 'Salvation' below in this list.

QUESTION: Is 'forgiveness' taught in the Baha'i Faith, particularly the forgiveness of sins that Christians believe can come about only through belief in Christ and the salvation received through that belief?

RESPONSE: Forgiveness is a constant and frequent theme in Baha'i Scriptures. Throughout Baha'u'llah's writings and those of His Son, 'Abdu'l-Baha, forgiveness is prominently mentioned as one of the attributes of God. Baha'u'llah speaks of God as being the *"ever forgiving"* and His predecessor, the Bab (similar but not identical to the role John the Baptist played in the life of Christ) said: *"Verily unsurpassed art Thou in granting forgiveness."* (The Bab: *Selections from the Bab*, Page: 200) Read Chapter three of this conversation/book for the history of the

Baha'i Faith. The Writings of the Bab are part of Baha'i Scripture, since Baha'u'llah said that the Bab was not simply a prophet Who announced Baha'u'llah's coming, but was a Manifestation of God in His own right.

Here is a prayer of the Bab about forgiveness:

"O GOD our Lord! Protect us through Thy grace from whatsoever may be repugnant unto Thee and vouchsafe unto us that which well beseemeth Thee. Give us more out of Thy bounty and bless us. Pardon us for the things we have done and wash away our sins and forgive us with Thy gracious forgiveness. Verily Thou art the Most Exalted, the Self-Subsisting.

"Thy loving providence hath encompassed all created things in the heavens and on the earth, and Thy forgiveness hath surpassed the whole creation. Thine is sovereignty; in Thy hand are the Kingdoms of Creation and Revelation; in Thy right hand Thou holdest all created things and within Thy grasp are the assigned measures of forgiveness. Thou forgivest whomsoever among Thy servants Thou pleasest. Verily Thou art the Ever-Forgiving, the All-Loving. Nothing whatsoever escapeth Thy knowledge, and naught is there which is hidden from Thee.

"O God our Lord! Protect us through the potency of Thy might, enable us to enter Thy wondrous surging ocean, and grant us that which well befitteth Thee.

"Thou art the Sovereign Ruler, the Mighty Doer, the Exalted, the All-loving. (The Bab: *Selections from the Bab*, Page: 178)

QUESTION: Christians believe in a 'forgiving' God, but they also believe that man is 'lost' in sin and will remain so unless he or she receives salvation through belief in Christ. What about that? And what about the fact that God sacrificed His only begotten

Son so that man could receive this gift of salvation? Christians believe that men and women are lost in their sinfulness until ransomed and redeemed by Christ and that it is through Christ's death on the Cross that salvation is offered to and obtained by sinful human beings.

RESPONSE: Baha'u'llah taught that every time a Manifestation is sent by God and 'steps forth' out of *"the invisible heaven,"* coming to earth and into human history in the form of a *"human temple"* that these Messengers (He calls them 'Manifestations of God') suffer for the sins of humanity, redeeming them from sin. These Manifestations bring the very 'Presence' of God into history. Since I am from a Christian background, I realize that Christians believe this has only happened in the case of Jesus. You can read chapter two of this conversation/book 'How a Christian became a Baha'i' for more detail on the Christian background of the author.

But Baha'u'llah also teaches that each and every One of the Manifestations suffered throughout their lives and several were crucified or martyred. This suffering, these deaths were for the purpose of redeeming mankind from sin and ransoming them from their 'lost,' sinful condition. Several quotes from Baha'u'llah may help. As you listen to them, keep in mind that although He is talking only about His own mission in this case, what He says applies to all the Manifestations that have stepped forth into history, out of the *"invisible heaven,"* including Jesus, Moses, Zoroaster, Buddha, Krishna, Muhammad and others.

If you read chapter three of this conversation/book, 'How it all Began,' you will get some important history of the Baha'i Faith, including the fact that

Baha'u'llah was imprisoned for much of His life. He said: *"My body hath endured imprisonment that ye may be released from the bondage of self"* and *"hath consented to be sorely abased that ye may attain unto glory"*. (Baha'u'llah: *Tablets of Baha'u'llah*, Page: 12)

The prison into which He had been cruelly thrown was a 'prison city' named Akka, the worst prison in the Ottoman Empire; it was a city across the bay from what is now Haifa, Israel, where the Baha'i Faith has its world center on the brow of the 'Mountain of the Lord' of the Old Testament—Mt. Carmel. (The same place where Elijah had that 'contest' with the prophets of Baal)

Baha'u'llah, in speaking of this prison-city, said: " *. . . He hath been made to dwell within the most desolate of cities, so that He may build up the hearts of Thy servants, and hath been willing to suffer the most grievous abasement, that Thy creatures may be exalted."* (Baha'u'llah: *Prayers and Meditations*, Page: 37) Baha'u'llah speaks to God, saying: *"I yield Thee thanks, O my God, for that Thou hast offered me up as a sacrifice in Thy path, and made me a target for the arrows of afflictions as a token of Thy love for Thy servants, and singled me out for all manner of tribulation for the regeneration of Thy people."* (Baha'u'llah: *Prayers and Meditations*, Page: 154)

**This is the Prison City of Akka. The two windows shown are
where Baha'u'llah was kept for many years. He called it
'The Most Great Prison.'**

And again, Baha'u'llah testifies to God: *"I swear by
Thy glory! I have accepted to be tried by manifold adversities
for no purpose except to regenerate all that are in Thy heaven
and on Thy earth"*. (Baha'u'llah: *Prayers and Meditations*,
Page: 198)

Baha'u'llah said He "... *hath consented to be bound with chains that mankind may be released from its bondage, and hath accepted to be made a prisoner within this most mighty Stronghold that the whole world may attain unto true liberty. He hath drained to its dregs the cup of sorrow, that all the peoples of the earth may attain unto abiding joy, and be filled with gladness. This is of the mercy of your Lord, the Compassionate, the Most Merciful.*

"We have accepted to be abased, O believers in the Unity of God, that ye may be exalted, and have suffered manifold afflictions, that ye might prosper and flourish. He Who hath come to build anew the whole world, behold, how they that have joined partners with God have forced Him to dwell within the most desolate of cities!" (Baha'u'llah: *Gleanings*, Pages: 99-100)

All of these quotations show how Baha'u'llah and all the other Manifestations of God sacrifice themselves for the redemption and renewal of individuals and of mankind as a whole. Their lives are the ransom for men and women who are caught in what Christians would call their sinful nature and what Baha'is would call their lower, animal nature; in either way of speaking, a condition of 'sin' produced by what Baha'u'llah calls *"evil and corrupt desires'"* and *"evil inclinations."*

As for salvation: There are very many quotations that could be given, but I will give you only one here: Baha'u'llah says He *"hast no desire except the regeneration of the whole world, and the establishment of the unity of its peoples, and the salvation of all them that dwell therein."*

(Baha'u'llah: *Gleanings*, Page: 243) Please see 'Salvation' below in this list.

Read Chapter Seven 'In the Garden a New Flower Hath Begun to Bloom': How a Christian Might Look at Baha'u'llah and His Place in History.'

GOD:

QUESTION: Do Baha'is believe in God?

RESPONSE: They do. You cannot read any portion of the Baha'i Scriptures without being reminded of the reality, power and majesty of God. Whether prayers, meditations or letters written to individuals, all of the Writings of Baha'u'llah extol the greatness of God.

QUESTION: I read in Chapter Five that Baha'u'llah referred to Himself as 'The Father' as if to say He is God Himself!? How can this be? How can 'God Himself' pray to God? Isn't that an inconsistency of logic?

RESPONSE: Well, first let's remember that Jesus prayed to God many times in the New Testament, and yet He said: *"I and My Father are one."* (John 10:30) How could Jesus, whom Christians believe to be God, pray to God? And the answer is the Trinity, according to Christians. Baha'is would agree, at least mostly, with a slightly different interpretation of the Trinity. I'll talk about this later on in this list of subjects. How could Jesus and Baha'u'llah have been the Presence of the reality of God, or Manifestations of God, as Baha'is would call Them, and still have been able to pray to God?

In both cases, you will find Jesus and Baha'u'llah denying, in one breath, that They are God, as when Jesus says to His disciples: *"Why do you call Me good? No one is good but One, that is, God."* (Mark 10:18) or stating that there are things that God knows, but He does not know, as when He speaks of His return, but says: *"But of that day and hour no one knows, not even the angels in heaven, nor the Son, but only the Father."* (Mark 13:32)

But in the next breath, both Jesus and Baha'u'llah

say things that indicate that when people hear Them, obey Them and respond to Them, they are responding to God. Baha'u'llah spoke of Himself as one Whom God had sent: *"Whom Thou hast sent down unto all Thy creatures and invested with Thy name, the All-Glorious, Whose will Thou hast ordained to be Thine own will, Whose self Thou hast decreed to be the revealer of Thine own Self"* (Baha'u'llah: *Prayers and Meditations*, Page: 131)

Finally, Baha'u'llah says of all the Manifestations of God (such as Moses, Krishna Jesus, Muhammad and Buddha): *"Whoso recognizeth them hath recognized God"* and further states *"God hath ordained the knowledge of these sanctified Beings to be identical with the knowledge of His own Self"* (Baha'u'llah: *Gleanings*, Page: 50)

QUESTION: When I went to a Baha'i meeting, I heard someone refer to Baha'u'llah as 'The Ancient of Days' and as 'The Lord of Hosts'. This sounds either ridiculous or blasphemous. Did they really mean to say that? These are names for God Himself!

RESPONSE: It would be helpful if you read chapter five of this conversation/book, but let me give you a short response. The Baha'i who told you that was correct and he quoted Baha'u'llah directly. Let me share with you what Baha'u'llah said, exactly: *"He, the Ancient of everlasting days is come, girded with majesty and power."* (Baha'u'llah: *Gleanings*, Page: 36)

He spoke of His disciples as those who heard *"the Call of their Lord, the Ancient of Days"*. (Baha'u'llah: *Tablets of Baha'u'llah*, Page: 250) and He spoke of Himself as *"Him Who is the Lord of all mankind"*. (Baha'u'llah: The *Kitab-i-Aqdas*, Page: 25) Finally, He said: *"The Promised Day is come and the Lord of Hosts hath appeared."* (Baha'u'llah: *Tablets of Baha'u'llah*, Page: 239)

QUESTION: I'm still amazed and a little angry that Baha'u'llah would make those claims! It makes me wonder about His integrity and even His sanity. I see that He definitely did say these things, but how can He have made these statements that sound so blasphemous, or even crazy!?

RESPONSE: If it were anyone other than Baha'u'llah saying these things, I too would see them as 'crazy' and 'blasphemous.' In chapter five of this conversation/book, I suggest that you place yourself in the shoes of a devout Jew who encounters Jesus for the first time. This Jew hears Jesus say, among other things, *"Most assuredly, I say to you, before Abraham was, I AM."* (John 8:58) Or, *"I and My Father are one"* (John 10:30) or *"I am the way, the truth, and the life. No one comes to the Father except through Me."* (John 14:6)

Or: *"All authority has been given to Me in heaven and on earth."* (Matt 28:18) Finally: *"He who has seen Me has seen the Father."* (John 14:9)

Now, continue to imagine yourself as that Jew, listening to Jesus. That Jew sees a wandering preacher, a sometime carpenter, he remembers that people say that nothing good comes out of Nazareth (the boyhood home of Jesus). He is told that Jesus has a habit of spending time with 'bad company,' including drunks and prostitutes (This is in the New Testament, let us not forget).

He knows that people accuse Jesus of being a blasphemer of God and someone who breaks the Holy Laws of the Sabbath. He hears many statements that make Jesus sound as if He is claiming to be God and when he hears that Jesus believes God has given Him *"authority"* over everything in heaven and on earth, what does this Jew conclude? Does he not feel and say exactly what you said when you heard the statements and claims of Baha'u'llah? Would you, as that Jew, not feel shocked, amazed, angry, disgusted?

Would you, as that Jew, not feel that you had heard something blasphemous and terrible? In fact, Jews of that time are reported in the New Testament to have felt exactly that way upon hearing Jesus speak. Some even felt that Jesus' teaching was 'of the devil' and a few felt so strongly they wanted to kill Jesus for His teachings, his ideas, which seemed so wrong, so destructive to the understanding of the 'true faith.'

Jesus clearly called Himself God when He said: *"I and My Father are one."* (John 10:30) and *"He who has seen Me has seen the Father."* (John 14:9) Those around Him, the Jews, definitely did think His statements were blasphemous. Jesus was finally crucified, largely on the basis of these kinds of statements. To further help you to be sure that I am not misquoting Baha'u'llah, here are the passages to which you were referring: *"From the dawning-place of testimony We have raised the Call unto all that dwell in the realm of creation."*

Baha'u'llah says some were perplexed by this 'Call' that He made to humanity. Others rejected it, but still others responded and *"Others have made haste, winged their way to answer the Call of their Lord, the Ancient of Days"* (Baha'u'llah: *Tablets of Baha'u'llah*, Page: 250)

In another passage Baha'u'llah says: *"The Divine Springtime is come . . . Take heed lest anything deter thee from extolling the greatness of this Day—the Day whereon the Finger of majesty and power hath opened the seal of the Wine of Reunion, and called all who are in the heavens and all who are on the earth."* (Baha'u'llah: *Gleanings*, Page: 28)

Further in the same passage, Baha'u'llah announces: *"We have, then, called into being a new creation, as a token of Our grace unto men. I am, verily, the All-Bountiful, the Ancient of Days."* (Baha'u'llah: *Gleanings*, Pages: 29-30) And: *"God is my witness! He, the Ancient of everlasting days is come, girded with majesty and power."* (Baha'u'llah: *Gleanings*, Page: 36)

It would probably help, also, to recall that Jesus said that others would soon see *"the Son of Man sitting at the right hand of the Power, and coming on the clouds of heaven."* (Matt 26:64)

When Jesus said this, He was standing before the Chief Priest, bound, on trial and accused with criminal acts. We probably think, though, that we understand Jesus, because we know He is talking spiritually and figuratively, not literally. Jesus was, in a spiritual sense, sitting at the right hand of 'Power' at that very moment. Baha'u'llah once said of Himself: *"He it is Who in the Old Testament hath been named Jehovah, Who in the Gospel hath been designated as the Spirit of Truth . . . "* (Quoted by Quoted in Shoghi Effendi: *World Order of Baha'u'llah*, Pages: 103-104) We must constantly remember that both Jesus and Baha'u'llah identified Their Beings with God when they were thinking of Their 'Divine' station. When thinking of Their 'Human' station, They saw themselves as just that, a human being, in many ways like others.

Christian doctrine, discussed in chapters four and five, is very clear that Jesus is 'fully God and fully man.' While Baha'i teaching, contained in Baha'u'llah's Revelation is slightly different from this, the two Faiths are not far apart in this area.

Baha'u'llah, like Jesus, is speaking in a figurative or metaphorical way, certainly not in a literal way. This is made clear when Shoghi Effendi, the Baha'i leader of the first half of the Twentieth Century (see Chapter Three for more detail) said: "Jehovah is a title of God, whereas

Baha'u'llah is the title of the Manifestation of God."
(Quoted in Shoghi Effendi: *Unfolding Destiny*, Page: 432)

There are, we repeat, times when Jesus is clearly
speaking figuratively, or metaphorically, as in the quote
several paragraphs above. In the same way that we understand Jesus, we can understand Baha'u'llah.

For more understanding, read the first few chapters
of this book/conversation. You may agree or disagree
with what is being said, but some things will become
clearer, as you read. At least, I hope so. I also think that
chapters Four, Five and Six of this book will be especially helpful.

GRACE:

QUESTION: Does Baha'u'llah talk about the Grace
of God, a concept so important in the Christian Faith?
Without God's Grace, there is no salvation, nor forgiveness, in Christian belief.

RESPONSE: When I looked in a concordance of
Baha'u'llah's writings, there were literally 'pages' of references to the Grace of God. Let me quote just several:

Baha'u'llah says that God's Mercy *"hath surpassed all
created things, and Thy grace...hath embraced the entire creation,"* (Baha'u'llah: *Prayers and Meditations*, Page: 149)
and prays to God in behalf of humanity *"Aid them, then,
by Thy strengthening grace, to exalt Thy word and to blazon
Thy praise"* (Baha'u'llah: *Prayers and Meditations*, Pages:
149-150) He entreats God, again in support of a needy
humankind, *"Thou art, however, the One Who is of great
bounteousness, Whose grace is immense. Look not down upon
them, O my God, with the glance of Thy justice, but rather
with the eyes of Thy tender compassions and
mercies."* (Baha'u'llah: *Prayers and Meditations*, Page: 137)

Baha'u'llah describes God's Grace as *"all pervasive"* and assures us that even with our sinful, lower natures, we will be redeemed by God, because, as He says (speaking of God) *"Thou art that All-Bountiful Who art not deterred by a multitude of sins from vouchsafing Thy bounty, and the flow of Whose gifts is not arrested by the withdrawal of the peoples of the world.*

And then Baha'u'llah, speaking of the *"wonders of Thy grace"* (Baha'u'llah: *Baha'i Prayers* (US), Page: 144), assures us of God's incredible bounty: *"From eternity the door of Thy grace hath remained wide open. A dewdrop out of the ocean of Thy mercy is able to adorn all things with the ornament of sanctity, and a sprinkling of the waters of Thy bounty can cause the entire creation to attain unto true wealth."* (Baha'u'llah: *Prayers and Meditations*, Page: 246)

In my opinion, many hundreds or even thousands of books will be written commenting on Baha'u'llah's announcement and explanation of the grace and mercy of God. Here are just two more comments from what Baha'u'llah called *"the ocean"* of His words, His Revelation: *". . . one drop out of the ocean of His bountiful grace is enough to confer upon all beings the glory of everlasting life."* (Baha'u'llah: The *Kitab-i-Iqan*, Page: 53)

And speaking of the 'Manifestations of God' (that is, of Jesus, Moses, Muhammad and others, including Baha'u'llah Himself): *". . . all else besides these Manifestations, live by the operation of Their Will, and move and have their being through the outpourings of Their grace."* (Baha'u'llah: *Gleanings*, Page: 179)

Finally, Baha'u'llah announces to all humankind: *"This is the Day in which God's most excellent favours have been poured out upon men, the Day in which His most mighty grace hath been infused into all created things."* (Baha'u'llah: *Proclamation of Baha'u'llah*, Page: 121)

Then, just as Christ spoke with power while bound

and on trial, Baha'u'llah speaks with 'spiritual power' from the Great Prison into which He had been thrown. Referring to His own appearance in human history, Baha'u'llah says: *"The door of grace hath been unlocked and He Who is the Dayspring of Justice is come . . . Thus commandeth thee He Who is the Dawning-Place of the Revelation of thy Lord, the God of Mercy, from His great Prison."* (Baha'u'llah: *Epistle to the Son of the Wolf,* Pages: 85-86)

Truly, Baha'u'llah took the prison into which He had been thrown, and turned it into a *"throne"* of God or, as He said in another passage, *"the seat of Glory."* We get a special insight into this 'spiritual power' when Baha'u'llah writes the following to a believer *"O my God! Thou beholdest the Lord of all mankind confined in His Most Great Prison, calling aloud Thy Name, gazing upon Thy face, proclaiming that which hath enraptured the denizens of Thy kingdoms of revelation and of creation.*

"O my God! I behold Mine own Self captive in the hands of Thy servants, yet the light of Thy sovereignty and the revelations of Thine invincible power shine resplendent from His face, enabling all to know of a certainty that Thou art God, and that there is none other God but Thee. Neither can the power of the powerful frustrate Thee, nor the ascendancy of the rulers prevail against Thee. Thou doest whatsoever Thou willest by virtue of Thy sovereignty which encompasseth all created things, and ordainest that which Thou pleasest through the potency of Thy behest which pervadeth the entire creation." (Baha'u'llah: *Tablets of Baha'u'llah,* Page: 233)

Baha'u'llah then calls out to the people of the world, saying: *"Hearken unto My voice that calleth from My prison."* (Baha'u'llah: *Epistle to the Son of the Wolf,* Page: 58 Baha'u'llah cries aloud to humankind: *"God grant that, in these days of heavenly delight, ye may not deprive yourselves of the sweet savors of the All-Glorious God, and may partake, in this spiritual Springtime, of the outpourings of His grace."*

Baha'u'llah continues: *"Arise in the name of Him Who is the Object of all knowledge,* [keep in mind as you read this that Baha'is believe Baha'u'llah's statement that He is the Return of Christ] *and, with absolute detachment from the learning of men, lift up your voices and proclaim His Cause."* Baha'u'llah then delivers an amazing promise: *"I swear by the Day Star of Divine Revelation! The very moment ye arise, ye will witness how a flood of Divine knowledge will gush out of your hearts, and will behold the wonders of His heavenly wisdom manifested in all their glory before you."* (Baha'u'llah: *Gleanings,* Page: 84)

GUILT:

Like Christ, Baha'u'llah discourages His followers from feeling 'guilty.' Rather, He asks them to be responsible and, when they have done wrong, to repent and to seek God's forgiveness and pardon, which He says is limitless. Both Baha'u'llah and Christ invited those around them to follow them and to accept the salvation they offered. Please see the 'Forgiveness/Salvation' section above and the section below on 'Salvation.'

HEALTH AND HEALING:

QUESTION: Is there anything in what you call 'the Baha'i Scriptures' about health and healing?

RESPONSE: Quite a lot. There is much that has been written by both Baha'u'llah and His Son, 'Abdu'l-Baha. A constant theme is that we are to concentrate first on our 'spiritual health,' but the health of our bodies and minds is also of great importance. Baha'is are told by Baha'u'llah to consult competent physicians.

Baha'u'llah says that spiritual and physical health are linked. Christians refer to Christ as the 'Great Physician.' And, Baha'u'llah (remembering that Baha'is believe Him to be Christ Returned) states that the world's ills will not be healed except *"through the power of a skilled, an all-powerful, and inspired Physician."* (Baha'u'llah: *Epistle to the Son of the Wolf,* Page: 62)

He then refers to Himself as *"the True Physician,"* the *"All-Knowing Physician"* and states that He, as the *"All-Knowing Physician hath His finger on the pulse of mankind. He perceiveth the disease, and prescribeth, in His unerring wisdom, the remedy."* (Baha'u'llah: *Gleanings,* Page: 213)

'Abdu'l-Baha, the Son of Baha'u'llah said: *"All true healing comes from God! There are two causes for sickness, one is material, the other spiritual. If the sickness is of the body, a material remedy is needed, if of the soul, a spiritual remedy.*

" If the heavenly benediction be upon us while we are being healed then only can we be made whole, for medicine is but the outward and visible means through which we obtain the heavenly healing. Unless the spirit be healed, the cure of the body is worth nothing. All is in the hands of God, and without Him there can be no health in us!" (`Abdu'l-Baha: *Paris Talks,* Page: 19)

And here is a prayer of Baha'u'llah, a favorite of mine, about healing. Though there are dozens of prayers revealed by Baha'u'llah for healing, this one is often referred to by Baha'is as 'The Healing Prayer':

"Thy name is my healing, O my God, and remembrance of Thee is my remedy. Nearness to Thee is my hope, and love for Thee is my companion. Thy mercy to me is my healing and my succor in both this world and the world to come. Thou, verily, art the All-Bountiful, the All-Knowing, the All-Wise." (Baha'u'llah: *Prayers and Meditations,* Pages: 262-263)

HEAVEN/HELL:

QUESTION: Do Baha'is believe in an afterlife, in Heaven and Hell?

RESPONSE: Very definitely, but Baha'i Teachings offer some new insights, as I think you will find. For the response on 'Afterlife,' please see below under 'Life after Death' and above, see 'Everlasting Life.' Briefly on the afterlife, however, Baha'is were taught by Baha'u'llah to believe in a life after death, in what Baha'u'llah called the *"many worlds of God."*

Teachings on Heaven and Hell mirror those of Christ, where Jesus seems to say that one begins to experience 'Heaven' by being a part of the Kingdom and 'Hell' as rejecting that same Kingdom of God. Some Christians believe in a very 'material' Heaven with 'Golden Streets' and a very material Hell, with 'fire and brimstone.' Many other Christians believe that Heaven and Hell are spiritual in nature, and this is closer to Baha'i belief.

Baha'u'llah teaches that Heaven is, literally 'nearness to God' while Hell is the opposite, the condition of being apart from or far away from God. As with Jesus, Baha'u'llah indicates that this condition of 'Heaven' and 'Hell' can and does begin here in this life. In the next life, Heaven and Hell will be measured literally by the reality of our 'nearness' to the Divine Being.

In the writings of Baha'u'llah, one will find symbolic language, such as a *"nethermost fire,"* which marks the condition of the unfaithful. Or, Baha'u'llah may ask God to *"open Thou their eyes,"* warning that not to do so will cause men to *"return unto the lowest abyss of the fire."* (Baha'u'llah: *Prayers and Meditations*, Page: 204) Baha'u'llah speaks of the *"fire of unbelief"* and speaks of acceptance of the Manifestation of God, Jesus for example or Baha'u'llah, in this way:

"Whoso hath recognized the Day Spring of Divine guidance and entered His holy court hath drawn nigh unto God and attained His Presence, a Presence which is the real Paradise, and of which the loftiest mansions of heaven are but a symbol"... "Whoso hath failed to recognize Him will have condemned himself to the misery of remoteness, a remoteness which is naught but utter nothingness and the essence of the nethermost fire. Such will be his fate, though to outward seeming he may occupy the earth's loftiest seats and be established upon its most exalted throne."

(Baha'u'llah: *Gleanings*, Pages: 70-71)

Let me repeat that while Baha'u'llah uses symbolic language (and, like Jesus, very strong language) the meaning of Heaven and Hell, is nearness to God or being shut out from God. The real 'state' of Heaven, according to both Christ and Baha'u'llah, is acceptance of Them, while Hell begins if one rejects Them. As to the state of those in the next world, Baha'u'llah says that those who have accepted the Manifestation *"shall associate and commune intimately one with another, and shall be so closely associated in their lives, their aspirations, their aims and strivings as to be even as one soul"* while the souls of the unfaithful will be *"made aware of the good things that have escaped them, and shall bemoan their plight, and shall humble themselves before God."* (Baha'u'llah: *Gleanings*, Pages: 170-171)

To close on this topic, let me give you several quotes from Baha'u'llah showing the hope and the power that exists in this new Day: *"A drop out of the ocean of Thy mercy sufficeth to quench the flames of hell, and a spark of the fire of Thy love is enough to set ablaze a whole world."* (Baha'u'llah: *Prayers and Meditations*, Page: 245)

"Death proffereth unto every confident believer the cup

that is life indeed. It bestoweth joy, and is the bearer of gladness. It conferreth the gift of everlasting life." (Baha'u'llah: *Gleanings*, Page: 345)

Finally, from the book '*Hidden Words*' of Baha'u'llah: "*O SON OF SPIRIT! With the joyful tidings of light I hail thee: rejoice! To the court of holiness I summon thee; abide therein that thou mayest live in peace for evermore.*" (Baha'u'llah: (Arabic) *Hidden Words*, Page: 33)

"*O SON OF THE SUPREME! I have made death a messenger of joy to thee. Wherefore dost thou grieve? I made the light to shed on thee its splendor. Why dost thou veil thyself therefrom?*" (Baha'u'llah: (Arabic) *Hidden Words*, Page: 32)

HOLY GHOST/HOLY SPIRIT:

QUESTION: I'm beginning to realize that there are some great similarities between the Christian and Baha'i Faiths. I wonder if, for example, the Baha'i Faith says anything about the 'Holy Ghost' or 'Holy Spirit'?

RESPONSE: It is certainly true that there are great similarities, as you will find if you read chapter nine: 'Similarities and Differences of the Christian and Baha'i Faiths.' As to the 'Holy Ghost,' Baha'u'llah makes frequent reference to the Holy Ghost and the Holy Spirit. I will cite just one reference, but it is an interesting and striking one. Baha'u'llah tells us of a personal experience: "*Whenever I chose to hold my peace and be still, lo, the voice of the Holy Ghost, standing on my right hand, aroused me, and the Supreme Spirit appeared before my face, and Gabriel overshadowed me, and the Spirit of Glory stirred within my bosom, bidding me arise and break my silence.*" (Baha'u'llah: *Gleanings*, Page: 103) There are many other references to the Holy Ghost. Read for yourself in *Glean-*

ings (from the writings of Baha'u'llah); see reading list above at beginning of this list).

In a striking and unusual passage from Baha'u'llah, we see the role that the Holy Sprit played in His Revelation: *"Methinks that I hear the Voice of the Holy Spirit calling from behind Me saying: Vary Thou Thy theme, and alter Thy tone, lest the heart of him who hath fixed his gaze upon Thy face be saddened."* (Baha'u'llah: *Gleanings*, Page: 37) Finally, Baha'u'llah said that His Revelation was brought *"so that He may infuse life eternal into the mortal frames of men, impart to the temples of dust the essence of the Holy Spirit and the heavenly Light, and draw the transient world, through the potency of a single word, unto the Everlasting Kingdom."* (Baha'u'llah: *Trustworthiness*, Page: 337) There are many references to the Holy Spirit in the Baha'i Revelation.

IMMACULATE CONCEPTION:
(See 'Mary')

INCARNATION:

QUESTION: What about the Incarnation? This is a core Christian belief.

RESPONSE: I really want to direct you to chapter five of this conversation/book, the chapter entitled: 'Manifestation: A New Way of understanding how God Reveals Himself." It is quite inadequate to give a short answer to this and that chapter deals with it in some detail. Baha'i teaching is very similar to Christian teaching regarding the Incarnation. Christians believe that God dwelt 'bodily' in Christ, while Baha'is believe that the fullness of God's Presence was in both Christ and Baha'u'llah, but that this 'fullness' was like the rays of the sun in a perfect mirror.

Whether one uses the concept of the 'incarnation' (never mentioned in the New Testament by name; it was a concept devised more than a hundred years later by Church Fathers and Church Councils) or whether one uses the new concept ('Manifestation') given by Baha'u'llah, what is meant in both cases is that the fullness of the presence of God was present in the Manifestations to such a degree that they could say to their followers, as both Jesus and Baha'u'llah did, that to see them was to see God.

I urge you to consult chapter five to hear what Baha'u'llah has to say about 'Manifestation' as a way of understanding how God reveals Himself. It gives us a way to see all of the Manifestations of history as being from one God. By doing this, it may lead the way, Baha'is believe, to human unity.

Baha'u'llah does use the word 'incarnate' once in His writings, when He says of His appearance in history: *"He* [that is, Baha'u'llah] *doth verily incarnate the highest, the infallible standard of justice unto all creation"* and *"were men to discover the motivating purpose of God's Revelation, they would assuredly cast away their fears, and, with hearts filled with gratitude, rejoice with exceeding gladness."* (Baha'u'llah: *Gleanings*, Page: 175)

Finally, although Baha'u'llah says that God, the Divine Being, is *"in His Essence, holy above ascent and descent, entrance and exit"*, (Baha'u'llah: *Seven Valleys and Four Valleys*, Pages: 22-23) He nevertheless speaks of His own appearance as a Manifestation of God as *"this glorious and manifest Being, that hath assumed a form subject to human limitations."* (Baha'u'llah: *Gleanings*, Page: 203) Read chapters five and seven of this conversation/book for more information.

INFALLIBILITY:

Just as Christians believe Jesus is 'infallible,' Baha'u'llah directly teaches Baha'is that Jesus and each and every one of the Manifestations of God have brought 'infallible' truth to mankind when They appear. Of His own Words, Baha'u'llah says: *"Give ear unto the verses of God . . . They are assuredly the infallible balance, established by God, the Lord of this world and the next. Through them the soul of man is caused to wing its flight towards the Dayspring of Revelation, and the heart of every true believer is suffused with light."* (Baha'u'llah: The *Kitab-i-Aqdas*, Page: 73)

Baha'u'llah, echoing the Words of Christ, said: *"What would it profit man, if he were to fail to recognize the Revelation of God? Nothing whatever."* He then appealed to the people of the world to recognize *"the Revelation sent down unto you in this Day, that the truth, the infallible truth, may be indubitably manifested unto you."* (Baha'u'llah: *Gleanings*, Page: 146) He called His teachings the *"infallible remedy for all the ills that afflict the children of men"* (Baha'u'llah: *Gleanings*, Page: 183) and referred to Himself as *"The Divine and infallible Physician."* (Baha'u'llah: *Gleanings*, Page: 213)

JEHOVAH:
(See 'God' in the list above)

JESUS CHRIST:
See the beginning of this list.

JUDGMENT/JUDGMENT DAY:

Baha'u'llah calls God *"The Lord of the Judgement Day,"* (Baha'u'llah: Trustworthiness, Page: 336) then refers to

His own Coming as *"this Day of Judgement."* (Baha'u'llah: Tablets of Baha'u'llah, Page 124) He tells us that the people of the world face judgment today, based upon whether they recognize and follow *"The Father"* of all mankind, in the same way that the people of Jesus' time faced 'judgment' based upon whether or not they recognized and followed *"The Son."*

Baha'u'llah's Son, 'Abdu'l-Baha, said of his Father: *"He hath brought forth a new creation on this day that is clearly Judgement Day—and still do the heedless stay fast in their drunken sleep . . . the Trumpet hath been blown . . . but still do the dead, in the tombs of their bodies, sleep on."* ('Abdu'l-Baha: *Selections*, 'Abdu'l-Baha, Page: 13)

KINGDOM OF GOD:

Baha'u'llah speaks in the same bold, forthright way that Christ spoke: *"Lo! He is come in the sheltering shadow of Testimony, invested with conclusive proof and evidence, and those who truly believe in Him regard His presence as the embodiment of the Kingdom of God. Blessed is the man who turneth towards Him, and woe betide such as deny or doubt Him."* (Baha'u'llah: *Tablets of Baha'u'llah*, Page: 12)

In words quite similar to those of Jesus, Baha'u'llah says: *"Behold ye the coming of the Glory; witness ye the Kingdom of God, the most Holy, the Gracious, the All-Powerful! .*
. . " (Baha'u'llah: Crisis and Victory, Page: 153) and speaks of Himself, as Christ spoke of Himself, of *"having on his right hand the Kingdom of God and on his left all the power and glory of His* [God's] *everlasting dominion . . . "* (Baha'u'llah: *Gleanings*, Page: 259) Finally, Baha'u'llah said that when He came, " . . . *He appeared with the Kingdom of God, thy Lord . . . "* Baha'u'llah speaks of the 'Kingdom of God' often. Read *Gleanings* (from the Writings of Baha'u'llah) mentioned in the reading list at the

top of these topics; you will find numerous mentions of 'the Kingdom of God.'

LAST DAYS:

QUESTION: Christians believe that Jesus will return in the 'Last Days' to build the Kingdom. Well, actually, Christians believe many different and even conflicting things about the 'Last Days' but all of them believe that there will come a time of renewal and resurrection of all mankind when Jesus returns. What does the Baha'i Faith say about this?

RESPONSE: This is one of the frequently recurring themes of Baha'u'llah. He tells us this is a 'New Day,' a Day of Resurrection for all mankind, that He, as *"the Father"* has come to usher in the time of reunion and renewal of the people of earth, drawing them from all cultures, religions, races, bringing them into unity and peace, and leading them to their task of building a new kingdom, as Jesus prayed, *"Thy kingdom come. Thy will be done in earth, as it is in heaven."* (Matt 6:10)

Referring to Himself as *"the Pen"* of God, writing or saying only what God wished Him to say, Baha'u'llah says that this *"Pen"* is *"driven by the fingers of Thy will"* and that *"from this Pen there floweth out unto all created things the water that is life indeed, and that the Pen itself hath been named by Thee the trumpet whereby the dead speed out of their sepulchers."* (Baha'u'llah: *Prayers and Meditations*, Pages: 280-281)

In another passage, Baha'u'llah says: *"The blast hath been blown on the trumpet"* and *"Speed out of your sepulchers. How long will ye sleep? The second blast hath been blown on the trumpet. On whom are ye gazing? This is your*

Lord, the God of Mercy." (Baha'u'llah: *Gleanings*, Page: 44)

Baha'u'llah explains in another place that the two 'blasts of the trumpet' were the appearance of His predecessor, the Bab and His own appearance as" the *Father*" of all mankind. To Christians, Baha'u'llah says, this 'trumpet blast' signals the 'Return of Christ,' for as Baha'u'llah said of Christ: *"He hath once more, in My person, been made manifest unto you.*" (Baha'u'llah: *Gleanings*, Page: 101)

Baha'u'llah was clear that His Coming was the 'Trumpet Blast,' signaling the Resurrection of all Mankind and the Call from the 'God of Mercy' for mankind to recognize their oneness and enact their unity. See also 'Apocalypse' in the list above.

There is more on the 'Time of the End' in Chapter Six of this conversation/book.

LAYING ON OF HANDS:

The Baha'i Faith has no rituals (with very few exceptions, those being a verse to be said at weddings and a prayer to be said at funerals). Thus, there is nothing similar to 'laying on of hands' since 'laying on of hands' refers primarily to ordination of clergy. Since the Baha'i Faith does not have a clergy, it seems not to apply.

However, the idea of passing down authority does exist in the Baha'i Faith, in that it was passed from the Bab to Baha'u'llah; from Baha'u'llah to His Son, 'Abdu'l-Baha; from 'Abdu'l-Baha to His grandson, Shoghi Effendi. Also, in Baha'u'llah's writings, He conferred great responsibility (see 'Infallibility' above in this list) on an institution He created that is called 'The Universal House of Justice.'

Baha'u'llah said of this Universal House of Justice

(first elected in 1963): *"God will verily inspire them with whatsoever He willeth"* (Baha'u'llah: *Tablets of Baha'u'llah,* Page: 68) and assures those who serve on this elected body that they are *"the recipients of divine inspiration from the unseen Kingdom. It is incumbent upon all to be obedient unto them."* (Baha'u'llah: *Kitab-i-Aqdas*: Other Sections, Page: 91)

Baha'u'llah appointed His Son, 'Abdu'l-Baha, to be the 'Center of His Covenant' with the Baha'is and with mankind and the official interpreter of the meaning of His Words. 'Abdu'l-Baha said of the Universal House of Justice that *"whatsoever they decide, is of God."* ('Abdu'l-Baha: Will and Testament, Page: 11) Because of these and many other similar statements, Baha'is feel that when the Universal House of Justice speaks or makes a decision, it has the force, for Baha'is, of God's Will and a continuing shower of what Baha'u'llah called *"divine inspiration from the unseen Kingdom."* See Chapter Three for some history: 'How it all Began.'

LIFE AFTER DEATH:

Here is one of the most well known sayings of Baha'u'llah: *"O SON OF THE SUPREME! I have made death a messenger of joy to thee. Wherefore dost thou grieve? I made the light to shed on thee its splendor. Why dost thou veil thyself therefrom?"* (Baha'u'llah: (Arabic) *Hidden Words*, Page: 32) That quote was from a book revealed by Baha'u'llah called *The Hidden Words*. I recommend it to you. Also from *The Hidden Words*: *"O SON OF SPIRIT! With the joyful tidings of light I hail thee: rejoice! To the court of holiness I summon thee; abide therein that thou mayest live in peace for evermore."* (Baha'u'llah: (Arabic) *Hidden Words*, Page: 33)

Baha'u'llah says: *"It is evident that the loftiest mansions in the Realm of Immortality have been ordained as the habitation of them that have truly believed in God and in His signs. Death can never invade that holy seat."* (Baha'u'llah: *Gleanings*, Page: 141)

Baha'u'llah gets as specific about the afterlife as any Manifestation has ever done: *"And now concerning thy question regarding the soul of man and its survival after death. Know thou of a truth that the soul, after its separation from the body, will continue to progress until it attaineth the presence of God, in a state and condition which neither the revolution of ages and centuries, nor the changes and chances of this world, can alter. It will endure as long as the Kingdom of God, His sovereignty, His dominion and power will endure. It will manifest the signs of God and His attributes, and will reveal His loving-kindness and bounty.*

"The movement of My Pen is stilled when it attempteth to befittingly describe the loftiness and glory of so exalted a station. The honor with which the Hand of Mercy will invest the soul is such as no tongue can adequately reveal, nor any other earthly agency describe. Blessed is the soul which, at the hour of its separation from the body, is sanctified from the vain imaginings of the peoples of the world. Such a soul liveth and moveth in accordance with the Will of its Creator, and entereth the all-highest Paradise." (Baha'u'llah: *Gleanings*, Pages: 155-156)

Then comes one of the most striking statements from Baha'u'llah, the 'Pen of God,' about the magnificence of the afterlife and the role that the 'true believer' will play in the next life. He reveals some information that is more specific than we have ever known: *"If any man be told that which hath been ordained for such a soul in the worlds of God, the Lord of the throne on high and of earth below, his whole being will instantly blaze out in his great longing to attain that most exalted, that sanctified and resplendent station . . . . The nature of the soul after death can never be*

described, nor is it meet and permissible to reveal its whole
character to the eyes of men."

Baha'u'llah then says that the purpose of the appearance of all of the Manifestations, including *"The Son"* of
God and His own Coming in *"the Glory of the Father"* has
been to *"educate all men, that they may, at the hour of death,*
ascend, in the utmost purity and sanctity and with absolute
detachment, to the throne of the Most High. The light which
these souls radiate is responsible for the progress of the world
and the advancement of its peoples. They are like unto leaven
which leaveneth the world of being, and constitute the ani-
mating force through which the arts and wonders of the world
are made manifest. Through them the clouds rain their bounty
upon men, and the earth bringeth forth its fruits.

"All things must needs have a cause, a motive power, an
animating principle. These souls and symbols of detachment
have provided, and will continue to provide, the supreme moving
impulse in the world of being. The world beyond is as differ-
ent from this world as this world is different from that of the
child while still in the womb of its mother. When the soul
attaineth the Presence of God, it will assume the form that
best befitteth its immortality and is worthy of its celestial habi-
tation." (Baha'u'llah: *Gleanings*, Pages: 156-157)

Finally: *"Death proffereth unto every confident believer*
the cup that is life indeed. It bestoweth joy, and is the bearer
of gladness. It conferreth the gift of everlasting life."
(Baha'u'llah: *Gleanings*, Page: 345)

Read more about 'Life After Death' under 'Soul'
below in this list.

LIMBO:

Baha'u'llah assures humanity, as has every other
Manifestation of God, that there is an afterlife. Jesus and
Baha'u'llah both refer to this life, which begins when

one recognizes the Manifestation, as 'life everlasting.' Baha'u'llah speaks specifically about this 'Life after Death' (see the section above by that title) and says that there are many 'worlds of God'. *"As to thy question concerning the worlds of God. Know thou of a truth that the worlds of God are countless in their number, and infinite in their range. None can reckon or comprehend them except God, the All-Knowing, the All-Wise."* (Baha'u'llah: *Gleanings*, Pages: 151-152)

The word 'Limbo' is not used, but Baha'u'llah speaks of those who will be closer to God or less close in the next world, so He clearly sees different 'stations' for those who enter the next life. He apparently also sees growth being possible, which is a concept at least indirectly related to the Catholic doctrine of 'Limbo.'

LORD AND SAVIOR:
(See 'Savior')

LORD OF HOSTS:
See 'God' in the list above.

MARRIAGE/DIVORCE:
(See 'Family')

MARY/IMMACULATE CONCEPTION:

QUESTION: My cousin is a Catholic. What do Baha'is believe about Mary, the Mother of Jesus?

RESPONSE: Mary is mentioned frequently in the Baha'i Scriptures. Baha'u'llah often refers to Jesus as *"Jesus, Son of Mary."* Mary occupies a high station in Baha'i writings and Baha'u'llah's Great Grandson, Shoghi

Effendi, the leader of the International Baha'i Community in the first half of the Twentieth Century, said that, based on Baha'u'llah's teachings, Baha'is believe in "the reality of the mystery of the Immaculacy of the Virgin Mary." (Citation below)

And, for the information of Catholic Christians, Shoghi Effendi added that "the primacy of Peter, the Prince of the Apostles, is upheld and defended," and "Peter is recognized as one whom God has caused (in the words of Baha'u'llah) *"the mysteries of wisdom and of utterance to flow out of his mouth."* Mary is described by Baha'u'llah as *"that veiled and immortal, that most beauteous, countenance"* and the station of Christ is spoken of as a *"station which hath been exalted above the imaginings of all that dwell on earth,"* (Quoted in Shoghi Effendi: The *Promised Day is Come*, Pages: 109-110)

There is much more about Mary in the Baha'i Writings. Explore! One way to do so is to purchase software called MARS, which contains all the scriptures of the Baha'i Faith that have been translated into English. Still another way is to buy software literally called 'Explore,' which allows you to explore the Baha'i Writings and Teachings in a beginning fashion, by arranging Baha'i Writings topically. There are numbers at the start of this chapter to use to find books and software.

MERCY:

QUESTION: You talked before about 'Grace', as it is understood by the Baha'is of the world. You said that there were pages of references in a concordance of Baha'u'llah's Writings about 'Grace.' What about 'Mercy'?

RESPONSE: Essentially the same with 'Mercy.' Many hundreds of references in Baha'u'llah's *"ocean"* of Revelation. I will offer only several of these numerous references. You can take the opportunity to read and study any portion of Baha'u'llah's Writings and it will be certain that before you read three or four paragraphs, you will hear Baha'u'llah talking about the 'Mercy' of God and His 'Grace'. I hope you will seize this opportunity. For now, here are several quotations to whet your interest.

Baha'u'llah implores God to give to humankind *"the breezes of Thy tender mercy"* (Baha'u'llah: *Prayers and Meditations*, Page: 215) and tells man to *"drink of the cup of Thy mercy that hath surpassed all things visible and invisible".* (Baha'u'llah: *Prayers and Meditations*, Page: 110) He says in a prayer given to Baha'is that they should pray to God to *"Cleanse me with the waters of Thy mercy, O my Lord, and make me wholly Thine."* (Baha'u'llah: *Prayers and Meditations*, Page: 139)

Baha'u'llah speaks of *"the precincts of Thy transcendent mercy"* and states that these *"precincts"* existed *"before the foundation of earth and heaven".* (Baha'u'llah: *Kitab-i-Aqdas*: Other Sections, Page: 101) He also speaks of *"Thy mercy whereby Thou didst invite all created things unto the table of Thy bounties and bestowals."* (Baha'u'llah: *Baha'i Prayers* (US), Page: 98)

The name most frequently used by Baha'u'llah for God is *"the All-Merciful".* He speaks of a God *"Whose mercy hath encompassed all things"* (Baha'u'llah: *Prayers and Meditations*, Page: 244) and says that *"A drop out of the ocean of Thy mercy sufficeth to quench the flames of hell, and a spark of the fire of Thy love is enough to set ablaze a whole world."* (Baha'u'llah: *Prayers and Meditations*, Page: 245)

Later, in the same passage, He continues: *"A dewdrop out of the ocean of Thy mercy is able to adorn all things with the ornament of sanctity, and a sprinkling of the waters of Thy bounty can cause the entire creation to attain unto true wealth.* " (Baha'u'llah: *Prayers and Meditations,* Page: 246)

The following quotation is representative of many others where Baha'u'llah talks about the 'Mercy' of God and His wondrous 'Grace.' *"What outpouring flood can compare with the stream of His all-embracing grace, and what blessing can excel the evidences of so great and pervasive a mercy? There can be no doubt whatever that if for one moment the tide of His mercy and grace were to be withheld from the world, it would completely perish.*

"For this reason, from the beginning that hath no beginning the portals of Divine mercy have been flung open to the face of all created things, and the clouds of Truth will continue to the end that hath no end to rain on the soil of human capacity, reality and personality their favors and bounties. Such hath been God's method continued from everlasting to everlasting. " (Baha'u'llah: *Gleanings,* Pages: 68-69)

Read Baha'u'llah's *Prayers and Meditations* or *Gleanings* from the writings of Baha'u'llah for more on God's Mercy and Grace. Meanwhile, let me close this section on God's Mercy with a prayer of Baha'u'llah:

"O my God, the God of bounty and mercy! Thou art that King by Whose commanding word the whole creation hath been called into being; and Thou art that All-Bountiful One the doings of Whose servants have never hindered Him from showing forth His grace, nor have they frustrated the revelations of His bounty.

"Suffer this servant, I beseech Thee, to attain unto that which is the cause of his salvation in every world of Thy worlds. Thou art, verily, the Almighty, the Most Powerful, the All-Knowing, the All-Wise. " (Baha'u'llah: *Prayers and Meditations,* Page: 251)

MIRACLES/VISIONS:

Both miracles and visions are described in the Baha'i Faith, but are not much talked about nor are they focused upon. Baha'u'llah specifically asked us not to talk about or focus on miracles because witnessing them does not create true faith and belief. Also, they are really only good for those who see them first hand, or for those who are emphasizing material things over the spiritual, inner meanings and belief that are important.

Baha'u'llah and all the other Manifestations of God had great power and all of Them did, in fact, do miraculous acts. But the real miracle, Baha'u'llah tells us, is the 'miracle' of Their appearance in human history. We participate in this miracle by recognizing Them. In this regard, there is an interesting passage in Baha'u'llah's Writings. He shows that God could choose to 'overwhelm' us with a miraculous act, almost like a magic trick, and we would have no choice but to believe. But this is not the way God chooses to act, says Baha'u'llah.

Here is the passage: *"Were the prophecies recorded in the Gospel to be literally fulfilled; were Jesus, Son of Mary, accompanied by angels, to descend from the visible heaven upon the clouds; who would dare to disbelieve, who would dare to reject the truth, and wax disdainful? Nay, such consternation would immediately seize all the dwellers of the earth that no soul would feel able to utter a word, much less to reject or accept the truth."* (Baha'u'llah: The *Kitab-i-Iqan*, Pages: 80-81)

Baha'u'llah says that the Manifestations are sent to us by God *"from their invisible habitations of ancient glory unto this world, to educate the souls of men and endue with grace all created things,* [and] *are invariably endowed with an all-compelling power, and invested with invincible sovereignty."* (Baha'u'llah: The *Kitab-i-Iqan*, Page: 97) So the

Manifestations have all power and sovereignty, but they don't prefer to have those who believe in them do so because of miracles. Jesus often asked those He healed not to tell anyone, if you recall.

Finally, there is the story of a man who spent many years collecting stories of the miraculous acts performed by Baha'u'llah. When He presented this collection to Baha'u'llah. He led him to a river, then proceeded to tear out pages from the book and throw them page-by-page into the river. Baha'u'llah thanked him for his thoughtfulness and service but gently explained what we have just been talking about, namely, that a decision to follow Christ or Baha'u'llah should be based on both rationality and an 'act of faith,' not upon being over-whelmed or impressed by a miraculous act.

NON-BELIEVERS:

If we take the Gospel of Christ as a starting point, we find it is very serious to fail to respond to the Manifestation of God. Jesus spoke of those who did not believe as *"dead"* by which we know He meant dead spiritually. Baha'u'llah made several similar statements, including: *" Speed out of your sepulchres. How long will ye sleep? The second blast hath been blown on the trumpet. On whom are ye gazing? This is your Lord, the God of Mercy. "* (Baha'u'llah: *Proclamation of Baha'u'llah,* Page: 98)

While both Christ and Baha'u'llah regard those who do not turn to them and accept them as spiritually 'dead,' it should be said that Baha'is are not intolerant toward those who do not believe as we do. It is true that we are trying to spread knowledge of Baha'u'llah's Coming and to broadcast His healing message and revitalizing teachings to the world, but we are forbidden by Baha'u'llah to pressure or proselytize.

QUESTION: In today's world, calling someone 'spiritually dead' is a sign of intolerance, in my opinion.

RESPONSE: I understand what you are saying, and I would never think to call someone 'spiritually dead.' However, the problem is that both Christ and Baha'u'llah did exactly that. It is a struggle that I think we must make to understand what they meant without becoming intolerant. I believe that you will find, when you investigate the Baha'is and the Baha'i community, that they are not an intolerant group; rather, that they put forth every effort to *"bring about concord and union among the people."* (Baha'u'llah: *Kitab-i-Aqdas:* Notes, Page: 209)

Baha'u'llah did ask us to teach His Faith to humanity, so there is a zeal to let people know that a great new Day has dawned upon humanity and an enthusiasm about the ingathering of humanity that is about to occur, but we do recognize that others will follow their own way. The task of Baha'is is to work for the betterment of the world and to do everything possible to bring about human unity. To think or act in a 'divisive' way would go against the core teachings of Baha'u'llah.

Finally, Baha'u'llah spoke often about the responsibility of every human being to think things through for themselves in an independent way. Therefore, Baha'is can give information and can enthusiastically present Baha'u'llah to the world as Christ Returned and as 'the Promise of All Ages' and as the appearance of *"the Father"* of all humankind, but they cannot cross a clear, bright line of each individual's responsibility for their life decisions.

ORIGINAL SIN: (See 'Sin')

PENANCE:

There is no idea of 'penance' in the Baha'i Faith. God's forgiveness is limitless and, as Baha'u'llah put it, no amount of wrongdoing can be greater than God's power to forgive. Forgiveness is free to all and can be obtained simply by asking God for pardon and forgiveness. Also there is no clergy in the Baha'i Faith, so there would be no one standing between God and the believer to decide penance.

It is, of course, true that any Baha'i, like any Christian or Jew or Moslem would want and should want to right any wrongs that they have done, if at all possible, but not on the basis of a 'penance' measured out by clergy or a religious institution. From the Baha'i writings, we learn that Baha'u'llah "prohibits slavery, asceticism, mendicancy, monasticism, penance, the use of pulpits and the kissing of hands" (Baha'u'llah: *Kitab-i-Aqdas*: Other Sections, Page: 14)

PRAYER:

QUESTION: Do Baha'is believe in prayer? How do they pray, and to whom?

RESPONSE: Baha'is do believe in prayer. It is central in the Baha'i Faith. Baha'is pray just as Christians do, to God. Sometimes, they address Baha'u'llah in their prayers, just as Christians sometimes address Jesus when they pray. Jesus taught His disciples to pray to God and Baha'u'llah did the same.

There are literally thousands of prayers from the Pen of Baha'u'llah and of His Son, 'Abdu'l-Baha (who is very central in the Baha'i Faith—see chapter three), and of His predecessor, The Bab (a figure not unlike John the Baptist, but Who, Baha'u'llah said, was also a Manifestation of God.)

Baha'u'llah refers to God as being one Who desires *"to answer the prayers of all men"* (Baha'u'llah: *Prayers and Meditations,* Page: 247) and Who *"hearest and art ready to answer."* (Baha'u'llah: *Prayers and Meditations,* Page: 248) Baha'is are commanded by Baha'u'llah to pray at least once a day, and in fact three special prayers are provided, including this 'Morning Prayer' that has always meant so much to me:

"I have wakened in Thy shelter, O my God, and it becometh him that seeketh that shelter to abide within the Sanctuary of Thy protection and the Stronghold of Thy defense. Illumine my inner being, O my Lord, with the splendors of the Day-Spring of Thy Revelation, even as Thou didst illumine my outer being with the morning light of Thy favor." (Baha'u'llah: *Prayers and Meditations,* Page: 251)

There is a prayer called the 'Long Prayer' in which Baha'u'llah describes prayer as being *"fire", "light"* and *"water."* We are encouraged by Baha'u'llah to ask God to *"make of my prayer a fire that will burn away the veils which have shut me out from Thy beauty, and a light that will lead me unto the ocean of Thy Presence"* and later in the same prayer to: *"Make my prayer, O my Lord, a fountain of living waters whereby I may live as long as Thy sovereignty endureth, and may make mention of Thee in every world of Thy worlds."* (Baha'u'llah: *Kitab-i-Aqdas:* Other Sections, Page: 93)

Baha'u'llah speaks of the Divine Being as *"the prayer-hearing, prayer-answering God!"* (Baha'u'llah: *Baha'i Prayers* (US), Page: 148) and the following prayer captures the essence of why Baha'u'llah taught His followers to pray, and for that matter, why Christians and the followers of all faiths have been taught to pray to God. It also speaks of the mystical effect that prayer has on the one praying and on the whole world:

"Intone, O My servant, the verses of God that have been received by thee, as intoned by them who have drawn nigh unto Him, that the sweetness of thy melody may kindle thine own soul, and attract the hearts of all men. Whoso reciteth, in the privacy of his chamber, the verses revealed by God, the scattering angels of the Almighty shall scatter abroad the fragrance of the words uttered by his mouth, and shall cause the heart of every righteous man to throb.

"Though he may, at first, remain unaware of its effect, yet the virtue of the grace vouchsafed unto him must needs sooner or later exercise its influence upon his soul.

"Thus have the mysteries of the Revelation of God been decreed by virtue of the Will of Him Who is the Source of power and wisdom." (Baha'u'llah: *Gleanings*, Page: 295)

PREDESTINATION:

QUESTION: Now and then, in this conversation/ book, you have said: "Let me tease you a little." Now, it's my turn. I want to see you give a 'short response' to 'Predestination'.

RESPONSE: Point well taken. Hundreds or thousands of books have been written by Christians, and for that matter, by Moslems, Jews and others on this topic. No, I can't give a meaningful 'short response' but I can give you a fascinating comment by Baha'u'llah and point you to the place where the quote appears.

Baha'u'llah is writing to a mother who is concerned about her son. He says to her: *"Let not thine heart grieve over what hath befallen thee. Wert thou to scan the pages of the Book of Life, thou wouldst, most certainly, discover that which would dissipate thy sorrows and dissolve thine anguish.*

"Know thou, O fruit of My Tree, that the decrees of the Sovereign Ordainer, as related to fate and predestination, are of two kinds. Both are to be obeyed and accepted. The one is irrevocable, the other is, as termed by men, impending. To the former all must unreservedly submit, inasmuch as it is fixed and settled. God, however, is able to alter or repeal it. As the harm that must result from such a change will be greater than if the decree had remained unaltered, all, therefore, should willingly acquiesce in what God hath willed and confidently abide by the same.

"The decree that is impending, however, is such that prayer and entreaty can succeed in averting it." (Baha'u'llah: *Gleanings*, Page: 133)

You can read this in its context in Baha'u'llah's *Prayers and Meditations.* It's not in the reading list, but I recommend it to you. Any Baha'i can tell you how to obtain a copy. And, when you do look this up, you can read the equally engaging prayer that Baha'u'llah gave to this mother to pray regarding her son.

QUESTION: If you don't mind, I don't want to wait. Let me hear that prayer right now, if you will.

RESPONSE: Yes, of course, at least a portion of it: *"O God, my God! Thou hast committed into mine hands a trust from Thee, and hast now according to the good-pleasure of Thy Will called it back to Thyself. It is not for me, who am a handmaid of Thine, to say, whence is this to me or wherefore hath it happened, inasmuch as Thou art glorified in all Thine acts, and art to be obeyed in Thy decree. Thine handmaid, O my Lord, hath set her hopes on Thy grace and bounty. Grant that she may obtain that which will draw her nigh unto Thee, and will profit her in every world of Thine. Thou art the Forgiving, the All-Bountiful. There is none other*

God but Thee, the Ordainer, the Ancient of Days."
(Baha'u'llah: *Gleanings,* Pages: 133-135)

Let's make one more observation on God's involvement in our 'Destiny.' In a prayer that Baha'u'llah taught His followers to pray, there is this thought: *"I have turned to Thee, forsaking mine own will and desire, that Thy holy will and pleasure may rule within me and direct me according to that which the pen of Thy eternal decree hath destined for me."* (Baha'u'llah: *Baha'i Prayers* (US), Page: 149)

PROPHECY:

Baha'u'llah's appearance in history has been foretold. He tells us that His coming" hath *been foretold in the Scriptures of old"* (Baha'u'llah: *Gleanings,* Page 344) and that it is *"this Day that hath been mentioned in all the Books, Scriptures, and Tablets."* (Baha'u'llah: *Epistle to the Son of the Wolf,* Page: 2) He continues about the 'Day of God' that we are witnessing today: *"Great indeed is this Day! The allusions made to it in all the sacred Scriptures as the Day of God attest its greatness. The soul of every Prophet of God, of every Divine Messenger, hath thirsted for this wondrous Day. All the divers kindreds of the earth have, likewise, yearned to attain it."* (Baha'u'llah: *Gleanings,* Page: 11)

In another passage: *"The Day, promised unto you in all the Scriptures, is now come. Fear ye God, and withhold not yourselves from recognizing the One Who is the Object of your creation. Hasten ye unto Him. Better is this for you than the world and all that is therein. Would that ye could perceive it."* (Baha'u'llah: *Gleanings,* Page: 314)

He specifically says: *"Whatever hath come to pass in this Day hath been foretold in the Scriptures of old"*(Baha'u'llah: *Tablets of Baha'u'llah,* Page: 244) and *"The Revelation which, from time immemorial, hath been acclaimed as the Purpose and Promise of all the Prophets of*

God, and the most cherished Desire of His Messengers, hath now, by virtue of the pervasive Will of the Almighty and at His irresistible bidding, been revealed unto men. The advent of such a Revelation hath been heralded in all the sacred Scriptures." (Baha'u'llah: *Gleanings,* Page: 5)

Also: "*He Whose advent hath been foretold in the heavenly Scriptures is come, could ye but understand it. The world's horizon is illumined by the splendours of this Most Great Revelation. Haste ye with radiant hearts and be not of them that are bereft of understanding. The appointed Hour hath struck . . .*" (Baha'u'llah: *Tablets of Baha'u'llah,* Page 244)

Then, He says something I believe you will find interesting: "*In this Day a great festival is taking place in the Realm above; for whatsoever was promised in the sacred Scriptures hath been fulfilled. This is the Day of great rejoicing.*" (Baha'u'llah: *Tablets of Baha'u'llah,* Page: 78) And,

Finally, an equally striking statement: "*The time foreordained unto the peoples and kindreds of the earth is now come. The promises of God, as recorded in the holy Scriptures, have all been fulfilled. Out of Zion hath gone forth the Law of God, and Jerusalem, and the hills and land thereof, are filled with the glory of His Revelation.*" (Baha'u'llah: *Gleanings,* Pages: 12-13)

PSALMS:

There are 'psalms' and hymns of praise, many of them, in the Baha'i Revelation. The best place to look for these is in Baha'u'llah's *Prayers and Meditations* where one will find some of the most moving and beautiful 'psalms' ever written. I am convinced that when the world discovers the devotional literature of the Baha'i Scriptures, they will be greatly attracted and even entranced. Let me quote one of the most widely known of

Baha'u'llah's prayers, which has the quality of a 'Psalm.'
It is often called 'The Sweet Scented Streams.'

*"From the sweet-scented streams of Thine eternity give
me to drink, O my God, and of the fruits of the tree of Thy
being enable me to taste, O my Hope! From the crystal springs
of Thy love suffer me to quaff, O my Glory, and beneath the
shadow of Thine everlasting providence let me abide, O my
Light! Within the meadows of Thy nearness, before Thy presence, make me able to roam, O my Beloved, and at the right
hand of the throne of Thy mercy, seat me, O my Desire!*

*"From the fragrant breezes of Thy joy let a breath pass
over me, O my Goal, and into the heights of the paradise of
Thy reality let me gain admission, O my Adored One! To the
melodies of the dove of Thy oneness suffer me to hearken, O
Resplendent One, and through the spirit of Thy power and
Thy might quicken me, O my Provider! In the spirit of Thy
love keep me steadfast, O my Succorer, and in the path of Thy
good-pleasure set firm my steps, O my Maker! Within the
garden of Thine immortality, before Thy countenance, let me
abide for ever, O Thou Who art merciful unto me, and upon
the seat of Thy glory stablish me, O Thou Who art my Possessor!*

*"To the heaven of Thy loving-kindness lift me up, O my
Quickener, and unto the Day-Star of Thy guidance lead me, O
Thou my Attractor! Before the revelations of Thine invisible
spirit summon me to be present, O Thou Who art my Origin
and my Highest Wish, and unto the essence of the fragrance of
Thy beauty, which Thou wilt manifest, cause me to return, O
Thou Who art my God! Potent art Thou to do what pleasest
Thee. Thou art, verily, the Most Exalted, the All-Glorious, the
All-Highest."* (Baha'u'llah: *Prayers and Meditations*, Pages:
258-259)

PURGATORY:
See the sections above on 'Limbo' and, especially, 'Life after Death.'

RANSOM:
See 'Forgiveness' above in this list.

RAPTURE:

QUESTION: Does Baha'u'llah say anything about the 'Rapture'?

RESPONSE: Yes, some things directly and many things indirectly. What Baha'u'llah does say is to indicate that the 'Rapture,' which some but not all Christians see as a 'physical' event is, in reality, a 'spiritual' event that is happening even as we engage in this conversation.

According to Baha'u'llah, there is a *"Resurrection"* of mankind now taking place. One might not think this is true, looking at the wars and the terrifying inhumanity of the Twentieth Century. Baha'u'llah asks us, rather, to look at the coming of the *"Father"* of all mankind, and the beginning of the gathering together of the people of earth. This is the true 'rapture,' according to Baha'u'llah. This is an actual 'Resurrection.' And it is happening now, as the Baha'i community spreads knowledge of the Baha'i Faith and its teachings, and as the people of Earth–person by person–arise to new life in recognition of Baha'u'llah and their commitment to follow Him to become 'Quickeners of Mankind.'

Baha'u'llah said in one prayer: *"O Thou the Lord of the visible and the invisible, and the Enlightener of all creation! I beseech Thee, by Thy sovereignty which is hid from the eyes of men, to reveal in all directions the signs of Thy manifold blessings and the tokens of Thy loving-kindness, that I may arise with exultation and rapture and extol Thy wondrous virtues, O Thou the Most Merciful, and stir up by Thy name all created things, and so kindle the fire of Thy glorification amidst Thy creatures, that all the world may be filled with the brightness of the light of Thy glory, and all existence be inflamed with the fire of Thy Cause.* "(Baha'u'llah: *Prayers and Meditations,* Page: 69)

If Baha'u'llah can call forth men and women from over the entire earth, who respond to the call stated in the paragraph above, there will be a true 'rapture' occurring and, come to think of it, it will have a physical as well as spiritual aspect. The physical aspect will be the building of a new earth and a kingdom that man has awaited and hoped for ever since Christ prayed for it, a 'Kingdom' of God and the Will of God to be done, *"on earth, as it is in heaven."*

Thus, not a 'rapture' in the traditional Christian sense, where two people would be driving a car and one would be 'taken up in the rapture' while the other one would be left behind. Rather, a 'rapture' in which millions upon millions of men and women will come into the knowledge of their true unity, the oneness of mankind, and will follow Baha'u'llah—Christ Returned—into a future of unity and peace, at once hoped for by man and planned for by God.

Baha'u'llah does not ignore man's capacity for inhumanity, which reached its zenith in the Twentieth Century. In a prayer, He states: *"Darkness hath encompassed every land, O my God, and caused most of Thy servants to tremble. I beseech Thee, by Thy Most Great Name* [a title of Baha'u'llah] *to raise in every city a new creation that shall turn towards Thee, and shall remember Thee amidst Thy servants, and shall unfurl by virtue of their utterances and wisdom the ensigns of Thy victory, and shall detach them-*

selves from all created things." (Baha'u'llah: *Prayers and Meditations*, Page: 171) This is what is happening right now in human history, the formation of a 'new creation' in cities and hamlets around the world, a true rapture, an actual coming to life, a resurrection of the people of the world.

REDEMPTION:
(See 'Forgiveness' above in this list)

RELICS:

When Christians, mainly Catholic Christians, but also some Orthodox and Protestants, revere relics, it seems to me to be a sincere attempt to connect with the historical Christ. A Christian preacher, the famous Harry Emerson Fosdick, had a well-known sermon about Jesus called: 'A Real Man, not a Myth.' Jesus was real and it was, at least to me, fully understandable that His followers would want to hold on to His memory in some physical ways.

Some Christian cynics have noted that there are enough small pieces of the original Cross of Calvary to make a thousand crosses, but I reject this cynicism, for the reason I have stated. And, Baha'is understand this impulse to hold onto the historical figure of the Manifestation of God. The Baha'is have kept every possible physical connection to Baha'u'llah, including clothing, a hat that He wore, pens that He used and numerous other things. They are kept carefully in an Archives building on Mt. Carmel (the Old Testament's 'Mountain of the Lord') in Haifa, Israel, which is the Baha'i International Center.

The Archives Building on Mt. Carmel, housing items associated with the central figures of the Baha'i Faith.

The prison cell of two rooms where Baha'u'llah was kept for several years with His family and seventy of His followers has been set aside by the government of Israel as a Holy Place of the Baha'is and you may see it in the 'Old City' of Akka, if you travel to Israel. Let me mention that if you do go to Israel, in addition to seeing the many wonderful historical places that remind one of Jesus and His life, you may also visit what the Israelis call 'The Baha'i Gardens' at the Baha'i World Center in the city of Haifa. There are many other interesting places to visit, including that prison cell, across the bay from Haifa, in the city of Akka.

Letters that Baha'u'llah sent to individuals are treated as priceless and Holy documents and are kept on Mt. Carmel as well, in a 'Center for the Study of the Texts.' As you may know, we have all the documents that Baha'u'llah wrote, in their original form, some in His handwriting, others in the hand of His secretary, but with His seal. The Baha'is are living with a great deal of excitement, since ten to twenty percent of Baha'u'llah's writings have not yet been translated from their original Persian or Arabic into English.

In the early Twenty-First Century, for example, an entirely new book of His letters, or as Baha'is call them, 'Tablets' will be translated and released to the world. This 'flow' of Baha'u'llah's Revelation into English translation will undoubtedly continue for many decades. Imagine the excitement that you would feel if you were a Christian living in Rome in the year 158 AD and you realized that next year a new book of Jesus' letters would be released in your native language. If you can imagine that, you know how Baha'is feel as the year turns to the new century. This Revelation is very close to us, Baha'u'llah having lived in the lifetime of your great, great grandfather, if you are twenty years old in 2000.

In closing, there are no 'relics' spoken of by Baha'is, other than those that one can see in the museum atmosphere of the Archives Building at the Baha'i World Center on Mt. Carmel. In this way, Baha'is can be assured of the absolute authenticity of those physical items connected to the historical person of Baha'u'llah.

RESURRECTION/ASCENSION:

QUESTION: What do Baha'is believe, or as you will probably remind me, what did Baha'u'llah teach about the Resurrection of Jesus Christ? Someone told me that Baha'is don't believe it occurred.

RESPONSE: This is certainly not the case. The Resurrection did occur and this very central event of Christianity is recognized by 'Abdu'l-Baha, Baha'u'llah's Son and main interpreter, as being all-important to early Christians and a central belief of Christians throughout the ages. The confusion may arise from 'Abdu'l-Baha's statement that the Resurrection is to be understood as a 'spiritual event' rather than a 'material event.'

He asked us to base our understanding of the Resurrection by focusing on the spiritual renewal of the disciples' Faith in Jesus rather than on a materialistic renewal. While 'Abdu'l-Baha said that the Resurrection of a Manifestation is not physical, He did not say anywhere that the disciples did not witness, in a spiritual way, the Risen Christ. In fact, 'Abdu'l-Baha, speaking of how the apostles responded after Christ's crucifixion, said: *"They saw Christ living, helping and protecting them."* ('Abdu'l-Baha: *Some Answered Questions*, Pages: 106-107)

Their important witness was spiritual, the event was spiritual and our understanding of it should be spiritual. In a similar manner, the Ascension of Christ and of Baha'u'llah are spiritual, not material events, for otherwise, we would focus on a miraculous, non-scientific, confusing belief and entirely miss the deep and beautiful spiritual meaning of their reunion with God at the end of their time on earth. Their triumph over the grave and their reunion with the Divine are the facts of a spiritual realm.

Here are the actual words of 'Abdu'l-Baha: *"The meaning of Christ's resurrection is as follows: the disciples were troubled and agitated after the martyrdom of Christ. The Reality of Christ, which signifies His teachings, His bounties, His perfections and His spiritual power, was hidden and concealed for two or three days after His martyrdom, and was not resplendent and manifest. No, rather it was lost, for the believers were few in number and were troubled and agitated.*

"The Cause of Christ was like a lifeless body; and when after three days the disciples became assured and steadfast, and began to serve the Cause of Christ, and resolved to spread the divine teachings, putting His counsels into practice, and arising to serve Him, the Reality of Christ became resplendent

and His bounty appeared; His religion found life; His teachings and His admonitions became evident and visible. In other words, the Cause of Christ was like a lifeless body until the life and the bounty of the Holy Spirit surrounded it. Such is the meaning of the resurrection of Christ, and this was a true resurrection. " ('Abdu'l-Baha: *Some Answered Questions*, Page: 104)

Anyone who had been around Jesus or Baha'u'llah knew that after physical death, their Spirit was very much 'alive' and was now with God, Who had sent them forth originally to earth for the 'salvation' and 'quickening' of mankind. For more information, read *Some Answered Questions by* 'Abdu'l-Baha or *Gleanings from the Writings of Baha'u'llah.* Also, read chapters six and ten of this book/conversation.

RETURN OF CHRIST:

QUESTION: Baha'i friends have told me that Baha'u'llah claimed to be the Return of Christ. I told them that this claim has been made literally hundreds of times in history, usually by people who are mentally deranged or pretenders or false prophets. How can I be sure that Baha'u'llah isn't in this category?

RESPONSE: You really can't be sure He is or isn't until you investigate. All I can tell you in this brief response is that He did make this claim, clearly and directly. He wrote to a community of Jews that if they wished to crucify Jesus again, then they should crucify Him. He said to them: *"O Jews! If ye be intent on crucifying once again Jesus, the Spirit of God, put Me to death, for He hath once more, in My person, been made manifest unto you."* (Baha'u'llah: *Gleanings*, Page: 101) Before we think that Baha'u'llah was being 'accusing' toward the Jews (as

Christians have sometimes been), let me share that this letter was very loving. Incidentally, many of the Jews of Hamadan, Iran (Persia) became Baha'u'llah's followers after receiving the letter that contained the above sentence.

Throughout this book, the greatest emphasis is put upon Baha'u'llah's claim to be the 'Return of Christ.' Since I come from a Christian background, I realize that this is more than anything what a committed Christian would want to know. Read chapters four, five and six, but this theme of the 'Return of Christ' runs throughout this conversation/book.

Baha'u'llah wrote a letter especially to Christians called 'Letter to the Christians' and you will be able to read it in its entire form in one of the chapters of this conversation/book. In the 'Letter to the Christians,' Baha'u'llah says: *"Tell Me then: Do the sons* [that is, the Christians] *recognize the Father, and acknowledge Him, or do they deny Him, even as the people aforetime denied Him (Jesus)?"*

And *"Open the doors of your hearts. He Who is the Spirit (Jesus) verily, standeth before them, We, in truth, have opened unto you the gates of the Kingdom. Will ye bar the doors of your houses in My face? . . . He, verily, hath again come down from Heaven even as He came down from it the first time."* (Baha'u'llah: *Tablets of Baha'u'llah*, Pages 10-11)

As you read this conversation/book, you will hear a theme that comes from a Christian theologian (J. B. Phillips) who once observed that Jesus is one of three things. He is either, the theologian said, a madman, or a charlatan/faker or, the only other choice is that He is Who He said He was. The same three choices exist for Baha'u'llah. Join the conversation and learn what Baha'u'llah has to say about Christ returning *"in My Person."*

REVELATION:

QUESTION: I've already heard you refer to Baha'u'llah's 'Revelation' and I must say to you that I object to the use of 'Revelation' to refer to Baha'u'llah's 'Writings.' Are they not simply the 'writings' of a man, who is perhaps wise and spiritual, but nevertheless, the writings of a mere man, not a Messenger of God, or as you Baha'is call it, a 'Manifestation'?

RESPONSE: This discussion came up above in this list under 'Baptism.' You may wish to review that section. I won't repeat it entirely, but let me remind you briefly of what was said there, namely, that both Jesus and Baha'u'llah said that the things they said did not come from themselves, but from God. Jesus directly said: *"The words that I speak to you I do not speak on My own authority; but the Father who dwells in Me does the works"* (John 14:10) and *"For I have not spoken on My own authority; but the Father who sent Me gave Me a command, what I should say and what I should speak."* (John 12:49) Clearly, Jesus felt His words were God's words, that is, 'Revelation.'

Baha'u'llah said the following: *"I can utter no word, O my God, unless I be permitted by Thee, and can move in no direction until I obtain Thy sanction."* (Baha'u'llah: *Prayers and Meditations*, Page: 208) Sounds very much like that quote from Jesus, doesn't it? He also told His followers that what He 'revealed' to them had been *"sent down unto thee from the Throne of thy Lord."* (Baha'u'llah: *Gleanings*, Page: 144) He described His Revelation as *"the Bread which cometh down from Heaven."* (Baha'u'llah: *Gleanings*, Page: 195)

So, it appears that both Baha'u'llah and Jesus felt their words were from God. They both felt that God was speaking through them. Baha'u'llah said: *"My holy, My divinely ordained Revelation may be likened unto an ocean in whose depths are concealed innumerable pearls of great price, of surpassing luster. It is the duty of every seeker to bestir himself and strive to attain the shores of this ocean . . . "* (Baha'u'llah: *Gleanings*, Page: 326)

At one point, Baha'u'llah wrote letters to many of the Kings and Rulers of the world, including Napoleon III. Later, He wrote to another person, suggesting that the other person read what *"God sent"* to Napoleon III. Evidently, when Jesus and Baha'u'llah and the other Manifestations of God speak (or write!) they feel that when they speak, write or act, it is God Who is acting . . . through them.

Is what Baha'u'llah wrote 'Revelation'? Everything depends upon Who Baha'u'llah is. If He is Christ Returned, if He is the *"Father"* of all mankind, sent and manifested by God to heal and unite a torn and failing world, then it is 'Revelation.' If not, it is just the 'Writings' of a wise and good man. Each man and woman and young person in the world has the opportunity now to decide Who Baha'u'llah is. If they recognize Him as the 'Promise of all Ages,' they will want to step toward *"the shores of this ocean"* of Baha'u'llah's Revelation.

SACRIFICE:

QUESTION: What about sacrifice? What does Baha'u'llah teach?

RESPONSE: Well, just several sentences above, we quoted Baha'u'llah saying that He had *"sacrificed His life that ye may be quickened."* In a prayer of thanks to God, Baha'u'llah says: *"I yield Thee thanks, O my God, for that Thou hast offered me up as a sacrifice in Thy path, and made me a target for the arrows of afflictions as a token of Thy love* *for Thy servants, and singled me out for all manner of tribulation for the regeneration of Thy people.* " (Baha'u'llah: *Prayers and Meditations*, Page: 154)

From His mid-thirties, until the end of His life (forty years later), Baha'u'llah was either banished from his native country or imprisoned, or under 'house arrest.' He was never again 'free' in the political sense. He was beaten, poisoned, imprisoned, tortured and chained as He brought God's healing message to the world and we hear Him say that He had *"consented to be bound with chains that mankind may be released from its bondage, and hath accepted to be made a prisoner within this most mighty Stronghold that the whole world may attain unto true liberty. He hath drained to its dregs the cup of sorrow, that all the peoples of the earth may attain unto abiding joy, and be filled with gladness.* " (Baha'u'llah: *Gleanings*, Page: 99)

Baha'u'llah suffered many tribulations over forty years of banishment from His homeland and imprisonment in one of the world's worst prisons. However, He said these *"tribulations"* had a Divine purpose: *"I have accepted to be tried by manifold adversities for no purpose except to regenerate all that are in Thy heaven and on Thy earth.* " (Baha'u'llah: *Prayers and Meditations*, Page: 198)

Baha'u'llah said this 'Regeneration' would take place as the men and women of earth realize that the *"Father"* of all mankind has come, bringing a Revelation that would *"recreate their hearts and immortalize their souls.* " (Baha'u'llah: *Prayers and Meditations*, Page: 198)

SALVATION:

QUESTION: I know already from reading the section above called 'Forgiveness' that Baha'is believe in 'Salvation.' But, as I said in a question before, Christians believe that salvation can only come through belief in

Jesus Christ. That is why He is called the 'Savior,' because He offers salvation. Christians don't believe this comes through anyone else or in any other way.

RESPONSE: I'm from a Christian background. So, I realize that Christians believe salvation can only come through Christ and that God's Appearance in history has happened only once (or twice, if Moses is counted). However, Baha'u'llah taught that salvation comes and is offered to women and men each and every time God manifests Himself in a full way in human history.

First, let me suggest you read chapters one and two: 'Why Questions from Christians was Written' and 'How a Christian became a Baha'i.' Baha'u'llah asks us to widen our understanding of God and His purpose in history to the point where we may be able to recognize that God has been guiding us all along, Manifesting Himself at many different times in history, to many different peoples. With plan and purpose, God has been shepherding us toward this moment of time in which we now live, during which a great ingathering of the people of earth will occur, and during which time we will realize our oneness and enact our unity. The result will be the peace that has been long prophesied, and awaited.

In this 'plan of God,' His purpose has been progressively revealed. (see chapter four of this conversation/book: 'Progressive Revelation: A New Way of Understanding History' and chapter five: 'Manifestation: A New Way of Understanding How God Reveals Himself.') God progressively reveals Himself, each time He sends a 'Manifestation of Himself. Whenever this 'Manifestation' appears in human history, 'salvation' of individuals and of the world is dependent upon individual men and women recognizing, accepting and following that Manifestation

The world is renewed as these men and women set

forth in their lives and in their communities the deeds and goals that the teachings of the Manifestation and His regenerating power have called forth. Baha'u'llah more than once referred to this process as the true meaning of 'Resurrection,' indicating that this is the way that a dead or dying world can be brought to new life.

As Baha'u'llah put it, the purpose of His Revelation was *"the regeneration of the whole world, and the establishment of the unity of its peoples, and the salvation of all them that dwell therein."* (Baha'u'llah: *Gleanings*, Page: 243) In a letter to a certain man, Baha'u'llah inserts a prayer to God to *"Suffer this servant, I beseech Thee, to attain unto that which is the cause of his salvation in every world of Thy worlds."* (Baha'u'llah: *Prayers and Meditations*, Page: 251) He told the people of the earth to enter the *"Ark"* which *"God hath ordained for the people of Baha."* [a short form of the name of Baha'u'llah] *"Verily, it passeth over land and sea. He that entereth therein is saved, and he that turneth aside perisheth."* (Baha'u'llah: *Epistle to the Son of the Wolf*, Page: 139)

In language reminiscent of Jesus, Baha'u'llah says: *"O ye who are as dead! The Hand of Divine bounty proffereth unto you the Water of Life. Hasten and drink your fill. Whoso hath been re-born in this Day, shall never die; whoso remaineth dead, shall never live."* (Baha'u'llah: *Gleanings*, Page: 213)

He further said that all His Revelation, His *"utterance"* exists only for the *"Regeneration"* and *"salvation"* of the people of the world and, as to salvation, Baha'u'llah tells us that He has *"come for your sakes"* and has *"borne the misfortunes of the world for your salvation."* He wonders aloud why we fail to recognize Him: *"Flee ye the One Who hath sacrificed His life that ye may be quickened?"* (Baha'u'llah: *Tablets of Baha'u'llah*, Page: 10) Finally, Baha'u'llah says: *"Blessed the soul that hath been raised to life through My quickening breath.*" (Baha'u'llah: *Tablets of Baha'u'llah*, Page: 16)

SATAN:
(See 'Devil' in the list above.)

SAVIOR:

Please read chapters one and two of this conversation/book. In them, I try to share with you the background I was privileged to experience in my early years, growing up in a parsonage, with two wonderful parents, both fully and wonderfully dedicated to Christ. At fifteen years of age, I gave my life to Jesus Christ in an experience of salvation, so that I have always regarded Jesus as my Lord and Savior. I would not be a Baha'i today if I did not believe that Baha'u'llah was the Return to the World of that 'Lord and Savior.'

In the Baha'i writings, Jesus is spoken of as 'Savior' numerous times and I want to direct you to the top of this list, where Jesus heads this list of topics. Please read that section for fuller information. Also, please read chapter six, which is 'A Baha'i Considers the Place of Jesus Christ in History.'

QUESTION: Well, the question I want to ask is whether Jesus is the one and only Lord and Savior of all the people in the world, as Christians believe.

RESPONSE: Jesus is Lord and Savior to me, as I explained. In my twenty-second year of life, I had to make a decision about Baha'u'llah, who said He was the Return of Christ to the world. I decided He was Who He said He was. Therefore, I had to follow my Jesus, wherever He led me. I'm glad I did. Where Baha'is and Christians probably differ is that Christians, as you say, believe Jesus is the 'one and only' Manifestation of God and therefore, the only possible Savior.

By contrast, Baha'u'llah has taught the Baha'is to believe that each time a Manifestation of God's Full Presence in history appears, that Person is a 'Savior' providing salvation to the people of that time. Baha'u'llah further says that the entire world into which a Manifestation is sent by God is greatly in need of a Savior (as ours is today).

Baha'u'llah speaks of Himself, saying: *"He hath come for your salvation"* and many other passages in His Writings indicate His role as 'Savior,' in bringing 'salvation' to the people of earth. (Baha'u'llah: *Proclamation of Baha'u'llah*, Page: 78) Baha'u'llah refers to Jesus as 'Savior' and He urges us to understand that 'salvation' comes from God, through the Manifestation of Himself in history *"in the form of the human temple."* When Moses or Buddha or Zoroaster, Muhammad, Jesus or Baha'u'llah appear, They offer God's gift of salvation to individuals and to the world. Those that turn away from them, He says, do not receive this salvation and are (as both Christ and Baha'u'llah said) spiritually 'dead.'

QUESTION: There is a question that has been bothering me for some time. I don't quite know how to phrase it, but it is this: Are you saying that if a new Manifestation appears, such as Baha'u'llah, offering salvation, does it mean that people cannot still find salvation in Christ?

RESPONSE: A good way to approach this question is to go to the New Testament and listen to Jesus carefully. When we do, we find that when a new Manifestation appears, such as Jesus Christ, one must (1) recognize Him, (2) accept Him, (3) then follow Him. We find

Jesus saying that salvation comes only through Him, don't we? However, that couldn't mean that Jesus invalidated the Old Testament, especially since He quoted the scriptures of Judaism dozens of times, as did St. Paul and Peter and other New Testament writers.

The other way to approach this question is to remember what Jesus said about the difficulty of putting the *"new Wine"* into *"old bottles."* Surely Jesus was not condemning the sincere Jew, but He did say that for those who met Him and turned away, that they were spiritually *"dead."* Baha'u'llah, like Jesus, indicated that those who became aware of Him and recognized that He was Jesus Returned would attain the 'Water of Life.' This is what He said: ***"O ye who are as dead! The Hand of Divine bounty proffereth unto you the Water of Life. Hasten and drink your fill. Whoso hath been re-born in this Day, shall never die; whoso remaineth dead, shall never live."*** (Baha'u'llah: *Gleanings*, Page: 213) Check John 11:25-6 for a statement from Jesus that is strikingly similar. Please consult chapters thirteen and fourteen for a much more full treatment of this issue.

SIN:

QUESTION: In my experience, Christianity is the one religion that takes the problem of human 'sin' seriously. To Christians, man is 'fallen' and has a sinful nature that causes individuals to make sinful choices and to do bad or evil acts. This is the explanation of why there is so much that is wrong with the world and with human beings. What does the Baha'i Faith, or what does Baha'u'llah say about 'sin'?

RESPONSE: Baha'u'llah says quite a bit about sin. But first, I have to tease you a little. Aren't you forgetting that the religion of Judaism practically invented the modern idea of sin? The story of Adam and Eve isn't from the New Testament, but from the Old Testament. And if we asked a Hindu, they would probably tell us that the idea of 'sin' goes still farther back, thousands of years before Moses.

I'm a student of the religions of the world, and I can assure you that the idea of 'sin' is in every one of the religions of the world. But, the Christian Faith bears the mark of its mother, the Jewish Faith, and follows very closely the Jewish idea of man having a sinful nature, even down to adopting the Jewish explanation of how that sinful nature got there in the first place. As I mentioned before, some early Church Fathers wanted to do away with the Old Testament, but finally were persuaded to keep it, not only because Jesus quoted it frequently, but also because they would have lost the story of Adam and Eve and the explanation given in that story as to why man has a nature 'inclined toward sin.'

The Christian and Baha'i ideas of man's nature differ somewhat, but not greatly. Read Chapter Nine, 'Similarities and Differences of the Christian and Baha'i Faiths.' Also, you might want to look at the list above where 'Evil' is discussed under the topic 'Devil.' Briefly, Christians believe in 'Original Sin,' a teaching stating that each and every baby born to man has a nature that is bent in the direction of sinful thought and expression. I'm well aware that not every Christian believes this, but it is in the creeds of almost all Christian denominations, including Catholic, Methodist, Baptist, Episcopal, Presbyterian, to name a few.

The Baha'i idea is that man has two natures, one a higher, spiritual nature, the other a 'lower,' animal nature. If individual souls experience salvation and are taught and led to the expression of their higher spiritual nature, and if they are taught and led to learn to control their lower, animal nature, they will more often express themselves in thinking and actions that are constructive and beneficial to them and to others. But, if their lower animal nature gains control, they will think and behave in a 'sinful' way.

Every human individual is 'loaded' both with that higher spiritual nature and the lower animal nature and the outcome of a life is whether or not the lower animal nature is properly controlled, managed and its energy directed toward constructive goals, while the higher, spiritual nature is strengthened and directed toward goals set forth by God, as seen in the teachings of the Manifestation of God, whether it be Jesus, Buddha or Baha'u'llah.

However, if salvation is not offered and accepted and the contest is between this 'higher' and 'lower' nature, then the lower, animal nature will often win the struggle. Unless mankind enters into salvation, as offered by God through the Manifestations of Himself, such as in Jesus and Baha'u'llah, then man will drift and slide into selfishness and sin and into the type of condition that we see in the world today.

Personally, I do not see much difference between the Christian and Baha'i teachings on the nature of man, except one important one, namely, that the Baha'is do not believe that the animal nature of man is inherently bad; rather, that it will turn into something positively destructive and even evil if it is not put under the control of the higher spiritual nature, strengthened and directed by 'salvation.'

The doctrine of original sin as being a 'genetic disease,' passed down from mother to son and daughter, and based on the choices made by ancient ancestors, Adam and Eve, is not part of Baha'i belief, but the realities of the story of Adam and Eve are very much the

same as what Baha'is believe, when one looks at the whole
picture. However, though Baha'is do not believe in 'original sin' as just described, 'Abdu'l-Baha (Baha'u'llah's Son)
did say that there are *"...instinctive human tendencies toward error."* So, while the 'sin' is not, in Baha'i belief
'passed down' genetically, it is still there in every human
individual in an 'instinctive' way.

So however we conceive it, 'Sin' is an important reality in the life of men and women and Baha'u'llah refers
to it often. Here are some gleanings from His Revelation
on the subject of 'Sin.'

In fact, let me begin with a statement of Baha'u'llah's
that sounds very much like the idea of 'Original Sin': ***"I
implore Thee, O my God, . . . not to abandon me unto my
self, for my heart is prone to evil."*** (Baha'u'llah: *Prayers and
Meditations*, Page: 210) Baha'u'llah acknowledges that
human beings will be ***"prone to evil"*** if their lower, animal nature is allowed to run unbridled, uncontrolled.
They must experience 'salvation' that only the Manifestations of God can provide to overcome their lower nature.

He speaks of man as having a ***"base and appetitive
nature."*** (Baha'u'llah: *Gleanings*, Page: 161) (Which again
does not sound 'too different' from the reality of the
meaning of the teaching of 'Original Sin,' does it?) He
tells His followers to pray to God to ***"draw me out of the
depths of my corrupt and evil desires."*** (Baha'u'llah: *Prayers
and Meditations*, Page: 216) Baha'u'llah's Son 'Abdu'l-
Baha reminds man of his own nature and the nature of
God by saying, *"We are all sinners, and Thou art the Forgiver of sins".* (`Abdu'l-Baha: *Promulgation of Universal
Peace*, Page: 176)

'Abdu'l-Baha speaks of a *"veil of sinfulness"* ('Abdu'l-
Baha: *Baha'i Prayers* (US edition), Page: 71) that man
has placed between himself and God. Baha'u'llah also

speaks hopefully of the Grace and Mercy of God, Who, He says is *"not deterred by a multitude of sins from vouchsafing Thy bounty, and the flow of Whose gifts is not arrested by the withdrawal* [away from God and into 'sin'] *of the peoples of the world. From eternity the door of Thy grace hath remained wide open."* (Baha'u'llah: *Prayers and Meditations,* Page: 246) I hear an echo of the God that Jesus described in the Parable of the Prodigal Son, don't you?

Later in the same passage, Baha'u'llah pleads to God: *"Deny not Thy servants the wonders of Thy grace. Cause them to be made aware of Thee, that they may bear witness to Thy unity, and enable them to recognize Thee, that they may hasten towards Thee. Thy mercy hath embraced the whole creation, and Thy grace hath pervaded all things."* (Baha'u'llah: *Prayers and Meditations,* Page: 246) Baha'u'llah assures man that God is the *"forgiver of sins," "the pardoner"* and even says that sinful man can turn to God's *"ocean of forgiveness and pardon."* (Baha'u'llah: *Baha'i Prayers* (US), Page: 149)

Before we leave this topic, and I hope that you will read and investigate at greater length to get a full understanding of what the Baha'i Faith has to say about 'Sin,' 'Forgiveness' and 'Pardon,' let's turn to the New Testament. Jesus did many things that angered the Pharisees, but the act, which absolutely enraged them, was when He healed a man and told him: *"Son, your sins are forgiven you."* (Mark 2:5) They pointed out to Jesus that He was being 'blasphemous' because only God can forgive sins. As you know, Jesus responded to them that He did this *"that you may know that the Son of Man has power on earth to forgive sins."* (Mark 2:10)

Baha'u'llah says that this power to forgive sins that is possessed by all of the Manifestations is *"the real sovereignty"* and *"the power of God's chosen Ones"* (Baha'u'llah: The *Kitab-i-Iqan,* Page: 134) He then makes an amazing statement, one that may be as challenging to you as Jewish ears were challenged by Jesus' statement that He could forgive sins.

Baha'u'llah tells us that a certain man came to the prison in which Baha'u'llah was held, asking for forgiveness. Baha'u'llah forgave his sins, saying: *"We have attired his temple with the robe of forgiveness and adorned his head with the crown of pardon . . . Say: Be not despondent. After the revelation of this blessed verse it is as though thou hast been born anew from thy mother's womb. Say: Thou art free from sin and error. Truly God hath purged thee with the living waters of His utterance in His Most Great Prison."* (Baha'u'llah: *Tablets of Baha'u'llah,* Page: 77) Baha'u'llah was writing from the terrible prison in Akka, Palestine— now Israel—into which He had been thrown by the forces opposing Him. These were, of course, the same forces that opposed Jesus Christ—clergy and kings.

In this last statement that He can forgive sin, Baha'u'llah challenges us more than ever to decide Who He is. The Pharisees said 'only God can forgive sin.' Jesus showed them that the *"Son of God"* also had that power, a power given Him by God. Now, Baha'u'llah tells us that in His appearance as *"The Father,"* He too is able to forgive sins and even to free men and women from *"sin and error"* to the point where they would be *"born anew"* as if coming straight from their *"mother's womb."*

SOUL:

QUESTION: What do the Baha'i teachings say about the soul?

RESPONSE: Baha'u'llah speaks of the 'soul' often in His Writings, His Revelation. For example: *"O SON OF MAN! I loved thy creation, hence I created thee. Where-*

fore, do thou love Me, that I may name thy name and fill thy soul with the spirit of life." (Baha'u'llah: (Arabic) *Hidden Words*, Page: 4) And, Baha'u'llah says that God has *"endowed every soul with the capacity to recognize the signs of God.*"(Baha'u'llah: *Gleanings*, Pages: 105-106)

The soul, He tells us, is indestructible, eternal and capable of growth not only in this life but also in *"all the worlds of God."* *"And now concerning thy question regarding the soul of man and its survival after death. Know thou of a truth that the soul, after its separation from the body, will continue to progress until it attaineth the presence of God, in a state and condition which neither the revolution of ages and centuries, nor the changes and chances of this world, can alter. It will endure as long as the Kingdom of God, His sovereignty, His dominion and power will endure. It will manifest the signs of God and His attributes, and will reveal His loving-kindness and bounty.*" (Baha'u'llah: *Gleanings*, Pages: 155-156)

In the following passage, Baha'u'llah speaks of the soul as a *"sign of God"*: *"Thou hast asked Me concerning the nature of the soul. Know, verily, that the soul is a sign of God, a heavenly gem whose reality the most learned of men hath failed to grasp, and whose mystery no mind, however acute, can ever hope to unravel. It is the first among all created things to declare the excellence of its Creator, the first to recognize His glory, to cleave to His truth, and to bow down in adoration before Him. If it be faithful to God, it will reflect His light, and will, eventually, return unto Him. If it fail, however, in its allegiance to its Creator, it will become a victim to self and passion, and will, in the end, sink in their depths.*" (Baha'u'llah: *Gleanings*, Pages: 158-159)

In a stunning passage describing the 'nature' of the soul after death and the continuing purpose of its existence, He says: *"The nature of the soul after death can never be described, nor is it meet and permissible to reveal its whole character to the eyes of men. The Prophets and Messengers of God have been sent down for the sole purpose of guiding mankind to the straight Path of Truth. The purpose underlying Their revelation hath been to educate all men, that they may, at the hour of death, ascend, in the utmost purity and sanctity and with absolute detachment, to the throne of the Most High.*

"The light which these souls radiate is responsible for the progress of the world and the advancement of its peoples. They are like unto leaven which leaveneth the world of being, and constitute the animating force through which the arts and wonders of the world are made manifest. Through them the clouds rain their bounty upon men, and the earth bringeth forth its fruits." (Baha'u'llah: *Gleanings*, Pages: 156-157)

We have, apparently, much to learn about the soul. Echoing the words of Jesus that *"I still have many things to say to you, but you cannot bear them now."* (John 16:12-13), Baha'u'llah says: *"Verily I say, the human soul is, in its essence, one of the signs of God, a mystery among His mysteries. It is one of the mighty signs of the Almighty, the harbinger that proclaimeth the reality of all the worlds of God. Within it lieth concealed that which the world is now utterly incapable of apprehending."* (Baha'u'llah: *Gleanings*, Page: 160)

For the person who recognizes the new Manifestation of God, Jesus in His Day or Baha'u'llah in this Day, He says: *"At that hour will the Mystic Herald, bearing the joyful tidings of the Spirit, shine forth from the City of God resplendent as the morn, and, through the trumpet-blast of knowledge, will awaken the heart, the soul, and the spirit from the slumber of heedlessness. Then will the manifold favors and outpouring grace of the holy and everlasting Spirit confer such new life upon the seeker that he will find himself endowed with a new eye, a new ear, a new heart, and a new mind. He will contemplate the manifest signs of the universe, and will penetrate the hidden mysteries of the soul."* (Baha'u'llah: *Gleanings*, Page: 267)

There are very many references to the soul in Baha'u'llah's *'ocean'* (as He calls it) of Revelation. Read for yourself in the *Gleanings* (from the writings of Baha'u'llah) and in *Prayers and Meditations*. Here are several *'pearls'* taken from this *'ocean'*: *"O MY SERVANT! Free thyself from the fetters of this world, and loose thy soul from the prison of self. Seize thy chance, for it will come to thee no more."* (Baha'u'llah: (Persian) *Hidden Words*, Page: 40)

And: *"Blessed the soul that hath been raised to life through My quickening breath and hath gained admittance into My heavenly Kingdom. Blessed the man whom the sweet savours of reunion with Me have stirred and caused to draw nigh unto the Dayspring of My Revelation."* (Baha'u'llah: *Tablets of Baha'u'llah*, Page: 16)

Finally: *"Cast away that which ye possess, and, on the wings of detachment, soar beyond all created things. Thus biddeth you the Lord of creation, the movement of Whose Pen hath revolutionized the soul of mankind."* (Baha'u'llah: *Gleanings*, Page: 139)

SUFFERING:
(See 'Tribulations' below in this list).

TIME OF THE END:
(See 'Last Days' in this list).

TITHING:

QUESTION: Do Baha'is 'tithe'? Are they expected to give a tenth of their income to the Lord, as Christians are expected to do?

RESPONSE: No, they do not. However, they are expected to contribute toward their Faith, in whatever amounts they choose. In addition to regular contributions, however, there is something Baha'u'llah called 'The Right of God.' It is a Baha'i law that, from time to time, each Baha'i will value their property and, taking certain deductions for what is needed, will then give nineteen per-cent of the 'net' amount to the Faith. This would be done only several times at most in a lifetime. No one watches over your shoulder to see if it is done, but all Baha'is look forward to the time when they can contribute to the 'Right of God,' over and above their regular contributions, which they can offer at any time, or at regular times of worship.

QUESTION: But you said earlier when talking about the Bible that the Bible was 'the Word of God.' Why then, do Baha'is not tithe if that is what the Bible says to do?

RESPONSE: Baha'u'llah teaches that when a new Manifestation of God comes to mankind and to history, that all must turn to Him, hear His teachings and obey His commands. In the case of Jesus, some laws and arrangements from the Old Testament continued to be in force, but Jesus changed some laws and practices too, didn't He? The law of the Sabbath was changed but the 'Great Commandment' was kept intact. The point is that all had to turn to the new Manifestation of God—Jesus— and obey His new teachings.

The same is true when any new Manifestation of God comes to humanity. All must turn to Him, hear His teachings and obey Him. Baha'is thus turn to Baha'u'llah, Christ Returned we believe, and obey His laws. Tithing is not a law, but the 'Right of God' is in place, representing for Baha'is the Will of God.

TONGUES:

QUESTION: Do Baha'is speak in tongues?

RESPONSE: In the way of a Pentecostal Church, no, they do not. Most Christians, of course, do not speak in tongues today; some do. This is not the way of the Baha'is, but one must always remember that the Baha'i Faith is very young as religions go, only 157 years old at the turn of the Christian millennium. We cannot at this time know all that may be expressed as the Baha'i Faith grows and is taken up by the thousands of cultures over planet earth. Certainly, we will be pleasantly surprised by some of the responses and expressions of Faith that will be seen.

I have always believed (just a personal belief) that Pentecostals are very close to the 'Spirit' of the Baha'i Faith and to Baha'u'llah and therefore may eventually respond more quickly to Baha'u'llah than anyone else. If a Pentecostal Church, in its entirety, became Baha'i almost overnight, it would seem unlikely to me that the members would suddenly lose their ability to 'speak in tongues,' but that is for the future. But to be clear in responding to your question, there is no tradition of 'speaking in tongues' among the Baha'is (but please read on for a further comment).

QUESTION: Isn't your idea of an entire church deciding to become followers of Baha'u'llah a bit of wishful thinking? I doubt that this would happen.

RESPONSE: Well, all I can tell you is that it has already happened. Re-read the Book of Acts. In the Christian era, entire synagogues, villages and, much later, entire ethnic groups of people came to Faith in Jesus

Christ in an 'entry by troops.' One of my favorites was the Christian missionary Ufilas (The Little Wolf) who entered German pagan villages in the fourth century. He preached Christ and, just for good measure, often topped off his sermon by personally chopping down 'sacred' trees that stood in the center of their community which were supposed to be the home of their god. When the god of that tree failed to strike down Ufilas, entire peoples of those regions instantly became followers of Christ. He also translated the Gospel into their languages, creating the first written expression of several of those languages.

This same phenomenon has occurred in the history of the Baha'i Faith. Large numbers of people from Churches, mosques, Muslim religious groups and theological schools in Iran, religious leaders, whole villages in Africa and India, entire groups of people have declared their Faith in 'entry by troops.' Baha'u'llah once wrote to a Jewish community of Hamadan, Persia (now Iran) and as a result of that letter and the Baha'i teaching there, nearly the entire community of Jews of that city became Baha'is. A great number of the Zoroastrians of Persia (Iran) became Baha'is within Baha'u'llah's lifetime. The Universal House of Justice (the Baha'i International body set up by Baha'u'llah) told the Baha'i world in the 1990's to expect the imminent 'entry by troops' of peoples and groups around the world.

The Universal House of Justice, at the center of an Arc of buildings on Mt. Carmel, the 'Vineyard' of the Lord.

However, as to the enthusiasm that is seen in the Book of Acts, where 'tongues' are mentioned, you may want to read an amazing document called '*The Dawnbreakers*,' which is a first-hand account of the early Baha'is. What you will see and hear in the 'Dawnbreakers' is strikingly similar to what you saw and heard in the Book of Acts. The enthusiasm (the very word means 'filled with spirit') of the early Baha'is is breathtaking. They truly did 'break the dawn' of a new Day. You may be very interested to read their story.

Baha'u'llah did say to a man who had just expressed his belief in Him that *"Whoso is enabled in these days to solemnly affirm this truth,* [that is, the recognition of Baha'u'llah] *hath attained unto all good, and the heavenly Spirit shall descend upon him in the daytime and in the night season, shall graciously assist him to glorify the Name of his Lord and suffer him to unloose his tongue and uphold with his words the Cause of his Lord, the Merciful, the Compassionate"* (Baha'u'llah: *Tablets of Baha'u'llah,* Page: 181) So, in the light of this passage, any 'speaking in tongues' that Baha'is will do will not be in strange unknown languages, but in brilliantly God-inspired words flowing forth from the enthusiasm they feel in 'breaking the dawn' of this New Day and announcing the coming of the *'Father of all Mankind.'*

This is the same passage where Baha'u'llah announces: *"Say, God is my witness! The Promised One Himself hath come down from heaven, seated upon the crimson cloud with the hosts of revelation on His right, and the angels of inspiration on His left . . . "* (Baha'u'llah: *Tablets of Baha'u'llah*, Page: 182)

Before we see this statement as fantastic or misguided, this would be a good time to remember that Jesus said, while standing at His trial, accused of criminal and blasphemous acts, that those in His presence would see Him *" . . . sitting at the right hand of the Power, [that is, God] and coming with the clouds of heaven."* (Mark 14:62) At another time He said: *"All authority has been given to Me in heaven and on earth."* (Matt 28:18) At the time that He said this, He was an unemployed, wandering carpenter, apparently powerless, standing on the shore of Kinnereth, the Sea of Galilee, talking to a group of uneducated, working-class disciples.

So, my question to myself and to you is this: What are we going to do with Jesus and Baha'u'llah (who claims to be Jesus returned)? They talk of 'riding on clouds,' being 'from heaven,' claiming 'oneness' with God, they say they have 'all power' and are 'sitting at the right hand of God.' Are we going to call them 'mad'? Cart them off to a mental hospital? Are we going to call them 'fakes,' 'charlatans'? What shall we think? What are we going to do? This question has to get answered, doesn't it?

I put my answer together, for Jesus, fifty years ago, and for Baha'u'llah, more than forty years ago. My answer, with Jesus and also with Baha'u'llah, is that Jesus, the *"Son of God"* and Baha'u'llah *"the Father"* were the sanest Beings ever to walk the earth. Their sanity is our salvation, in my understanding. What do you think?

TRANSFIGURATION:

Here is a passage from 'Abdu'l-Baha, Baha'u'llah's Son, which explains the Baha'i belief in the 'transfiguration' as a 'spiritual vision and a scene of the Kingdom':

"Thou didst ask as to the transfiguration of Jesus, with Moses and Elias and the Heavenly Father on Mount Tabor, as referred to in the Bible. This occurrence was perceived by the disciples with their inner eye, wherefore it was a secret hidden away, and was a spiritual discovery of theirs.

"Otherwise, if the intent be that they witnessed physical forms, that is, witnessed that transfiguration with their outward eyes, then there were many others at hand on that plain and mountain, and why did they fail to behold it? And why did the Lord charge them that they should tell no man? It is clear that this was a spiritual vision and a scene of the Kingdom. Wherefore did the Messiah bid them to keep this hidden, 'till the Son of Man were risen from the dead,'-that is, until the Cause of God should be exalted, and the Word of God prevail, and the reality of Christ rise up." ('Abdu'l-Baha: *Selections*, Page: 162)

TRIBULATION:

QUESTION: I don't exactly know how to ask this question. I'm wondering what Baha'is think or what Baha'u'llah taught about suffering and tribulation, about the 'tests' of life. Part of my question is about the suffering of Christ and I suppose you would broaden it out to the suffering of all the Manifestations of God, but really I am focused—I'm sure you understand—on the suffering of Jesus.

But is there some way that the suffering of Jesus and

others relates to the suffering, the tribulation that all human beings must go through, or do go through?

RESPONSE: You have touched on a major theme of the Baha'i Faith. You may want to turn to chapter six: 'Who do Men Say that I am?': A Baha'i considers the Place of Jesus Christ in History.' This chapter includes an important statement that Baha'u'llah made about Christ that is one of the most beautiful tributes to Christ and His teachings, His suffering and His influence upon history, that has ever been given, even by any Christian. Take a look, if you like. Meanwhile, here is just the beginning of that statement.

"Know thou that when the Son of Man yielded up His breath to God, the whole creation wept with a great weeping. By sacrificing Himself, however, a fresh capacity was infused into all created things. Its evidences, as witnessed in all the peoples of the earth, are now manifest before thee. The deepest wisdom which the sages have uttered, the profoundest learning which any mind hath unfolded, the arts which the ablest hands have produced, the influence exerted by the most potent of rulers, are but manifestations of the quickening power released by His transcendent, His all-pervasive, and resplendent Spirit." (Baha'u'llah: *Gleanings*, Pages: 85-86)

There is more to the statement, but you can read the rest in Chapter Six. Baha'u'llah teaches that the suffering of Jesus, and of Buddha, and of Muhammad and others have all contributed a *"quickening power"* to humanity. However, it is true, as far as I can tell, that no such statement as the one about Christ has even been penned by Baha'u'llah about any other Manifestation of God.

We must be careful, though, since Baha'u'llah cautioned the people of the world not to compare the Manifestations of God in their spiritual power, since: *"If thou*

*wilt observe with discriminating eyes, thou wilt behold Them
all abiding in the same tabernacle, soaring in the same heaven,
seated upon the same throne, uttering the same speech, and
proclaiming the same Faith. "* (Baha'u'llah: *Gleanings,* Page:
52) In the strictly spiritual sense, Baha'u'llah tells us we
are to make *"no distinction whatsoever between them. "*
(Baha'u'llah: *Gleanings,* Page: 187)

As for trials, tests and tribulations of the Manifestations, Baha'u'llah made it clear that Christ's suffering
and that of Muhammad and others, and of Himself, are
for the salvation of humanity. He said that His own 'tribulations' and suffering had a meaning and a purpose. He
prayed: *"O Lord my God! I yield Thee thanks for that Thou
hast made me the target of divers tribulations and the mark of
manifold trials, in order that Thy servants may be endued
with new life and all Thy creatures may be quickened. "*
(Baha'u'llah: *Prayers and Meditations,* Pages: 146-147) In
another prayer, He offers up His very life to God, *"so
that the world might be quickened, and all its peoples be
united. "* (Baha'u'llah: *Epistle to the Son of the Wolf,* Page:
53)

Baha'u'llah's entire life was completely devoted to
the renewal of humanity, to 'quickening' the entire human race, literally building a new world by bringing it
into unity and peace. Because His message was so challenging, clergy and kings alike did everything possible to
still His voice. Chains, manacles, banishment from His
native land, life-long imprisonment, beatings, torture;
but nothing worked to keep Him away from His God-
appointed task. He tells us that for most of His life, He
was *"sitting under a sword hanging on a thread,"*
(Baha'u'llah: *Epistle to the Son of the Wolf,* Page: 94) that
He had been *"hemmed in by sorrows which no tongue can
describe. "* (Baha'u'llah: *Prayers and Meditations,* Page: 5)

Speaking of Himself, He said: *"Thou wast immersed*

all the days of Thy life beneath an ocean of tribulations. At one time Thou wast in chains and fetters; at another Thou wast threatened by the sword of Thine enemies. Yet, despite all this, Thou didst enjoin upon all men to observe what had been prescribed unto Thee by Him Who is the All-Knowing, the All-Wise." (Baha'u'llah: *Prayers and Meditations*, Page: 312)

Had Baha'u'llah been a mere man, He surely would have been discouraged. He would have turned back, retreated. But Baha'u'llah had been commissioned by God to appear in human history as *"the Father"* of all mankind, with the task of bringing all men and women, all the religions, all the cultures of earth into unity and fulfillment. Thus, Baha'u'llah could say, even in the face of so much discouragement and opposition: *"Should they hide Me away in the depths of the earth, yet would they find Me riding aloft on the clouds."* (Baha'u'llah: *Epistle to the Son of the Wolf*, Page: 53)

Baha'u'llah had been infused with the Divine Spirit, as is seen in this prayer: *"I know not what the water is with which Thou didst create me, or what the fire Thou didst kindle within me. I swear by Thy glory! I shall not cease to mention Thee, though all that are in Thy heaven and on Thy earth rise up against me. Thee will I magnify, in all circumstances, with a heart wholly rid of all attachment to the world and all that is therein."* (Baha'u'llah: *Prayers and Meditations*, Page: 182)

With this kind of inner experience, Baha'u'llah could say: *"Neither the hosts of the earth nor those of heaven can keep me back from revealing the things I am commanded to manifest. I have no will before Thy will, and can cherish no desire in the face of Thy desire. By Thy grace I am, at all times, ready to serve Thee and am rid of all attachment to any one except Thee."* (Baha'u'llah: *Prayers and Meditations*, Page: 184)

TRINITY:

QUESTION: I believe you said that Baha'is believe in the Trinity. Is that really true? Surely their belief is not exactly the same?

RESPONSE: You're right. Not exactly the same, but close! Baha'is obviously do believe in God, in the Divinity of Christ and Baha'u'llah mentions the Holy Spirit often. Baha'is believe that God is absolutely indivisible. He is One. God is an *"unknowable essence,"* says Baha'u'llah, Who nevertheless finds a way for man to know 'about' Him by manifesting Himself from time to time in human history. When God 'manifests' Himself in a Jesus or a Baha'u'llah, men can then see God and hear God, as when Jesus says *"He who has seen Me has seen the Father"* (John 14:9) or as when Baha'u'llah says: *"If it be your wish, O people, to know God and to discover the greatness of His might, look, then, upon Me . . . "* (Baha'u'llah: *Gleanings*, Page: 272)

When God manifests Himself in the Manifestations, it is as if God is the Sun and the rays of the Sun have found themselves reflected in a *"perfect mirror."* This perfect reflection of God manifested in what Baha'u'llah called *"the human temple"* is what Christians would call the second 'person' of the Trinity. And the third 'person' of the Trinity is the Holy Spirit, which God uses to communicate to man and to infuse the Manifestation of God with power and truth.

On one occasion, Baha'u'llah gave us an unusual glimpse of the inner workings of the mind of a Manifestation, when He said that if it had been only His choice as to whether to speak out to the world, He would have remained silent. But, He said, whenever *"I chose to hold my peace and be still, lo, the voice of the Holy Ghost, stand-*

ing on my right hand, aroused me, and the Supreme Spirit appeared before my face, and Gabriel overshadowed me, and the Spirit of Glory stirred within my bosom, bidding me arise and break my silence" (Baha'u'llah: *Gleanings,* Page: 103)

Read more on this and other Christian topics in *Baha'u'llah and the New Era* and *Some Answered Questions* from the reading list above.

TRUMPET:

You can read more on this in the list above under 'Last Days.'

VIRGIN BIRTH:

QUESTION: Do Baha'is believe in the Virgin Birth?

RESPONSE: They do. Baha'u'llah doesn't seem to speak to this directly, but there are several indirect references that give some understanding and guidance. Baha'u'llah speaks of the *"plight"* of Mary, saying: *"Reflect, what answer could Mary have given to the people around her? How could she claim that a Babe Whose father was unknown had been conceived of the Holy Ghost? Therefore did Mary, that veiled and immortal Countenance, take up her Child and return unto her home."* (Baha'u'llah: The *Kitab-i-Iqan,* Page: 56) From this quotation, we see that Baha'u'llah supported the role of the *"Holy Ghost"* in the birth of Jesus.

Then, His Son, 'Abdu'l-Baha, talks about the Virgin Birth in *Some Answered Questions* (See 'Reading List' at top of this list). He does not deny the existence of the Virgin Birth, but points out:

"The honor and greatness of Christ is not due to the fact that He did not have a human father, but to His perfections,

bounties and divine glory" and *"Christ was born and came into existence from the Holy Spirit."*

Both Baha'u'llah and 'Abdu'l-Baha always encourage us to look at the spiritual rather than the materialistic explanation of things, possibly because one of the central Baha'i teachings is the unity of science and religion. Looking at things in a materialistic way is what the ancient Greeks and Romans and other ancient religions did, where they needed to believe that their kings or leaders were produced by a human mother and a 'god' who came down to earth to father a child. This was their way of understanding how a great general or poet or playwright could be produced.

As a result, a number of Roman and Greek emperors, generals and poets were considered to have been born of a 'virgin' through contact with a 'god' or a divine being. By contrast Baha'i Teachings show that the spiritual understanding is to focus not on the 'miraculous' nature of Christ's birth, but on the life He lived, the teachings He brought and the salvation He offered to human individuals.

It is probably worth noting in passing that the greatest of the New Testament writers, St. Paul, must have agreed with this emphasis on the spiritual over the material meaning, since he never mentions the Virgin Birth. Also, that one of the two New Testament genealogies of Jesus is traced through Joseph, His father, which could not possibly have had a 'material' meaning in light of the Virgin Birth. I always took this to mean that the Gospel writers wanted to show that both the Father and Mother of Jesus had a spiritual 'connection' to Father Abraham, as they traced both sides of this family back to Abraham and even to Adam. See chapter nine for the interesting fact that Baha'u'llah is also descended from Abraham, as is Muhammad.

Notwithstanding all that has been said, the Baha'i Teachings on the Virgin Birth of Jesus Christ are quite clear, indicating at one point in the Writings that the Baha'i Faith is "in entire agreement" with Christian teaching on the subject of the Virgin Birth. (Quoted in Shoghi Effendi, *High Endeavors*, page 70) Shoghi Effendi, Baha'u'llah's Great-grandson, further quotes from a letter of 'Abdu'l-Baha that "Christ was not begotten in any ordinary way, but by the Holy Spirit." (Shoghi Effendi, Letter dated 22 December, 1948)

In that same letter, he again quoted 'Abdu'l-Baha saying that the Virgin Birth, according to Baha'i Teachings, is 'the great miracle of the Christian Faith.' The importance of the Virgin Birth, however, lies not in the physical fact, but in its spiritual significance as a sign of Christ's Sonship, of His Spirit's relationship with God's Spirit.

Finally, Baha'is would say that most arguments over different 'beliefs' occur when we focus on the material, literal aspects of things, rather than looking deeper at the true, spiritual meaning that lies hidden in a belief or an event. In this light, and taking into consideration the other items we have mentioned, it would seem that Christians and Baha'is believe nearly alike on the subject of Virgin Birth.

Baha'i belief never supports a conflict between science and religion, but says, rather, that they must agree. In this light, our understanding of the Virgin Birth would have to be in some terms that could be understood and accepted by a scientific mind. Even if that understanding may not be available today, a Baha'i would say that this belief must someday be in accord with scientific truth.

WILL OF GOD:

First, the Baha'i Faith has a strong belief that God does have a 'Plan' for mankind. This plan has been in existence all along, for the many eons of time that man and man's predecessors have been on our earth. The plan envisions, according to Baha'u'llah, that all human beings will come closer and closer to unity, finally realizing our oneness. And, Baha'u'llah tells us, this consummation of God's Plan for our human unity is now to be accomplished in the 'Day of God', the very day in which we now live.

How will this be accomplished? Baha'u'llah said that the spiritual energy released by His coming, His Teachings, and the community that He called into being will stimulate men and women to claim their oneness. But humankind is not alone in its struggle to accomplish this task. Baha'u'llah said: *"Verily I say, whatever is sent down from the heaven of the Will of God is the means for the establishment of order in the world and the instrument for promoting unity and fellowship among its peoples."* (Baha'u'llah: *Tablets of Baha'u'llah*, Page: 67)

And just as Jesus promised to aid His followers with *"power from on high"* (Luke 24:49), Baha'u'llah says to those who follow Him: *"We are with you at all times, and shall strengthen you through the power of truth. We are truly almighty. Whoso hath recognized me will arise and serve Me with such determination that the powers of earth and heaven shall be unable to defeat his purpose."* (Baha'u'llah: *Kitab-i-Aqdas*, Page: 33)

Baha'u'llah tells us that the *"Will of God is not limited by the standards of the people, and God doth not tread in their ways. Rather is it incumbent upon everyone to firmly adhere to God's straight Path."* (Baha'u'llah: *Tablets of Baha'u'llah*, Page: 109) This seems to be His way of reminding us that we don't know the answers, but God does, and that God is constructing the broad outlines of our future through the sending of a Manifestation of Himself in our own time. This new Manifestation–Baha'u'llah—will inspire us, direct us, lead us and infuse us with the energy and the will to build Christ's *"Kingdom of God"* and to do His will *"on earth, as it is in heaven."*

The following passage from the *Prayers and Meditations* of Baha'u'llah, is a meditation in which Baha'u'llah is teaching mankind about His own identity, His appearance in the world, and what this appearance means in terms of the 'Will of God'.

"Glorified be Thy name, O Lord my God! I beseech Thee by Him . . . Whom Thou hast sent down [that is, Baha'u'llah] *unto all Thy creatures and invested with Thy name, the All-Glorious, Whose will Thou hast ordained to be Thine own will, Whose self Thou hast decreed to be the revealer of Thine own Self, and His essence the Day-Spring of Thy wisdom, and His heart the treasury of Thine inspiration, and His breast the dawning-place of Thy most excellent attributes and most exalted titles, and His tongue the fountain-head of the waters of Thy praise and the well-spring of the soft-flowing streams of Thy wisdom, to send down upon us that which will enable us to dispense with all else except Thee, and will cause us to direct our steps towards the sanctuary of Thy pleasure and to aspire after the things Thou didst ordain for us according to Thine irrevocable decree.*

"Empower us, then, O my God, to forsake ourselves and cleave steadfastly to Him Who is the Manifestation of Thy Self, the Most Exalted, the Most High." (Baha'u'llah: Prayers *and Meditations*, Pages: 131-132)

Baha'u'llah closes this passage by saying: *"Powerful art Thou to do what Thou pleasest and to ordain what Thou willest."* (Baha'u'llah: *Prayers and Meditations*, Page: 132)

WORD OF GOD:

John 1:1 begins with the striking words: *"In the beginning was the Word, and the Word was with God, and the Word was God."* Christians believe, as do Baha'is, that this 'Word' is the motive force for the world being called into being, as the means for the 'creation' of the world. Christians would say, as in John 1:14: *"And the Word became flesh and dwelt among us,"* while Baha'u'llah similarly says that God causes this *'Word'* to be 'Manifested' to men in the form of the *"human temple."* Baha'u'llah continues to say that God, *"through the potency of His sublime Word, hath called into being the entire creation."* (Baha'u'llah: *Tablets of Baha'u'llah*, Page: 161)

This *'Word'* of God, Christians believe to be Christ, and Baha'is believe that the 'Word' does represent Christ but also that the *'Word'* was also in all of the other Manifestations of God. In fact, one of the best ways to understand Baha'i belief is to begin to see that the *'Word'* of God is the powerful, divine, generating force within not only Jesus, but also Moses, Buddha, Muhammad and others, and in this day, Baha'u'llah.

Baha'u'llah said that this *"word"* of God was indeed the force behind the creation, not only of the earth, but of the heavens as well. He speaks of: *"Thy Word which was hidden in Thy wisdom and whereby Thou didst create Thy heaven and Thy earth"* (Baha'u'llah: *Prayers and Meditations*, Pages: 219-220) and *"all else besides Him have been created through the potency of a word from His presence."* (Baha'u'llah: *Tablets of Baha'u'llah*, Page: 110)

Baha'u'llah tells us that this *'Word'* has *"animating energies, stirring within all created things"* that can *"instill new life into every human frame."* (Baha'u'llah: *Gleanings*, Page: 141) Stating that the world is in great need of healing and change, He says that only this new 'Word of God' *"has been endowed with capacity for such change."*

He tells us of the mission which God has given Him: *"Perplexing and difficult as this may appear, the still greater task of converting satanic strength into heavenly power is one that We have been empowered to accomplish. The Force capable of such a transformation transcendeth the potency of the Elixir itself.* ['Elixir' being the 'medicine' that the world needs] *The Word of God, alone, can claim the distinction of being endowed with the capacity required for so great and far-reaching a change."* (Baha'u'llah: *Gleanings*, Page: 200)

Baha'u'llah even says that it is this new 'Word' of God *"upon which must depend the gathering together and spiritual resurrection of all men . . . ."* (Baha'u'llah: *Gleanings*, Page: 97)

Baha'u'llah teaches us that this 'Word' of God is sent to humankind from time to time in human history to renew us, to provide 'salvation,' to point us in the right direction, to 'resurrect' us from the 'death' of our failures, and this time to lead us into earth-wide unity. He says this great event of God 'manifesting Himself' has occurred again in our time in His own appearance. Here is a passage of Baha'u'llah that is taken from a letter written specifically to Christians in which He dramatically announces His coming to the world.

"Lo! The Father is come, and that which ye were promised in the Kingdom is fulfilled! This is the Word which the Son [that is, Jesus] *concealed, when to those around Him He said: 'Ye cannot bear it now.' And when the appointed time was fulfilled and the Hour had struck, the Word shone forth above the horizon of the Will of God."* [He then speaks directly to Christians]: *"Say, verily, He* [that is, Jesus] *hath testified of Me, and I do testify of Him. Indeed, He hath purposed no one other than Me."* (Baha'u'llah: *Tablets of Baha'u'llah*, Page: 11)

Finally, Baha'u'llah counsels Christians: *"Beware, O followers of the Son, that ye cast it not behind your backs. Take ye fast hold of it. Better is this for you than all that ye possess. Verily He is nigh unto them that do good. The Hour which We had concealed from the knowledge of the peoples of the earth and of the favoured angels hath come to pass."* (Baha'u'llah: *Tablets of Baha'u'llah*, Page: 11)

We can wonder how this 'Word of God' will be able, in this day, to recreate and renew mankind? Baha'u'llah tells us that the 'Word' that existed before the creation of the world and which has now been manifested to men in His coming *"is the master key for the whole world, inasmuch as through its potency the doors of the hearts of men, which in reality are the doors of heaven, are unlocked"* (Baha'u'llah: *Tablets of Baha'u'llah*, Page: 173) and writes to a believer that this *'Word'* will *"quench . . . the lamp of idle fancy, of vain imaginings, of hesitation, and doubt, and mayest kindle, in the inmost chamber of thine heart, the newborn light of divine knowledge and certitude."* (Baha'u'llah: The *Kitab-i-Iqan*, Page: 49)

In an unforgettable prayer from the book *Prayers and Meditations*, Baha'u'llah shares with us what happens when God manifests Himself, telling us that God has *'called Him into being'* and showing us the part that the *'Word'* of God plays in this process. Let me quote a major portion of this prayer:

"Praised be Thou, O Lord my God! I supplicate Thee by Him Whom Thou hast called into being, [that is, Baha'u'llah] *Whose Revelation Thou hast ordained to be Thine own Revelation and His Concealment Thine own Concealment. Through His Firstness Thou hast confirmed Thine own Firstness, and through His Lastness Thou hast affirmed Thine own Lastness.*

"Through the power of His might and the influence of His sovereignty the mighty have apprehended Thine omnipotence, and through His glory they who are endowed with au-

thority have acknowledged Thy majesty and greatness. Through His supreme ascendancy Thy transcendent sovereignty and all-encompassing dominion have been recognized, and through His will Thine own will hath been revealed. Through the light of His countenance the splendors of Thine own face have shone forth, and through His Cause Thine own Cause hath been made manifest.

"Through the generative power of His utterance the whole earth hath been made the recipient of the wondrous signs and tokens of Thy sovereignty, and the heavens have been filled with the revelations of Thine incomparable majesty, and the seas have been enriched with the sacred pearls of Thine omniscience and wisdom, and the trees adorned with the fruits of Thy knowledge. Through Him all things have sung Thy praise, and all the eyes have been turned in the direction of Thy mercy. Through Him the faces of all have been set towards the splendors of the light of Thy countenance, and the souls of all have been inclined unto the revelations of Thy divine greatness.

"How great is Thy power! How exalted Thy sovereignty! How lofty Thy might! How excellent Thy majesty! How supreme is Thy grandeur—a grandeur which He Who is Thy Manifestation hath made known and wherewith Thou hast invested Him as a sign of Thy generosity and bountiful favor. I bear witness, O my God, that through Him Thy most resplendent signs have been uncovered, and Thy mercy hath encompassed the entire creation. " (Baha'u'llah: *Prayers and Meditations*, Pages: 294-295)

Then, Baha'u'llah gives us the clearest statement ever made in any scripture of exactly how the *'Word'* that is in the Manifestation of God acts to *"revolutionize"* the whole creation and begins to give birth to *"a new creation."* Here is the full quote:

"I testify that no sooner had the First Word proceeded, through the potency of Thy will and purpose, out of His mouth,

[that is, out of the mouth of Baha'u'llah] *and the First Call gone forth from His lips than the whole creation was revolutionized, and all that are in the heavens and all that are on earth were stirred to the depths.*

"Through that Word the realities of all created things were shaken, were divided, separated, scattered, combined and reunited, disclosing, in both the contingent world and the heavenly kingdom, entities of a new creation, and revealing, in the unseen realms, the signs and tokens of Thy unity and oneness." (Baha'u'llah: *Prayers and Meditations*, Page: 295)

Finally, in that same prayer, Baha'u'llah prays that God will: *"Rain down, therefore, upon us from the heaven of Thy mercy and the clouds of Thy gracious providence that which will cleanse us from the faintest trace of evil and corrupt desires, and will draw us nearer unto Him Who is the Manifestation of Thy most exalted and all-glorious Self. Thou art, verily, the Lord of this world and of the next, and art powerful to do all things."* (Baha'u'llah: *Prayers and Meditations*, Pages: 299-300)

Allow me to close this list of Christian topics and our conversation with two brief prayers of Baha'u'llah:

"O my Lord! Make Thy beauty to be my food, and Thy presence my drink, and Thy pleasure my hope, and praise of Thee my action, and remembrance of Thee my companion, and the power of Thy sovereignty my succorer, and Thy habitation my home, and my dwelling-place the seat Thou hast sanctified from the limitations imposed upon them who are shut out as by a veil from Thee.

"Thou art, verily, the Almighty, the All-Glorious, the Most Powerful." (Baha'u'llah: *Prayers and Meditations*, Page: 261)

And, this beloved, oft-quoted prayer:

"Blessed is the spot, and the house, and the place, and the city, and the heart, and the mountain, and the refuge, and the cave, and the valley, and the land, and the sea, and the

island, and the meadow where mention of God hath been made, and His praise glorified."
(Baha'u'llah: Family Life, Page: 385)

This ends the list of Christian subjects with *short answers* to questions that you may have had as to what the Baha'i Faith has to say on these subjects. Let me say once again that these answers are *brief* and do not give proper attention to any one of these items. Therefore, I refer you to the reading list at the beginning of this list and to the chapters in this conversation/book.

Take a look at chapter one. Join the conversation! And if you have a suggestion for the author regarding some subject that you think has been left out of this list of Christian topics, or if you just want to contact him, please take a look at chapter fifteen. Addresses, including email address are included. Please use them to be a participant of this book. The next and final chapter describes the acknowledgments I wish to make connected with the writing and production of this conversation/ book.

CHAPTER SEVENTEEN

ACKNOWLEDGMENT

My dear friend Gary Matthews has said that there can be no really good book without the contribution of many people. My experience in writing this conversation book has amply confirmed his judgment. From the time one is conceived and born, there are numerous persons whose input will show throughout one's life, but especially so when one attempts to write a book, and especially a book of this type.

My parents—though now with the Christ they loved, followed and served—were, in an emotional and spiritual way, intimately involved in the production of this book. I felt as if they were looking over my shoulders as I wrote. I am indebted to them not only for life itself but also for introducing me to the One Who was and is *"the way, the truth, and the life."* (John 14:6) I pray every day a prayer of Baha'u'llah's Son, 'Abdu'l-Baha: *"O God! Forgive my father and my mother their trespasses! Cast a glance of providence and usher them into Thy Kingdom. They educated me from the beginning of my life, but I was unable to compensate them for their labor. Do Thou reward them and grant them eternal life and make them dear in Thy Kingdom.* " (From *Star of the West*)

Baha'u'llah has assured me in His writings that He will indeed reward and 'compensate' them.

He says: *"One of the distinguishing characteristics of this most great Dispensation is that the kin of such as have recognized and embraced the truth of this Revelation...will, upon their death, if they are outwardly non-believers, be graciously invested with divine forgiveness and partake of the ocean of His Mercy."* (Baha'u'llah: *Family Life*, Page: 386)

My high-school English teacher, Mrs. Green, was here within me as I attempted, with whatever failings, to write clearly and correctly. My college teachers in Psychology, Philosophy, Religion, English, Shakespeare, all so stimulating and inspiring, were right here within, too. There were three that must be named: Dr. Wilfred George, Dr. Gavin Doughty, Sr. and Dr. Alfred Martin. I owe a debt to Mrs. Green and to these college professors and to others that simply cannot be repaid. Only God can reward them and I plead with Him to do so. I can't blame any of them for my failings or for any mistakes, but to the degree that something of worth has been created, I must share any credit with them and so many others that I cannot take the time to name.

There was a coterie of people who helped me find Baha'u'llah. They too were with me as I wrote this book. If I had not read Nels F. S. Ferre's *The Sun and the Umbrella*, I would never have gone to Vanderbilt University School of Divinity to study under his tutelage. If I had not gone to Vanderbilt, I would not have lived with a retired minister and his wife who so graciously offered their home free of charge to a penniless divinity student.

Had I not been in that home, I would not have read Stanwood Cobb's *Security for a Failing World*, the first book that explained the Baha'i Faith to me and introduced me to Dr. Cobb, with whom I would later have a lengthy, enduring relationship. Had I not been at Vanderbilt, I would not have met professors Dr. Nels F. S. Ferre, Dr. Bard Thompson, Dr. Kendrick Grobel, Dr. Roger Shinn and especially Dr. George Mayhew, all such excellent scholars and mentors. Had I not been in Dr. Mayhew's class, I would have missed meeting the person described below, who was invited to the class by Dr. Mayhew to speak on the Baha'i Faith.

That person—also departed to be with Christ and Baha'u'llah—has been present in my feelings, my thoughts and in my attempt to understand the best way to present the Baha'i Faith to Christians. While writing this conversation, it was as if he were constantly oversee-ing my efforts in a loving, caring way. His name is Win-ston Evans. He was commissioned in the 1930's by Shoghi Effendi, the Great-Grandson of Baha'u'llah and the Guardian of the Baha'i Faith, to contact Christian lead-ers and theologians, informing them of the message of the Baha'i Faith and of the Coming of Baha'u'llah.

He carried out this task so well from the mid 1930's until his death in 1973, that there was no theologian, Christian writer or teacher of note who had not learned of Baha'u'llah. Winston taught me the Baha'i Faith, in-troducing me to Baha'u'llah, 'Abdu'l-Baha and the Guardian of the Baha'i Faith—Shoghi Effendi. Without Winston's help, both then and now, I would have been unable even to attempt to produce this 'conversation with a Christian.' It is my hope that this book is a continua-tion of sorts of Winston's lifelong effort, and a fulfill-ment of a promise made to him to continue his work.

Other persons stood behind me as I worked. I was

aware of their spiritual presence. The Baha'is in the Nashville, Tennessee Baha'i Community in 1957, when I declared my Faith in Baha'u'llah were outstanding, memorable people. Among them, Nellie Roche, Maude Barnes, Dr. Sarah Pereira, Mary Watkins, Susie Langford, Casey and Alice Walton and especially Georgia and Roy Miller. The Millers, in particular, were so inspiring, that I named a daughter—Georgine—after Georgia Miller.

A Baha'i 'sister,' Lucia Sims, played a crucial role, both directly and indirectly, in the production of this book and, in fact, in my becoming a Baha'i. Had I not had her guidance and spiritual support, I may not have been able to recognize the Baha'i Faith in 1957 for what it was. She led the way and I am grateful. In a direct way, she is one of the 'readers' of the near to final draft of this book, along with numerous others mentioned below.

A Baha'i 'brother,' Bill Hatcher, was an inspiration as he declared his faith in Baha'u'llah at about the same time—1957—in Nashville. Bill was an honors student in Mathematics at Vanderbilt and had been given a full scholarship to go to Yale Divinity School when Baha'u'llah called him into discipleship. His enthusiasm, spirit and intellect meant a great deal to me. His contributions to the Faith, both in the past and currently, both philosophical and literary, have inspired me as I as I made my attempt to produce this book.

My dear wife Dorothy Lemon-Thompson has supported me strongly as I put in the major effort to write this conversation. She deserves special mention and thanks. At every turn, she was behind this project, including reading the pre-final draft. I cannot find the right words to tell you how important this was to me, but let me simply say that I do not think that I would have been able to complete this book without her understanding, love and support.

My adult children were thoughtful, helpful and supportive. One of them—Patricia—was a reader. The others, Hunter, Tahirih and Kent, gave constant support and encouragement. I want to certify that it is certainly true that one is changed in the most positive way by the experience of parenthood. I am grateful for the 'input' into my character and personality that all my children have offered. I had an extra 'helping' of children in my second marriage, with stepchildren Charlie and Adrienne, who have also taught me about life. Grandchildren, thirteen of them (!) have also contributed greatly to my happiness and illumination, and my hopefulness about life.

Numerous people agreed to read a pre-final draft. Their names are Jim Booth, Margery Clarke, Rev. Ralph Cook, Patricia Gant, John Huddleston, Phil Kurata, Daniel Illari, Dr. Carl Lee, Gary Matthews, Sandy Messina, Fred Myers, Dr. Bernie Nebel, Lucia Sims, Dorothy Thompson, Steve Vance and David Willard. Each one contributed numerous important suggestions or corrections and several of them must be singled out for the many hours of labor that went beyond mere reading of the book. They acted as editors, each making many suggestions for change and enhancement. These 'editors' were Phil Kurata, Dr. Carl Lee, Sandy Messina, Dr. Bernie Nebel and Lucia Sims. Each one of them went over the entire text, making hundreds of comments that resulted in distinct improvement of this conversation. Dr. Elmer Martin, a Christian friend, made suggestions for questions.

I must single out author and friend John Huddleston who gave the text a meticulous reading, making many suggestions for improvement. He also provided valuable technical information about world financial matters and arms expenditures. Susie Clay offered statistics on the current world situation with regard to the elementary education of girls. Phil Kurata, a professional writer, provided literary criticism that was sorely needed.

Beyond the suggestions for change and after all the corrections and additions were made, the book was read in final draft by two other persons, who gave it the strong 'going over' that is needed by any book being made ready for publication. These two persons are Nancy Lee and Phyllis Reis, two of the most meticulous people I know and their willingness to comb through this conversation gave me the confidence to send it out to the world. Without all the readers and editors and these two final readers, I would have suffered with uncertainty as the book went to publication. None of these readers is to be held accountable for any mistake that may still slip through, a misspelling or a grammar error, or whatever.

Baha'i Review Committees in Australia and the United States read the manuscript and, in the case of the United States Review Committee, one of their reviewers was Gary Matthews, mentioned above as one of the original twelve readers. Gary, therefore, got the dubious privilege of having to read the book twice in three months. Gary's suggestions were numerous and important. Lynnea Yancey, of the United States Baha'i Literature Review Office was helpful and supportive and, as a part of the Review Process, was another reader of the entire manuscript, as was her spouse. A dear friend and talented graphics designer, Aria Mansuri, helped to locate the pictures and prepared them for the manuscript. Other images were supplied by Iraj Radpour of Images International. Still others were supplied by the Audio Visual Department of the Baha'i International Center.

I am immensely grateful to all of the people mentioned above for their efforts and fully thankful for their willingness to take on this task. Only after seeing the efforts of all the people mentioned above, did I realize what a large task I had asked of them. Had I known, I might have been less willing to ask. However, they have assured me that it was one of those famous 'labors of love' and each of them wanted such a book to be as good as it could be, in light of the fact that it might be the first introduction of the Baha'i Faith to many Christian readers.

In summary, many people, hundreds really, contributed directly and indirectly to the writing of this book. I am acutely aware of their contribution, their presence, and spiritual guidance. I have mentioned only a few of the many that could be mentioned, but as for the rest, I know who you are and you know who you are. I salute all the people who contributed to this effort and I thank them with a full and grateful heart. As you read and participate in this conversation, you are talking not only with me, but also with all of them.

Thom Thompson